MW00826758

State Violence and Genocide in Latin America

This edited volume explores political violence and genocide in South America during the Cold War, examining this in light of the United States' hegemonic position on the continent.

Using case studies based on the regimes of Argentina, Chile, Guatemala, Peru, and Uruguay, this book shows how US foreign policy – far from promoting long-term political stability and democratic institutions – has actually undermined them. The first part of the book is an inquiry into the larger historical context in which the development of an unequal power relationship between the United States and Latin American and Caribbean nations evolved after the proliferation of the Monroe Doctrine. The region came to be seen as a contested terrain in the East–West conflict of the Cold War, and a new US-inspired ideology, the National Security Doctrine, was used to justify military operations and the hunting down of individuals and groups labelled as "communists." Following on from this historical context, the book then provides an analysis of the mechanisms of state and genocidal violence, demonstrating how in order to get to know the internal enemy, national armies relied on US intelligence training and economic aid to carry out their surveillance campaigns.

This book will be of interest to students of Latin American politics, US foreign policy, human rights and terrorism, and political violence in general.

Marcia Esparza is an Assistant Professor in Criminal Justice Department at John Jay College of Criminal Justice in New York City. **Henry R. Huttenbach** is the Founder and Chairman of the International Academy for Genocide Prevention and Professor Emeritus of City College of the City University of New York. **Daniel Feierstein** is the Director of the Center for Genocide Studies at the Universidad Nacional de Tres de Febrero, Argentina, and is a Professor in the Faculty of Genocide at the University of Buenos Aires, Argentina.

Series: Critical Terrorism Studies
Series Editors: Richard Jackson, Marie Breen Smyth and
Jeroen Gunning
Aberystwyth University, UK

This book series will publish rigorous and innovative studies on all aspects of terrorism, counter-terrorism and state terror. It seeks to advance a new generation of thinking on traditional subjects and investigate topics frequently overlooked in orthodox accounts of terrorism. Books in this series will typically adopt approaches informed by critical-normative theory, post-positivist methodologies and non-Western perspectives, as well as rigorous and reflective orthodox terrorism studies.

Terrorism and the Politics of Response
Edited by Angharad Closs Stephens and Nick Vaughan-Williams

Critical Terrorism Studies
Framing a New Research Agenda
Edited by Richard Jackson, Marie Breen Smyth and Jeroen Gunning

State Terrorism and Neoliberalism
The North in the South
Ruth Blakeley

Contemporary State Terrorism
Theory and Practice
Edited by Richard Jackson, Eamon Murphy and Scott Poynting

State Violence and Genocide in Latin America
The Cold War Years
Edited by Marcia Esparza, Henry R. Huttenbach, and Daniel Feierstein

State Violence and Genocide in Latin America

in Latin America

The Cold War years

**Edited by Marcia Esparza,
Henry R. Huttenbach, and
Daniel Feierstein**

Routledge
Taylor & Francis Group

LONDON AND NEW YORK

First published 2010
by Routledge
2 Park Square, Milton Park, Abingdon, Oxon, OX14 4RN

Simultaneously published in the USA and Canada
by Routledge
711 Third Avenue, New York, NY 10017

Routledge is an imprint of the Taylor & Francis Group, an informa business

First issued in paperback 2011

© 2010 Selection and editorial matter, Marcia Esparza, Henry R. Huttenbach
and Daniel Feierstein; individual chapters, the contributors

Typeset in Times by Wearset Ltd, Boldon, Tyne and Wear

All rights reserved. No part of this book may be reprinted or reproduced or
utilized in any form or by any electronic, mechanical, or other means, now
known or hereafter invented, including photocopying and recording, or in
any information storage or retrieval system, without permission in writing
from the publishers.

British Library Cataloguing in Publication Data
A catalogue record for this book is available from the British Library

Library of Congress Cataloging in Publication Data
p. cm.
1. State-sponsored terrorism–Latin America–History–20th century.
2. Political violence–Latin America–History–20th century.
3. Genocide–Latin America–History–20th century. 4. Latin America–
Politics and government–1948–1980. 5. United States–Relations–Latin
America. 6. Latin America–Relations–United States. I. Esparza, Marcia.
II. Huttenbach, Henry R. III. Feierstein, Daniel, 1967–
HV6322.3.L29S73 2009
303.6098′09045–dc22

2009015183

ISBN10: 0-415-49637-3 (hbk)
ISBN10: 0-415-66457-8 (pbk)
ISBN10: 0-203-86790-4 (ebk)
ISBN13: 978-0-415-49637-7 (hbk)
ISBN13: 978-0-415-66457-8 (pbk)
ISBN13: 978-0-203-86790-7 (ebk)

Contents

Contributors

Gabriela Aguila is a historian. She has a PhD in History from the University of Rosario, Argentina and is Professor in Contemporary Latin American History and Contemporary European History, School of History and School of Anthropology, University of Rosario. Recently, she published *Dictatorship, Repression and Society in Rosario (1976–1983)*, a study about repression, social behaviours, and social attitudes during the Argentine dictatorship (2008).

Marc Drouin is a doctoral candidate studying Latin American history at the Université de Montréal. He is presently carrying out his dissertation research on memory, violence, first-person accounts of atrocity crimes, and recently released police and military archives in Guatemala.

Marcia Esparza is an Assistant Professor in Criminal Justice Department at John Jay College of Criminal Justice in New York City. Her work with the Guatemalan Truth Commission (1997–2000) led her to create the Historical Memory Project, a resource center documenting state violence and genocide in the Americas. Her work on the aftermath of war has been published in leading English and Spanish journals. She is currently collecting court transcripts from human rights cases in Chile and working on a book manuscript on post-war violence in Guatemala. She is currently a Fulbright Senior Specialist.

Daniel Feierstein holds a PhD in Social Sciences at the University of Buenos Aires. He directs the Center for Genocide Studies at the Universidad Nacional de Tres de Febrero, Argentina, and is Professor of the Faculty of Genocide at the University of Buenos Aires, Argentina. He is also the director of the *Revista de Estudios sobre Genocidio*, the first scholarly journal on genocide in Spanish. In the last years he has published *Genocidio como practica social* (2007), *Seis estudios sobre genocidio* (2000), and many articles on the subject in Spanish, English, and Hebrew.

Andrei Gómez-Suárez is Associate Tutor and DPhil candidate in International Relations at the University of Sussex, Brighton. His articles on the genocide of the Unión Patriótica in Colombia have been published in the *Journal of Genocide Research* and *Revista de Estudios sobre Genocidio*. He is currently researching the relationship between geopolitics and genocide.

Juan Guzmán Tapia is currently the director for the Center of Human Rights of the Universidad Central of Chile. Amongst its various activities, the Center is charged with the defense and promotion of human rights as well as the teaching of human rights courses to local and foreign universities. The Center's mission also encompasses the teaching of human rights to law enforcement agents in Chile and abroad with the aim of promoting a human rights culture within a framework of human dignity. He is the author of *Corte Penal Internacional, posición del gobierno de algunos Estados respecto a su jurisdicción* (Barcelona: Real Academia de las Ciencias Económicas y Financieras, 2008).

Jennifer K. Harbury is a Harvard University scholar and a Radcliffe Institute Fellow. She is an activist and attorney who has spent much of the past 20 years working to promote human rights in Guatemala. Her husband, Efrain Bamaca Velasquez, was a Mayan leader who was "disappeared" by the Guatemalan military in 1992. Since learning of her husband's death, Harbury has dedicated much of her time to pressing for human rights reforms for both the United States and Guatemalan governments. She is the author of *Searching for Everardo* (2000) and *Truth, Torture and the American Way* (2005).

Maureen S. Hiebert is Assistant Professor in the Law and Society Program at the University of Calgary. Her research interests includes Holocaust and genocide studies, comparative genocide theory, genocide and elite decision-making, the Cambodian genocide and the Holocaust, and international criminal law. She is the author of "The Three 'Switches' of Identity Construction in Genocide: The Nazi Final Solution and the Cambodian Killing Fields" (*Genocide Studies and Prevention*, April 2008) and "Theorizing Destruction: Reflections on the State of Comparative Genocide Theory" (*Genocide Studies and Prevention*, December 2008).

Henry R. Huttenbach is founder and principal editor of the *Journal of Genocide Research*, founder and Chairman of the International Academy for Genocide Prevention, and Professor Emeritus of City College of the City University of New York.

J. Patrice McSherry is Professor of Political Science and Director of the Latin American and Caribbean Studies Program at Long Island University in New York. She is the author of two books and numerous published works on military regimes, Cold War politics, Operation Condor, and human rights issues. Her book *Predatory States: Operation Condor and Covert War in Latin America* (2005) was selected as a Choice Outstanding Academic Title in 2006.

Raúl Molina Mejía is a former civil engineer and University of San Carlos professor who was forced to leave Guatemala in 1980. He worked with Rigoberta Menchú and others in Representación Unitaria de la Oposición Guatemalteca in the 1980s, bringing attention to Guatemala's human rights situation before the United Nations and other international fora, and he has remained involved in the struggle for democracy in Guatemala. He teaches history at Long Island University and serves as the international secretary of the Guatemala Peace and Development Network.

Pablo Policzer is an Assistant Professor in Political Science and holder of the Canada Research Chair in Latin American Politics at the University of Calgary. He obtained his PhD in political science from the Massachusetts Institute of Technology, and his BA in political science from the University of British Columbia. His book *The Rise and Fall of Repression in Chile* was published in 2009.

Luis Roniger is a comparative political sociologist, Reynolds Professor of Latin American Studies at Wake Forest University, North Carolina. Among his books are *Patrons, Clients and Friends* (1984); *Hierarchy and Trust in Modern Mexico and Brazil* (1990); *Democracy, Clientelism and Civil Society* (1994); *The Legacy of Human Rights Violations in the Southern Cone* (1999); *Globality and Multiple Modernities* (2002); and *The Politics of Exile in Latin America* (with Mario Sznajder, 2009).

Guillermina S. Seri is Assistant Professor in the Department of Political Science at Union College, Schenectady, NY, where she teaches Latin American politics and political theory. Her research focuses on the practices of everyday governance embedded in policing, and she is preparing a book manuscript, "Little sovereigns: police, security, and governmentality in present Argentina." Before coming to Union, Seri was a Postdoctoral Fellow and a Visiting Assistant Professor in the Program of Peace and Conflict at Colgate University, NY, and taught at various universities in Argentina.

Ernesto Verdeja is Assistant Professor of Political Science and Peace Studies in the Department of Political Science and the Joan B. Kroc Institute for International Peace Studies at the University of Notre Dame. He has published in *Constellations, Res Publica, Metaphilosophy, Contemporary Political Theory*, the *European Journal of Political Theory*, and *Contemporary Politics*, and has co-edited two books, one on transitional justice and the other on civil society in Cuba. His forthcoming book, *Unchopping a Tree: Reconciliation in the Aftermath of Political Violence*, develops a theory of political reconciliation following mass violence. He is currently working on a book-length project on comparative genocide and moral bystanders.

Preface*

Juan Guzmán Tapia

In the twentieth century, there were numerous left- and right-wing dictatorships, or totalitarian governments, or just dictatorships, plain and simple. These corrupt forms of government are characterized by traits which arise in the wake of the following circumstances: civil or foreign wars; from occupation by a foreign power; from a revolution; from a *coup d'état*; and as the result of corruption within a democratic context. Against this background, doctrines are imposed upon the nationals of that country, without their consent.

The truth is that, in any event, the state is deified over the real common interest of the citizens; formulas are used that tend to exclude opinions and beliefs; and they often lead to the expulsion, exclusion, or eradication of individuals belonging to a specific race, religion, or ethnic or national group, or of those who belong to banished political parties. Hence the principle that anything goes when it comes to imposing the interest of the winning, dominant, or supreme group.

The methods of exclusion range from those that prevent someone from doing something, as in the case of censorship, to the point of going as far as the extermination of entire groups. During Hitler's and Stalin's eras, that is how millions of men, women, the elderly and children, were annihilated for no other reason than being Jews or Ukrainians.

During the most recent dictatorships in the Americas, kidnapping, torture, and the forced disappearance of people became institutionalized; doctrines were established and defended under the pretext of an extreme degree of nationalism, or national security, or, sometimes, merely on a dictator's whim.

Nowadays thanks to the "global village," we are shocked when we watch in our living rooms how in some African towns thousands of people are victims of starvation, disease, filth, and infestations, and how thousands of women, the elderly and children die due to the international agencies' inability to provide the resources for a decent and humane livelihood, while wars of ethnic "cleansing" are being fought in which millions of dollars and euros are spent that could alleviate so much poverty.

Let us not forget that in Ukraine, Stalin ordered the ever-increasing massacre of millions of peasants simply because they had not been able to produce all the flour needed by the USSR. A paragraph in the introduction to the complete works of Vasilli Grossman illustrates the punishments the state meted out for the this lack of production. There, Tzvetan Todorov states:

> In the most fertile lands of the Ukraine, once the best performing peasants had been expelled, an infernal machine was implemented: Due to the absence of the former landowners, the crops became scarce; nonetheless, the Party delegates had to report that everything was working fine. However, the peasants who had remained in those lands were not able to deliver their quota of wheat required by the State.
>
> Government agents seized them in order to forcibly acquire all the nourishing resources they held and, to punish the peasants' resistance. They prevented them from stocking up on provisions at the local town markets. So the peasants exhausted their meager supplies; then, their seedlings; later on, their potatoes; and, finally, their livestock. When winter arrived, they were feeding themselves with acorns from oak trees; and once they had exhausted them, they ate dogs, cats, rats, snakes, ants, and worms. In the spring, famine was so endemic that, before dying, they became insane and tried to escape. However, in their attempt to flee, they were hunted down by the police, who forced them to succumb to acts of cannibalism. Everybody starved. Immediately afterwards, they started dying – first the children, then the old, and, eventually, the middle aged. In the beginning, they buried their bodies; then, they stopped, and there were vast numbers of corpses scattered all over the streets and backyards. ... The last ones died in their beds. Silence blanketed all. In this way, the whole population was wiped out.
>
> Today, it is estimated that nearly six million people perished in the afore-mentioned circumstances.[1]

Hitler used gas chambers; Stalin, repression, hunger, and harrowing Siberian exile. In Rwanda, several decades afterward, there were no ovens or gas chambers – they used machetes. In that country, which was the setting for one of the last genocides in the twentieth century, from April to July 1994, 800,000 indigenous Tutsis were killed by their neighbors, the Hutus. Journalist Jean Hatzfeld, in his book *Machete Season: The Killers in Rwanda Speak*,[2] tells us about the murderers' own confessions, who, far from being ashamed, bragged about the skills they were acquiring from slaughtering their neighbors. Killing with a machete became part and parcel of their everyday lives. It was considered something natural, something that had to be done.

In Chile, during Pinochet's dictatorship, in one of the worst places of torture and extermination known as Villa Grimaldi, the torturers and killers kept a work schedule, just as in Rwanda, during which they tortured and killed. Usually, they had their weekends off. During those free days, their children visited the famous villa for a swim in its pools and to enjoy its park. Hearing the children playing and having fun, people who had been recently tortured, as well as the rest of the imprisoned population, thought that they were about to lose their minds. If faced with those torturers, Jesus would have once again said: "Father, forgive them for they know not what they do...."

In Argentina, the Mothers of Plaza de Mayo made their stance known to the whole world: "Never again!"

This entreaty implies many things. It says never again to genocide, to crimes against humanity, to dictatorships, and to impunity.

Argentina and the rest of the countries of Latin America except Chile (which still subjects itself to the orders of the United States), as well as the majority of the United Nations member states, apart from the United States, Israel, and a few others, ratified the Rome Statute of the International Criminal Court, which makes them part of that treaty and therefore subject to the jurisdiction of the Court. Most of the world has responded thus far to the cry of "never again."

> In most countries, where there has been a bloody dictatorship (as is the case with most of them), a civil war, or whatever form of systematic violation of human rights, their populations need a "never again" to be guaranteed to them. They need justice and reconciliation. In Chile, this justice has been incomplete and reconciliation is nonexistent. Hence, the need for a permanent court, with jurisdiction over crimes against humanity, against the most horrible violations of human rights.[3]

The legal notion of genocide has remained unchanged regarding what basically constitutes this crime. In the international treaties and even in the Rome Statute (Art. 6), genocide continues to be associated with a number of serious events, from the forced relocation of children from one group to another, up to the killing of members of a group. However, when scholars indicate what typifies this crime, they only include national, ethnic, racial, and religious groups, leaving out political ones, which have been the most affected in the twentieth century and in what has elapsed of the twenty-first.

Due to this legal restriction, numerous criminal acts, which implicitly constitute genocide, have gone unpunished. Many of these criminal acts have evaded being classified as genocide by subjecting them to formulas/definitions that make them seem less than suicide. We were able to see an illustration of this in the case of the forced displacement of the Pehuenche groups in the zone of Alto Bío-Bío in Chile due to the construction of a dam and hydroelectric power plant. This displacement involved the eviction of numerous members of the Mapuche nation from their ancestral lands, which were densely populated by *pehuenes* (Araucaria pines that produce a pine nut with which the Mapuche fed themselves). They used to reside at an altitude that did not affect them. They were relocated to a place on the mountain range above 2,000 meters (more than 6,500 feet) in altitude, which gave rise to famine, disease, cold, and the worst imaginable quality of life. As a result of this displacement, the group was broken up, their animals died, and their members either emigrated or perished. However, these acts carried out in a fully fledged democracy are considered important contributions to progress. Moreover, their leading promoters continue to run as candidates for the posts of representatives, senators, and even presidents.

This book, *State Violence and Genocide in Latin America: The Cold War Years* constitutes a fundamental contribution to the study, research, and struggle against blindness – the kind of blindness that is generated when one refuses to recognize, at the political and jurisdictional levels, the new forms of genocide, its constant advancement, and the little efforts made by the members of the international community to fight against this unpunished crime.

This anthology emphasizes the most dramatic formula of genocide suffered in Latin America during the last half of the twentieth century. It was encouraged by successive US administrations, when they were trying to fight the so-called "enemy within," inspired by the regional security doctrine.

Lastly, this compendium constitutes another milestone in the analysis of a very dark period of the law, and it is an incentive to understand the need to eradicate all the paths that lead to the corruption of the democratic system. Ultimately, it allows us to thoroughly understand the importance of putting an end to this impunity, which has permitted so much excess and inhumanity.

Notes and references

* Translated by Miguel Falquez-Certain.
1 Tzvetan Todorov, "Les combats de Vassili Grossman," introduction to Vassili Grossman, *Œuvres*, Paris: Laffont, 2006, p. xvii.
2 J. Hatzfeld, *Machete Season: The Killers in Rwanda Speak*, New York: Farrar, Straus and Giroux, 2005.
3 "Corte Penal Internacional, Posición del gobierno de algunos estados respecto a su jurisdicción [International Criminal Court: Official Stance of Some States Concerning Jurisdiction]." Speech of admittance to the Real Academia de Ciencias Económicas y Financieras, Barcelona, read on January 17, 2008 by the corresponding member for the Republic of Chile, Dr Juan Guzmán Tapia. Copy in Judge Guzmán's possession.

Acknowledgments

We would like to acknowledge several people who have kindly assisted us in this project.

Many thanks to contributors who worked diligently to meet deadlines and to the anonymous reviewers for their excellent suggestions. Our gratitude also goes to Rebecca Brennan from Routledge for her kind assistance throughout the many months it took to compile this book.

Because this book-project was housed at John Jay College of Criminal Justice in New York City, we owe our gratitude to the students who enthusiastically participated in research and editing tasks: Lina Rojas and Arie Braizblot whose very presence at John Jay College reminds us of the history of state violence and genocide in Colombia and Latin America. Special thanks to Geetangali Ramdeo for her relentless enthusiasm to bring this project to fruition. The larger John Jay community was always ready to support the project.

To friends for their support in what sometimes felt like a never-ending task: Pierre-Yves Linot, Stephanie Alfaro, Olga Teploukhova, Barry Spunt, Mary E. Sanger, and Carol Colmenares, for their continuous support in bringing the Latin American experience with state violence and genocide to the wider New York City area and beyond.

The publisher and the authors would like to thank the copyright holders for granting permission to reprint the following material:

Daniel Feierstein, "Political Violence in Argentina and Its Genocidal Characteristics," *Journal of Genocide Research* 8, 2, June 2006, Special Issue: "Confronting Genocide: New Voices from Latin America," pp. 149–68.

Gabriela Aguila, "Dictatorship, Society, and Genocide in Argentina: Repression in Rosario, 1976–1983," *Journal of Genocide Research* 8, 2, June 2006, Special Issue: "Confronting Genocide: New Voices from Latin America," pp. 169–80.

Introduction

Globalizing Latin American studies of state violence and genocide

Marcia Esparza[1]

In the last two decades, studies of genocides have multiplied.[2] European and Anglo-American scholarship has focused on investigating prominent cases such as the extermination of Armenians under the late Ottoman Empire, the Jewish Holocaust, and the mass killings in Rwanda. There has been, however, a virtual silence over the question of whether or not genocide was committed in Latin America against left-wing groups during the Cold War years (mid-1940s to early 1990s).[3]

The primary reason for this dearth of research is that scholars of genocide often follow the 1948 United Nations Convention on the Prevention and Punishment of the Crime of Genocide, which excludes political groups as a category of victims protected by the Convention.[4] In 1998, Spanish Judge Baltasar Garzón, however, interpreted the Convention in ways that allowed him to issue a warrant for the arrest of Chilean dictator General Augusto Pinochet on charges of crimes against humanity, including genocide, widespread and systematic torture, and "disappearance." While Garzón set an undeniable precedent for future indictments based on notions of universal jurisdiction,[5] General Pinochet's detention took the scholarly community by surprise since Chileans (and non-Chileans) killed during the dictatorship (1973–90) were considered to be political victims and thus lacked the features of a group protected by the Convention.[6]

Another reason for the relative silence over genocidal violence in Latin America is the fact that episodes of extreme violence continue to be measured against the organized destruction of European Jews during the Holocaust. This bias reinforces a standing notion of the uniqueness of the Final Solution. The current Eurocentric debates on genocide deter us from even questioning whether or not genocidal violence in Latin America did, in fact, take place.

If we are to investigate the occurrence of genocide in Latin America, we must question the purpose of this violence, what left-wing groups represented ideologically, what the mechanisms of violence were, and how Cold War violence differed from prior forms of state violence. Until these questions are raised, we run the risk of falsely assuming that Latin America is somehow immune from genocidal processes – and that this was the case during the late twentieth century. This anthology suggests that without investigating the Latin American experience of extreme forms of political violence, the global study of genocide remains incomplete.[7] Thus, this book delves into the sociological and historical recurrence of state violence, of which the deliberate destruction of particular political groups is one modality, and aims to place it within a global context. Furthermore, as Henry R. Huttenbach has noted, until we include a broader range of case studies, it is premature to proclaim a theory of genocide.[8]

The case studies analyzed here, from Argentina, Chile, Colombia, and Guatemala, represent two significantly different areas, given the variations in their economic and political development.[9] State violence in these regions has also differed significantly, with Colombia enduring the longest armed conflict in the hemisphere, and Central American nations continuing to wrestle with the lingering effects of internal armed conflicts.[10] Regardless of their differences, the regions share a common history of an unequal economic and political relationship with the United States and a shared history of state-organized violence that can be traced back to colonial times (see Roniger in this volume).

In the remainder of this introduction, and in light of the scarcity of scholarship dealing with extreme forms of destruction of particular groups in Latin America's societies, I examine elements that together can serve as a platform for discussion when analyzing state violence and genocide in the region. Two of these elements, social polarization and the role of the United States in facilitating the mechanisms of violence, are thoroughly examined in this volume. The inclusion of a third element, *el pueblo*, seeks to provide an overarching concept that encompasses victimized groups and people based on their ideological views. This discussion is followed by a brief summary of each chapter.

Towards a Latin American paradigm of state violence and genocide

An examination of the bloodshed and crimes against humanity perpetrated against Latin America's left-wing collectives during the Cold War years is not new. Scholars of Latin America have long examined state terrorism. Political scientists and historians have provided us with a body of literature explaining the breakdown of democracy and the rise of authoritarian regimes as well as the historical involvement of the US in the region since the 1823 Monroe Doctrine. Sociologists and anthropologists have examined the construction of a culture of fear and the rise of human rights groups led by women as worldwide symbols of resistance to military power.[11] Since these models for studying state violence already exist, how can the study of Latin America's Cold War violence through the prism of genocide add to the established literature?

First, through the lens of genocide, the region's extreme class, ethnic, and racial polarization is brought to light, all traits characterizing other societies that have suffered from genocide.[12] This societal fragmentation is largely due to efforts to control economic resources – copper, oil, nitrate, lithium, natural gas, cotton, and coffee, to name a few. According to a 2008 World Bank Report, Latin America, together with sub-Saharan Africa, are the "most unequal [socio-economic] regions of the world."[13] At the same time, because studies of genocide raise particular questions about the identity of the victims the study of Latin America offers an example of state crimes primarily against political groups that embodied the demands of *el pueblo*, a group that has been long "excluded from the universe of obligation of the dominant group."[14] *El pueblo* is composed of popular organizations from the poor and exploited lower classes like peasant leagues, migrant workers, shantytown organizations, miners' and workers' unions, village teachers, and economically disadvantaged populations of urban cities.[15]

Through the lens of genocide, the ideological justification for the elimination of undesirable groups, and the methods employed, can also be elucidated. This view uncovers the ways in which the US anticommunist crusade transformed the region's old class conflicts into new ones. Mexican philosopher Leopoldo Zea has suggested that the East–West ideological race was largely used as the pretext to deal with social problems that long preceded the anticommunist era. For Zea, the Cold War justified further US intervention in a region where "Any action incompatible with these interests [i.e. the interests of the US] [was] interpreted as an expression of communist intervention in America, and on that account, a menace to the security of the continent."[16] As a result, local armies, fueled with patriotic values to defend *la patria* (the fatherland) from an alleged communist menace, adapted notions of the Cold War ideology to disguise military assaults against *el pueblo*.[17]

The proposed paradigm views state-led violence as a continuum along a range of years that extends beyond the Cold War era, where the state organization of widespread killings must be seen as the outcome of cumulative "complex historical processes."[18] A detailed account of the region's long-term history of political violence is a monumental task, one that is outside the scope of this introduction. Nevertheless, this discussion hopes to highlight the need to recognize Latin America's long history of class, political, and ethnic confrontation. This recognition is crucial if we want to elucidate the extent to which state terrorism has institutionalized the use of violence to resolve social conflicts. These claims find an echo in Fernando Mires' analysis of seven Latin American revolutions with his conclusion that it is fruitless to examine the Nicaraguan uprising of the 1970s, and the state's response, without exploring the country's history.[19]

In laying out this paradigm, three interrelated parameters can be considered: (1) the region's broader colonial and postcolonial historical background and the formation of highly polarized societies based on class, race, and ethnicity;[20] (2) the social construction of the "other," of *el pueblo* as a separate political subject; and (3) the role the United States plays in promoting violent doctrines of national security to resolve deep-seated class and ethnic conflicts in the region, further polarizing extremely divided societies. National security doctrines that developed under the Cold War asserted that nations were at war with an internal enemy as opposed to an external one, an ideology that justified local armies' aggression against their own people.[21]

Colonial and postcolonial polarization: the preexisting conditions in Latin America

Leo Kuper's analysis of plural societies bears particular relevance to the discussion of state violence and genocide in Latin America.[22] According to Kuper, those nations characterized as extreme plural societies – that is, fragmented by deep divisions that are often the result of colonialism – "offer the necessary conditions for domestic genocide."[23] In divided societies, dominant groups discriminate socially and economically against subordinate minorities, or "hostage" groups, marginalizing them and often making them victims of genocidal attacks. Genocide then becomes the ultimate expression of the state's aim to annihilate the hostage groups.[24] For Kuper, genocide is not a random or spontaneous outbreak of lethal violence. Rather, it is an outgrowth of decisions made by powerful economic and political elites who have access to significant state resources to exploit the long-standing social divides between groups and ultimately destroy them.

Latin America's colonial background fits the description Kuper proposes. Above all, its history shows that European colonization helped create fault lines that divided societies along class, racial, and ethnic lines. Western colonization imposed a vertical order of social castes based on self-defining parameters of what it meant to be "civilized" in order to legitimize its dominion in indigenous territories. To accomplish their task, the colonizers went on to dehumanize the indigenous population. Considered savages, an inferior race, by the *criollos* (people of Spanish descent), and viewed as the "external" social group, the "other" indigenous peoples became easy prey for policies of annihilation.[25] The Europeans strategically manipulated this differentiation between indigenous and non-indigenous groups, asserts Argentinean philosopher Walter Mignolo, to establish its own hegemonic order in the Americas, as indigenous leaders and their communities insisted upon upholding their distinctive ethnic heritages.[26]

Latin American scholars agree that nineteenth-century political emancipation from Spain did little to eliminate the new nations' internal cleavages. On the contrary, Leopoldo Zea argues, it left Latin America divided into two bands: those who aspired to build a model society radically different from the Spanish motherland, and those who dreamt of copying the colonizer's regime.[27] Zea further argues that the profound ethnic and class divisions formed during the colonial period remained largely intact, particularly in areas where indigenous land conflicts were unresolved. Most problematic for Zea, however, was the fact that the social customs and cultural practices of the colonizers also remained intact in the minds of elites and of the colonized.

Unable to break away from their colonial past and to transform their colonial mind-set, the ruling classes (always light-skinned) have inescapably reproduced systems of exclusion over marginalized groups, who are seen as "inferior" classes and considered unruly. According to Esteban Echeverria, in the eyes of the elites, the lower classes lacked civic culture, which justified calling for "a strong hand" (a euphemism for ruthless dictators) to discipline them, particularly as a workforce for economic exploitation.[28] This internal colonization by the elites, as criticized by Latin American thinkers, has continued to reinforce patterns of social exclusion through *caudillismos* (strongmen) and tyrannies, and the perpetuation of military and ecclesiastic power. Moreover, postcolonial oligarchy, merchant elites, and Church officials continued to exercise control over "darker-skinned under-classes" more ruthlessly than ever before, further reinforcing the colonial heritage.[29]

Latin American observers also agree that the emancipation from Spain did not lead to real economic and political independence.[30] Instead, those who hoped to throw off the economic, political, and cultural legacy of European colonialism witnessed the rise of the second wave of colonization, this time by the United States.[31] The formulation of the 1823 Monroe Doctrine and later, the 1893 Manifest Destiny credo (aimed at keeping European economic influence off the shores of the continent) established a US presence in the territory. The military occupations in the Caribbean and Central America added another layer of economic, ethnic, and political polarization in this region.

Against this colonial and postcolonial divide, US efforts at communist containment in the twentieth century were accomplished rather easily. They were superimposed, following Kuper's logic, on deeply polarized and dependent societies. The initiation of the US National Security Doctrine radicalized preexisting local, long-standing internal conflicts while providing the ideological pretext to eliminate political opposition.

Two factors should be considered when accounting for the state's new forms of widespread violence against left-wing, organized sectors of *el pueblo* during the Cold War years: the rise of the labor and peasant movements, and the Cuban revolution of 1959.

First, historians have noted that until World War I, few workers in the region were organized in trade unions and left-wing groups.[32] This changed dramatically with the advent of the Great Depression, as national industries turned to the development of local industries (a policy known as import substitution) that encouraged the massive immigration of rural peasants into urban centers in the 1930s, particularly in South America. For James Petras, the radicalization of political organization is often associated with economic development. The introduction of capitalist modes of production, he argues, has encouraged "the concentration of workers [that] have usually generated social forces for mass radical political organization."[33] Thus, pockets of the labor movement, in the absence of state repression, "have become the foundations for larger revolutionary movements in situations where they were able to communicate with one another and to organize."[34]

This growth in the size of the working class was accompanied by a widespread expansion of unions.[35] The Brazilian case illustrates this point: Some 351,000 workers were unionized in 1940; by 1947, this had more than doubled to 798,000. This increase reflected a "trend toward more centralized organization, the search for greater autonomy from the state, and militancy over wages" signaling a new era for workers and *el pueblo*'s organized segments.[36]

Since the 1950s, vibrant popular movements with "heavy anti-US overtones"[37] have erupted into the political landscape. Broad mass movements also contested severe dire economic conditions that resulted from failed nationalistic development policies and ironically brought further dependency on the US. During this time, James Cockcroft reports, "Latin America had more hungry people than India, Pakistan, and Bangladesh."[38] The triumph of Cuba's leftist revolution, and new left and indigenous philosophies, mainly liberation theology,[39] fueled these grassroots movements and left-wing insurgencies, as in Guatemala.[40]

A second explanation for the escalation of state violence is found in the success of the Cuban revolution of 1959, which elites and the US feared to be a precursor to a larger Latin American revolution. An alleged menace of a "second Cuba" gave the United States further justification to protect its hemispheric hegemony and economic stronghold against Soviet invasion. At the same time, nationalist models and agrarian reforms under Guatemalan President Arbenz in 1950 and the 1970 election of socialist Salvador Allende in Chile were deemed by elites and Washington to be utterly intolerable. Thus the threat of the "domino effect" (if one country fell prey to communism, the rest would follow) was used to justify US military aid to Latin American armies in their purge of popular groups with criminalized political views.

The ultimate objective of military campaigns launched against organized pockets of *el pueblo* was to physically eliminate a generation of left-wing political leadership and its supporters and sympathizers necessary to pave the way for new free market policies. According to Alain Rouquie, a scholar of Latin American armed forces,

> The reorganization of society and the restoration of capitalism was to permit the establishment of a democracy … Politics was to be eliminated in order to liberate the economy. National security coincided with the laws of capitalism and the new international division of labor.[41]

Fearing the success of mass mobilizations that could impede the reorganization of wealth in society, military campaigns of war and terror were aimed at disarticulating *el pueblo* as a political force, which, like a cancer, had to be "surgically extracted."[42]

The "other": *el pueblo* in the history of Latin America

Rafael Lemkin, the founding father of genocide studies, concluded that violence could be defined as genocidal to the extent that it is planned to eradicate essential features of the victimized group. He argues:

> Genocide does not necessarily mean the immediate destruction of a nation … It is intended rather to signify a coordinated plan of different actions aiming at the destruction of essential foundations of the life of national groups, with the aim of annihilating the groups themselves.[43]

What remains a rather heated controversy is what, in fact, constitutes a group.

For the most part, scholars argue that a victimized group must possess stable features, such as ethnicity or nationality, which can easily set them apart from other national groups.[44] According to this argument, unlike the markers of political ideology, racial and ethnic identifiers are immutable identities to which the victimized group is bound, with no chance to escape from being seen as the "other." Harff and Gurr[45] have used the term politicide to refer to the killing of political opponents, to distinguish the crime from genocide, thereby offering a tool to examine this specific form of destruction (see Feierstein, Chapter 2, and Hiebert and Policzer, Chapter 3, for nuanced discussions of the literature). Others, such as Israel Charny, have called for a definition of genocide that includes the extermination of human beings regardless of any identity, a definition that would include political adversaries.[46] The discussion as to whether political markers are mutable needs to be contextualized in different historical and political settings.

In light of Latin American polarization among class, ethnic, and political lines, left-wing groups and popular movements had long been labeled as a threat to the state's capitalist projects and singled out for elimination. *El pueblo* was a large threat to capitalist and US ideals because of its ability to draw together many different kinds of people; therefore, political groups within *el pueblo* had to be eliminated.[47] When popular movements allied with guerrilla groups, as in Guatemala, states employed a genocidal strategy to eliminate potential support to armed groups.[48] Pablo Gonzalez has further concluded that it is only when *el pueblo* erupts into the political landscape that revolutionary projects in the region can prove fruitful. Moreover, for the pro-capitalist ruling elites, members from the lower classes are seen with disdain,[49] as their organizations are perceived as the embodiment of anti-capitalism and anti-modernity.[50]

A brief examination of Latin America in the twentieth century shows a quasi-uninterrupted century of massacres and bloodshed claiming the lives of *el pueblo* mostly in disputes over the nation's resources. This long-ranging history shows episodes of revolutionary uprisings and the resulting state efforts to crush them. In Chile, at the end of the 1890s, over 300 strikes took place, and in Iquique (1907), sodium nitrate miners refusing to abandon their strike were gunned down by state soldiers, as documented in Lessie Jo Frazier's *Salt in the Sand.*[51] In 1919 in Argentina, labor unrest was crushed by bloody army repression, known as the "tragic week."[52] In El Salvador, violence against *el pueblo* claimed an estimated 30,000 lives in a 1932 slaughter of peasants and indigenous people who were organized under communist leader, Agustin Farabundo Marti. In Trujillo, Peru, an APRA (Alianza Popular Revolucionaria Americana) uprising and brutal military retaliation in 1931 initiated a long period of political violence in the country. In 1940s Colombia, "*La Violencia*" pitted conservative and liberal peasants in a civil war where "one-quarter of a million people in a population of 10 million perished."[53] The Mexican revolution led by Emiliano Zapata in 1910 is yet another example of the struggles to overhaul the stratification of landed societies.

Even with the threat of armed subversion in the Southern Cone, the evidence suggests that states frequently and incorrectly equated non-armed mobilization with subversion.[54] In Argentina, for example, Rolando Munck argues, the state went beyond targeting guerrillas to include the workers' movement.[55] During this time, Penny Lernoux reports, left-wing politics were perceived to be so threatening that even those sympathizing with the popular sectors and working on behalf of the poor were perceived to be left-wing supporters.[56]

For the most part, it can be said that left-wing political groups were set apart from other national groups through rituals, traditions, and values transmitted from one generation to the next. Regardless of their internal class interests and respective local histories in each country, members and organizations from *el pueblo* have shared political and cultural traits distinguishing them from other groups.[57] The only guarantee a social class will remain homogenous is their shared historical memory, concludes French sociologist Maurice Halbwachs.

Focusing on the transmission of rituals and cultural practices, Halbwachs studied the transformation of classes in Europe and argued that each social class subscribes to a particular collective memory constructed over long periods of time. Each class group is heir to a particular consciousness, a reservoir of events, ideologies, and cultural practices of past groups – the embodiment of the "frameworks of memory."[58] Left-wing groups were also identified by a reservoir of social practices brought to bear in the mobilization of popular movement. This reservoir included: workers' ideologies of popular power, strikes, the take-over of buildings, rallies, street demonstrations, soup kitchens, popular songs, arts and crafts, and anniversaries of significant events within *el pueblo*. These signifiers have all become part of the consciousness of *el pueblo* and have served to galvanize the mobilization of political groups demanding an end to the quasi-feudal living conditions of large segments of the Latin American population, particularly where indigenous peoples are the majority.

Confronted with organized discontent, when the anti-communist hunt came to the regions' doorsteps, states' disguised military attacks against undesirable groups from *el pueblo* under the pretext that nations were at war against alleged "terrorist communists." To this end, they deployed their military forces against the poor who were now labeled as the internal enemy. As Leopold Zea has argued, the Cold War was the ideological pretext military regimes used to dehumanize, imprison, torture, and kill anyone demanding higher salaries or land reforms. Lesley Gill has noted that "demands for better living conditions constitute evidence for the military of an innate propensity for violence and unruliness among peasants and indigenous and working-class people."[59] According to numerous official (such as Truth Commissions) and non-official investigations, political victims included socialist and communist parties, landless peasants, truck drivers, university professors and students, rural teachers, leaders of port unions, construction workers, miners, indigenous peoples – all members of the popular classes.[60]

The Cold War largely transformed political opposition into targets of military campaigns where the enemy was not a foreigner but a fellow countryman. Institutions of violence were created, military bases were expanded, techniques of torture were redefined, and organized criminal intelligence networks decimated peasants and workers' political groups. As in Chile in 1907 and *La Violencia* in Colombia in the 1940s, the victims represented the poorest of society. This time local armies found the ideological justification to physically break the backbone of *el pueblo* labor and peasant militancy. As suggested earlier, by destroying the leadership and cadres of left-wing political groups, the state weakened the possibilities for political opposition and the ability for *el pueblo* to reconstitute their key social networks, which are fundamental elements in the preservation of the group as a social force. A historical memory of political vindications can only be transmitted and recovered in relation to other individuals who have shared similar experiences, because, as Halbwachs has suggested, memory is a collective process. Part three of this book deals with the extent societies have recovered and broken away from their legacy of state violence and genocide.

The mechanisms of violence and the "United States factor"

Authors in this anthology emphasize the "US Factor" in shaping political violence.[61] A few caveats, however, should be mentioned before the organization of this anthology is laid out for the reader.

First, any discussion of the politics of extermination in the region, the selection of victims, and the making of perpetrators needs to consider the imperial projects of foreign powers. State violence is intrinsically related to the capitalist economic project and the notion that the liberalization of markets will bring about political democracy.[62] As Gregg Grandin has noted, Latin America has been pivotal in the creation of the US as an empire. Since early on, the region was seen as

> bountifulness ... throughout the nineteenth century but especially after the economic contradictions and corporate mergers of the 1890s, many of America's largest international corporations got their start in Latin America, as capitalists poured billions into the region, first in mining, railroads, and sugar, then in electricity, oil, and agriculture.[63]

Naked economic exploitation by local elites has been coupled with U.S complicity in supplying the mechanisms of state violence in order to create a favorable business climate for multinationals.[64] Grandin further notes that Latin American countries have been used as a workshop where military intervention *coups d'état* have been orchestrated. A classic example of US intervention is Guatemala where the Eisenhower administration, through Operation Success, orchestrated the overthrow of democratically elected president Jacobo Arbenz in 1954.

Second, as Grandin has suggested, the region has been used as a laboratory where the mechanisms of violence, such as torture, have been widely used even before the world became aware of torture techniques used in Iraq (documented later in this anthology). To win the war against communism in the region, the

US also provided training for top Latin American military personnel and death squads.[65] One of the most infamous US institutions providing courses to foreign militaries is the recently renamed western hemisphere Institute for Security Cooperation (WHISC), formerly the Army's School of the Americas (SOA), located at Fort Benning Military Base in Columbus, Georgia.

This book

The contributors in this book address some of the questions and formulate others that reshape existing definitions of genocide. Though there are disagreements among authors that reflect larger theoretical debates, their essays address three main themes: the long history of economic, political, ethnic, and racial polarization, the role of the US in shaping the mechanisms of violence, and the long-term implications of colonialism and the Cold War era in the destruction of organized segments of *el pueblo*'s political projects. While references to *el pueblo* and their allying groups are addressed indirectly, the majority of victimized groups in Argentina, Chile, Colombia, and Guatemala belonged to the most vulnerable segments of the population.

State Violence and Genocide in Latin America: The Cold War Years is divided into three parts, corresponding with three broad areas of scholarly research. Part I explores the roots of the problem and theoretical underpinnings, Part II explores the mechanisms of political violence, and Part III considers the rebuilding of peace in deeply polarized societies. Each of the chapters included here reshapes the frame of reference that circumscribes the discussion laid out in this introduction.

In Part I, Chapter 1, by Reynolds Professor of Latin America, Luis Roniger, discusses the long-standing unequal relationship between the Latin American region and the United States. Roniger's essay, "US Hemispheric Hegemony and the Descent into Genocidal Practices in Latin America," explores the historical facts and precipitating factors behind political violence. He traces the rise of the US as the world imperial power back to the nineteenth century. This rise involved the expansion and conquest of territories, populations, and riches from Mexico, Central America, and Caribbean lands, and the coalescence of wealthy oligarchy and bourgeoisie interests with the interests of the United States, as suggested by Jennifer Harbury in a later chapter. Without this long-term perspective, a narrative of the region's harrowing experience with state violence cannot be fully grasped. In this leading chapter, Roniger reminds us that among the legacies of the region's "dirty wars" are the "well-trained local constabularies to protect the interests of US corporations."

Daniel Feierstein, Director of the Center on the Study of Genocide in Buenos Aires, authors the second chapter. In "Political Violence in Argentina and its Genocidal Characteristics," Feierstein examines the occurrence of political violence in Argentina and argues that the latest military repression (1976–83) amounted to genocide. Feierstein traces state-sponsored terrorist practices back to previous experiences of genocide and argues that Argentinean juntas appropriated French and US counterintelligence practices used in Algeria and Vietnam. In his essay, Feierstein offers a new definition of genocide to account for the reorganization of social relationships. In so doing, he argues that the exclusion of political groups from the definition of genocide ends up privileging certain criminal events and populations while excluding others.

Whether or not political violence can be characterized as genocide is the focus of the third chapter, written by Calgary University professors Maureen S. Hiebert and Pablo Policzer. "Genocide in Chile? An Assessment" identifies three debates found in the literature on genocide that should be considered when evaluating the state violence of Chilean dictator General Augusto Pinochet (1973–90). Like the rest of authors included in this volume, Hiebert and Policzer discuss the role played by National Security Doctrine ideas and provide scenarios to evaluate US complicity in human rights crimes. For the authors, the study of US involvement is unfinished, and they suggest alternative models for reconsidering the occurrence of "degrees of genocide" when evaluating the Chilean case.

Marc Drouin's "Understanding the 1982 Guatemalan Genocide" is also a theoretical contribution to the field. In Chapter 4, Drouin's nuanced analysis traces the evolution of military campaigns in Guatemala (1954–96), contesting the view that the Guatemalan genocide is a "borderline case." He explores how war crimes and crimes against humanity evolved into "full-blown genocide by 1982," eliminating an entire generation of indigenous leaders and professionals. Drouin places the Maya genocide along the continuum of "atrocity crimes" to demonstrate that genocidal violence should be seen within a range of political violence perpetrated by states, "from such crimes against humanity as extermination and persecution to full-blown genocide."

In the second part of the book, authors examine the mechanisms of violence. J. Patrice McSherry, professor of political science and Director of the Latin American and Caribbean Studies Program (Long Island University) places Operation Condor, an intra-American criminal network facilitated by the US, within the larger "continental counterinsurgency regime." In, " 'Industrial Repression' and Operation Condor in Latin America," McSherry shows how secret cooperation between the dictatorships of Argentina, Bolivia, Brazil, Chile, Paraguay, Uruguay, and to a lesser extent, Peru and Ecuador, was crucial to eliminating political opposition. Through an analysis of declassified US documents, McSherry concludes that "Condor operations, and the larger campaigns of state terrorism, reflected intent to destroy."

Through her own prosecution of her husband's torturers and killers in Guatemala, Harvard scholar Jennifer K. Harbury examines the close, long-term, working liaisons between the CIA and death squads in Central America. In "The United States and Torture: Lessons from Latin America," Harbury focuses on the prevailing notions of justifying the use of torture techniques to successfully extract information from prisoners. Harbury concludes that this grim history is hardly unique, but rather "is the history of the hemisphere, from the rich farmlands of El Salvador and Honduras, to Panama with its priceless canal, to the mines and natural resources of Brazil and Chile." At the same time, her personal account demonstrates the epistemological value of emotions when documenting mass atrocities.[66]

In her essay, "State Violence and Repression in Rosario during the Argentine Dictatorship, 1976–83," historian Gabriela Aguila (Universidad Nacional de Rosario) contributes to the historiography of the region. Aguila examines genocidal practices in the city of Rosario against the larger continuum of violence in Argentina. She elucidates the sophisticated operations carried out by the Anti-Communist Argentine Alliance (the Triple A) a para-police group charged with hunting down so-called subversives. Chapter 7 is also a reminder of how people witnessing the atrocities – the bystanders – were silenced by fear as some sectors provided their support to Argentina's *proceso de reorganización* (reorganization process) and its genocidal politics.

In Chapter 8, University of Sussex scholar Andrei Gómez-Suárez focuses on the destruction of the Unión Patriótica (UP) to analyze the different geopolitical discourses underpinning US foreign policy and their central role in defining the violent strategies designed by Colombian statecraft. In, "US–Colombian Relations in the 1980s: Political Violence and the Onset of the Unión Patriótica Genocide," the author discusses the elimination of UP members. The UP was a political front bringing the Communist Party and other leftist and centrist political forces together. Like Feierstein, Drouin and Molina Mejía, Gómez-Suárez also examines genocidal practices as processes. Within this framework, he utilizes the term "perpetrator bloc" to include the network of criminal groups in charge of the second stage of the UP elimination: the armed forces, drug traffickers, government officials, paramilitary, and the so-called self-defense groups.

The last section of this anthology, Part III, includes essays examining the aftermath of state violence and the quest for justice and reconciliation. This section sheds light on how civil society's capacity to rebuild depends on both the recovery of truth and the historical memory of both victims and perpetrators of violence. It also suggests that polarized societies' capacity to heal will depend on the ability of the criminal justice system to carry out transparent legal proceedings against all who participated, directly or as accomplices, in a state's repressive and genocidal policies.

Notre Dame Professor Ernesto Verdeja's, "Political Violence, Justice, and Reconciliation in Latin America," is based on case studies from Argentina, Chile, Guatemala, and Peru. In Chapter 9, Verdeja shows that in spite of important efforts to confront atrocities, democracies remain incomplete. It is against a backdrop "of highly constrained democratic transitions," or pacted-transitions, that reparations, forgiveness, and reconciliation should be evaluated. He concludes by asserting that international actors, such as the United States, can play an important role in the quest for reconciliation by releasing confidential information kept about the Cold War years.

Union College professor Guillermina S. Seri's, "Vicious Legacies? State Violence(s) in Argentina" sheds light on the legacies of terror in Argentina. Not surprisingly, she finds similarities and continuities between past and ongoing widespread violence, a point worth considering when drafting new law enforcement policies. Currently, these policies tend to view political violence as something from the distant past, and fail to see the tight relationship between past and current criminal violence. Her focus on the violent reactions of police in the aftermath of larger violence allows her to place institutionalized repression from the "dirty war" years in a broader context.

My own chapter, "Courageous Soldiers (*Valientes Soldados*): Politics of Concealment in the Aftermath of State Violence in Chile," examines the lingering effects of complicity and secret collaboration in the aftermath of long-term violence. It looks at testimonies from court proceedings of criminal cases where Chilean perpetrators were sentenced after the restoration of political democracy. This analysis of court files obtained in Chile is offered as a critique of Truth Commissions in the region, which have failed to account for perpetrators' voices.

In Chapter 12, former Dean of the University of San Carlos in Guatemala, Raúl Molina Mejía argues that, although giant steps have been taken towards criminal accountability and reconciliation, particularly in Chile and Argentina, the problem of impunity continues to haunt Latin America. This is particularly true in Guatemala where a peace process has failed to assign responsibility for crimes against humanity. In "Bringing Justice to Guatemala: The Need to Confront Genocide and Other Crimes Against Humanity," Molina Mejía proposes the creation of a special tribunal for Guatemala, in combination with the work of the International Criminal Court (ICC). In Mejía's view, criminal accountability needs to occur in order to heal extremely polarized societies.

No other book to date has been devoted to the study of genocide during the Cold War years in Latin America. This book is a pioneer and as such, it has left the definition of genocide open for each author to wrestle with. All the authors' contributions are original works except for two chapters that were thoroughly expanded (Feierstein and Aguila's chapters have previously appeared in a special volume commissioned by the *Journal of Genocide Research* in 2006).

There are at least three important lessons that can be drawn from an examination of Latin America's Cold War violence through the lens of genocide.

One of them is that local elites, whose contempt for the dark-skinned lower classes can be traced back to colonial times, have continued to reproduce systems of inequalities. Their neocolonial mentality has been transmitted from generation to generation and has coincided with US notions of racial supremacy. Second, extreme class, race, and ethnic polarization in the region has led to the construction of *el pueblo* as an entity that can be considered as the "hostage group." The inclusion of *el pueblo* in the typology of "the other" (the victims of genocide) helps us reframe studies of genocide in the region because it contextualizes organized violence against the majority of the Cold War victims who are dark-skinned, indigenous and poor. It can thus be said that state violence and genocide in the region encompassed victims with various identity markers. Lastly, an examination of Latin American history shows the long-standing implications of US-led geopolitical projects that include powerful multinationals and corporations.

Authors in this volume provide the groundwork to understanding the flourishing of state violence and genocide in Latin America. Each essay provides a vast array of empirical evidence (from declassified information, court files, and oral testimonies) for the integration of Latin America within genocide studies. In each case presented here, scholars wrestle with historical interpretations and concepts laid out in this introduction, and thus subscribe to various interdisciplinary frameworks. The role of the US in promoting democracy and security and in shaping the methods of destruction, and the extent of US complicity are all part of this ongoing debate.

There are still, of course, many scholarly gaps. In particular, this anthology lacks case studies from the Caribbean, an area largely impacted by US dominance. Primarily, this is due to space limitations, but also because the heterogeneity of this sub-region calls for an in-depth analysis in its own right. Further hemispheric research should also scrutinize how pockets of the population became rescuers by saving thousands of people, even in the midst of extreme violence. Moreover, scholarship should carry out comparative analysis of postcolonial state violence and genocide in Africa and Latin America and other areas of the so-called developing world in order to uncover particular factors that can contribute to the growth of genocide studies. Genocide as a criminal process is fluid and takes new forms depending on the larger political scenario. The historical record of Latin America undoubtedly exemplifies this pattern of genocides committed by states, and thus can certainly enhance the already rich typology of existing genocidal studies.

Notes and references

1 Many thanks to Stephanie Alfaro, Jaime Hidalgo, Henry R. Huttenbach, Suzanne Oboler, Anani Dzidzienyo, Mary Ellen Sanger, and Liza Rosas Bustos for their insightful comments on earlier versions of this chapter. Many thanks also to Kristy Eldredge for her editorial assistance and to Sarah Scott for her thoughtful suggestions on the final version of this chapter.

2 The extensive literature includes, among others, R. Lemkin, *Axis Rule in Occupied Europe: Laws of Occupation, Analysis of Government, Proposals for Redress*, Washington, DC: Carnegie Endowment for International Peace, 1944; L. Kuper, *The Pity of It All: Polarization of Racial and Ethnic Relations*, Minneapolis, MN: University of Minnesota Press, 1977; H. Fein, *Accounting for Genocide: National Responses and Jewish Victimization During the Holocaust*, New York: The Free Press, 1979; Z. Bauman, *Modernity and the Holocaust*, Ithaca, NY: Cornell University Press, 1989; E. Staub, *The Roots of Evil: The Origins of Genocide and Other Group Violence*, Cambridge: Cambridge University Press, 1989; F. Chalk and K. Jonassohn. *The History and Sociology of Genocide: Analyses and Case Studies*, New Haven, CT: Yale University Press, 1990; Raul Hilbert, *Perpetrators, Victims, Bystanders: The Jewish Catastrophe, 1933–1945*, New York: Harper, 1992; C. Browning, *Ordinary Men: Reserve Police Battalion 101 and the Final Solution in Poland*, New York: HarperCollins, 1992; H. Fein, *Genocide: A Sociological Perspective*, London and Newbury Park, CA: Sage Publications, 1993; S. Katz, *The Holocaust in Historical Context*, Volume 1: *The Holocaust and Mass Death Before the Modern Age*, Oxford: Oxford University Press, 1994; M. Mamdani, *When Victims Become Killers: Colonialism, Nativism, and the Genocide in Rwanda*, Princeton, NJ: Princeton University

Press, 2001; A. Hinton, *Annihilating Difference: The Anthropology of Genocide*, Berkeley, CA: University of California Press, 2002; M. Shaw, *War and Genocide: Organized Killing in Modern Society*, Cambridge: Polity Press, 2003; E. Weitz, *A Century of Genocide: Utopias of Race and Nation*, Princeton, NJ: Princeton University Press, 2003; J. Semelin, *Purifier et détruire: usages politiques des massacres et genocides*, Paris: Le Seuil, 2005; M. Levene, *The Rise of the West and the Coming of Genocide*, London: I. B. Tauris & Co. Ltd, 2005; T. Ackam, *A Shameful Act: The Armenian Genocide and the Question of Turkish Responsibility*, New York: Metropolitan Books, 2006; S. Totten and S. W. Parsons, *A Century of Genocide. Critical Essays and Eyewitness Accounts*, London: Routledge, 2009.

3 Notably, an emerging literature examining genocide in the region is illustrated in the works of D. Feierstein: *Seis estudios sobre genocidio: analisis de las relaciones sociales: otredad, exclusion y exterminio*, Buenos Aires: Eudeba Publishers, 2000; E. P. Roorda. *The Dictator Next Door: The Good Neighbor Policy and the Trujillo Regime in the Dominican Republic, 1930–1945*, Durham, NC: Duke University Press, 1998. Yet, with the exception of the Center for the Study of Genocide in Buenos Aires, led by Daniel Feierstein, the absence of educational centers for the study of the phenomenon of genocide in the region still prevails.

4 For an overview of the antecedents excluding the political category out of the Convention, see E. D. Weitz, *A Century of Genocide: Utopias of Race and Nation*, Princeton, NJ: Princeton University Press, 2003; See also D. Feierstein, M. Hiebert and P. Policzer, and J. P. McSherry in this volume.

5 For a discussion on universal jurisdiction used by Judge Garzón in the Pinochet case, see N. Roth-Arriaza, *The Pinochet Effect: Transnational Justice in the Age of Human Rights*, Philadelphia, PA: University of Pennsylvania Press, 2006; see also E. Verdeja in this volume for a general discussion of trials and accountability in the region.

6 W. Schabas argues that this broader definition of genocide has also been used in Ethiopia where the former Derg regime has been charged with genocide. Online, available at: www.usip/org/pubs/specialsreports/sr99017.html (accessed on July 28, 2008).

7 The exclusion of the Latin American experience from genocide studies is most dramatically exemplified in Samantha Power's acclaimed book, *A Problem from Hell: America and the Age of Genocide*, New York: Basic Books, 2002. Here, Power explores US

> policy of nonintervention in the face of genocide ... No US president has ever made genocide prevention a priority, and no US president has ever suffered politically for his indifference to its occurrence. It is thus no coincidence that genocide rages on
>
> (p. xxi)

While her detailed account of how the US has failed to prevent genocidal violence is remarkable, her exclusion of Latin America from her universe of case studies renders invisible the role the US has played in backing genocidal violence in the region.

8 See H. Huttenbach, "From the Editor: Towards a theory of genocide? Not Yet! A Caveat," *Journal of Genocide Research*, 6, 2, June 2004, pp. 149–50.

9 For a full review of the regions' economic development, readers should particularly refer to the dependency school exemplified in the work of F. H. Cardoso and E. Faletto, *Dependency and Development in Latin America*, Berkeley, CA: University of California Press, 1979; O. Ianni: *Imperialismo y cultura de la violencia en América Latina*. México: Editorial Siglo XXI, 1969; C. Furtado, *El poder economico: Estados Unidos y America Latina*. Buenos Aires: Centro Editor de Latinoamerica, 1971.

10 With the exception of Costa Rica, the Central American region was engulfed in bloody armed conflicts. For a discussion of Costa Rica's exceptionalism, see J. Booth, *Costa Rica: Quest For Democracy, Nations of the Modern World: Latin America,*

Boulder, CO: Westview Press, 1998; See Gómez-Suárez in this volume for a nuanced discussion of genocide in Colombia.

11 See, for example, P. C. Schmitter (ed.), *Military Rule in Latin America: Function, Consequences and Perspectives*, Beverly Hills, CA: Sage Publications, 1973; G. O'Donnell, P. Schmitter, and L. Whitehead (eds), *Transitions from Authoritarian Rule* (4 vols), Baltimore, MD: Johns Hopkins University Press, 1986; B. Loveman, *Por La Patria: Politics and the Armed Forces in Latin America*. Wilmington, DE: SR Books, 1999; J. P. McSherry, *Incomplete Transition, Military Power and Democracy in Argentina*, New York: St Martin's Press, 1997. C. Menjivar and N. Rodriguez, *When States Kill: Latin America, the US, and Technologies of Terror*, Austin, TX: University of Texas Press, 2005.

12 Though his work emphasizes extreme racial polarization above all, Kuper examines cases from Rwanda and Burundi. See Kuper, *The Pity of It All*.

13 Online, available at: www-wds.worldbank.org/servlet/WDSContentServer/WDSP/IB/2008/02/01/000158349_20080201123241/Rendered/PDF/wps4504.pdf) (accessed on December 14, 2008). Also, David de Ferranti, World Bank Vice-president for Latin America and the Caribbean, notes,

> Latin America and the Caribbean is one of the regions of the world with the greatest inequality. The richest one-tenth of the population of Latin America and the Caribbean earn 48 percent of total income, while the poorest tenth earn only 1.6 percent.
>
> (Online, available at: web.worldbank.org/WBSITE/EXTERNAL/COUNTRIES/LACEXT/0,,contentMDK:20384897~pagePK:146736~piPK:146830~theSitePK:258554,00.html (accessed on January 27, 2009))

14 H. Fein, *Accounting for Genocide: National Responses and Jewish Victimization during the Holocaust*, New York: Free Press, 1979.

15 The term *pueblo* can have different anthropological, sociological, and political meanings. For the most part, however, it is associated with particular political identities and relationships, representing the lower classes.

16 L. Zea, *Latin America and the World*, Norman, OK: University of Oklahoma Press, 1963, p. 57.

17 According to Cockcroft, "only a minority of Latin Americans shared the prevalent US view of an "East–West" (communist–capitalist) conflict shaping their destinies. Most Latin Americans, including presidents taking office during the new democratic dawn of the mid-1980s, believed the main axis of conflict, as well as of wealth and poverty, was 'North–South' (rich–poor)." J. Cockcroft, *Neighbors in Turmoil: Latin America*, New York: Harper & Row Publishers, 1989, p. 5.

18 Weitz, *A Century of Genocide*, p. 2.

19 F. Mires, *La rebelion permanente. Las revoluciones sociales en America Latina.* Mexico: Siglo XXI Editores, 1988; see all authors in this volume, particularly L. Roniger (Chapter 1).

20 Considering the deep class cleavages, racial subordination is often less acknowledged and examined, which hinders discussions of the racial and ethnic overtones of state terrorism. Yet, as Latin American thinkers have noted, "Racial inequality was another of the evils of Hispanic America, especially in countries like Peru and Mexico" (L. Zea, *The Latin American Mind*, Norman, OK: University of Oklahoma Press, p. 185). Preexisting racial prejudices in the Caribbean, for example, have led to acts of genocide against the Haitians by General Rafael Leonidas Trujillo in 1932. See Roorda. *The Dictator Next Door.*

21 The National Security Doctrine gave rise to national security states defined as states that resorted to the use of terror to subdue their populations. See J. Patrice McSherry, "Death Squads as Parallel Forces: Uruguay, Operation Condor and the United States," *Journal of Third World Studies*, 24, 20, 2007, pp. 13–52.

22 See L. Kuper, *Genocide: Its Political Use in the Twentieth Century*. New Haven, CT: Yale University Press, 1981; L. Kuper, *The Prevention of Genocide*. New Haven, CT, and London: Yale University Press, 1985.

23 Kuper, *Genocide: Its Political Use*, p. 57.

24 Kuper, *Genocide: Its Political Use*.

25 The "whitening" of the population was also seen as a solution. In Argentina, for example, the mixed blood between Spanish and the native population was seen as one cause for economic stagnation, a problem which could be, according to Argentinean thinker Domingo Sarmiento, fixed through the immigration of white races into the country. See Zea, *The Latin-American Mind*.

26 W. Mignolo, "La colonialidad a lo largo y a lo ancho: el hemisferio occidental en el horizonte colonial de la modernidad," in *La colonialidad del saber: eurocentrismo y ciencias sociales. Perspectivas latinoamericanas*, ed., Edgardo Lander, Buenos Aires: CLASCO), 2000. Online, available at: http://waltermignolo.com/publications (accessed on March 19, 2009).

27 Zea, *The Latin American Mind*.

28 Elites' contempt for the lower classes coincides, as noted by Lars Schoultz, with long-standing US views of Latin Americans as incapable of governing themselves. See L. Schoultz, W. C. Smith, and A. Varas (eds), *Security, Democracy, and Development in US–Latin American Relations*. Miami: North-South Center Press. Thomas C. Mann, assistant secretary of state for economic affairs during the Eisenhower administration (1953–61), once said, "I know my Latinos ... they understand only two things – a buck in the pocket and a kick in the ass" (P. H. Smith, *Talons of the Eagle. Dynamics of US–Latin American Relations*, Oxford: Oxford University Press, 2000, p. 157).

29 Cockcroft, *Neighbors in Turmoil*, p. 6.

30 Zea, *Latin American Mind*.

31 J. Gonzalez, *A History of Latinos in America: Harvest of Empire*, New York: Viking, 2000; G. Grandin, *Empire's Workshop. Latin America, the United States, and the Rise of the New Imperialism*, New York: Metropolitan Books, 2006.

32 J. Petras, *Politics and Social Structure in Latin America*, New York: Monthly Review Press, 1970.

33 Petras, *Politics and Structure*, p. 22.

34 Petras, *Politics and Structure*, p. 23.

35 Melvyn P. Leffler and David S. Painter have noted:

> An independent feature of the post post-war years was the emergence of orga-nized labor as a major social and political actor in Latin America. By the late 1930s, the exports sectors had largely recovered from the world depression and import substitution industrialization had accelerated in the more economically developed countries of the region. The Second World War gave a further impetus to industrial development. Combined with population growth and rural–urban migration, the size of the working class had expanded considerably. And its char-acter was being rapidly transformed: besides the important nuclei of workers in the agricultural and mining export sectors, – many of them state employees, and industrial workers were increasingly important. In Mexico the number of workers in manufacturing had risen from 568,000 in 1940 to 938,000 in 1945.

> See M. P. Leffler and D. S. Painter, *The Origins of the Cold War: An International History*, New York: Routledge, 2005, p. 305.

36 Leffler and Painter, *The Origins of the Cold War*, p. 305.

37 Cockcroft, *Neighbors in Turmoil*, p. xii.

38 Cockcroft, *Neighbors in Turmoil*, p. 4.

39 See for example, L. Boff and C. Boff, *Introducing Liberation Theology*, New York: Orbis Books, 1998; G. Gutierrez, *Teología de la liberación: perspectivas*, Salamanca: Ediciones Sigueme, 1982.

40 In Argentina, the military junta soon eliminated the Montoneros and Ejercito Revolucionario del Pueblo (ERP). In Uruguay, the military eradicated the Tupamaro Movement of National Liberation (MLN) as President Juan Maria Bordaberry declared a state of internal war. See A. Rouquie, *The Military and the State in Latin America*, Berkeley, CA: University of California Press, 1987; J. P. McSherry, *Incomplete Transition.*

41 Rouquie, *The Military and the State*, p. 261.

42 P. F. Weiss, "Repression and State Security," in J. Corradi, P. F. Weiss, and M. A. Garreton (eds), *Fear at the Edge: State Terror and Resistance in Latin America*, Berkeley, CA: University of California Press, 1992, p. 44.

43 R. Lemkin, *Axis Rule in Occupied Europe: Laws of Occupation, Analysis of Government, Proposals for Redress*, Washington, DC: Carnegie Endowment for International Peace, 1944, p. 79.

44 For Alex Hinton, categories such as ethnicity also lack enduring characteristics and these "seemingly stable categories refer to sets of social relations that have fuzzy boundaries and vary across time and place." A. Hinton, *Annihilating the Difference: The Anthropology of Genocide*, Berkeley, CA: University of California Press, 2002, p. 5.

45 B. Harff and T. Gurr; "Toward Empirical Theory of Genocides and Politicides," *International Studies Quarterly*, 32, 3, September 1988, pp. 359–71.

46 I. W. Charny (ed.), *Genocide: The Critical Bibliographic Review*, London: Mansell Publishing, 1988.

47 For Latin American scholars' discussions of *el pueblo*, see Gonzalez, *A History of Latinos in America*; D. Camacho, and R. Menjivar (eds), *Los movimientos populares en America Latina*, Mexico: Siglo XXI Editores, 1989; R. Lanz, "Lo político transfigurado. Estrategias para entrar al mundo postmoderno [The Transfiguration of Politics. Strategies For Entering the Post-Modern World]." Online, available at: www.serbi.luz.edu.ve/scielo.php?pid=S1315–52162006001000007&script=sci_arttext&tlng=es (accessed on February 4 2009).

48 See the chapters by M. Drouin and R. Molina Mejía, this volume.

49 According to Lesley Gill, notions of "dirty" "lazy," and "ignorant" are commonly used to define the popular classes. L. Gill, *The School of the Americas*, Durham, NC: Duke University Press, p. 55.

50 This is particularly so in Guatemala, where *el pueblo*'s political exclusion is largely the result of ethnic and racial discrimination of the Mayan people. See the chapters by M. Drouin and J. Harbury, this volume.

51 L. J. Frazier, *Salt in the Sand: Memory, Violence, and the Nation-State in Chile, 1890 to the Present*, Durham, NC: Duke University Press, 2007.

52 Cockcroft, *Neighbors in Turmoil*, p. 501.

53 Cockcroft, *Neighbors in Turmoil*, p. 352.

54 Corradi *et al.*, *Fear at the Edge.*

55 R. Munck, *Latin America: The Transition to Democracy*, London: Zed Books, 1985.

56 P. Lernoux, *Cry of the People: United States Involvement in the Rise of Fascism, Torture, and Murder and the Persecution of the Catholic Church in Latin America*, New York: Doubleday & Company, 1980.

57 For Ricardo Melgar Bao, until the mid-twentieth century the history of Latin America's workers' movements was driven by a discordant array of groups. R. Melgar Bao, *El movimiento obrero latinoamericano*, Mexico, DF: Alianza Editorial Mexicana, 1988. See also F. Calderón, *Movimientos sociales y politica: la decada de los ochenta en Latinoamerica*. Mexico: Siglo XXI Editores, 1995.

58 In his account of the frameworks of memory and the transformation from feudalism to modern social structures, Halbwachs writes:

> But what difference is there really, apart from the title, between a lawyer, a public prosecutor, and a rich, active, and cultivated merchant, a member of Parliament,

or the titular incumbent of one of these offices that confer a nobility of dignity? They are united by family relations and alliances, meet in the same salons, read the same books, and participate equally in the type of social life in which one is concerned with a person's function. They participate in a society that is interested only in itself, in all that qualifies its members to gain admittance, and in what enables them alike to animate, sharpen, and renew the consciousness that it has of itself.

See M. Halbwachs, *On Collective Memory*, Chicago: University of Chicago Press, 1992, p. 136.

59 Gill, *The School of the Americas*, p. 55.
60 Victims in Argentina, as Daniel Feierstein shows in his chapter in this volume, were also identified by their ethnic memberships as Jewish; See also Lernoux, *Cry of the People*, pp. 341–5.
61 France also has significantly participated in facilitating the methods of state terrorism. See Marie-Monique Robin, *Escuadrones de la muerte, la escuela francesa*, Buenos Aires: Editorial Sudamericana, 2005. Also, in 2003, a top Chilean intelligence commander, Manuel Contreras, now in prison for charges of crimes against humanity, declared in a television interview broadcast in France that the Pinochet regime had received military assistance from France under the administration of Valéry Giscard d'Estaing (1974–81). *La Nacion*, September 2, 2001.
62 Smith, *Talons of the Eagle*.
63 Grandin, *Empire's Workshop*, pp. 16–17.
64 Calderón, *Movimientos sociales*. For a discussion of American involvement, Grandin has also included Christian evangelical missionaries preaching the gospels of capitalism. See Grandin, *Empire's Workshop*.
65 See the chapter by J. P. McSherry in this volume.
66 For a discussion of the epistemology of emotions, see the ethnographic work of R. Behar, *The Vulnerable Observer: Anthropology that Breaks your Heart*, Boston: Beacon Press, 1996.

Part I

The roots and theoretical underpinnings

1 US hemispheric hegemony and the descent into genocidal practices in Latin America[1]

Luis Roniger

This chapter aims to provide a long-term perspective on the rise of the US to hemispheric hegemony in the Americas, and to discuss some of the consequences of such a rise in the second half of the twentieth century, in particular, those consequences which resulted in the genocidal repression by military and authoritarian rulers of their own countrymen in the Southern Cone during the 1970s and 1980s, and in Central America in the 1980s and early 1990s. While providing such a background, this chapter aims to be synoptic and not exhaustive. For further information and to test the general arguments presented here, readers are referred to an extensive literature that follows a continental scope of analysis,[2] and monographs devoted to the study of relationships between the US and other countries in the Americas.[3]

The rise of the US to hemispheric hegemony

By the onset of the twentieth century, President James Monroe's address made on December 1823 seemed ominous. Voiced under the protective maritime umbrella of Great Britain, the clear-cut line it predicated between Europe – and its remaining colonies in the New World – and the independent republics of the Western hemisphere could be seen as a foreboding doctrine, when perceived from the perspective of its corollary by President Theodore Roosevelt in 1904. According to that corollary, the US would be forced to intervene in the Western hemisphere when chronic unrest and political corruption would demand it. In the interval between Monroe's address and Roosevelt's era, the US had expanded its territory through a series of successful wars, most notably the incorporation of Texas, the defeat of Mexico in the 1846–8 war, and the defeat of Spain in the so called Spanish–American War of 1898. Immediately following the Spanish–American War, Cuba was occupied and had to accept the terms of the Platt Amendment that conditioned its sovereignty until the early 1930s. Also since 1898, Puerto Rico has remained dependent on and connected to the US. By the late 1890s, the US had also managed to curtail or contain German and French inroads in Central America and the Caribbean. Moreover, by 1901, Britain tacitly accepted – in the Hay-Pauncefote Treaty signed with the US – that Central America was already within the US sphere of influence. By 1903, the

US supported Panama's independence from Colombia, in return for the exclusive rights to build the Panama Canal and control the Canal Zone.[4]

The twentieth century witnessed further reinforcement of US hemispheric hegemony, sustained by policies aimed at controlling access to resources deemed strategic by the US's investments in the Americas. The US took an active role in the "liberation" of Panama from Colombia, and established control through pacts and military occupations. The pursuit of US interests and investments often implied influencing or controlling the destinies of other states and nations in the hemisphere, initially in Central America and the Caribbean. According to Jan Knippers Black, "gunboat and dollar diplomacy helped to keep other Central American states submissive, and the owners of United Fruit and other companies openly boasted of buying and selling presidents."[5] Increasingly, such strategy was followed also in the Andean region and the Southern Cone.

The first three decades of the twentieth century were characterized by the recurrent and in some cases permanent US presence in the Caribbean and Central America. This is what has come to be known as Big Stick interventionism, which was practiced in Cuba, Puerto Rico, and for years by marines occupying Nicaragua, Haiti, and the Dominican Republic. Such interventionism cannot be attributed exclusively to the expansionist drive of the US. The weak institutionalization of national states generated a situation in which domestic contenders called the US to serve as the transnational actor that could intervene, supporting them in their power struggles. As Robert H. Holden indicates, under such situations of hollow legitimacy and fragmented authority, the US easily became

> a kind of transnational *patrón* who distributed favors and bought clients by playing on divisions within and among the governments of Central America. As early as 1911, Adolfo Díaz, the US-installed president of Nicaragua, offered the US *chargé* in Managua a treaty that would permit Washington "to intervene in our internal affairs in order to maintain peace."[6]

It is this complementarity of interests that brought about the recurrent direct intervention of US forces in Central America and the Caribbean in the early twentieth century. Following three decades of interventionism, the US elaborated on a strategy for containing or controlling political change by leaving behind well-trained local forces to protect the claims of US corporations and the governments and political leaders favored by US policy-makers.[7]

The 1930s and early 1940s were thus a hiatus in direct intervention, dictated by Franklin D. Roosevelt's idea of the 'Good Neighbor' policy. This model contributed paradoxically to the growth of US trade and direct investments in the region, as well as to the alignment of most Latin American elites and armed forces with the US. The principle of nonintervention was strongly supported by the Inter-American system, which saw in it a delayed recognition of the Bolivarian principles that set the major norms of the Latin American international regime. Promulgated by Simón Bolivar in the early 1820s, they included the norms of equality of sovereign states, non-recognition of territorial gains following wars, the peaceful settlement of international disputes by mechanisms of arbitration, and a system of collective security, including mutual defense and neutrality. Since the 1820s, Bolivarianism could be seen as a generalized expression of Latin American transnational commitment, which was affected by the launching of the Pan-American movement after 1889, which recognized the leading role of the US in shaping the agenda and establishing the continent's common norms.[8] While the new US policy did not obliterate the memory of earlier interventions, it was perceived as a more egalitarian recognition of Latin American national sovereignty.

During the course of the two world wars, the influence of Great Britain, France, Germany, and other European countries diminished. In the 1930s, sympathy with Germany and the Axis countries was still widespread, along with distrust of the US. A process of alignment with the US took place, however, before and during World War II, even in countries such as Mexico, which sent troops to the front.[9] The process accelerated in Brazil, a country that sent soldiers to fight alongside the American Fourth Army in Italy during World War II, and that received US support in the form of equipment and military training and in establishing military academies. Countries in the Western hemisphere granted air and naval bases to the US. World War II put aside the former pattern linking Latin American armed forces to European armies. The cooperation during the war – reflected in the Inter-American Defense Board (1942) – led to multilateral cooperation and optimism, as expressed in the Inter-American Treaty of Reciprocal Assistance signed in Rio de Janeiro in 1947 and the launching of the Organization of American States in Bogotá, Colombia, the following year. By then, Latin America was firmly locked within the US sphere of influence, as the nuclear standoff of the Cold War led the US and the USSR to accept each other's established spheres of influence.[10]

By the end of World War II, the US had established strong bilateral military ties and had acquired a near monopoly of training and equipping Latin American armed forces. Since 1951, a series of bilateral agreements for military assistance had been signed. These agreements defined grants and credits for the acquisition of US military equipment, the stationing of US military missions in Latin America, and the training of Latin American officers in military schools both in the US and in the Panama Canal Zone. In tandem with the move of the political pendulum towards authoritarian and military governments in the 1950s throughout most of the region (exceptions being Brazil, Costa Rica, Chile, Uruguay, and somehow also Cuba), the US placed increasing emphasis on ties with the Latin American military, police, and national guard forces. By 1960 nearly 7,000 officers had been assigned to Military Assistance Advisory Groups in Latin America and police forces were trained in counterinsurgency methods. In the early 1970s military grants and credit sales more than tripled to over $218 million, while the size of the Latin American armed forces grew exponentially, especially in those countries in which the military had seized power.[11]

The agreements of military cooperation were originally set within the framework of the multilateral arrangements, with the US reassuring Latin American countries that the new format of assistance neither was intended to trigger an arms race between these countries, nor would it lead to US intervention, e.g. in the form of entrenching dictatorships.

Respecting the national sensibilities of the military was key to enabling such a rise in military relationships. Latin American military professionals saw themselves as the heirs of the founding fathers of their states as they had engaged in the construction of national identity during independence. Like many officers elsewhere – and most civilian leaders in their societies – they believed in their vocation for leadership. In some countries, perhaps most notably Brazil, Argentina, Peru, and Panama, they felt committed by vocation to fight against their societies' underdevelopment, illiteracy, poverty, and national fragmentation.[12]

In the context of the Cold War, this vision focusing on their society's unity and development became an increasing concern with national security and a need to fight internal enemies. Gradually, the latter became identified as leftist groups who, with their revolutionary discourse and activities, were destabilizing the political arena and colonizing public spaces and culture in a detrimental and anomic way. This of course was seen as inimical to the "true" values of the nation. Their professional training added to their corporate consciousness and gave them a sense of alienation from these disorderly civilians and their foreign ideas.

In order to fully assess the impact of the US backing of the military that would take power during the 1960s, one should take into consideration the progressive decline of alternative models of US influence in Latin America. In conjunction with military cooperation in the 1950s and early 1960s, US policy tried to project its model of development onto Latin American countries. This was a model that promised modernization and political development once economic change was achieved. It also claimed to lead to an eventual decline of inequality and polarization, and to the promotion of democracy. Bolivia stands out among the countries where this model was attempted. As stressed by Kenneth Lehman, Bolivia had been a favorable place to test these premises since the April 1952 revolution by the MNR (National Revolutionary Movement) managed to bring to power leaders who, in spite of their rhetoric, were genuinely interested in modernization along capitalist lines. Motivated by ideological visions that were more liberal than Marxist, the new elites sought US assistance as the driving force of this change. Increasingly, the US provided the desired assistance on conditional terms, demanding that Bolivia should become open to private initiative, foreign investment, and the logic of free markets. Unable to operate such changes in the short term and with both Bolivians and Americans disappointed, the US came to recognize by the early 1960s the increasing importance of state regulation, as envisioned in the Alliance for Progress.[13]

Similarly, following the military coups that started with the CIA-orchestrated removal of President Jacobo Arbenz in Guatemala in 1954, the Cuban revolution of 1959, and Che Guevara's commitment to create as many Vietnams as he could, the US moved to condone and often support authoritarian rule in the name of national security.[14]

If Latin American countries were unfit to follow the US model of development and, in the context of the Cold War, were on the brink of political breakdown and the threat of revolution, perhaps it was time to make room for a renewed domestic model of "order and progress" resembling that which, in the late nineteenth and early twentieth centuries, had been successfully adopted by the followers of positivism in Latin America.

From a geopolitical perspective and in terms of resources, small countries depended heavily on US decisions. Partnerships however were rather unequal. While it is true that in the early 1960s leaders such as Victor Paz Estenssoro of Bolivia used their connections with Washington to try to maneuver domestic political forces, the US relied even more strongly on the result of local cohorts of power struggling to dominate the political and public arena. In some cases, confrontations occurred between factions of the armed forces, foreshadowing the rise to power of the military, for example, the confrontations in Argentina in the early 1960s, which eventually led to military dictatorships spanning 1966–73 and 1976–83.

In the early 1960s, President Kennedy increased US support for hemispheric security forces in parallel to the Alliance for Progress. President Johnson continued that orientation. In early April 1964 this shift in emphasis became evident as the US supported the Brazilian coup that deposed João Goulart. Paradigmatic of the ever-increasing US shift to support military options, too, is the case in neighboring Bolivia on the eve of General René Barrientos' deposing of Bolivian president Paz Estenssoro in November 1964. Both the US embassy and the State Department moved to support military intervention, motivated by fears that Paz could be assassinated and vice-president Juan Lechín, a leftist, made president.[15]

So ended a period in which the US had supported the reformist option, which – despite idealistic perceptions – failed to trigger democracy and capitalism in the client states. In the case of Bolivia, the shift to military rule and the provision of US military training paid off, at least in the short term. General Barrientos, through the use of populist and paternalist means, built broad support among Bolivian peasants and succeeded in isolating Che Guevara's guerrilla forces, and subsequently capturing and executing the revolutionary leader in October 1967, in a joint CIA–Bolivian operation.

Starting in the 1960s, the impact of US hemispheric policy combined with domestic trends, primarily the increasing socio-economic mobilization and polarized political arenas. Having the supportive vision of being on the frontline of defense of Western civilization, as led by the US and encoded in doctrines of national security, Latin American governments slipped into a renewed use of regimes of exception, military interventions in public life, and suspension of constitutional freedoms and guarantees, with severe consequences in the realm of human rights. I turn now to analyze these dimensions, which along with the role of the US as hegemonic power, were crucial factors in the descent to genocidal practices in the region.

Domestic trends and polarized political arenas

Latin American societies shared a dual cultural dynamic. On the one hand, there was a substratum of respect for hierarchy, authority and order, of Roman Catholic origins, with corporatist leanings. On the other hand, from an early stage, elites looked to the centers of world development, absorbing secular Western ideas and ideologies and adapting them as part of their models of nation-building, though only as far as they befitted their views and local realities. From early on, elites, both liberals and conservatives, interpreted their societies in terms of a struggle between civilization and barbarism. This legitimized their policies of annihilating indigenous populations, repressing rural social forces, and privatizing communal lands and releasing them to the markets, where lands were appropriated mostly by large landholders, thus creating a spiraling concentration of lands along with a multitude of minifundia peasants and landless rural workers.

With the adoption of formal models of constitutional liberal democracy, the elites interpreted them in ways which stressed their authority and endorsed formal equality only as long as this did not affect the hierarchical structure of society. For instance, while they responded to popular pressures by widening the scope of suffrage laws, elites organized the electoral processes in ways which were tainted by fraud, patronage, and vote-buying. This ensured the elites' continued control over the polity, its institutions, and resources. The political realm was organized in a republican presidentialist way, with electoral systems that allowed greater electoral participation and generated popular mobilization among substantial sectors of the middle and lower classes. The models incorporated by the political classes formally ensured the recognition of basic rights and liberties, according to the European and North American pattern, and yet for many decades politics were accompanied in practice by fraud, clientelism, and the manipulation of the electorate by the political elites.[16]

In most Latin American countries, institution building was supported by the development of an agro-export economic model, which was sometimes coupled with financial markets, e.g. in Uruguay, or, as in the cases of Chile or Bolivia, with a mineral-export model. The agro-export and mineral-export models provided the resources for the growth of state bureaucracies and sometimes the expansion of state benefits, which in cases such as Argentina and Brazil had strong populist characteristics. By the mid-twentieth century these societies underwent processes of modernization and late industrialization, massive rural–urban migration and a rise in unfulfilled expectations, which led to increasing socioeconomic mobilization and political polarization.

Against the backdrop of the Cold War and the inability of ruling elites to lead their countries to peaceful coexistence and more equal development, a growing sense of support for radical change dominated intellectual circles and the younger generations. Many in the latter group supported the feeling, expressed by Eduardo Galeano in one of the most widely read essays in that period, that Latin American should be radically transformed, if necessary by force:

There is much rottenness to be thrown to the sea in the way to the reconstruction of Latin America. The deprived, the humiliated, the damned, they
have this task in their hands. The Latin American national cause is, before
anything else, a social cause. In order that Latin America should be reborn,
there is a need to throw down the lords of the land, country by country.
Times of rebellion and change are beginning. There are those who believe
that destiny rests on the knees of the gods, but the truth is that it works, as a
constant challenge, in the conscience of men.[17]

The potential for violence was imbued in the ideological polarization between
public spheres and civil society. As Ana Pizarro observed, for the Left, the 1960s
and early 1970s were years of practicing "criteria" in the social sciences, of discussing the theory of dependency as opposed to development approaches, criticism and counter-criticism, of launching a dialogue with Africans who were
emerging from decolonization processes, of assessing the significance of the
Cuban revolution and the prospects of Caribbean and Latin American integration.[18] Influencing the political climate during this epoch were anti-imperialist
feelings, the spread of liberation theology, demands to protect the rights of
minorities, and the rise of feminism.

The messages contained in the elaborations of the Left were rejected by
others who held diametrically opposed visions of their society, and who were no
less passionate in their own views and positions.[19] The very principled positions
of these circles and the semi-sacredness with which they cognitively structured
and evaluated the forces of society contributed to the clash that tore apart these
societies in the period leading to the military takeovers.

Formal democracy broke down and was replaced by military rule in a domino
effect that originated in Brazil in 1964, where it signaled the defeat of the legacy
of populist mobilization and radicalization. Historian José Murilo de Carvalho's
research shows, contrary to accepted truism, that two factors were detrimental to
sustaining democracy. First, the breakdown of civilian rule was not the result of
the lack of democratic support by the citizens as reflected in voting patterns, but
rather the lack of democratic conviction in the elites. The elites were undermining democracy by precluding any compromise and negotiating arrangements in
Congress and in the parties. Second, the lack of communication between the
masses and the politicians failed to capture the popular mood. That is, the elitist
and hierarchical character of political articulation in these societies was detrimental to the health and continuity of democracy during this period.[20]

The biggest move toward the revolutionary option and its subsequent suppression took place in Salvador Allende's Chilean "peaceful road to socialism,"
which could have been seen as the radicalization of Frei's program of "revolution in liberty." Allende attempted what turned out to be impossible in the framework of the Cold War: to move a country in the Western hemisphere toward
socialism by constitutional and legal means. This was thought as ridiculous by
radical leftists such as Castro and was unacceptable to the US. Already in 1970,
following Chilean elections and foreseeing the probable nomination of Salvador

Allende as president by the Chilean Congress, the US attempted to prevent it by supporting military plotters who eventually assassinated General René Schneider, the top commander of the Chilean armed forces. During Allende's administration, the US, under the leadership of Henry Kissinger, who served first under Richard Nixon as national security advisor and later as secretary of state, encouraged and supported destabilizing maneuvers by parties opposed to Allende's Popular Unity (UP) coalition and by the military plotters who, under the top command of General Augusto Pinochet, ended the unique experience of the Chilean move towards socialism on September 11, 1973.

The coup in Chile gave credence to the claim by the revolutionary Left that only violence would open the door to socialism in Latin America. With the election of Juan D. Perón, Argentina became a haven for political exiles and revolutionary organizations. Uruguayan Tupamaros, Bolivian ELN (National Liberation Army), Paraguayan groups within the Colorado party, and Chilean MIR (Revolutionary Left Movement) joined Argentinean Montoneros and ERP (Revolutionary Popular Army), convinced that they would trigger a process leading to an irreversible path towards socialism. With mass mobilizations at their peak, these groups thought they could galvanize public opinion and bring about either insurrection or a military takeover of the country. Engaged in a partially successful series of kidnappings of corporate CEOs for huge ransoms, and some military actions in remote areas such as the rural hinterlands of Tucumán in Argentina, as well as terrorist attacks on military personnel, the revolutionary groups passed from an initial phase of euphoria to being decimated by paramilitary networks and later on by the military in power. The August 1973 decision by such groups to coordinate their actions and provide mutual logistical, financial, and military support across borders through a Revolutionary Coordinating Junta (JCR) augmented the concern in military circles and further enabled the latter to use their actions to taint the nonviolent opposition with the violent tactics of the guerrilla groups.[21] The military in Brazil, Paraguay, and the various countries of the Southern Cone managed rather early on to marginalize the radical Left, after launching their own network of counterintelligence coordination and following the capture of some key Southern Cone activists in Paraguay. However, they continued to use the actions of the radical revolutionary Left as central to their own discourse of salvation of their nations from the threat of international communism and moved to coordinate transnational repression in the framework of Operation Condor.[22]

Within a shared process of the breakdown of democracy and the transition to military rule in much of Latin America, each country entered the authoritarian period in a different way, which is beyond the purview of this chapter. Many factors influenced the breakdown of democratic rule, foremost the character of political struggle and polarization; the high levels of mass mobilization; the increasing political violence and the perceived menace of leftist onslaught; the prevailing doctrines of national security diffused during the Cold War; and the relative capacity of the political classes to confront the ongoing crises.[23] All these factors affected the specific timing and road to authoritarianism, as they were played out against the background of distinct political paths and patterns of civil–military relationships. These factors would affect the patterns of repression and massive human rights violations followed by the various governments as well.

Yet, beyond these differences, there was coordination in the war against "subversion," most significantly spearheaded by Operation Condor, which was launched by then Colonel Manuel Contreras of the DINA, Chile's state security agency. While preparing such a move, Contreras traveled to the US to ask for training, and subsequently, the Chileans benefited from US military advisors in counterintelligence. Secluded from the public eye, Operation Condor was designed to coordinate the exchange of intelligence and the launching of combined operations against political activists in exile, many of whom were abducted, assassinated, or transferred for interrogation and later disappeared, with the most complete secrecy and lack of accountability.[24]

It may be claimed that, in the short term, some top US officials and agencies welcomed the initiative of Chile and its partners in Operation Condor, overlooking the genocidal policies adopted, at least before its agents struck in Washington, DC, assassinating former Chilean Foreign Minister, Orlando Letelier and his secretary Ronni Moffitt, a US citizen. Yet, in the view of several Latin American high officers, the US was passive and not aggressive enough in the fight against communism during the Cold War. I would accordingly claim that, even taking into account the training and support of the US, one should look for a no less fundamental source of conviction of the military commands in their shared, albeit nuanced, belief in doctrines of national security.

Doctrines of national security

These societies, which in the 1960s and 1970s had experienced processes of massive popular mobilization and increased (disordered and almost "anarchical") participation, were forcefully demobilized under military rule. In many cases, political parties were banned or their activities frozen by decree; educational systems were regimented and disciplined after major military interventions in the universities and school programs were reshaped according to the new ideological parameters; heavy censorship was imposed upon the media and cultural expression was "purified" of any leftist orientations; trade unions were attacked, with many of their activists jailed and assassinated; professional and entrepreneurial associations were co-opted, "cleansed" of hostile elements; and self-censorship crystallized as the result of a highly repressive situation. Policies of annihilation of the radical Left and its supporters were carried out both domestically and beyond the national borders.[25]

Because of their functional role, their formation, and their professional training, the military saw themselves as guardians of the nation's values and traditions, especially in times of crisis. The National Security Doctrines, shared by the military establishments of the Latin American countries in the framework of the Cold War, posited a link between the concepts of nation and state, and the central role of the armed forces in connection to both. Military leadership considered itself the most qualified and perhaps the only capable institutional actor for achieving the defense and promotion of national interests. Under the political and institutional challenges posed by the generation dreaming of accomplishing a Socialist Revolution, with groups of armed radical leftist guerrillas using violent means to bring about a revolution, the armed forces believed they had the right and obligation to redefine and organize their nations according to the guidelines of the doctrines of national security.[26]

According to that doctrine, the basic values of a nation are anchored organically within Western civilization (interpreted in terms of Christian values), the defense of private property and initiative, and opposition to communist and Marxist ideas. As Manuel Antonio Garretón indicated, national unity was sought and interpreted in terms of a tradition or "soul," consisting of "freezing certain historical facts or universalizing particular features that are defined outside the freely expressed collective will."[27]

The military leaders thought they were most qualified to channel the "true" national spirit through the state machinery, safeguarding the nation. Paradoxically enough, this state-centric vision that centralized the role of the state in shaping the direction of society was also shared by the revolutionary Left.[28]

The organic conception of the nation implied a binary view of the world that resembled the categories of the Cold War. Eliminating the enemy was the only option, since these individuals were considered to be beyond redemption due to their irreparable ideological and flawed political views (a concept denoted in Spanish as *irrecuperabilidad*). By exterminating these "contaminated" cells or organs, both physically and ideologically, society could manage to retain its basic parameters of national values and traditions. If necessary, the armed forces would extirpate the threat, following the ideological visions they incorporated from the French theorists of counterinsurgence developed in the Algerian war and reinforced by the strong anti-communist visions taught in the School of the Americas and other US training centers of anti-guerrilla warfare attended by Latin American officers. The local idioms of organicism gave further credibility to the doctrines of national security that stressed the primacy of national well-being over individual rights. According to this logic, individual rights, including the most basic human rights, should be subordinate to national aims and goals whenever necessary.[29]

In Argentina, this vision was a guideline for eliminating the enemies of the nation; the terms used were organic in nature and projected a medical discourse that demanded the "extirpation of ill tissues" from the national body. This hinted at the genocidal practices adopted to decimate a generation and its dreams of radical political change, as indicated by writer Ricardo Piglia.[30]

On the basis of the doctrines of national security, the top commanders of the armed forces thought their society was penetrated by a secluded enemy that aimed at destroying the moral values of the nation. It is precisely from these doctrines that confrontation arose that made use of genocidal practices and a systematic technology of terror and repression aimed not only at physical destruction but also at eradicating its memory from the annals of the nation. This led to the dehumanization of those detained or abducted. These individuals were denied the most basic needs and brutally tortured, with thousands summarily executed and "disappeared." In almost contradictory terms, the enemy was defined in ambiguous terms that could be elastically broadened to include not only active supporters but even remote sympathizers or citizens apathetic enough not to support the policies of the military governments, as in the famous threat launched by the then military governor of the province of Buenos Aires in Argentina during the first junta regime, Ibérico Saint-Jean: "First we kill the subversives; then we kill their collaborators; then … their sympathizers; then those who remain indifferent; and finally we kill the timid."[31] In a binary world such as the one envisioned by the military, there was no room for indecision or lack of full commitment.[32] In such a binary and extreme definition of the situation, all means were deemed legitimate in the fight against subversion. Flagrant human rights violations were ignored, while the armed forces claimed to have saved their countries from being destroyed from within.[33]

The genocidal turn and US influence

The confrontation with communism and with the vernacular forms of radical socialism generated policies that condoned genocidal practices whenever they could be justified in terms of saving the national soul and structure of society. As a result, this confrontational vision, supported by the National Security Doctrine and its related counterinsurgency methodologies, led to the denial of individual rights and the killing of thousands of individuals, including many completely unrelated to any armed movement but only concerned with improving life conditions or attempting to promote social justice, agrarian reform, healthcare, education, or fair working conditions.

In Argentina 30,000 persons were abducted and later vanished without a trace. Chile has officially recognized a death toll of over 3,000 as the result of state and politically motivated violence. Other countries in the Southern Cone made use of long-term imprisonment, torture, and forced exile as was typical of Uruguay and Brazil. In Nicaragua the National Guard was responsible for some 40,000–50,000 murders before the fall of Somoza. Due to the mounting pressure in international and transnational fora in Europe and North America, the actions of the military governments were under scrutiny starting in 1976 and became increasingly so under the Carter administration.

Yet, the pendulum shifted again to counterinsurgency support when President Ronald Reagan came to office in 1981. With communist Cuba just to the south, and the recent triumph of the Sandinista revolution in Nicaragua in 1979, the new administration envisioned a Soviet–Cuban campaign aimed at generating a domino effect throughout Central America and the Caribbean. The Reagan administration began combating the perceived threat by developing interventionist policies, which claimed to be promoting democracy in Central America. The primary focus of these policies was the destabilization of the Sandinista government in Nicaragua and the consolidation of anti-communist political forces in El Salvador, a country where the entrenched elites were unwilling to compromise with the moderate opposition and the rebels had begun to seriously challenge the authoritarian regime.

The Reagan administration swiftly resolved that it would stand firm in El Salvador against "Soviet expansion," by supporting a substantial military and economic assistance program that would prevent the communist rebels from seizing power as they had in Nicaragua. The second part of Reagan's plan involved removing the Sandinistas from power. He terminated all economic aid to Nicaragua and supported the formation of counterrevolutionary guerilla groups, the Contras, with a base of logistic support in neighboring Honduras. Reagan initially rationalized the use of such groups as a means of preventing arms shipments to El Salvador, and later promoted their image as a pro-democracy force that sought to topple the Sandinista regime. Reagan's Cold War policies toward El Salvador and Nicaragua resulted in massive violence and violations of human rights in both countries. In El Salvador, the US funneled hundreds of millions of dollars in military aid to fund a repressive military government's bloody war against communism; and in Nicaragua, the United States' Contra guerillas engaged the government in a war that cost thousands of lives and ruined the country's infrastructure. In El Salvador, during the civil war, state forces were responsible for killing an estimated 75,000 civilians, or well over 1 percent of the total population. The conflict spilled over also to Guatemala, where guerrillas had been in existence since the 1950s. The civil war lasted until 1996 with over 250,000 persons assassinated, including up to 50,000 *desaparecidos*, and hundreds of thousands of displaced individuals, either at the hands of the armed forces or of the militarized civilian units known as the PACs.[34]

Since many of those responsible for launching such genocidal practices and massive human rights violations had some training at US academies, we need to address the issue of US influence and responsibility in such atrocities against humanity. While the issue of direct influence is rather clear for the case of Central America under the Reagan administration, the picture is more complex when assessing the US impact on the genocidal practices carried out in the Southern Cone, and reflecting on the impact of US military training. Of course, the US had economic, military, and diplomatic leverage over many of the countries of the Americas, and was confident of its capacity to dictate the course of history south of the Rio Grande. In a recent article, Steven Volk mentions a paradigmatic instance of such self-perception among policy-makers in the US:

> Henry Kissinger once famously lectured Gabriel Valdés, Chile's Minister of Foreign Relations to the United States, on the direction of history. "You come here speaking of Latin America," he chided Valdés, "but this is not important. Nothing important can come from the South. History has never been produced in the South."[35]

In the cases of Chile and Argentina, however, the US discovered to its dismay the limits of its power. During the Nixon and Ford terms, the administration refrained from joining those countries who criticized Pinochet, maintaining cordial relations with the military regime, while circumventing the US Congress's limitations on economic assistance by ordering its delegates to support loans from international banks to Chile. By late 1976, when Chilean repression and blatant abuse of civil rights gained awareness in US public opinion, the US tried to pressure Pinochet to change Chile's domestic policies, to no avail.[36]

Nonetheless, the image of the Pinochet regime was seriously tarnished following international campaigns of denunciation led by a strong network of Chilean activists and committees of solidarity. These campaigns led to the disclosures of international terrorist actions led by DINA agents in cooperation with the intelligence and security units of sister countries against the democratic opposition in exile, such as the assassination of General (retired) Carlos Prats and his wife in Buenos Aires, the attempted assassination of Bernardo Leighton, a prominent Christian Democrat exile, in Rome and last but not least the murder of Allende's former ambassador to the US and minister of Defense, Orlando Letelier in Washington DC. Progressively, these had an impact on the US. In the words of Peter Kornbluh,

> In the United States, Chile joined Vietnam as a catalyst for national debate over the corruption of American values in the making and exercise of US foreign policy. During the mid 1970s, events in Chile generated a major political reevaluation of human rights, covert action, and the proper place for both in America's conduct abroad. The Kissingerian disregard for Pinochet's mounting atrocities prompted an outraged Congress to pass precedent-setting legislation curtailing foreign aid to his regime, and to mandate human rights criteria for all US economic and military assistance. Public revulsion of Washington's ongoing association with Pinochet's brutality prompted a widespread political effort to return US foreign policy to the moral precepts of American society – creating a groundswell that helped elect Jimmy Carter as the "human rights president."[37]

For the Southern Cone, the ascent of Jimmy Carter to the presidency in 1977 projected human rights as a centerpiece of US foreign policy. Carter supported various UN declarations condemning Chile for its curtailment of human rights, the State Department invited many of the General's foes for briefings, and the US accepted a large number of political exiles. Once in the country, these exiles energized public opinion against their repressive home government. Following this, Carter temporarily withdrew his ambassador and reduced the embassy's staff. Military assistance was stopped, and the Chilean navy was not allowed to participate in maneuvers with the US fleet. The US canceled credits destined for Chile, refused to insure private investments there, and vetoed Chilean loan applications. The pressure led to some cosmetic concessions, such as the release of a few political prisoners, and the promise to return Chile to democracy by 1991. While this was a major step, Pinochet planned his way out in a way that would institutionalize core aspects of its regime. In 1980 Chilean citizens approved a new constitution devised by Pinochet's legal advisors, which created a series of authoritarian mechanisms that ensured the irreversibility of some of the main institutional and structural transformations established under the military regime. Moreover, US pressure had its own limitations: as William Sater stresses, General Pinochet proved to be capable of sidestepping Carter's human rights stance. Moreover, Washington's efforts to isolate Chile achieved its goals in antagonizing General Pinochet. After a while, the Pinochet regime criticized Washington for "not taking the lead in a world crusade against communism."[38]

Under Reagan, many of Carter's actions were annulled, as Reagan advocated a quiet diplomacy toward Chile. By the late 1980s, the domestic and international pressure against Pinochet contributed to the acceleration of the protracted yet planned transition back to democracy, yet under the constitutional terms of the 1980 charter that secured authoritarian enclaves and the maintenance of the economic model in the democratic period starting in 1990.

In the case of Argentina, the pressures of the Carter administration in the 1970s only marginally impacted the junta's genocidal practices. First, Kissinger gave his support for the goals and methods of the "dirty war," without criticizing its repressive methods, at the very same time that the US administration was praising the economic direction of the de facto government. Second, the military junta moved to project a false international image of respect for human rights in Argentina, in the belief that they could overcome its critics, that Cold War optics would prevail, and that Carter meant only a temporary shift in US policy. Third, while Argentina supported the US on disarmament issues, it reinforced international relationships with Cuba, Yugoslavia, and other non-aligned states. The Cubans claimed to understand the need for military intervention in Argentina and the Soviets did not put pressure on Argentina due to their own human rights record. A series of miscalculations – the last of which was the Malvinas/Falklands war – served to undermine the capacity of the Argentine regime to institutionalize itself on lines resembling the Chilean success story. It is, however, unclear whether the end of military training programs in Argentina in 1977 and of sales of military equipment by the US had a serious impact on human rights policies. Although the figures of vanished individuals declined by 1978, it was also clear by then that the radical Left had been annihilated and the Argentinean junta continued to pursue its repressive policies, including the mission of military advisors training counterinsurgency forces in El Salvador and Central America between 1978 and 1982.[39]

Equally important to consider is the training received by Latin American high officers and soldiers at the School of the Americas, or SOA. The School was originally established in the Panama Canal Zone by the US in 1946, catering since 1949 to Latin American students. The US opened the door to Latin American alliances by modernizing outdated military equipment and offering courses on US weaponry. In this way, Latin American militaries became dependent on replacing and purchasing weapons from the US, guaranteeing Latin American allies and also an increased market for the US weaponry industry. After the Cuban revolution, the School changed into the School of the Americas, which opened in 1963. It moved to Fort Benning, Georgia, in 1984 and operated there until its replacement by the Western Hemisphere Institute for Security Cooperation in 2001. The objective of the SOA included the discouragement of any type of leftist power in Latin America, particularly power inspired by the Soviets or the Cubans. Increasingly, the SOA launched witch-hunts to expel and punish left-leaning civilians who were supposed communist threats. Accordingly, the curriculum of the SOA centered on counterinsurgency operations. Officially, the school was attempting to "create professional soldiers," while encouraging Latin Americans to learn from the modern, professional US forces. Similarly, the SOA taught courses that encouraged values such as a free democracy and a stable economy in a "well organized society."[40] In practice, the SOA indoctrinated the military studying there to repress left-leaning civilians who were supposed communist threats. Accordingly, the curriculum of the SOA centered on counterinsurgency operations. A review of training manuals prepared by the US military and used between 1987 and 1991 for intelligence training courses in Latin America and at the SOA reveals, according to a first-hand analysis, that they advocated:

> tactics such as executing guerrillas, blackmail, false imprisonment, physical abuse, use of truth serum to obtain information and payment of bounties for enemy dead. Counterintelligence agents are [were] advised that one of their functions is "recommending targets for neutralization," a term which is defined in one manual as "detaining or discrediting" but which "was commonly used at the time as a euphemism for execution or destruction," according to a Pentagon official (*Washington Post*, September 21, 1996). What is *not* included in these excerpts, however, is the larger context. The seven army manuals train[ed] Latin American militaries to infiltrate and spy upon civilians, including student groups, unions, charitable organizations and political parties; to confuse armed insurgencies with legal political opposition; and to disregard or get around any laws regarding due process, arrest and detention.[41]

The training manuals did not differentiate between guerilla insurgents and peaceful civilian protestors. Ambiguity was ensconced in the SOA training manuals, according to which a target was "someone that could be hostile or not." Furthermore, there was explicit instruction on the art of "wheedling," the SOA term for an inhumane set of interrogation techniques. Other torture mechanisms recommended by the manuals were "prolonged constraint, prolonged exertion, extremes of heat, cold, or moisture, deprivation of food or sleep, disrupting routines, solitary confinement, threats of pain, deprivation of sensory stimuli, hypnosis, and use of drugs or placebos."[42]

Graduates of the SOA have been implicated in massive human rights violations. In El Salvador, more than half of all officers cited for human rights violations in a major massacre, including 83 percent of those implicated in the massacre of El Mozote, were graduates of SOA. The UN Truth Commission report of March 1993 found that two of the three assassins of Archbishop Oscar Romero – also implicated in other human rights abuses, including the organiza- tion of death squads – had been graduates of the SOA. In Nicaragua, Father Fer- nando Cardenal indicted 26 members of the Nicaraguan Guardia with human rights violations including torture, the use of electric shock, and rape. Of the 26 accused, 25 were graduates of the SOA. Among renowned graduates of SOA were General Hugo Banzer who ruled Bolivia between 1971 and 1978; Colom- bian General Hernán José Guzmán Rodríguez, about whom it is claimed that he protected and aided a paramilitary death squad, MAS, between 1987 and 1990, responsible for the deaths of nearly 150 individuals; Omar Torrijos and Manuel Noriega of Panama, Rafael Videla, Roberto Viola and Leopoldo Galtieri of Argentina, Humberto Regalado Hernández of Honduras, and Manuel Antonio Callejas of Guatemala. Some of these graduates and others were inscribed in the Hall of Fame of SOA, leading critics of the school to claim that "if the SOA held an alumni meeting, it would bring together some of the most unsavory thugs in the hemisphere."[43]

Members of the Latin American armed forces were attracted to the SOA for various reasons. Many considered traveling abroad a valued perk or attendance at the School a *sine qua non* for rising in the ranks once back in the home country. Students did not attend SOA because of their desire to further human rights or promote democracy in their home nation. In fact, students had a poor understanding and lack of regard for human rights, considering it a nuisance or focus of jokes.[44] Due to the sharing of experiences with fellow military officers, the mutual reinforcement of attitudes predicating the use of violent means was probably reinforced. One should conclude that the SOA experience probably increased the likelihood of human rights violations being followed by its gradu- ates as part of the campaign against the radical Left and its supporters.

Conclusion

Students of international relations have observed with perplexity that during the Cold War period, US leaders were "trying to reconcile the irreconcilable by embracing repressive and corrupt elites while simultaneously attempting to foster democracy and social justice."[45] This was not a story of deceit. It rather reflected a crucial contradiction in US policy during the Cold War. Interested in curtailing the advance of the revolutionary Left and radical insurgency in the Americas, the US interest was to find allies interested in supporting the same liberal democratic principles dear to American citizens, starting with the rule of law and individual rights. However, US policies of backing, training, and strengthening the armed forces in Latin America encouraged the forceful take- over of power and the adoption of counterinsurgency methods that tore apart these societies, undermined the rule of law, and produced some of the most atro- cious records of crimes against humanity.

In recent decades, democracy has been restored in all these nations. The restored democracies have not been able to undo the long-term effects of such genocidal practices not only on the victims, their relatives, friends, and peers, but also on these societies and cultures at large. Latin American societies will likely continue to struggle with the grim legacies of their past genocidal practices, and face challenges in a widespread spectrum of issues: from acknowledgment and the construction of collective memory, through psychological healing and reparations, to truth and a sense of unmet justice.[46] With the progressive declassification of secret documents, the US will likely continue to confront its role and accountability as a hegemonic power responsible in part for the descent of Latin American state rulers into the use of brutal and often even genocidal practices against their own citizens during the last phases of the Cold War.

Notes and references

1 I am grateful to Melissa Velarde for her editorial assistance.
2 See, among others, P. Smith, *Talons of the Eagle*, Oxford: Oxford University Press, 2000; B. Loveman and T. Davies Jr (eds), *The Politics of Anti-Politics*, Wilmington, DE: Scholarly Resources, 1997; B. Loveman, *Constitution of Tyranny*, Pittsburgh, PA: University of Pittsburgh Press, 1993; F. M. Nunn, *The Time of the Generals: Latin American Professional Militarism in World Perspective*, Lincoln, NE: University of Nebraska Press, 1992; G. Weeks, *US and Latin American Relations*, New York: Pearson, 2008; and notes below.
3 See, for example, the outstanding monographs in the series on the United States and the Americas, directed by Lester D. Langley and published by the University of Georgia Press.
4 R. H. Holden and E. Zolov, *Latin America and the United States: A Documentary History*, New York: Oxford University Press, 2000.
5 J. K. Black, *Sentinels of Empire: The United States and Latin American Militarism*, New York: Greenwood Press, 1986, pp. 27–8.
6 Illustrative also is the following case, mentioned by Robert Holden:

> When the *jefe máximo* of Guatemala, Manuel Estrada Cabrera, began to see night fall on his 22 years in power in 1920, he summoned the US minister to his office and, in the latter's words, "placed the entire situation and the fate of the country in our hands and would agree to abide by any decision which we make."

See R. H. Holden, *Armies without Nations: Public Violence and State Formation in Central America, 1821–1960*, New York: Oxford University Press, 2004, p. 27.
7 Black, *Sentinels of Empire*, p. 4.
8 A. M. Kacowicz, "Latin America as an International Society," *International Politics* 37, 2000, pp. 143–62.
9 The belated exception is Argentina, which did not break diplomatic relations with the Axis until 1944 and only declared war in 1945 as an implicit condition for joining the United Nations. Similarly, Argentina remained economically attached to the UK longer than other sister-nations, as exemplified in a 1933 preferential commercial agreement known as the Roca-Runciman Agreement.
10 Smith, *Talons of the Eagle*, p. 121.
11 P. García, *El drama de la autonomía militar*, Madrid: Alianza Editorial, 1995.
12 F. Nunn, "The South American Military and (Re)democratization: Professional Thought and Self-Perception," *Journal of Interamerican Studies and World Affairs*, 37, 2, 1995, pp. 7–9.
13 K. D. Lehman, *Bolivia and the United States: A Limited Partnership*, Athens, GA: University of Georgia Press, 1999.

14 The US did so especially since the discourse that attributed corruption to the civilian administrations in Latin America struck a chord in the minds of decision-makers in Washington. J. Johnson, *Latin America in Caricature*, Austin, TX: University of Texas Press, 1980.

15 Lehman, *Bolivia and the United States*, p. 141. Juan Lechín (1914–2001), a leftist political figure of Trotskyist leanings, was head of the Federation of Bolivian Mine Workers from 1944 to 1987 and served as vice-president of Bolivia in 1960–4.

16 This was either in the form of a political system centered on parties, or in the form of contention between an elitist pattern and a populist mobilization pattern. The pivotal force in the political system has been traditionally the executive, which has often overridden the formal powers of the legislature and has exercised strong influence on the judicial system, often curtailing the autonomy of the latter. See L. Roniger and C. H. Waisman (eds), *Globality and Multiple Modernities: Comparative North American and Latin American Perspectives*, Brighton: Sussex Academic Press, 2002. See especially the chapters by S. N. Eisenstadt, L. Whitehead, and L. Roniger, pp. 7–28, 29–65 and 79–105.

17 E. Galeano, *Las venas abiertas de América Latina*, Montevideo: Ediciones del Chanchito, 1987, pp. 435–6.

18 A. Pizarro, *De ostras y caníbales. Ensayos sobre la cultura latinoamericana*, Santiago: Editorial Universidad de Santiago, 1994, p. 173.

19 G. V. Correa, "Otros rasgos históricos de la derecha," *La Segunda*, Santiago, February 27, 1966.

20 J. M. de Carvalho, *Cidadania no Brasil: O longo caminho*, São Paulo: Civilização Brasileira, 2001.

21 J. Dinges, *The Condor Years*, New York: The New Press, 2005. See especially pp. 41–81.

22 The initiative was Chilean. See letter by Manuel Contreras, head of National Intelligence in Chile, inviting South American police and intelligence delegations to a secret meeting aimed at coordinating cross-national intelligence, to be held in Santiago on November 25–December 1, 1975. M. Contreras, *Document 00143F0011–0022*, 1975. Online, available at: www.pj.gov.py/cdya (accessed September 26, 2008).

23 These factors have been thoroughly studied by political scientists and Latin Americanists such as Giovanni Sartori, Laurence Whitehead, Guillermo O'Donnell, Philippe Schmitter, Juan Linz, and Alfred Stepan.

24 According to J. Patrice McSherry,

> Condor employed complex infrastructures and covert elimination mechanisms (such as burning bodies or throwing them into the sea).... The Condor apparatus bypassed the official state judicial and penal structures that remained functioning during the military regimes.... Top US officials and agencies, including the State Department, the Central Intelligence Agency, and the Defense Department, were fully aware of Condor's formation and its operations from the time it was organized in 1975 (if not earlier). The US government considered the Latin American militaries to be allies in the Cold War and worked closely with their intelligence organizations. US executive agencies at least condoned, and sometimes actively assisted, Condor 'counter-subversive' operations.

See J. P. McSherry, "Operation Condor: Clandestine Inter-American System," *Social Justice* 26, 4, 1999, pp. 144–5; and see also J. P. McSherry, *Predatory States: Operation Condor and Covert War in Latin America*, Lanham, MD: Rowman and Littlefield, 2005.

25 There were differences in the way de facto rulers carried out policies in tandem with a lack of political freedoms and civil rights. In Brazil, authoritarian rulers did not obliterate all the formalities of democracy, such as the Congress and political parties, in order to retain legitimacy. Instead, they carried out intermittent repression along with

attempts to enlarge social rights while restricting political rights (the suspension of habeas corpus, violation of privacy, censure of media, etc.). In addition, there were exceptions to such visions, as in the case of the Peruvian developmental military rule by General Juan Velasco Alvarado, especially in the first years following the 1968 coup. L. Roniger and M. Sznajder, *The Legacy of Human Rights Violations in the Southern Cone*, Oxford: Oxford University Press, 1999.

26 J. T. Valdés, *El terrorismo de estado*, México: Nueva Sociedad, Editorial Nueva Imagen, 1980; D. Pion-Berlin, *The Ideology of State Power*, Boulder, CO: Lynne Rienner, 1989.
27 M. A. Garretón, *The Chilean Political Process*, Boston: Unwin Hyman, 1989, p. 70.
28 See the declarations of Colonel Juan Deichler Guzmán in P. Politzer (ed.), *Fear in Chile: Lives under Pinochet*, New York: Pantheon Books, 1989, pp. 20–39; and A. J. Letelier, "Los intelectuales-políticos chilenos," in W. Hofmeister and H. C. F. Mansilla (eds), *Intelectuales y política en América Latina*, Rosario: Homo Sapiens Ediciones, 2003, pp. 171–98, especially pp. 171–9.
29 M. Sznajder, "Entre autoritarismo y democracia: El legado de violaciones de derechos humanos," in L. Senkman and M. Sznajder (eds), with the cooperation of E. Kaufman, *El legado del autoritarismo*, Buenos Aires: Grupo Editor Latinoamericano, 1995, pp. 16–17; and L. Roniger, "Sociedad civil y derechos humanos: Una aproximación teórica en base a la experiencia Argentina," in ibid., pp. 37–54.
30 Piglia has concluded that,

> During the dictatorship, a 'medical' story circulated: the country was ill; a virus had corrupted it; a drastic intervention was needed. The military state defined itself as the only surgeon able to operate without delays and without demagoguery. To survive, society had to endure major surgery. Some parts had to be operated on without anesthetic. That was the kernel of the plot: a sick country and a group of physicians ready to save its life. In fact, the story covered up a criminal reality of mutilated bodies and bloody operations. But at the same time the story referred to that reality explicitly. The structure of the terror story conveyed and secluded everything [at the same time].

See R. Piglia, "Los pensadores ventrílocuos," in R. Angel, *Rebeldes y domesticados*, Buenos Aires: Ediciones el Cielo por el Asalto, 1992, p. 32.
31 J. Simpson and J. Bennett, *The Disappeared: Voices from a Secret War.* London: Robson Books, 1985, p. 66.
32 D. Feierstein, "Political violence in Argentina and its genocidal characteristics," *Journal of Genocide Research* 8, 2, 2006, pp. 149–68. On the ambiguity of defining the enemy and its genocidal consequences in Argentina see G. Levy, "Considerations on the Connections between Race, Politics, Economics and Genocide," *Journal of Genocide Research* 8, 2, 2006, pp. 137–48.
33 Nunn, *The Time of the Generals*, p. 201; J. Simpson and S. Bennett, *The Disappeared*, London: Robson Books, 1985, p. 66. In recent years, the armed forces left behind this narrative of saving the nation and their views of society's collective blame. Their sustained effort to project blame onto others was reflected in their attempt to assume a new narrative according to which they too had been victims of terrorism, a fact often overlooked by society and which determined an unpaid public debt due to their contribution to society at large. See V. Salvi, "Memoria y justificación. Consecuencias de la auto-victimización del ejército Argentino," paper presented at the Second International Congress on Genocidal Practices, Buenos Aires, Universidad Tres de Febrero, November 2007.
34 C. Menjívar and N. Rodríguez, *When States Kill*, Austin, TX: University of Texas Press, 2005; and especially A. Lauria-Santiago, "The Culture and Politics of State Terror and Repression in El Salvador" and R. Sieder, "War, Peace and Memory Politics in Central America," both in A. B. de Brito, C. Gonzalez-Enriquez, and P. Aguilar

(eds), *The Politics of Memory: Transitional Justice in Democratizing Societies*, Oxford: Oxford University Press, 2001, pp. 85–114 and 161–89 respectively.

35 S. S. Volk, "Chile and the United States Thirty Years Later: Return of the Repressed?," in S. Nagy-Zekmi and F. Leiva (eds), *Democracy in Chile: The Legacy of September 11, 1973*, Brighton: Sussex Academic Press, 2005, pp. 24–40.

36 Accordingly,

> Henry Kissinger declared that Santiago's human rights abuses strained Chile's diplomatic relations with the United States. If the Moneda's policy failed to change, Kissinger warned, the damage would be considerable. By then, however, Washington had lost much of its leverage on Chile. So much foreign private capital – nearly three billion dollars from 1974 to 1978 [*sic*] – had flowed into Santiago that Pinochet not only did not require American economic assistance, but he even publicly belittled the American offer of twenty-five million dollars in aid. Nor did the US arms embargo discommode Santiago.... Santiago encountered little difficulty in replacing American weapons [with German, British, French, Spanish and Brazilian acquisitions].... Increasingly Santiago manufactured its own weapons as well as assault and armored vehicles.

See W. F Sater, *Chile and the United States: Empires in Conflict*, Athens, GA: University of Georgia Press, 1990, pp. 191–2.

37 P. Kornbluh, "Finding the Pinochet File: Pursuing Truth, Justice, and Historical Memory through Declassified US Documents," in Nagy-Zekmi and Leiva, *Democracy in Chile*, p. 16. See also P. Kornbluh, *The Pinochet File*, New York: The New Press, 2003.

38   Much to Carter's dismay, Brady Tyson, an aid to UN Ambassador Andrew Young, publicly apologized for America's supposed role in upending the Allende regime. Since such statements complicated Washington's foreign relations, the State Department ordered Tyson to resign.... [T]he White House [also] discovered that the international community, contrary to public statements ... opposed Carter's attempt to mix morality and assistance.... Washington's abortive attempt to isolate Chile succeeded only in antagonizing General Pinochet ... after flaying US imperialism, the Moneda then criticized Washington for not taking the lead in a world crusade against communism.

(Sater, Chile and the United States, pp. 194–5)

39 D. Sheinin, *Argentina and the United States: An Alliance Contained*: Athens, GA: University of Georgia Press, 2006, pp. 150–80.

40 National Security and International Affairs Division, *School of the Americas US Military Training for Latin American Countries*, Washington, DC: US General Accounting Office, 1996 (by N. Toolan, M. Forster, K. Handley, F. J. Shafer, and N. Ragsdale). Online, available at: www.fas.org/asmp/resources/govern/gao96178.pdf (accessed on January 30, 2008); L. Gill, *The School of the Americas*, Durham, NC: Duke University Press, 2004, especially pp. 71–3.

41 L. Haugaard, "Declassified Army and CIA Manuals Used in Latin America: An Analysis of Their Content," Latin American Working Group, February 18, 1997. Online, available at: www.lawg.org/misc/Publications-manuals.htm (accessed on January 30, 2008).

42 Gill, *School of Americas*, p. 212; Haugaard, "Declassified Army and CIA Manuals."

43 B. Brown, "School for Scandal," *Commonwealth* 22, 125, 1998, pp. 10–11; K. E. McCoy, "Trained to Torture? The Human Rights Effects of Military Training at the School of the Americas," *Latin American Perspectives* 32, 6, 2005, pp. 47–64.

44 Gill, *School of Americas*, p. 152.

45 D. E. Schulz, "Ten Theories in Search of Central American Reality," in D. E. Schulz and D. H. Graham, *Revolution and Counterrevolution in Central America and the*

Caribbean, Boulder, CO: Westview Press, 1984, p. 55. See also M. Sikkink, *Mixed Signals*, Ithaca, NY: Cornell University Press, 2004, pp. 79–105.

46 On some of these lasting problems in the Southern Cone see, among others, M. Feitlowitz, *A Lexicon of Terror*, Oxford: Oxford University Press, 1998; Roniger and Sznajder, *The Legacy of Human Rights Violations in the Southern Cone*; A. C. G. M. Robben and M. Suárez-Orozco (eds), *Cultures under Siege: Collective Violence and Trauma*, Cambridge: Cambridge University Press, 2000. On Central America see M. Esparza, 'Post-war Guatemala: Long-Term Effects of Psychological and Ideological Militarization of the K'iche Mayans," *Journal of Genocide Research* 7, 3, 2005, pp. 377–91; R. Sieder, *Guatemala after the Peace Accords*, London: Institute of Latin American Studies, 1999; Menjívar and Rodríguez, *When States Kill*. On the long-term impact of ostracism in the region, see M. Sznajder and L. Roniger, *The Politics of Exile*. New York: Cambridge University Press, 2009.

2 Political violence in Argentina and its genocidal characteristics

Daniel Feierstein[1]

The National Security Doctrine promoted throughout Latin America by US strategists during the Cold War inspired the military repression in Argentina between 1974 and 1983. This anticommunist ideology gave the armed forces of the region the messianic mission of rebuilding their societies by eliminating political "subversion."

Because the repression in Argentina was directed against political groups, the question arises whether it is appropriate to describe these events as genocide. I will argue that it was precisely the attempt to transform Argentine society through partial annihilation of the national group that justifies the use of the term, both legally and sociologically. By considering genocide as a social practice, we gain a deeper insight into the underlying purposes of genocide in the modern world, of which the distortion of collective memory is only one.

Processes of repression in Argentina, 1974–83

The so-called "dirty war" in Argentina began around mid-1974 and reached its height between 1976 and 1979 after the military coup that overthrew President Isabel Martínez de Perón on March 24, 1976. In fact, the "dirty war" was far from being a war; but to understand its true nature together with the political and social context in which it occurred, we need to trace events back to the military coup that ousted President Juan Domingo Perón in 1955 and outlawed Peronism, the political movement based on his ideas and programs.

Peronism was the most important political development in Argentina in the twentieth century and one that still defies definition. Perón himself was a pragmatist, describing his policies as a "third position" between capitalism and communism. His regime introduced numerous benefits for the poor, including a comprehensive public health system, as well as attempting to bring about a more equitable distribution of income by strengthening the labor unions. Argentina's conservative elite found these policies unacceptable and tried to reverse them after Perón was forced into exile in 1955.

One of Perón's achievements had been to promote a new sense of self-esteem and political consciousness among the working classes, including the ability to challenge authority on a regular basis. Consequently, the succession of military regimes and controversial pseudo-democratic governments that attempted to destroy Perón's legacy between 1955 and 1973 met with increasing popular resistance in the form of strikes, boycotts, and other forms of protest. At the same time, the now clandestine Peronist movement splintered into various factions, left-wing and right-wing, each supported by the exiled Perón from Franco's Spain. As social agitation increased, repression grew harsher and divisions within the Peronist movement deepened. When Perón was finally allowed to return from exile in June 1973, a crowd of three and a half million gathered at Buenos Aires's main airport to welcome him. However, he was unable to land when right-wing snipers belonging to the Argentine Anti-communist Alliance, or Triple A, opened fire on the crowd, killing 13 people and wounding 365.

One reason why political conflicts in Argentina and the rest of Latin America had become more radical was the success of the Cuban revolution of 1959. Fearing that Marxist revolution would spread to the rest of Latin America, US strategists encouraged the Latin American military to think in terms of ideological rather than territorial boundaries and to maintain "armies of occupation" within their own countries to control the population. Under the US National Security Doctrine Latin America's armed forces were trained to wage a "new type of war" using the counterinsurgency methods developed by the French in Algeria and the US in Vietnam.

In Argentina, several armed left-wing groups, both Peronist and Marxist, had emerged during the 1960s while labor union bureaucrats were mostly conservatives. Perón was elected president with his wife Isabel as vice-president on September 23, 1973 but even Perón was unable to reunite the Peronist movement. Only two days after the elections, José Ignacio Rucci, the secretary general of CGT (Argentina's largest labor union) was murdered, allegedly by members of the left-wing Peronist guerrilla group Montoneros, and Perón ordered his minister for social welfare, José López Rega, to eliminate left-wing militants. López Rega obliged by transforming the Triple A into a death squad and enlisting members of the security forces.[2] When Perón died suddenly in July 1974 and his wife Isabel assumed power with López Rega as her de facto prime minister, the atmosphere of violence and uncertainty increased.[3]

Some authors describe the run-up to the military coup as a period of "civil war"[4] and others, as one of "political radicalization and repressive escalation."[5] Nevertheless, although state violence had clearly gone beyond traditional political repression by the end of 1975, it would be wrong to speak of civil war. It is true that, shortly after Perón began attacking left-wing Peronism, the Guevarist People's Revolutionary Army (ERP) began a guerilla war in the northwest province of Tucumán. But the ERP never numbered more than 300 men and women and was unable to control even the rural mountain areas. Nevertheless, in February 1975, the government issued Decree No. 261/75 ordering the army's commander-in-chief to "execute all military operations necessary for the effects of neutralizing or annihilating the action of subversive elements acting in the Province of Tucumán." These operations, known as *Operativo Independencia*, had in fact already begun the previous year and were to provide a blueprint for repression after the military coup of March 24, 1976.

The repression carried out by General Jorge Rafael Videla's military junta was meticulously planned. After the coup, Argentina was divided into five areas and 19 sub-areas, under the operational control of the armed forces. More than 500 clandestine detention centers were set up in a country with only 25 million inhabitants.[6] There was not a single city which did not have a detention center nearby. Kidnapping, torture, and murder were carried out with a ruthlessness and efficiency, which suggested years of ideological and practical preparation.[7] Many of the victims disappeared without trace, their bodies buried in unmarked graves or dumped in the sea. Although there are more than 13,000 confirmed reports of murders and forced "disappearances," human rights organizations calculate the real number at between 15,000 and 30,000. The majority were killed before the Inter-American Commission on Human Rights visited Argentina in 1979.

Most victims were not members of left-wing armed organizations, who together never numbered more than a thousand, but anyone with vaguely left-wing views, including labor union militants, students, doctors, lawyers, and social workers running soup kitchens and neighborhood centers. They were not killed for their political ideas but because they participated in social movements ranging from left-wing and Peronist groupings to independent groups without any clear political affiliation.

The detention centers themselves combined the worst horrors of the Nazi concentration camps, the French camps in Algeria, and US counterintelligence practices in Vietnam. Victims were routinely tortured with the *picana* (an electric prod) or the "submarine" (whereby the victim's head was repeatedly submerged in buckets of water) as well as suffering humiliation, abuse, overcrowding, and hunger. There were also some specifically Argentine refinements of cruelty, such as torturing prisoners in front of their children or spouses, torturing prisoners' children in front of their parents, and the illegal appropriation and subsequent "adoption" by military families of more than 500 children of the disappeared. The consequences of this dark chapter in Argentine history linger on. Despite over 500 reported cases of illegal appropriation, only 90 children have been returned to their original families.

The ideological origins of these practices are undeniable. Numerous eyewitnesses have described the presence of swastikas and other Nazi emblems at these detention centers, the identification of many Argentine officers with Nazism and the "special treatment" given to Jewish prisoners. One eyewitness, Daniel Eduardo Fernández,[8] states that "every kind of torture was applied against the Jews, but in particular there was one which was extremely sadistic and cruel: the "rectoscope," which consisted of inserting a tube into the victim's anus, or into a woman's vagina, and then releasing a rat into the tube. The rodent would look for a way out and try to go forward by gnawing at the victim's internal organs."[9] Another eye-witness, Pedro Miguel Vanrell, tells how "the torturers would laugh, take the prisoners' clothes off and paint swastikas on their backs with spray paint."[10]

Other testimonies, such as that of journalist Jacobo Timerman, describe how the repressors repeatedly attempted to dehumanize Jewish prisoners by forcing them to bark like dogs and walk on all fours.[11] Barrera and Ferrando recall that in the El Atlético detention center, prisoners were forced to shout "Heil Hitler," and recordings of speeches by Nazi leaders were played during the night.

Peregrino Fernández, a Federal Police inspector who collaborated with Harguindeguy, Videla's interior minister, indicates clearly the institutionalization of state terror during this period: "Villar and Veyra (Federal Police officers) acted as the ideologues: they indicated literature and commented upon books about Adolf Hitler and other Nazi and Fascist ideologues."[12] It was not that individual repressors committed "excesses"; these practices were institutionalized within the security forces. However, the repression was not guided by anti-Semitism as such, but rather by the "fight against subversion" as defined by the National Security Doctrine.

In 1999, Spanish Judge Baltasar Garzón of the Fifth Central Court of Instruction in Madrid filed charges against 98 members of the Argentine armed forces for the crimes of genocide and terrorism. In his indictment, Garzón quoted declarations made by Admiral Mendia just before the coup in March 1976, in which Mendia explained to his officers in Puerto Belgrano that the orders of the military leaders were "to combat everything that goes against Western and Christian ideology. For this purpose," Mendia added, "we have the approval of the Church." Mendia went on to outline the method the navy would follow:

> Wearing civilian clothing, we shall act in quick operations, intense interrogations, practice of tortures and physical elimination by means of operations in aircraft from which, during the flight, the living and narcotized bodies of the victims will be dropped into thin air, thus giving them a Christian death.

Speeches like these were accompanied by sermons from the Argentine Catholic pulpit calling the armed forces to a "holy war." For example, on September 23, 1975, the military vicar, Vitorio Bonamin, said in the presence of General Viola:

> I salute all the men of the Armed Forces who have come here to the River Jordan to cleanse themselves of blood in order to take charge of the country. The Army is expiating the impurities of our country. Wouldn't Christ want the Armed Forces to go beyond their function one day?

On June 27, 1976, the archbishop of Bahía Blanca, Jorge Mayer, said in a statement justifying the repression, "The subversive guerilla wants to steal the cross, the symbol of all Christians, to crush and divide the Argentine people with the hammer and sickle."

Thus, the perpetrators explicitly stated that this was not simply a military war. They believed society was under attack from individuals seeking to revolutionize social relationships. In 1977, the Ministry of Education distributed a pamphlet entitled *Subversion within the Educational System* warning of "the evident offensive in the area of children's literature, the aim of which is to send a type of message enabling children to educate themselves to be free and to choose for themselves." The same pamphlet states that

> the intention of Marxist publishers is to offer books to accompany children in their struggle to discover the real world and the world of adults, to help them not to be afraid of freedom, to help them to love, to fight, to assert themselves, to defend their ego against the ego which parents and institutions often try to impose upon them, consciously or unconsciously victims of a system which has tried to make them in its own image.[13]

In short, the misnamed "dirty war" was really an attempt to reshape social relationships through terror and death. The perpetrators sought to destroy individual freedom, whether or not the victims supported a particular political party, and thus impose a hierarchical vision of society which was not only economic but religious – a vision the perpetrators called "Western and Christian." This is the background against which we will now consider whether it is legally, historically, and sociologically appropriate to categorize these events as genocide.

Law as a producer of truth: the legal definition of genocide

Law plays a key role in the construction of collective memories of historical events. In the case of the military repression described above, legal definitions not only determine the way these events are construed but also the possibility of bringing the perpetrators to justice.

The most widely accepted legal definition of genocide even today is the one approved by the United Nations in the Convention on the Prevention and Punishment of the Crime of Genocide in December 1948. Article 2 of this Convention defined genocide as follows:

> In the present Convention, genocide means any of the following acts committed with intent to destroy, in whole or in part, a national, ethnical, racial or religious group, as such:
>
> a   Killing members of the group;
> b   Causing serious bodily or mental harm to members of the group;
> c   Deliberately inflicting on the group conditions of life calculated to bring about its physical destruction in whole or in part;
> d   Imposing measures intended to prevent births within the group;
> e   Forcibly transferring children of the group to another group.

In the aftermath of the Holocaust, the essential elements of this definition – an "intent to destroy" either "in whole or in part" groups defined in terms of nationality, ethnicity, race or religion – seemed like a reasonable compromise given that several countries such as the USSR and Great Britain had a recent history of domestic and/or colonial repression and had insisted on the exclusion of social and political groups as targets of genocide

Nevertheless, in 1946 the United Nations General Assembly had called upon member states to define this new criminal category, stating (Resolution 96 (I)) that:

> Genocide is a denial of the right of existence of entire human groups, as homicide is the denial of the right to live of individual human beings; such denial of the right of existence shocks the conscience of mankind, results in great losses to humanity in the form of cultural and other contributions represented by these groups, and is contrary to moral law and to the spirit and aims of the United Nations. Many instances of such crimes of genocide have occurred when racial, religious, political and other groups have been destroyed, entirely or in part. The punishment of the crime of genocide is a matter of international concern.

This resolution contained two significant elements. First, it contemplated the genocide of political groups; and second, it defined genocide through an analogy with homicide. The definition established the characteristics of the event through the type of crime committed (collective killing against individual killing) and not through the characteristics of the victims: "racial, religious and political" were simply examples and the term "other" completed the categorization.

It is true that later, at the drafting stage of the Convention, even Raphael Lemkin, who had coined the term genocide in 1933, expressed doubts as to whether political groups should be included. It was argued that political groups lacked the cohesion or permanence of other groups. In addition, it was clear that the inclusion of political groups would jeopardize the acceptance of the Convention by a large number of states that did not want the international community to become involved in their internal political struggles.

However, Donnedieu de Vabres, the primary French judge during the Nuremberg trials after World War II, argued that the express exclusion of political groups might be interpreted as legitimizing crimes against political groups. Thus, three discussions were on the table:

a   whether the definition of genocide should be universal (like any other criminal categorization) or limited to certain groups;
b   whether the limitation was an aid to facilitate the approval of the Convention by the largest possible number of states; and
c   whether leaving certain groups explicitly out of the categorization might not represent a way of legitimating their annihilation.

After arduous negotiations and disagreements, the final decision was that the protection of political groups and other excluded groups should be ensured outside the scope of the Convention by member countries' national legislations and by the Universal Declaration of Human Rights. Thus, the United Nations defined genocide practices as a new legal typology, explicitly stated in Article 2 of the Convention. But by excluding political groups, the definition of genocide became arbitrarily restrictive. Why, we must ask, should religious ideology carry more weight than political ideology when both constitute systems of beliefs?

The principle of equality before the law: inequality before death?

It is unlikely that genocide would have become an everyday concept, much less a crime under international law, had it not been for the Holocaust. Europeans had always considered comparable acts less alarming when they took place in the colonies – that is, in places where victims were perceived as "others." After World War II, however, Europeans could neither ignore the massacres that had taken place on European soil nor treat them as mere accumulations of individual murders. The targeting of whole population groups was clearly different from repeated homicide or multiple murders. It was this particular reason which drove the United Nations to codify a new type of international crime as genocide.

However, by focusing on the characteristics of the victims, this codification violated fundamental legal principles, such as "equality before the law" and the impossibility of assigning relative values to human lives. By restricting genocide to four groups (ethnic, national, racial, or religious), the Convention created a differentiated (non-egalitarian) law. The same practices, undertaken with the same systematization and viciousness, would only be recognized for what they are if the victims shared certain characteristics and not others.

With the exception of "aggravating circumstances," the laws of most countries, including Argentina, define criminal acts not in terms of the victim but in terms of the behavior itself. In the Argentine Criminal Code, for example, each article usually begins with a hypothesis such as "anyone who kills another person" (Article 79: Homicide). The characteristics of the "other person" do not alter the basic nature of the criminal act: homicide is homicide, regardless of who is killed. Aggravating circumstances, such as a family relationship between killer and victim, and mitigating circumstances, such as extreme provocation, may increase or decrease the sentence but these do not create separate legal categories. In other words, this connection between aggravating or extenuating circumstances and the characteristics of the victim is established in such as way as not to alter the principle of equality before the law.

On the other hand, by creating protected and unprotected groups of persons, the 1948 Convention actually legitimated the fundamental hypothesis underlying all acts of genocide, namely, that some have less right to life than others. We might call this restrictive perspective the dominant or "hegemonic" discourse since it has been incorporated by many states into their legal codes. The advantage of adopting this discourse is that it focuses attention away from the essentially political purposes of all modern genocides. Once the perpetrators have been punished, events can be relegated to history without the need to ask which sectors of society benefited and continue to benefit from genocide.

Truth and justice for the dead: the end of impunity

Over the last 30 years, however, many jurists have challenged the hegemonic legal classification of genocide, as have historians and sociologists (see below). Four cases worth highlighting are: the Whitaker Report, published by United Nations Economic and Social Council Commission on Human Rights in 1985; the indictment of members of the Argentine military in 1999 by Spanish judge Baltasar Garzón; the discussions and analyses over the last 15 years of the International Criminal Court regarding events in the Balkans and Rwanda; and, finally, some Argentine sentences during 2006 and 2007 recognizing that genocide was committed in Argentina. This section will focus mainly on the arguments of Garzón and the Argentine judges.

Under its domestic law, Spain has universal jurisdiction over serious crimes such as genocide even when these are committed outside Spain by foreign citizens. An action may be brought in the public interest by any Spanish citizen and an investigating judge then gathers evidence and interviews witnesses to determine whether there is sufficient basis for the claims alleged in the complaint. After studying depositions by several human rights organizations of Madrid in 1997, Judge Baltasar Garzón as prosecuting magistrate started proceedings against 98 Argentine military for crimes of "terrorism and genocide."

The legal arguments contained in his 156-page indictment of November 2, 1999 can be summarized as follows:

a   The requirement that victimized national groups be defined in terms of ethnicity in order to prove that genocide has taken place is unconstitutional under Spanish law (subsection one);

b   The extermination of "political groups" may be termed genocide in spite of the explicit exclusion of such groups under Spanish law (subsection two);

c   The term "national group" is appropriate to classify the victims in Argentina (subsection three);

d   The term "religious group" is also appropriate to classify the victims, bearing in mind the ideological nature of religious belief and the Argentine military's explicit aim of establishing a "Western and Christian" order (subsections three and four);

e   Racist thinking is essentially political in nature. "Racial groups" are imaginary constructions that always refer in fact to "political groups" (subsection five);

f   The term "ethnic group" is also appropriate to classify the victims given the specific nature of the "special treatment" given to the Judeo-Argentine population and its symbolic nature (subsection five).

We have already discussed the inconsistency of excluding "political groups" from legal and theoretical definitions of genocide and we have also described the "special treatment" to which Argentine Jews were subjected in various detention centers. We will now examine Garzón's arguments (c), (d) and (e) in more detail.

Argument (c) is based on the fact that the perpetrators sought to *destroy structures of social relationships within the state, in order to substantially alter the life of the whole.* This is in line with Article 2 of the 1948 Convention (cited above), which defines genocide as "intent to destroy, in whole or in part, a national ... group." The Argentine national group had been annihilated "in part," substantially altering the social fabric of the country. The continuation of the dictatorship's neo-liberal policies during the 1990s – policies that "nationalized" corporate debts but cut social benefits for the poor – is a poignant example of the extent to which the destruction of part of a national group can affect post-genocide economic, social, and political development.

The case of Yugoslavia is particularly relevant to this discussion since it involved a series of overlapping genocide processes and the International Criminal Tribunal for the Former Yugoslavia (ICTY) was faced with the problem of determining "which part" of the population must be annihilated in order to classify the situation as "genocide." Lemkin had already suggested that "in part" meant the destruction of a "substantial part" of the group; but how do we define "substantial"?

In a sentence published on December 14, 1999, ICTY stated that a "substantial part" could mean either (i) "a large majority of the group in question"; or (ii) "political and administrative leaders, religious leaders, academics and intellectuals, business leaders and others ... regardless of the actual numbers killed," and that "[t]he character of the attack on the leadership must be *viewed in the context of the fate or what happened to the rest of the group.*"[14] This clearly corroborates Garzón's argument (c) about the appropriateness of the term "national group" to classify the victims in Argentina.

Garzón's argument (d) highlights the "religious" and ideological purpose of the repression. As Garzón himself explains, the military government not only justified the repression as a defense of "Christian and Western" values, explicitly describing it as a "crusade," but also enlisted members of the Catholic Church to run detention centers. This religious worldview of "us" and "them" was clearly political and ideological, and such belief systems make the Convention's definition of genocide even more problematic – a definition which privileges religious beliefs but not political ones.

Beyond its legal usefulness, an analysis of the repression that took place in Argentina between 1974 and 1983 as an ideologically motivated genocide with religious characteristics provides a much more authentic and comprehensive historical account than that provided by the concepts of "politicide" (discussed below) or "political genocide." This is because the aims of the repressors were not only political. Even the name the dictatorship gave to its campaign – "Process of National Reorganization" – clearly shows that it sought to radically transform morality, ideology, the family, and other institutions that regulate social relationships. To do so, the perpetrators eliminated anybody who embodied an alternative way of constructing social identity.

Even faced with the amount of evidence that Garzón gathered, which runs to thousands of pages, countries are often unwilling to recognize that genocide has taken place on their territory and Argentina was no exception. Spain does not try individuals *in absentia* and the Argentine government rejected all Spain's requests for extradition. So, until Lieutenant Commander Adolfo Scilingo traveled to Spain voluntarily to testify, it seemed unlikely that the case would ever be heard.

Nevertheless, Madrid's Central Criminal Court sentenced Scilingo to 640 years for crimes against humanity. In its judgment of April 19, 2005, the Court argued that under article 607 of the recently revised Spanish Penal Code, the crimes fitted the definition of crimes against humanity "better" than that of genocide. According to the Court, the new article 607, which follows the terms of the Genocide Convention of 1948 and protects only the victims of "national, ethnic, racial and religious groups," did not allow for the inclusion of the victims within the category of a "national group."

In fact, the dividing line between these supposedly different crimes is unclear. For example, the same judgment recognized that:

> [T]he Court is applying this super-stringent and restricted interpretation of the crime of genocide at the present time precisely because the broader concept of crimes against humanity has now been included in the [Spanish] Penal Code, forcing us to reinterpret this crime accordingly. However, at the moment when it was committed and until this rule took effect, its definition in criminal law as a crime of genocide was correct.[15]

The Court's decision became even more confusing when it went on to state that although it supported the use of the concept of genocide only in those cases where crimes against humanity did not exist as a legal concept, it recognized that the United Nations had excluded political groups from its definition of genocide because of political pressures. In my opinion, this is something that should never be admitted as a basis for legal definitions.

In the meantime, however, the genocide thesis has gained ground in Argentina. In September 2006, the Federal Criminal Oral Court No. 1 of La Plata, Argentina, found Miguel Osvaldo Etchecolatz (former director general of investigations for the Buenos Aires police) guilty of "crimes against humanity within the framework of the genocide that occurred in Argentina between 1976 and 1983." In October 2007, it sentenced Christian von Wernich (a police chaplain) for the same crime.

In the case of Etchecolatz, the Court recognized that the charge of genocide had been rejected on a technicality known as the "principle of congruity" (the charge had not been included in the original investigations) but went on to give a lengthy justification of why the genocide label should be applied to the Argentinean experience. The grounds of the sentence included the following points:

a   Political groups were included in all drafts of the Convention on Genocide following United Nations Resolution 96/1 of the General Assembly, December 11, 1946. Political groups were not excluded from the Convention for legal reasons but because of "the prevailing political circumstances at the time," a reason not supported by the philosophy of law.

b   Even though the Convention excludes political groups, the Court considered that "there is no impediment to the use of the term genocide" in describing what happened in Argentina, namely, the "partial annihilation of a national group," since Argentina's Supreme Court ruled (in Causa 13/84 against the Argentine military juntas) that "we consider as proven the practices of mass destruction implemented by those calling themselves the Process of National Reorganization ..., a process that was practically identical throughout the country and prolonged in time."

c   The Court also deemed that "the plural and pluripersonal acts alleged were acts against a group of Argentineans or residents of Argentina that could be differentiated, and which no doubt were differentiated by those who organized the persecution and harassment" and these actions "consisted of deaths, prolonged illegal detentions ..., tortures, confinements in clandestine detention centers ..., removing detained children and giving them to other families – forcibly transferring children of the group to another group, so that the idea is clearly present of the extermination of a group of the Argentinean population. This was not done in a random or indiscriminate fashion, but with the intention of destroying a section of the population ... composed of those citizens who did not fit the type pre-established by the promoters of the repression as necessary for the new order to be installed in the country."

d   Developing this argument, the Court further considered that those targeted for extermination were not specific individuals; rather, "thousands were disappeared or killed for no political or ideological reason other than the fact that they belonged to certain communities, sectors or groups of the Argentinean nation (national group) which [the perpetrators] considered, in their inconceivable criminal logic, to be incompatible with the Process."

e   Finally, the Court considered that "the term 'national group' is absolutely valid for analyzing what happened in Argentina since the perpetrators set out to destroy part of the social fabric in order to produce a sufficiently substantial change so as to affect the State in its entirety. Given the inclusion of the term 'total or partial' in the definition of the 1948 Convention, it is evident that the Argentinean national group has been annihilated 'partially' and to a sufficiently substantial extent as to alter the social relations within the nation ... the annihilation in Argentina was not spontaneous, was not fortuitous, was not irrational: this was the systematic destruction of a 'substantial part' of the Argentine national group, with the intention of transforming it as such, redefining its way of life, its social relations, its destiny, its future."

For this reason, the sentence concludes that "from all that has gone before it is indisputable that we are not dealing as we previously expected with a mere succession of crimes, but rather with something significantly greater that deserves the name of genocide."[16]

The specific charge presented in all these cases has been the partial destruction of the Argentinean national group, in accordance with Article Two of the Genocide Convention. However, labeling the crimes committed in Argentina as genocide has been controversial, especially outside Argentina. One of the main arguments of the lawyers and international organizations that have rejected Garzón´s argumentation and the Argentine sentences has been that,

> [T]he victims were individually chosen for their political beliefs and not because they belonged to a group, which would imply that those responsible for their disappearance and/or murder did not have the necessary criminal intent as they did not intend to destroy a group but only to eliminate political dissidents.[17]

At the moment of writing, lawyers and human rights organizations continue to argue about these two ways of understanding the facts: genocide or crimes against humanity. Researchers and lawyers who support the idea that genocide happened in Argentina say that there is ample evidence that the vast majority of the victims were social activists belonging to trade unions, student organizations, or neighborhood associations, and so the notion of "individual political dissidence" has proved difficult to sustain because of the group dimension. Also, there are more than 500 cases in which the children of activists were kidnapped and, in some cases, tortured, murdered, or "disappeared" – children who by no stretch of the imagination could be classed as "political dissidents."

Nevertheless, it is insufficient to prove that political activists and their children were systematically persecuted and murdered or even that a network of over 500 concentration camps was set up all over Argentina for this purpose. Indeed, the defenders of the "genocide" position say that focusing too narrowly on the fact that the victims belonged to certain groups distracts attention from the real intentions of the perpetrators – the transformation of the rest of Argentinean society by eliminating these groups and what they represented.

For a better understanding of the debate, we turn now to public declarations made by some of the perpetrators themselves which are widely quoted in the academic literature and, particularly, as a "proof of genocide" in the Argentine Court sentences.[18]

The voice of the perpetrators

Nine months after the military coup, Jorge Rafael Videla, who headed the military government between 1976 and 1980, explained in an interview in the magazine *Gente* the objectives of the new regime:

> Argentina is a Western and Christian country, not because a notice at Ezeiza Airport says so, but because of its history. It was born Christian under Spanish rule; it inherited its Western culture from Spain and it has never renounced this condition; on the contrary, it has defended it. It is to defend

this Western and Christian condition as a way of life that this struggle has begun against those who have not accepted this way of life and have tried to impose a different one.[19]

A year later, in a newspaper interview published in *La Prensa*, Videla expressly defined the struggle against "subversion":

Within our way of life, nobody is deprived of freedom just because they think differently; but we consider it a serious crime to attack the Western and Christian way of life and try to change it for one that is completely alien to us. The aggressor in this type of struggle is not just the bomber, the gunman or the kidnapper. At the intellectual level, it is anyone that tries to change our way of life by promoting subversive ideas; in other words, who tries to subvert, change or disrupt [our] values ... A terrorist is not just someone who kills with a gun or a bomb, but anyone who spreads ideas that are contrary to Western and Christian civilization.[20]

Many similar declarations by the repressors are on record. But perhaps the clearest indication of the military dictatorship's intention to systematically reorganize Argentinean society is to be found in the name the regime gave itself – "Proceso de Reorganización Nacional" ("Process of National Reorganization"). The process was worked out in detail by General Diaz Bessone, the minister of planning, in his "National Project," which argued that "the real objective is to organize a new and viable political system and to make the achievements of [our] armed intervention irreversible."

Going on to analyze what he calls "the foundational stage" of the Process of National Reorganization, Diaz Bessone emphasized the following:

Founding a new republic is no easy matter ... The armed forces must be sufficiently alert, determined and resourceful to act simultaneously as an efficient fighting force against guerrillas and terrorists; an efficient surgeon that will remove the evil from all social classes and walks of life; an efficient government that will steer the ship of state skillfully and prudently; and last but not least, parents of the new republic, strong, united, just, free, supportive of others, clean, exemplary ... The political project, the creative project of life in common, will have no meaning, nor will it illuminate Argentina's path ahead, unless it is applied now. Otherwise, we run the risk of going astray or falling behind those nations that actively determine the course of history. Moreover, our failure so far to solve the basic problems may give our opponents the chance to regroup as long as those who create and sustain subversion remain alive.[21]

In short, Diaz Bessone is arguing that this regime, which defines itself as a "Process of National Reorganization," must supplement military action against guerrilla forces with "surgery" to "remove the evil" from every part of society and so make way for a "New Republic." In other words, a series of individuals and groups must be annihilated to achieve the transformation and guarantee the security and purity of the new society.

The conceptual debate: thinking beyond the law

We have already argued that defining genocide in terms of the characteristics of the victims has no precedent in modern criminal law and clearly damages the principle of equality before the law. It is now time to consider the implications of such a definition from a historical and sociological point of view.

In legal terms, a homicide is always, in principle, a homicide. For the social sciences, however, some homicides are so extraordinary that they justify the development of a specific name to label them. Sociologists use the term Holocaust or Shoah to refer to the systematic annihilation of Europe's Jewish population under Nazism because of the unique characteristics of this historical tragedy. Nevertheless, just as the 1948 Convention's definition of genocide is insufficient to explain the nature of the Shoah, the specific characteristics of the Shoah do not in themselves define the limits of the term "genocide."

In the social sciences, the important element for constructing a concept such as genocide is what we might call the "structural similarities" of unique events. Each historical event is unique so we need to go beyond its specificities in order to categorize social phenomena which are equivalent in terms of purpose, design, implementation, and consequences. One issue that tends to overlap with and influence legal definitions is whether different historical processes fit the same category (e.g. genocide), or whether they are different enough to justify the creation of new categories.

Historians and sociologists have proposed various criteria for defining the term genocide, which can be summarized as follows:

a   Genocide is an action. Therefore, any systematic annihilation of a group because of its characteristics (whatever those may be) constitutes genocide (Chalk and Jonassohn, Henry R. Huttenbach, or Mark Levene);[22]

b   Genocide is the intention to systematically destroy the entire group, and not only a part of it (Steven Katz);[23]

c   Genocide is any systematic annihilation of significant numbers of the population as long as the population is in a situation of "defenselessness" or does not constitute a "real threat" to the perpetrator (Israel Charny or Helen Fein);[24]

d   There is a qualitative difference between genocide and politicide because of the characteristics of the victims (Barbara Harff and Ted Gurr);[25]

e   There is a qualitative difference between destruction/subjugation processes of massacre (where victims are almost always political) and destruction/eradication processes of massacre (where victims are almost always ethnic or national) (Jacques Semelin).[26]

Let us now consider in turn the general implications of these five definitions as well as what they contribute to our understanding of the Argentine repression in particular.

a   Genocide as the annihilation of a group

This definition is clear and inclusive. The Argentine state defined different political organizations and individuals as "subversive." These people, in the eyes of the perpetrators, formed a group because they posed a threat to Christian and Western values. "Western" referred to Argentina's political alignment during the Cold War, while "Christian" referred to the state religion of Roman Catholicism. Thus, the group was explicitly defined in both political and religious terms. The annihilation was clearly "one-sided," taking into account that most armed left-wing groups had been completely defeated by the time the military seized power, and was so effective that social autonomy, social criticism, and solidarity were to vanish from Argentine society for at least two generations.[27]

b   Genocide as the intention to systematically destroy the entire group

To my mind, Katz's definition is too subjective, making it unusable for sociological purposes. Assessing "intent" to destroy totally is a complex task due to the different groups of perpetrators involved in a particular instance of genocide. Also, it is difficult to kill an entire group, especially a large one. If applied literally, this definition might even exclude the Holocaust itself – as members of targeted groups did in fact survive.

The number of people murdered in Argentina – between 15,000 and 30,000 – was obviously quite small in relation to the total population of 25 million. On the other hand, annihilation of the group was "practically total" in the sense that autonomy, political opposition, and critical thinking were eliminated from Argentine society almost entirely for two generations. Even Peronism, which was revived after the military dictatorship, has little to do in terms of policies either with early Peronism (1946–55) and the Peronist resistance (1955–73), or with late Peronism (1973–6).

c   Genocide as the annihilation of the "defenseless"

The critical element in Fein's and, to a certain extent, Charny's definitions of genocide is the "defenselessness" of the victims. Although "defenselessness" is also a debatable category, the Argentine case, in principle, does not seem to fit this type of definition.

Again, the problem lies in how the victimized group is defined. Many of the political groups persecuted by the dictatorship were armed organizations but their ability to defy state power was always limited. Armed struggle in Argentina cannot be compared with that in Cuba, Nicaragua, El Salvador, or Guatemala, where left-wing armed organizations were able effectively to resist state forces.

Nevertheless, the category of "defenselessness" does not seem to apply to groups which had a military organization, however weak they may have been, and a philosophy of armed conflict. The process could be defined as "one-sided," but that does not imply that the victims were "defenseless."

To complicate matters still further, most of the victims in Argentina were members of political organizations that sympathized to a greater or lesser extent with or opposed various armed organizations, or individuals with no clear political affiliation. The relationship of the victims with those who decided to engage in armed conflict was unclear, ranging from armed sympathizers with left-wing organizations to militants who were strongly opposed to violence.

On the other hand, most of the murders were carried out by kidnapping victims from their homes, on the street, or at work, and transporting them to concentration camps, subjecting them to torture, and subsequently executing them. This happened regardless of the victim's affiliations and "in a situation of defenselessness," even though many of the victims had, at various times and in various ways, supported the idea of armed conflict. This is what sets the Argentine repression apart from many civil wars fought in the Third World.

Therefore, if we accept this third type of definition, we might say that those victims who were not members of armed organizations qualify as victims of genocide, while those who were members of armed organizations but were kidnapped in a situation of defenselessness fall into an ambiguous category; and finally, a small percentage of the victims – those who died in armed confrontations – do not qualify as victims at all.

This approach, in my view, does more to expose the problems inherent in the concept of "defenselessness" than it does to clarify the Argentine case. Furthermore, it raises difficult and undesirable questions about the degree of activism of the victims, which may even result in criminal charges against them. The need to prove "defenselessness" reverses the burden of proof, forcing an investigation into how defenseless each victim actually was.

d Qualitative difference between genocide and politicide

Harff and Gurr apply the term politicide not only to political groups but also to anyone who is targeted for opposing a regime. In their view, the Argentine case was one of politicide, not genocide, since "victim groups [were] defined primarily in terms of their hierarchical position or political opposition to the regime and dominant groups." Those persecuted by the Argentine repressors were clearly members of groups that engaged in "political opposition to the régime," regardless of the fact that a minority expressed opposition only in the obtuse imagination of the perpetrators.

We need to question the usefulness of this distinction. Harff and Gurr's work is clearly a response to the exclusion of "political groups" from Article 2 of the 1948 Convention. Their aim is to analyze different modalities in mass annihilation and the fundamental discussion revolves around whether genocide and politicide are different types of persecution that require different concepts or whether politicide is simply a subcategory within the larger category of genocide. If the two are qualitatively different, then so is ethnocide, defined as genocide against a national group, or genocide against a religious group or any other specific group, such as a sexual or economic group.

e Subjugation vs. eradication

I believe that genocide perpetrated against political groups does, in fact, have its own particular characteristics, and that the processes of destruction/subjugation are different from the processes of destruction/eradication. If we accept Semelin's distinction between destruction/subjugation processes and destruction/eradication processes as valid, the Argentine repression conforms to the first type. However, in practice we generally find a mixture of both. In Argentina, the destruction/subjugation processes were mixed with the total "destruction/eradication" of some political movements and their complete disappearance from the Argentine political arena.

The problem with Semelin's distinction is that it allows the term genocide to be applied only to destruction processes, but not to subjugation processes, thus creating a fragmented picture made up of genocidal and non-genocidal events. This tends to obscure the wider historical context and distort the true meaning of events. In the Argentine case, eradicating certain political, social, and cultural groups was intended to subjugate society as a whole.

In conclusion, the military repression in Argentina between 1974 and 1983 would seem to be best described by the genocide processes Harff and Gurr categorize as "politicide" and to the massacre processes Semelin calls "destruction/subjugation." On the other hand, these different varieties of genocide are, in reality, often interwoven, and so are difficult to differentiate.

Moreover, as discussed above, the "Western and Christian" ideology of the Argentine perpetrators introduced a religious as well as a political dimension. Now, genocidal processes based on an ideological construct combining two belief systems, politics and religion, differ in some respects from those based on national or ethnic criteria. However, their "structural elements" – polarization into "us" and "them," the demonizing of the enemy, modality of operation, the concentration camp system, dehumanization of otherness, destruction of social relationships, among many other symbolic processes – are all very similar.

Conclusions or "a debate with ongoing political consequences"

The preamble to the 1948 Convention states that "at all periods of history genocide has inflicted great losses on humanity." And yet genocide as a form of annihilation distinct from war is a peculiarly modern phenomenon. The need for a specific term to define it was not generally felt until the middle of the twentieth century and since then politicians have seemed more concerned about the stigma of genocide rather than preventing or punishing genocide itself.

Describing different historical processes as genocide does not mean that these are identical. Clearly, different contexts and ideologies surround the annihilation of Armenians, Greeks, and Assyrians during the World War I; or the annihilation of Jews, Roma and Sinti, Slavs, homosexuals, Jehovah's Witnesses, and political opponents under Nazism; or the extermination processes in Indonesia, East Timor, Cambodia, the Balkans, Rwanda, and Argentina, to name but a few. Nor do we wish to ignore the differences, both quantitative and qualitative, between the industrialized mass murder and incineration of millions of human beings under the Third Reich and the artisan extermination of tens of thousands of people buried in common graves or thrown into the ocean from military airplanes in Argentina.

In using the concept of genocide to describe these various events, we wish to point out the connecting thread between them – a technology of power based on the "denial of others," their physical disappearance (their bodies) and their symbolic disappearance (the memory of their existence). The disappearance of the victims is intended to have a profound effect on the survivors: it aims to suppress their identity by destroying the network of social relations that makes identity possible at all (a particular type of identity defined by a particular way of life). In short, the main objective of genocidal destruction is the transformation of the victims into "nothing" and the survivors into "nobodies." Unlike war, genocide does not end with the deaths it causes, but begins with them.

Notes and references

1 This chapter is a broadened version of the text published as "Political Violence in Argentina and Its Genocidal Characteristics," *Journal of Genocide Research* 8, 2, 2006, pp. 169–80.

2 For an analysis of the operations of the Triple A, see I. González Janzen, *La Triple A*, Buenos Aires: Contrapunto, 1986.

3 For the period after 1955, it is important to highlight the work of D. James, *Resistencia e integración: El Peronismo y la clase trabajadora Argentina, 1946–1976*, Buenos Aires: Sudamericana, 1990. For a different perspective, see the work of Juan Carlos Marín, *Los hechos armados. Argentina 1973–76. La Acumulación Primitiva del Genocidio*, Buenos Aires: La Rosa Blindada and PI.CA.SO., 1996. For a third perspective, among many others, see Eduardo Luis Duhalde, *El estado terrorista argentino. Quince años después, una mirada crítica*, Buenos Aires: EUDEBA, 1999.

4 J. C. Marin, *Los hechos armadas. Argentina, 1973–1976. La acumulacíon primitive del genocidio*, Buenos Aires: PI.CA.SO/La Rosa Blindada, 1996.

5 C. Hilb and D. Lutzky, *La nueva izquierda argentina: 1960–1980 (Politica y violencia)*, Buenos Aires: CEAL, 1984.

6 For details of the location and characteristics of the clandestine detention centers, as well as the operation of the repressive structure and its levels of organization and responsibility, see José Luis D'Andrea Mohr, *Memoria debida*, Buenos Aires: Colihue, 1999.

7 See the different sources in the trials made in Argentina, from the "Nunca más" Report (CO.NA.DEP, *Nunca más: Informe de la Comisión Nacional sobre Desaparición de Personas – Report of the National Commission on the Disappearance of Persons*, Buenos Aires: EUDEBA, 1984) to the last trials against Héctor Julio Simón,

Miguel Osvaldo Etchecolatz, Christian von Wernich, among others trials over the last three years.

8 File No 1131 of the CONADEP (Comisión Nacional sobre la Desaparición de Personas – National Commission on the Disappearance of Persons), created by the first post-dictatorship democratic government in order to investigate the events which had taken place during the years of repression.

9 CONADEP, *Nunca más.*

10 Ibid., File No. 1132.

11 Jacobo Timerman; *El caso Camps. Punt inicial,* Buenos Aires: El Cid Editor, 1982. For a revised and extended version by the same author, see *Preso sin nombre, celda sin número,* Buenos Aires: Ediciones de la Flor, 2000.

12 CONADEP, *Nunca más.*

13 Mohr, *Memoria debida,* p. 70.

14 Case No. IT-95-10-T, para. 82. Emphasis in the original.

15 The same sentence also states:

> It should be noted that the Court has finally decided that the specific statute applicable in this case is that of 'Crimes against Humanity' as contained in Article 67-bis of the current Penal Code. ... The question, then, is: How were these crimes punished in the past under Spanish National Law? Was it correct to describe them as crimes of Genocide? The answer that we believe most likely is that it was indeed [correct].
>
> (Sentencia N° 16/2005 del Juzgado de Instrucción N° 5, Sala de lo Penal, Sección Tercera, Audiencia Nacional Española, del 19 de abril de 2005)

16 All the quotes are from the sentence against Echetcolatz by the Federal Oral Criminal Court No. 1 of La Plata, September 2006, available in Spanish at www.ladhlaplata. org.ar/juicios.htm.

17 The *amicus curiae* presented by the human rights organization Nizkor in the trial against Adolfo Scilingo requested he be sentenced for "crimes against humanity," and not under the concept of "genocide." For the complete *amicus curiae* and the sentence of Spain's Audiencia Nacional, see www.nizkor.org.

18 This is just a small sample of the declarations that have been collected. A much larger sample can be found in the grounds of the accusations and sentences against Miguel Osvaldo Etchecolatz and Christian von Wernich at www.ladhlaplata.org.ar/juicios. htm For an analysis of these declarations see D. Feierstein, *El genocidio como práctica social,* Buenos Aires: Fondo de Cultura Económica, 2007.

19 Jorge Rafael Videla, in *Gente,* December 22, 1976.

20 Jorge Rafael Videla, in *La Prensa,* December 18, 1977.

21 A fundamental part of the "National Project" – including the passage cited above – is reproduced as an annex by Enrique Vázquez in *La última. Origen, apogeo y caída de la dictadura militar,* Buenos Aires: EUDEBA, 1985, pp. 299–327.

22 See F. Chalk and K. Jonnasohn; *History and Sociology of Genocide: Analysis and Case Studies,* New Haven, CT: Yale University Press, 1990; Henry R. Huttenbach; "Towards a Conceptual Definition of Genocide," *Journal of Genocide Research* 4, 2, 1991, pp. 167–176.

23 See S. Katz; *The Holocaust in Historical Context,* Oxford: Oxford University Press, 1994, p. 24.

24 See I. Charny; "Toward a Generic Definition of Genocide," in George Andreopoulos; *Genocide: Conceptual and Historical Dimensions,* Philadelphia, PA: University of Pennsylvania Press, 1994 and H. Fein; *Genocide. A Sociological Perspective,* London: Sage Publications, 1993.

25 See B. Harff and T. Gurr; "Toward Empirical Theory of Genocides and Politicides," *International Studies Quarterly,* 37, 3, 1988.

26 J. Semelin; *Purify and Destroy. The Political Uses of Massacre and Genocide*, New York: Columbia University Press, 2007.

27 However, it is important to point out that at the beginning of the conversations I had the opportunity to hold with both Henry R. Huttenbach and Frank Chalk regarding the appropriateness of their categorizations to define the Argentine case, the use of the concept of genocide was not at all obvious to them. The content of this chapter is based partly on conversations I have held with them, as well as with Eric Markusen, Enzo Traverso, Bruno Groppo, Barbara Harff, and Ted Gurr, among others.

3 Genocide in Chile?

An assessment

Maureen S. Hiebert and Pablo Policzer

Did the Chilean military dictatorship commit genocide? The Chilean Truth and Reconciliation Commission Report (known as the *Informe Rettig*) documented some 3,200 victims over the course of the 17-year dictatorship ushered in by the 1973 military coup which overthrew the left-wing government of Salvador Allende; yet it avoided using the term genocide.[1] In Argentina, the Report of the National Commission on the Disappearance of Persons (CONADEP), which documented some 9,000 victims, also avoided it;[2] yet in that country the accusation of genocide is gaining increasingly wide acceptance in official documents and sources.[3] Should the same happen in Chile?

Chile is an ambiguous case because state-directed killing in and of itself does not necessarily constitute genocide. Further, the victims in Chile were primarily political actors and groups rather than ethnic, "racial," national, or religious groups as has been the case in most genocides.[4] To evaluate whether the political killings in Chile may be considered genocidal we must review the debates in the literature on genocide studies over how to define genocide and how these debates can help illuminate the status of the Chilean case.

Like others in the social sciences, genocide is a highly contested concept about which scholars in the field continue to strongly disagree. Unlike most social science concepts (with the exception of those in law and criminology), genocide is also a legally codified crime in international and domestic law. It has also become a normative label that victims of human rights abuses wield to draw attention to their suffering, and that perpetrators deny in their own efforts to neutralize accusations that they have committed the most heinous of crimes. It is for these reasons that there is no one widely accepted definition of genocide against which we can measure the Chilean experience. Rather, we must evaluate the Chilean case in the context of three key debates in the literature over how to define genocide. These debates revolve around the identity of the victim group (who are the victims of genocide?), the intention of the perpetrators (does genocide require a specific "intent to destroy"?), and the extent and methods of destruction (is there a numerical or proportional threshold of destruction and/or manner of destruction that is unique to genocide?). Our review of these debates suggests that the violence directed by the Chilean regime against its opponents was closer to genocide than commonly assumed.

Identity of the victim group

The most obvious grounds upon which we might disqualify Chile as a case of genocide is the identity of the victim group, insofar as the targets of the regime were political groups (members of left-wing parties and movements), and not ethnic, national, or religious groups.[5] The 1948 United Nations Convention on the Punishment and Prevention of the Crime of Genocide (UNGC) and some noted genocide scholars exclude political groups from their definitions because these groups are considered to be too amorphous and transitory.[6] The UNGC stipulates that genocide is the "attempt to destroy" four specific kinds of groups: "national, ethnical, racial, and religious groups as such."[7] Political groups are obviously absent from this list. When it was being negotiated, the Soviet and Iranian delegations argued for leaving political groups out of the final draft of the UNGC. It was this position, adopted largely to prevent the Convention from being scuttled, which ruled the day. For the Soviets, genocide was not applicable to political groups because they understood genocide as a crime inherent to Nazism, a fundamentally race-based ideology and political system. The Soviet delegation further argued that from a "'socialist scientific' perspective political groups do not have identifiable 'objective characteristics' as do racial or ethnic groups."[8]

While the Soviet position reflected their own contemporary preoccupations – namely the regime's ideological proclivities and the self-serving goal of removing anything from the Convention that resembled the Great Purges of the 1930s – the Iranian delegation provided an argument that is still found in the current literature that rejects the inclusion of political groups. The Iranians contended that a distinction had to be made "between those groups, membership of which was inevitable, such as racial, religious or national groups, whose distinctive features were permanent, and those, membership of which was voluntary, such as political groups, whose distinctive features were not permanent." Destruction of the former should be recognized as the most heinous of crimes since it was committed against "human beings whom chance alone had grouped together."[9] This position implies that the victims of political killing can change their political affiliation, and thus group membership, in order to save themselves. By contrast, members of racial, ethnic, national, or religious groups cannot escape their more "primordial" identity and their resulting genocidal victimization.

Scholars who reject the idea that the victimization of political groups can be genocidal argue that not only are political groups mutable, but also that they are targeted for political or ideological reasons. Therefore, the use of violence against them, while obviously wrong, constitutes violations of human rights such as the safety and security of the person, freedom of expression and of assembly and the like, but not genocide. Manus Midlarsky, for example, argues that genocide involves the "systematic mass murder of people based on ethnoreligious identity" only, because this kind of killing "tap[s] into much deeper historical roots of the human condition" than does the targeting of "designated enemies of the state based on socioeconomic or political criteria."[10] Political or socioeconomic victims of state-sponsored mass murder, he argues, are "attributable to more detailed ideological considerations."[11]

Analysts like Midlarsky follow Barbara Harff's contention that the victimization of political and socioeconomic groups constitutes a separate but related phenomenon to genocide called "politicide." For Harff, both genocides and politicides are characterized by the intent to destroy "a communal, political, or politicized ethnic group." The difference between genocide and politicide rests on how the perpetrators define the identity of the victim group. In genocide the victim groups are identified by the perpetrator along "communal characteristics," while in politicides "groups are defined primarily in terms of their political opposition to the regime and dominant group."[12]

Although the preceding understanding of genocide would seem to preclude the Chilean case, it is important to remember that the original formulation of the crime of genocide by the Polish-American jurist Raphael Lemkin, along with the work of many contemporary genocidal scholars, suggests that political groups are essentially no different than the more "primordial" victim groups commonly associated with genocide. Moreover, the historical record shows that radical regimes have not been shy about targeting their political opponents, real and imagined, for genocidal destruction. For Lemkin, genocide included the extermination of groups "because of their political beliefs and/or practices."[13] The 1946 United Nations General Assembly Resolution 96 (I), calling on member states to draw up a convention to prevent and punish genocide, included the assertion that "[m]any instances of such crimes of genocide have occurred when racial, religious, political, and other groups have been destroyed, entirely or in part."[14]

The ultimate exclusion of political and socioeconomic groups from the final version of the 1948 UNGC was not because genocide by its nature only involves communal groups into which individuals are born. While the Soviet, Iranian and other delegations argued otherwise, most Western states, including the United States, supported the inclusion of political groups, noting that membership in such groups was no more mutable than in religious groups, and that history has shown that states have been "easily able to identify political groups they wished to destroy."[15] Before being voted off the Convention at Soviet insistence, political groups remained in successive drafts of the Convention until November 29, 1948. Political groups were recognized in these drafts as victims of genocide with the caveat that the Convention was only applicable "to the most horrible form of crime against a group, that of physical destruction."[16] Western and other delegations that supported the inclusion of political groups relented to the Soviet position not because of the latter's superior logic, but as a matter of political expediency to save the Convention, imperfect though it was.

Following on some of the debates presented at the UN when the UNGC was being negotiated, scholars who support the recognition of political groups have not only reiterated the idea that there is no objective difference between political and communal groups – since both the latter and the former categories can be constructed by the members themselves and the perpetrators of genocidal killing – but they also argue that ideological motivation is not a credible basis upon which to exclude political groups. Chalk and Jonassohn, for example, note that although political and socioeconomic groups have been targeted for destruction based on ideologically derived conceptions of the victims as "enemies of the people," these alleged enemies "are mythical to begin with" and, therefore, "it is futile to search for rational and objective boundaries to define them.... Millions of human beings have died because of their alleged membership in these 'mutable' groups."[17] Recognizing that ethno-communal groups are not primordial collectivities with "objective" boundaries and characteristics, and that political elites construct victims of genocide as threatening "enemies" requiring destruction – be they ethnic, national, political, or socioeconomic – Chalk and Jonassohn in their definition of genocide leave the identity of the victim group up to the perpetrators themselves,[18] while Helen Fein simply refers to the destruction of "collectivities."[19] This more open-ended socially constructed approach to the question of the victim group seems to be the most logical since it is the perpetrators of genocide, not legal scholars or social scientists making *ex post* analyses, who choose their victims, define the victims' alleged characteristics, and draw the boundary between the victim group and the rest of society. By not limiting the identity of the victim group we can acknowledge the victimization of political groups and whole socioeconomic classes in the past as well as the targeting of other groups who may become the victims of genocide in the future.

As for the concept politicide, it is essentially a distinction without a difference. The killing of defenseless former political opponents or completely innocent individuals who are perceived or alleged to be members of an opposing political group is virtually identical to the status of ethno-communal victims of genocide, so long as the perpetrator imputes threats that do not really exist to objectively powerless groups grounded in an intention to destroy the group as such. The mass killing of actual political opponents who possess real power capabilities, on the other hand, is not genocide. Rather, it is a bloody contest between two opposing forces, albeit a contest in which killing, repression, and atrocities are perpetrated by one or both sides. Here, the victims of state-sponsored political killing are genuine political opponents, rebels, or insurgents who really do want to undermine, destroy, or replace the existing political order. Political victims of genocide do not act this way nor do they possess real power capabilities. Instead, it is the fact that the perpetrator defines them as members of a threatening group who must be destroyed, despite all objective evidence to the contrary, which constitutes the basis of genocide.

The Chilean case must be analyzed carefully in this light. Chilean military leaders since 1973 have claimed that they were fighting a "war" against an armed opponent, and have continuously argued that any "excesses" that may have been committed must be understood in this context. As noted above, genocides are not perpetrated against armed combatants, or against political opponents who possess real power vis-à-vis the perpetrators.

It is true that the Chilean military overthrew a sitting government before unleashing its repression, and that at least some of the opponents it faced were armed. The MIR (Revolutionary Left Movement), for example, mobilized for armed revolution. It did not join the Allende government's Popular Unity (UP) coalition, because it was critical of what it argued was Allende's preference for reformism through peaceful and constitutional means over revolution. And even inside the UP, some sectors (e.g. inside the Socialist Party) also favored taking up arms, and pushed Allende in this direction. The final period of the Allende government was also marked by growing unrest and insecurity: strikes, business nationalizations, land and factory takeovers, and sometimes armed clashes between Allende supporters and opponents.[20] The *Informe Rettig* describes the insecurity in this period by noting that

> no side had a monopoly on violence, and that violence flared up because the extent of polarization already underway encouraged each individual to believe he or she was overstepping the bounds of the legal framework only in response to, and defense against, someone else who had already done so ... In any case it would have been illusory to expect that the armed forces and security forces could see in these circumstances anything but a threat to break their monopoly on weapons and their internal unity, once more conjuring up the specter of division and civil war.[21]

Nevertheless, several reasons disqualify the military's rationalization of their activities. First, the most significant power available to any government is the coercive power of the state – i.e. the armed forces themselves. In Chile, with the exception of some individual officers, the armed forces withdrew their support from the Allende government. Second, while there was some armed resistance after the coup (e.g. from the MIR and other armed combatants from other parties), this was minimal, and ultimately no match for the awesome and overwhelming power of the Chilean armed forces, one of the best armed and trained in Latin America. The official records indicate that any remaining armed resistance against the military after the coup was effectively dealt with in a matter of days.[22] Third, the military regime continued to target victims well after the end of the armed resistance it encountered upon taking power. The claim that the military had to use overwhelming force to defeat well-armed opponents might (as the *Informe Rettig* suggests) have made sense in the months and weeks leading up to the September 11 coup. But after encountering such minimal armed resistance after taking power, these claims fail to explain the military's continued targeting and elimination of unarmed civilians. And finally, while they would almost certainly have opposed the regime, a significant portion of the regime's victims were not directly connected to any political party or movement,[23] were unarmed, and posed no direct (or even indirect) threat to it.

Intention of the perpetrator

The second criterion against which we can evaluate the status of the Chilean case is the intention of the perpetrator. There continues to be a vigorous debate in the genocide literature over whether genocide should be characterized primarily by outcomes – that is, obvious evidence of killing and other forms of victimization of specific groups of people[24] – or by the intention of the perpetrator to destroy the victim group as a group. If we choose the first approach then evidence of killing and other forms of abuse is enough to suggest that genocide did take place in Chile. If we take the second intentionalist approach then we will have to show that the dictatorship intended to destroy political groups as such.

The outcome-oriented approach argues that intention should not be a central component of a definition of genocide or a foundation for determining which cases of gross human rights violation constitute genocide, for two reasons. First, it is extremely hard to empirically prove the intention of the perpetrator; and second, it is morally wrong to narrowly define genocide based on intent. The first argument suggests that the true intentions of elite actors over sometimes lengthy periods of time, or during the chaos of war or revolution, can be extremely hard to prove or the evidence may simply never become available. Moreover, genocidal political elites more often than not go to great lengths to obscure their true intentions by using dissembling or euphemistic language – even in confidential documents or private discussions – to refer to their genocidal destruction of specific groups. In what the Nazis themselves called the "Final Solution to the Jewish Question," for example, deportation to the death camps was publicly and privately called "deportation to the East" or transfer for "special treatment," while mass shootings of Jews in the occupied East were referred to as *Aktions* (actions). Individuals who were slated for torture and execution by the Khmer Rouge were "invited to study with *Angkar*" (literally the "Organization"). In Rwanda, Hutus were exhorted in radio broadcasts to do their "work" and kill their Tutsi neighbors.

The second outcome-oriented argument contends that even if the destruction of a group was not the primary intent of political elites, the destruction of the members of a group is no less real, and political elites, by virtue of the objective policies they pursue, are no less responsible for the inflicting of mass suffering and death. To rest a definition of genocide on intent would, therefore, exclude a number of serious instances of the deliberate causing of mass death. In making this argument Israel Charny, for example, defines genocide as the causing of death to defenseless people. He deliberately leaves out the issue of intent not only for methodological reasons (i.e., the problem of available evidence), but also because he believes that to argue that the causing of mass death to innocents is not genocide is simply morally wrong. Charny thus defines genocide "in the generic sense" as the "mass killing of substantial numbers of human beings, when not in the course of military forces of an avowed enemy, under conditions of the essential defenselessness and helplessness of the victims."[25]

Other genocide scholars argue, on the other hand, that intent to destroy a group of people because of their collective identity must be central to a definition of genocide precisely because it is this very specific intention that differentiates genocide from all other crimes, and is the characteristic that gives genocide its terrible signature. Citing the *Akayesu* decision at the International Criminal

Tribunal for Rwanda, Payam Akhavan notes that the crime of genocide requires a "special intent" (*dolus specialis*) to destroy the victim group as such where the perpetrator "clearly intended the result, signifying a psychological nexus between the physical result and the mental state of the perpetrator."[26] In their definition of genocide, Chalk and Jonassohn explicitly refer to the "intent to destroy" a victim group,[27] while Steven Katz suggests that genocide, as distinct from other atrocities and mass murder, only occurs when there is an "actualized intent" to physically destroy an entire group.[28] Helen Fein deals with the problem of proving intent by suggesting in her definition that intent is demonstrated by the "purposeful action by a perpetrator to physically destroy a collectivity."[29]

Whether genocide is conceptualized as a means to another political end[30] or as a policy goal in and of itself, the intention-oriented approach emphasizes that genocide is not a method of collective punishment for what are actual illegal acts (even if the allegations of such crimes are often made by the perpetrators), nor is it an accidental or unintended consequence of some other kind of military action or political policy. Genocide is an intentional and systematic attempt to physically eliminate an innocent, defenseless group of people who are ultimately targeted for who they are and not because of the power they really possess or what they have done.

The outcome-oriented approach, in which intention is eschewed in favor of evidence of group victimization, is a relatively easy test for the Chilean case, insofar as there is evidence of the victimization of individuals who belonged largely to left-wing political parties or groups.[31] The intention-oriented approach is a harder test. But if we can show, either through direct evidence or a pattern of purposeful actions, that the dictatorship possessed a "special intent" to bring about the physical destruction of political groups as such, and if we can demonstrate that the regime regarded their victims as implacable enemies of the people whose continued existence was perceived to threaten the state and the wider society, then the killings committed by the dictatorship in Chile were not just dirty, they were genocidal.

Direct evidence and patterns of purposeful actions do suggest both the regime's special intent and the fact that they regarded their victims as implacable enemies. During the 1960s, the Chilean military (along with others in the region) was influenced by the National Security Doctrine, a set of American-inspired cold war principles which held that the primary threats to national security were internal rather than external, and that national security itself was the primary yardstick to assign government priorities and evaluate government policies. The critical areas involved counterinsurgency policies to target "insurgents" or "subversives," geopolitical policies to align domestic priorities with a global fight against communism, and security and development policies targeted at industrialization and growth.[32]

Influenced by these principles, the region's armed forces increasingly turned their attention away from preparation for possible attacks by other countries, and toward domestic issues, including the threats posed by Marxist or Marxist-inspired parties and groups.[33] Although anti-communism has deep historical roots in the Chilean armed forces, as it does in others in Latin America, the National Security Doctrine provided the clearest military doctrinal framework for such views, turning them from personal opinions to purposeful actions. Reflecting this influence, soon after taking power on September 11, 1973, junta member and air force commander-in-chief, General Gustavo Leigh, argued that the primary purpose of the dictatorship would be to "extirpate the Marxist cancer" from the Chilean body politic, applying even extreme measures to do so.[34]

Other military commanders had similar intentions. In October 1973, Augusto Pinochet sent a small group of loyal army officers on a mission to visit the military's prison camps, located throughout the country, to ensure that all officers adopted a uniformly hard line against the prisoners under their control. In most places the local commanders had taken prisoners and were holding trials. The mission, led by General Sergio Arellano, faced resistance from local commanders who were applying military rules ensuring due legal process for prisoners, or were working to normalize relations with the local population. As Arellano's mission passed through the regiments, dozens of prisoners who were awaiting trial were summarily executed, mostly without the knowledge of the local commander. Typically, Arellano's team would remove prisoners from the detention centers to take them to "interrogations" in a different camp. The prisoners would be summarily executed in an isolated spot.[35]

The *Informe Rettig* points out that Arellano's mission, with its official and extraordinary character, with the highest authority – originating in the commander-in-chief – that backed it up, with its aftermath of astonishing extralegal executions, and with its blatant impunity, could not fail to give the officers of the armed forces and the carabineros (*Fuerzas Armadas y de Orden*) one clear signal: that there was only one command and that it would have to be carried out ruthlessly.[36]

The pattern of targeting victims is consistent with this description, and suggests similar intentions. Figure 3.1 shows that most victims were killed between September and December 1973, with substantial killings (mostly disappearances) committed in the period between 1973 and 1977.

Table 3.1 shows that most of the victims came from the three major left-wing parties: socialist, communist, and MIR. While roughly half of the total victims had no recorded party affiliation, the major official reports on the crimes committed by the dictatorship suggest that they were targeted because of their suspected links to left-wing parties and activities. In other words, the targeting of political victims was not random or part of a general policy to repress the entire population. Nor was the victimization of real or imagined left-wing members and supporters a by-product of another policy or an accidental or unforeseen outcome. Rather the killing was a systematic and organized policy directed at a specific element of Chilean society whom the regime intended to destroy.

The official reports also indicate that victims were selectively targeted at different periods. The *Informe Rettig* reports that most "of the killings and the arrests that ended in disappearance [between September and December 1973]

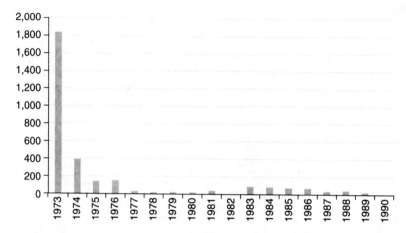

Figure 3.1 Number of victims (killed) per year (source: adapted from the Comisión Nacional de Verdad y Reconciliación (1991), and the Corporación Nacional de Reparación y Reconciliación (1996)).

Table 3.1 Victims according to party affiliation

Socialist Party	482
Movement of the Revolutionary Left (MIR)	440
Communist Party	427
Movement of Unitary Popular Action (MAPU and MOC)	36
Manuel Rodríguez Patriotic Front (FPMR)	22
Radical Party	17
Christian Democratic Party	12
Christian Left	7
National Party	4
Radical Left Party	3
Fatherland and Liberty	3
Party for Democracy	2
Social Democratic Party	1
Independent Democratic Union	1
Other parties	16
No information regarding affiliation	1,724
Total	3,197

Source: adapted from the Corporación Nacional de Reparación y Reconciliación (1996, 591).

were the result of actions aimed at outstanding officials of the overthrown government," and other party, union, neighborhood, and student leaders deemed to sympathize with the ousted government.[37] In 1974, the regime created a special secret police (the National Intelligence Directorate, DINA), which aimed to more selectively and systematically eliminate the regime's enemies, targeting the MIR as its first priority. The DINA held its victims in secret locations, where they were interrogated and tortured.[38] The bodies of those who were killed were disposed of so as to disappear.

In 1974, most of those disappeared by the DINA belonged to the MIR, and by 1975 the DINA began to systematically target the Socialist and later the Communist Parties.[39] The DINA was also instrumental in setting up a counterinsurgency network among the other military dictatorships in the region (including Argentina, Paraguay, Uruguay, Bolivia and Brazil), "Operation Condor." Condor was designed to facilitate the collaboration of the region's military regimes to exchange information about their internal enemies, and to eliminate them.[40] As suggested above, this pattern of repression indicates a deliberate and systematic intention to eliminate specific groups of people deemed by the regime to be its enemies.

Methods and outcomes of destruction

The final criterion upon which we can assess Chile as a case of genocide (or not) is the method of destruction and the outcome of that destruction. The first part deals with how the UNGC defines the methods of destruction while the latter revolves around two related debates: whether genocide should be defined by a body count; and, if the numbers of dead are part of a definition, what should be the number or proportion.

Article II of the UNGC states that genocide involves the following methods of destruction:

a   Killing members of the group;
b   Causing serious bodily or mental harm to members of the group;
c   Deliberately inflicting on the group conditions of life calculated to bring about its physical destruction in whole or in part;
d   Imposing measures intended to prevent births within the group;
e   Forcibly transferring children of the group to another group.[41]

The first three methods are all forms of physical destruction in which the existing members of the group are killed or irreparably harmed directly or indirectly either over a short period of time or over the long term or both. The last two methods are intended to bring about the biological destruction of the group by ensuring that the group cannot reproduce itself (preventing births) or that a new generation cannot grow up as members of the group (forcible transfer of children). Genocide can involve one, all, or a combination of these methods. Particularly extreme forms of genocide, such as the Nazi extermination of Europe's Jews or the genocide in Rwanda aimed at annihilating the Tutsi minority, are marked by a "root and branch" strategy in which the perpetrator seeks to destroy a significant number of members of the group as well as its capacity to reproduce itself. Hence the targeting not just of men who might come together to defend the group and fight back, but women and children. Women are targeted because they are the bearers of the next generation, and children because they are the next generation.

The first two methods are clearly evident in Chile. As indicated above, the military dictatorship killed members of political opposition groups, as well as those it suspected of belonging to or sympathizing with such groups. The causing of serious bodily or mental harm to such groups is also evident. Figure 3.2 indicates the number of people imprisoned by the dictatorship, per year, with data drawn from the *Comisión Valech* report. The report documents that in the majority of imprisonments, especially under the DINA and its successor, the CNI, victims suffered often brutal physical and mental torture, including beatings, electric shocks, and sexual violations.

The combination of killings and brutal torture is arguably also evidence of the third method stipulated by the UNGC. Those targeted were killed outright, or suffered traumatic conditions intended to ensure they did not return to their former political activities, or consider taking them up in the first place. In the latter case one could argue that the regime tried to bring about the destruction of political groups by fundamentally undermining the ability of members to function as a group.

By contrast to Argentina, where the forcible transfer of children from one group to another was a more common strategy of repression,[42] there is little evidence of this kind of systematic "root and branch" strategy in Chile. Family members (e.g. wives or husbands) were targeted in many cases, but largely because they were themselves also seen to be political enemies, and not because of their potential to reproduce.

More controversial in the genocide literature is the debate over whether genocide should be defined in terms of the number of victims. The Genocide Convention does not provide an absolute number or specific proportion but rather refers to the destruction of a group "in whole or in part."[43] Following the Convention, Kuper argues that genocide must involve a "substantial" or "appreciable" number of victims although he does not give us a number or percentage of victims.[44] Midlarsky is more specific, arguing that genocide is characterized by the destruction of ethno-national groups where the death toll among members of

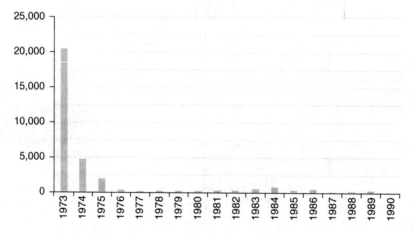

Figure 3.2 Number of detainees per year (source: adapted from the Comisión Nacional sobre Prisión Política y Tortura (2004)).

the group reaches between 66 and 77 percent.[45] For Valentino "mass killing" (a concept he uses instead of genocide) is defined by "at least fifty thousand intentional deaths over the course of five or fewer years."[46] Each of the authors believes that an absolute number or proportion of victims is crucial for establishing the scale of the crime of genocide and to differentiating it from other less destructive forms of violence and abuse.

By these criteria, Chile is a less likely candidate for genocide. A comparison between Figures 3.1 and 3.2 indicates that most of those detained were not killed. In this sense, as we have suggested earlier, Chile is a less straightforward case of genocide than others, in which few detainees survived. It falls far below Valentino's threshold of 50,000 victims, and it does not meet the two thirds threshold suggested by Midlarsky. Notwithstanding the significance of torture as one method of genocide, the quantification of death as part of a definition of genocide, however, raises important issues that call the utility and desirability of this approach into question. If we can establish "intent to destroy" should the destruction of members of a group not be considered genocide if the absolute number or proportion of members killed is relatively low? What about a scenario in which a successful outside intervention prevents the implementation of a planned genocide or interrupts its execution before the casualty rate could climb to a specifically defined "genocidal" level? Is the partial destruction of a subsection of a victim group as defined by gender, geographical location, or some other subgroup characteristic – for example the mass murder of the male population of Srebrenica during the Bosnian war – genocide or simply an isolated massacre, or a "genocidal massacre"[47] or "gendercide"?[48] Lastly, what are the ethics of determining genocide by the numbers? There are no satisfactory answers to these questions. Consequently, we suggest that establishing a precise number or threshold is a poor guide for determining whether the Chilean military regime committed genocide.

Conclusion

Our aim in this brief essay has not been to document the extent to which genocide occurred in Chile, but to suggest how it may be possible to begin to think about whether it did or not. By contrast to Argentina, where the claim of genocide has been increasingly accepted in official circles, the Chilean case continues to be understood as one of massive human rights violations and political violence (including detentions, torture, killings, and disappearances), but not genocide. Our assessment of how scholars understand the phenomenon of genocide suggests that the Chilean regime's crimes should be reconsidered. While it is a less obvious case of genocide than others in Latin America (such as Guatemala, where large numbers of victims were targeted because of their identity as members of indigenous communities, or Argentina, where a larger number of political opponents were killed than in Chile, often using "root and branch" methods), it demonstrates both the clear intention to eliminate a specific group of political opponents deemed to be a threat to national security, and their deliberate and purposeful targeting in order to achieve this outcome.

At the same time, although our focus is on the direct perpetrators of genocide – the Chilean military authorities – our assessment also raises questions about the more indirect role of the United States in this period. We have noted that the Chileans (along with others in Latin America) were influenced by National Security Doctrine ideas, which refocused their attention toward internal enemies. American authorities also lent political, economic, and military support to the Chilean regime during this early period when most of the violence occurred, and were for the most part well apprised of the Chileans' actions against their political enemies.[49] The question is how to assess the Americans' possible complicity in the Chilean (and other Latin American regimes') crimes. We would suggest three possible scenarios.[50] The first is a case of direct complicity, analogous for example to that of Nazi officials who directed their allies in other regimes to help them carry out their plans of extermination. The second is a somewhat more indirect complicity, where American officials actively encouraged but did not direct the Latin Americans' actions against their political enemies, because it helped them advance their geopolitical goals in the Cold War, namely to eradicate Marxism. The third scenario is where the Americans were aware of the Latin Americans' actions but did nothing to discourage or challenge them, and where their silence could be interpreted as a form of tacit encouragement. Although none of these scenarios can be completely ruled out without more thorough research, the available evidence suggests some combination of the second and third scenarios. Establishing the precise nature of American officials' complicity in genocide in Chile is beyond the boundaries of this chapter, but we would urge this as an important area for future research.

One possible counterargument to this suggestion may be that the crime of genocide – arguably the most serious accusation that can be leveled against any government or regime – should be reserved for only the gravest of cases: the least ambiguous, which leave no doubt about the number and the types of killings. The idea here is that by including more ambiguous cases, like the Chilean, the value of the term is "banalized" as Michael Ignatieff has put it.[51] Our response to this is two-fold. First, we are not arguing that the Chilean military regime definitely and unambiguously committed genocide. We are claiming that the reasons for excluding it from the list of regimes that did are poor, and that there are very good reasons for reconsidering it – e.g. in a revisionist history perspective – in light of how scholars have come to understand this phenomenon. The premise here is that genocide is not a nominal but an ordinal category. Unlike being pregnant, it is possible for regimes to commit *degrees* of genocide. In this sense, the claim is that the Chilean regime committed genocide to a certain degree; less than other regimes (such as the Khmer Rouge or the Nazi), to be sure, but more than commonly assumed.

Second, determining that some aspects of the atrocities committed by the Chilean dictatorship were genocidal does not necessarily imply any specific legal or political consequence. It is conceivable for there to be an increasing consensus around the fact that the regime committed genocide along with the determination that this does not make much legal or political difference. While this is possible, we would suggest it is unlikely. Chilean society continues to struggle with how to deal with the legacy of the military regime and with fundamental questions such as how to bring to justice those who perpetrated atrocities. This struggle has been hampered by continuing divisions over the extent to which the violence during the dictatorship was justified or not. It is in this context that a reexamination of the Chilean case along the lines we are suggesting here should be understood. Any choices made by Chileans and others about how to deal with the crimes of the dictatorship – whether to redouble the efforts to bring perpetrators to justice or not – should be made on the basis of full information, and in light of the best available knowledge about what did, in fact, occur.

Notes and references

1 Comisión Nacional de Verdad y Reconciliación, *Informe Rettig: Informe de la Comisión Nacional de Verdad i Reconciliación*, 2 vols, Santiago: La Nación and Ediciones Ornitorrinco, 1991. Also see www.ddhh.gov.cl/ddhh_rettig.html, and www.ddhh.gov.cl/estadisticas.html. The more recent National Commission on Political Imprisonment and Torture (known as the Comision Valech), which published its report in 2004, also avoided the term. Comisión Nacional sobre Prisión Política y Tortura, *Informe de la Comisión Nacional sobre Prisión Política y Tortura*, Santiago, Chile: Ministerio del Interor, 2004.

2 The *Informe Rettig* did, however, use analogous language:

> the [military] regime which considered it necessary to change our legal tradition by introducing capital punishment, never used it as such. Instead, it organized a collective crime, a veritable mass extermination, on which the evidence is now coming to light in the morbid form of hundreds of nameless corpses and the testimony of the survivors, telling of those who died in agony. It was not an excess of repressive activity, it was not a mistake. It was the implementation of a cold-blooded decision. There are so many examples and proofs that there can be no doubt about this conclusion.

CONADEP, *Nunca Más: Informe de la Comisión Nacional sobre la Desaparición de Personas*, Buenos Aires: Editorial Universitaria de Buenos Aires, 1995. CONADEP, *Nunca Más*, 1984. Online, available at: http://web.archive.org/web/20031013232413/nuncamas.org/english/library/nevagain/nevagain_155.htm (accessed on February 13, 2008).

3 E.g., in 2006 Miguel Etchecolatz, former investigations director of the Buenos Aires police during the military dictatorship, was convicted of "crimes against humanity committed under the framework of a genocide." W. Pertot, "Delitos cometidos en el marco del genocidio," *Página/12*, September 20, 2006.

4 This is true for most cases of genocide. The possible exceptions are the Cambodian genocide in the 1970s and the Stalinist purges of the 1930s. For sources on the Cambodian genocide see B. Kiernan, *The Pol Pot Regime: Race, Power, and Genocide in Cambodia under the Khmer Rouge, 1975–79*. New Haven, CT: Yale University Press, 1996; B. Kiernan, *Blood and Soil: A World History of Genocide and Extermination from Sparta to Darfur*, New Haven, CT: Yale University Press, 2007, pp. 539–69; E. D. Weitz, *A Century of Genocide: Utopias of Race and Nation*, Princeton, NJ: Princeton University Press, 2003, pp. 144–89; and A. L. Hinton, *Why Did They Kill?: Cambodia in the Shadow of Genocide*, Berkeley, CA: University of California Press, 2005. For the Soviet Union see R. J. Rummel, *Lethal Politics: Soviet Genocide and Mass Murder since 1917*, New Brunswick, NJ: Transaction Publishers, 1990; Kiernan, *Blood and Soil*, pp. 486–511; and Weitz, *A Century of Genocide*, pp. 53–101.

5 The Chilean regime targeted a number of left-wing opponents belonging to different groups or parties (e.g. the Communist Party, Socialist Party and Movement of the Revolutionary Left [MIR]). Not all the regimes' victims, however, belonged to a specific party.

6 As noted below, some scholars suggest that the destruction of political groups is a related but separate phenomenon called "politicide."

7 Office of the United Nations High Commission for Human Rights, *United Nations Convention on the Prevention and Punishment of the Crime of Genocide, United Nations General Assembly Resolution A (III), 9 December 1948*, 1948. Online, available at: www.OHCHR.org/english/law/genocide.htm (accessed June 13, 2008).

8 L. Kuper, *Genocide: Its Political Use in the Twentieth Century*, New Haven, CT: Yale University Press, 1981, pp. 24–9.

9 United Nations Economic and Social Council, *Session 7, 26, August 1948*, p. 712; as quoted in Kuper, *Genocide*, p. 26.

10 M. I. Midlarsky, *The Killing Trap: Genocide in the Twentieth Century*. Cambridge: Cambridge University Press, 2005, p. 22, fn. 21.

11 Ibid., p. 310.

12 B. Harff, "No Lessons Learned from the Holocaust? Assessing Risks of Genocide and Political Mass Murder Since 1955," *American Political Science Review* 97, 1, 2003, p. 58.

13 L. Chorbajian, and G. Shirinian, *Studies in Comparative Genocide*, New York: St Martin's Press, 1999, p. xvi.

14 United Nations, *United Nations General Assembly Resolution 96 (I), 11 December, 1946*, 1946. Online, available at: http://daccessdds.un.org/doc/RESOLUTION/GEN/NRO/033/47-IMG/NR003347.pdfOpenElement (accessed June 1, 2008).

15 Kuper, *Genocide*, pp. 28–9.

16 Ibid., p. 29.

17 F. R. Chalk and K. Jonassohn, *The History and Sociology of Genocide: Analyses and Case Studies*. New Haven, CT: Yale University Press, 1990, p. 10.

18 Ibid., p. 23.

19 H. Fein, *Genocide: A Sociological Perspective*. London: Sage, p. 24.

20 The classic sources on the internal disputes that led to the breakdown of the Chilean democratic regime in 1973 remain A. Valenzuela, *The Breakdown of Democratic Regimes: Chile*, ed. J. J. Linz and A. Stepan, Baltimore, MD: Johns Hopkins University Press, 1978, and the film by P. Guzmán, *The Battle of Chile*, Icarus Films, 1976.

21 Comisión Nacional de Verdad y Reconciliación, *Informe Rettig*, Part II, Chapter 1.

22 Comisión Nacional de Verdad y Reconciliación, *Informe Rettig*; R. J. Barros, *Constitutionalism and Dictatorship: Pinochet, the Junta, and the 1980 Constitution*, Cambridge: Cambridge University Press, 2002.

23 See Table 3.1.

24 I. Charny, "Toward a Generic Definition of Genocide," in G. Andreopoulos (ed.), *Genocide: Conceptual and Historical Dimensions*, Philadelphia, PA: University of Pennsylvania Press, 1994.

25 Ibid., p. 75.

26 According to Akhavan, *dolus specialis* refers to the degree of intent rather than the scope. *Dolus generalis* or general intent was defined in *Akayesu* as a circumstance in which "the perpetrator means to cause a certain consequence or is aware that it will occur in the ordinary course of events." P. Akhavan, "The Crime of Genocide in the ICTR jurisprudence," *Journal of International Criminal Justice* 3, 4, 2005, p. 992.

27 Chalk and Jonassohn, *The History and Sociology of Genocide*, p. 23.

28 S. T. Katz, *The Holocaust in Historical Context*, New York: Oxford University Press, 1994.

29 Fein, *Genocide*.

30 Benjamin Valentino, for example, argues that mass killing, of which genocide is in

his view a distinct but related phenomenon, is a "strategic" means for elites to use their power capabilities to achieve radical policies and/or to counter "the most dangerous threats." B. A. Valentino, *Final Solutions: Mass Killing and Genocide in the Twentieth Century*, Ithaca, NY: Cornell University Press, 2004, pp. 3–4.

31 As indicated above, while a minority of these individuals were armed, a majority were not, especially after the brief initial period immediately after the coup.

32 G. Lopez, "National Security Ideology as an Impetus to State Violence and State Terror," in M. Stohl and G. Lopez (eds), *Government Violence and Repression: An Agenda for Research*, Westport, CT: Greenwood Press, 1986; D. Pion-Berlin, "The National Security Doctrine, Military Threat Perception, and the 'Dirty War' in Argentina," *Comparative Political Studies* 21, 3, 1988, pp. 382–407.

33 G. O'Donnell, *Modernization and Bureaucratic-Authoritarianism: Studies in South American Politics*, Berkeley, CA: Institute of International Studies, University of California, 1973; A. Stepan, *Authoritarian Brazil: Origins, Policies, and Future*, New Haven, CT: Yale University Press, 1973; G. Arriagada Herrera, *La política militar de Pinochet*, Santiago, Chile: n.p., 1985; Lopez, "National Security Ideology"; B. Loveman, and T. M. Davies Jr, *The Politics of Antipolitics: The Military in Latin America*, Wilmington, DE: Scholarly Resources, 1997; J. S. Fitch, *The Armed Forces and Democracy in Latin America*, Baltimore, MD: Johns Hopkins University Press, 1998, ch. 4; B. Loveman, *For* La Patria: *Politics and the Armed Forces in Latin America*, Wilmington, DE: SR Books, 1999.

34 S. Huidobro, *Decisión naval*, Valparaíso: Editorial Impresa de la Armada, 1989, p. 263. See also C. Huneeus, *El regimen de Pinochet*, Santiago: Sudamericana, 2000, pp. 98–100. In Argentina, General Ibérico Saint, governor of Buenos Aires province during the dictatorship, expressed a similar intent when he stated in 1977: "First we kill all the subversives; then, their collaborators; later, those who sympathize with them; afterward, those who remain indifferent; and finally, the undecided."

35 P. Verdugo, *Caso Arellano: Los zarpazos del puma*, Santiago: Ediciones Chile América CESOC, 1989; J. Escalante Hidalgo, *La misión era matar: el juicio a la caravana Pinochet–Arellano*, Santiago: LOM Ediciones, 2000. See also P. Policzer, *The Rise and Fall of Repression in Chile*, South Bend, IN: Notre Dame University Press, 2009, ch. 3.

36 Comisión Nacional de Verdad y Reconciliación, *Informe Rettig*, p. 123.

37 Ibid., Part III, Chapter One, A.1.e.

38 Comisión Nacional sobre Prisión Política y Tortura, *Informe De La Comisión Nacional sobre Prisión Política y Tortura*.

39 Comisión Nacional de Verdad y Reconciliación, *Informe Rettig*, Part III, Chapter Two, A.1.a. See also Barros, *Constitutionalism and Dictatorship*, pp. 124–31; and Policzer, *The Rise and Fall of Repression in Chile*, ch. 4.

40 P. Kornbluh, *The Pinochet File: A Declassified Dossier on Atrocity and Accountability*, New York: New Press, 2003; J. Dinges, *The Condor Years*, New York: New Press, 2004; J. P. McSherry, *Predatory States: Operation Condor and Covert War in Latin America*, Boulder, CO: Rowman & Littlefield, 2005.

41 United Nations Convention on the Prevention and Punishment of the Crime of Genocide, *United Nations General Assemby Resolution A (III), 9 December, 1948*, Office of the United Nations High Commission for Human Rights. Online, available at: www.OHCHR.org/english/law/genocide.htm (accessed May 30, 2008).

42 L. Oren, "Righting Child Custody Wrongs: The Children of the 'Disappeared' in Argentina," *Harvard Human Rights Journal* 14, 2001, pp. 123–95; A. Kletnicki, "Disappeared Children in Argentina: Genocidal Logic and Illegal Appropriation," *Journal of Genocide Research* 8, 2, 2006, pp. 181–90.

43 Despite the lack of clarity in the Convention itself, the International Criminal Tribunal for the Former Yugoslavia rejected Serbian General Radislav Krstic's appeal that he was not guilty of aiding and abetting genocide in the slaughter of approximately

7,000 Muslim men and boys in Srebrenica, Bosnia, in July 1995 because the number of victims was "too insignificant" to be genocide (BBC News, April 19, 2004. Online, available at http://news.bbc.co.uk/2/hi/europe/3638473.stm).

44 Kuper, *Genocide*, p. 32.

45 Midlarsky, *The Killing Trap*, pp. 10, 25.

46 Valentino, *Final Solutions*, pp. 11–12.

47 Kuper uses the term "genocidal massacre" for the slaughter of a substratum of people within a victim group, for example, the obliteration of whole villages by the French in Algeria after the riots in Setif in 1945 or the destruction of Lidice and Lezaky as reprisals for the assassination of German officials in World War II. He does, however, concede the essential arbitrariness in drawing the line between genocidal massacre and genocide proper. Kuper, *Genocide*, p. 32.

48 First coined by Mary Anne Warren, *Gendercide: The Implications of Sex Selection*, Totowa, NJ: Rowman & Allanheld, 1985, p. 22. "Gendercide" is gender-selective mass killing defined as "the deliberate extermination of persons of a particular sex or gender." Warren stresses that gendercide, unlike "gynocide" and "femicide" is a gender-neutral term in that the victims can be male or female. Drawing on Warren, Adam Jones emphasizes the gender-selective killing of what he calls "battle-aged" men (ages 15–55) in genocides and wars, A. Jones, *Gendercide and Genocide*, Nashville, TN: Vanderbilt University Press, 2004.

49 Lopez, "National Security Ideology"; Kornbluh, *The Pinochet File*; Dinges, *The Condor Year*; L. Gill, *The School of the Americas: Military Training and Political Violence in the Americas*, Durham, NC: Duke University Press, 2004; McSherry, *Predatory States*.

50 H. Fein, "Accounting for Genocide After 1945: Theories and Some Findings," *International Journal on Minority and Group Rights* 1, 2, 1993, p. 99.

51 M. Ignatieff, "Lemkin's Legacy," Washington DC: United States Holocaust Memorial Museum, 2000. Online, available at: www.ushmm.org/conscience/analysis/details/php?content=2007–12–27 (accessed June 15, 2008). For a similar argument see H. Fein, "Genocide, Terror, Life Integrity, and War Crimes: The Case for Discrimination," in G. J. Andreopoulos (ed.), *Genocide: Conceptual and Historical Dimensions*, Philadelphia, PA: University of Pennsylvania Press, 1994, pp. 95–108.

4 Understanding the 1982 Guatemalan genocide

Marc Drouin

We have created a more humanitarian, less costly strategy, to be more compatible with the democratic system. We instituted civil affairs (in 1982) which provides development for 70 percent of the population, while we kill 30 percent. Before, the strategy was to kill 100 percent.

General Héctor Alejandro Gramajo Morales[1]

If someone wanted to understand the 1982 Guatemalan genocide, what would that person study? The country's history is certainly a good place to start and there are many fine historians of Guatemala. Many have drawn our attention to the country's geography, from the cold and temperate highlands to the tropical lowlands and Pacific coast. Because early Spanish settlers in the region preferred easily cultivated land in the lower, more fertile parts of the mountains, Indians tended to occupy the colder and higher areas. According to Murdo McLeod, this arrangement resulted in Indians concentrating in the western highlands, and non-Indians in the eastern lowlands and Pacific piedmont. Since as far back as the sixteenth century Indians have left their towns and villages in the *altiplano* to work seasonally *en la costa*.[2] Students of history interested in indicators of change and continuity would discern the recurrence and prevalence of such settlement and migratory labour patterns over centuries.

Another constant in the historiography is the notion that Indians can somehow be, and indeed should be, transformed into something other than who they are on a collective and individual basis. Such change is usually imposed to make Indians do something they are resisting.[3] But, as Luis Cardoza y Aragón has rightly pointed out, the theme of induced Indian transformation is a pervasive one throughout the Americas and is not unique to Guatemala.[4] What seems worthy of attention, however, is the fact that as discussions take place over time about Indians and their fate, little if anything seems to ever improve in terms of their actual social or material conditions. Though there have been and are exceptions, as Greg Grandin and Irma Alicia Velásquez have demonstrated,[5] Indians' living standards today remain deplorable in Guatemala,[6] as in many parts of the continent.[7]

By examining the massacres of highland Indian communities carried out by Guatemalan security forces in the early 1980s, this chapter will attempt to

explain how and why the historical exclusion of the country's indigenous majority led to genocide in 1982. Often considered a borderline case, if considered at
all, the Guatemalan genocide should be of interest to scholars because it allows
for a nuanced discussion of state violence as it escalates from such crimes
against humanity as extermination and persecution to full-blown genocide. Identifying and describing this process, including perpetrator intent and motive, may
contribute to a better understanding of genocide while drawing attention to an
often overlooked example taken from a country which lies, quite literally, on
North America's doorstep.

Turning Indians into non-Indians

David McCreery's masterful account of life in rural Guatemala demonstrates an
historical record replete with discussions pertaining to the country's Indians,
how they should be treated and how they were expected to behave. Non-Indian
decision-makers in the nineteenth and early twentieth centuries, for instance,
agreed that Indians should be worked hard, not only to civilise them, but to
ensure the prosperity of planters and elites. Enlightenment liberals preferred
public instruction and integration in order to overcome what they considered the
Indians' backwardness, an obstacle to progress and development. To this effect
the pages of the *Diario de Centro América* carried the debates between those
who wished to improve Indians through education and those who believed that
only forced labour could do them any good. Either way, the Indians were not
consulted. If they had been, they probably would have flatly rejected the *North
American* solution suggested by some, consisting in either their physical extermination or their "whitening" through European immigration.[8]

Many among Guatemala's elite believed that turning Indians into non-Indians
was a worthwhile endeavour, and *ladinisation* was the term used to describe the
process. The idea was to have Indians become *ladino* by adopting the most
outward signs of European culture, such as speaking Spanish, wearing Western
clothing or owning private property.[9] For many throughout the twentieth century,
24 to 30 months of obligatory military service was considered the best way to
transform Indians in this way, to give them, in one officer's words, "a new per-
sonality". Indian conscription, wrote the colonel, "was only the beginning of an
often painful physical metamorphosis given the violent change from one way of
life to another". The objective of this transformation ultimately was to have dis-
charged conscripts continue the process of *ladinisation* in their villages, thereby
changing their communities' social and cultural configuration.[10] One general
likened the process to "what a blacksmith does to make horseshoes. So we must
forge *el pueblo*," he believed.[11] Another general, who became president in 1983,
explained to reporters that "we must do away with the words 'indigenous' and
'Indian'. Our mission requires the integration of all Guatemalans."[12]

Turning Indians into *ladinos* was a long, difficult process, of course, and
some officers doubted that change in the Indians' exterior appearance could
reflect actual change in their way of thinking. In the early 1980s the Ixil Indians

of Quiché department, for example, were considered especially reluctant to cooperate with *ladino* authorities and the military knew this because the Ixil were the subject of study and debate. While some *ladino* officers considered ways of "rescuing the Ixil mentality", others would have preferred to see the Ixil population simply "disappear as a cultural subgroup, estranged to the National way of being".[13] Regardless of the options at hand, officers generally tended to suspect the Indians' loyalty and usually preferred working with troops recruited in the eastern, non-indigenous areas of the republic.[14]

In terms of elite mentality, research conducted in the late 1970s by Marta Casaús Arzú demonstrates a marked historical continuity in the way that Guatemala's colonial elite families and their descendants thought of Indians. Three quarters of respondents among the country's most influential families considered themselves white, some of them supporting their claim with a written colonial heirloom attesting to their purity of blood (*pureza de sangre*). Interestingly, participants in the study with the highest levels of formal education expressed the greatest racial intolerance. Many recommended Indians abandon their way of life and adopt Western lifestyles, others recommended strict segregation, while still others believed Indians could be improved racially through cross-breeding and artificial insemination. Ethnic cleansing was also considered an option, 5 to 10 per cent of respondents approving of such extreme solutions as the extermination of the Indians altogether.[15]

Indian agency and repression

As the Cold War heated up in the Caribbean in 1959 with the overthrow of the Batista dictatorship in Cuba, anti-communism in Guatemala was already considered a pathological obsession.[16] United States intervention in 1954 had put an abrupt end to a period of democratic reform that began in 1944. Scholars have written extensively on the provoked demise of Guatemala's electoral democracy and hundreds if not thousands of documents from American archives have since been released, detailing US responsibility.[17] When the Guatemalan government agreed to support US actions against Cuba, however, almost a third of the military revolted in November 1960. The effort failed to overthrow the regime and a handful of rebels sought refuge in the mountains of eastern Guatemala, firing the opening rounds of a 36-year internal armed conflict.[18]

By the late 1970s there were a number of protagonists setting the stage for what soon became a human rights tragedy. On one hand, there were four factions of armed leftist guerrillas attempting to violently overthrow a string of corrupt and brutal military governments. The number of actual armed combatants in the early 1980s varies according to sources, from the US State Department's number of 3,500 to as many as 12,000. Although this last figure (from a top-ranking military strategist) is considered exaggerated, small bands of rebels, organised into regional fronts, were nonetheless present in Guatemala's highlands, northern lowlands, Pacific coastal areas and capital.[19] Said to be present in more than half of the country's 22 departments, and counting on what was perceived as growing popular support, small bands of insurgents would still have had to defeat Central America's best trained, best-equipped and most professional army. Army numbers, in fact, grew steadily from an estimated 22,000 troops to as many as 48,000 at the conflict's apex.[20]

In 1981 a general explained the conflict from a regional perspective. He believed the entire Caribbean basin was threatened by international communism, Fidel Castro in Cuba and the Sandinistas in Nicaragua being obvious and dangerous points of dissemination. In Guatemala, the general recommended keeping an eye on local political pathogens threatening the country's health and stability. Like the single tropical amoeba, he said, leftist guerrillas were parasites that would continue to multiply unless appropriate measures were taken to eradicate them completely.[21] The Guatemalan army at the time was extremely worried that the insurgents would spark an open rebellion in the Indian highlands. One captain believed rebels were making headway not by converting a mass of illiterate Indians to Marxism, but by explaining the reasons for their desolation and by "offering them a dignity they had never received from governments that have always treated them as a backward subgroup, brutalised by ignorance and alcohol".[22]

Massacres of Indian men, women and children in Guatemala began in earnest in May 1978, a stone's throw away from a major Canadian nickel mine, culminating in 1982.[23] By 1981 the US Central Intelligence Agency (CIA) was reporting on the indiscriminate killing of civilians in rural areas, government soldiers being "forced to fire at anything that moved".[24] In 1982 the CIA reported several villages being burned to the ground while Guatemalan commanding officers were "expected to give no quarter to combatants and non-combatants alike".[25] Such acute repression of course raises the question as to what Indians in Guatemala could possibly have done to merit such violent attention – apart from *being* Indians, which, in the minds of some authorities, was problematic in and of itself.

In terms of agency, studies carried out in Guatemala indicate that by the late 1970s some Indian communities had acquired 20 years of solid organising experience, successfully experimenting with peasant leagues and unions, literacy campaigns and municipal politics. According to Shelton Davis, grass-roots initiatives in the 1960s, supported by progressive sectors within the Catholic Church, became the basis of an important rural revitalisation movement. With donated funds and technical assistance, the agricultural cooperative movement in Guatemala became one of the fastest growing of its kind in Central America. By 1976 there were an estimated 500 rural cooperatives organised into eight federations with a combined membership of more than 132,000. Close to 60 per cent of these cooperatives were located in the highlands where they were reportedly having a major impact on the Indians' political attitudes, regional marketing strategies and agricultural techniques.[26]

Under conditions more conducive to political democracy and social reform, writes Davis, such tangible gains in rural areas, reached through entirely legal means, could have evolved into greater Indian participation in many aspects of

Guatemalan society. Instead, these initiatives often drew violent opposition from conservative authorities who were not prepared to allow Indians to participate as independent actors in national politics or partake as full-fledged members of that society.[27] Adapting the Cold War to local circumstances, non-Indian authorities and landowners accused indigenous leaders of being communists and wanting to overthrow the rural status quo.[28]

Counterinsurgency in the highlands

If rural cooperatives and peasant unions became the locus of mediation between Indian rural labourers and non-Indian merchants and planters, they also became collective means for many Indian communities to strengthen their economies, improve living conditions and make reformist demands heard. When the Committee for Peasant Unity (CUC) began organising in rural areas in the early 1970s more than 300,000 Indian farmers left the highlands every year to work on Pacific coast plantations in order to supplement their meagre incomes.[29] The two to six months they spent there every year made them, according to one observer, "the largest migratory labour stream as a percent of total population of any nation in the world".[30] CUC was Guatemala's first Indian-led national labour organisation and the first to bring highland Indians and poor *ladino* farmworkers together. When the organisation made its public debut in the capital's May Day demonstration in 1978, the sight of thousands of Indians marching together in the streets of the capital is said to have made a lasting impression on many urbanites unaccustomed to such an organised Indian presence.[31]

Violence against indigenous farmers, whether affiliated to CUC or not, soon reached catastrophic proportions. At the end of May 1978, soldiers and landowners massacred some 50 K'eqchi Indian men, women and children in the town of Panzós, in the department of Alta Verapaz.[32] When General Romeo Lucas García became president in July, he is said to have begun a frontal attack on the rural cooperative movement, targeting its leaders, national support structure and local membership.[33] In January 1980, when Indians and their student supporters occupied the Spanish Embassy in Guatemala City to denounce widespread government repression in the highlands, not one of the demonstrators was left alive.[34] Later that year, an Indian farmer in the department of Quiché told Robert Carmack how heavily armed men from eastern Guatemala went house to house in his highland community using lists to single out Catholic, CUC and cooperative leaders. Fifteen people were assassinated in the incident. The man's brother, a CUC leader, was found stabbed in his side, crucified between two trees.[35]

It is in this repressive context that CUC struck Pacific coast plantations in February 1980: over 70,000 sugarcane cutters in 60 plantations, followed by 40,000 cotton pickers, brought harvests to a standstill. As Indian and *ladino* labourers paralysed the countryside, the spectre of peasants lined up along the Pan-American highway brandishing machetes shook the country and forced the minimum wage for farm labourers up from US $1.12 to $3.20 a day. After many landowners refused to pay the new minimum wage, CUC brought the coffee harvest to a halt in September.[36] This kind of repeated, unified action across racial barriers was, according to George Black, utterly unheard-of in Latin America.[37] The strike also came on the heels of the July 1979 Sandinista revolution in Nicaragua, making Guatemalan planters sit up and notice.

In July 1981 the military government of General Romeo Lucas García dismantled a network of guerrilla safe houses in Guatemala City. Based in part on information gathered from its efforts, it then initiated a campaign in rural areas against indigenous communities suspected of supporting the guerrillas.[38] The initiative, according to secondary sources, was called Ceniza 81 (Ashes 81)[39] and it was directed by the army's new chief of staff, General Benedicto Lucas García, the president's brother, who, in the 1950s, trained in Algeria with French paratroopers as a student of counterinsurgency.[40] Counting on a recent contribution of US jeeps and trucks from the Reagan administration, the army mobilised thousands of foot soldiers into the countryside on an unprecedented scale.[41]

Ashes 81 reportedly began on the economically important Pacific coast in August before moving into the central highlands by October.[42] At that time, the National Institute of Cooperatives (INACOOP) reportedly declared 250 rural cooperatives illegal because of their alleged Marxist inspiration. The organisation's official membership lists were then said to be used to single out, disappear or assassinate the most active and dedicated people living in Indian communities.[43] In what was perceived at the time as a marked change in strategy, large-scale killing of real or suspected guerrillas began to characterise military operations in the highlands.[44] According to Church and other sources, the government's counterinsurgency efforts resulted in 11,000 to 13,500 deaths in 1981 alone.[45] Most, according to the *New York Times*, "were Indians and peasants, victims of the army's 'scorched-earth' strategy".[46] According to Robert Carmack, only three or four of the original 40 founders of CUC are said to have survived the army's offensive.[47]

An important component of the 1981 campaign was the creation and deployment of a new strategic and highly mobile strike force, organised by gathering 3,000 to 5,000 troops from other areas of the country and redeploying them in the highlands to carry out search and destroy missions.[48] Another innovation was the creation of rural militias to support these troops and to fight subversion in the countryside. This made some people nervous since arming civilians, let alone Indians, was not a very common occurrence in Guatemala and was, in fact, illegal according to the country's constitution.[49] One of the first rural militias was created in the municipality of Rabinal, located in the highland department of Baja Verapaz. On 20 October 1981, military officials gathered approximately 1,000 Indian men and organised them into the first civil defence patrols.[50] Starting as a pilot project in two or three highland areas, the patrols became strategic extensions of the Guatemalan army throughout the region in a matter of months. They also had the added benefit of replacing local forms of governance with structures subservient to *ladino* military authority.[51]

The patrols caught the attention of a US journalist who travelled with top military officials to the Ixil Indian town of San Juan Cotzal, in northern Quiché.

There, the reporter found Indian patrolmen standing at attention armed with 12-gauge shotguns, and a humble schoolhouse where 360 children were busily learning the rudiments of the Spanish language.[52] In all, as many as 800,000 to one million Indians may have been part of these patrols by 1983, typically organised into groups of 10 or 12 men between the ages of 15 and 60, serving 24-hour shifts every 10 days or so. In Rabinal, punishment for a lack of adherence to the patrols ranged from torture, for being late or missing a shift, to death for repeat offenders.[53]

The patrols were presented to sceptics as part of a bold new ultranationalist *Guatemality* doctrine. One of the doctrine's proponents described the San Juan Cotzal patrollers in fervently patriotic terms, extolling all things Indian, from classical Mayan architecture to the contemporary private ownership of small farm plots, and the bearing of arms against international communism.[54] In Rabinal, army explanations of this international menace drew on local idioms, essentialising differences between good Indians and bad Indians, and legitimating brutal acts of violence against those who stood in the way of the nation's greater well-being. According to one anthropologist, subversion was explained to highland Indians in terms of a virus infecting men, women and children, and, like the virus, those infected by it were to be annihilated. In and around the Rabinal area, subversives were referred to in the local language as subhuman beasts and demons, clearly lying outside Helen Fein's universe of human obligation.[55]

Studying massacres

A sensitive indicator of imminent genocide that scholars seem to agree on is the indiscriminate massacre of defenceless victims, regardless of their age or gender. Leo Kuper has been credited with coining the term *genocidal massacre* in 1981 to designate "acts falling short of full-blown genocide" in qualitative and numerical terms.[56] Helen Fein and others also used the term to describe cases in which perpetrators lacked the capacity to kill a significant part of a group, or in cases in which massacres were episodic rather than continuous. Fein, like Kuper, also believed genocidal massacres could constitute an incremental step toward full-blown genocide.[57]

Important research is being carried out today in Guatemala to determine the nature and extent of massacres committed in the early 1980s. Among existing studies is the 1999 UN-sponsored truth commission report on the causes and consequences of Guatemala's internal armed conflict. Beginning in 1960 and lasting until December 1996, when a peace agreement was signed, the conflict was Central America's longest. The commission estimated that over 200,000 Guatemalans had lost their lives, including 40,000 victims of enforced disappearance. The commission also documented a total of 669 massacres in which more than five people lost their lives simultaneously. Of those, 626 were attributed to state forces, 32 were imputed to leftist insurgents while in 11 cases responsibility could not be assigned. For the critical years from 1981 to 1983 the commission concluded that government troops had committed acts of genocide against distinct groups of the Mayan people.[58]

In its analysis, the commission developed a typology which included massacres of a selective nature and those committed indiscriminately against settled and displaced populations.[59] Based in part on this typology, I studied over 100 first-person accounts of massacres perpetrated in Guatemala's highlands and northern lowlands between December 1981 and October 1982. The testimony in question was gathered by legal investigators working for the non-governmental Center for Human Rights Legal Action (CALDH) between 1996 and 2001. In-depth interviews with survivors of 21 massacres were carried out following a standard format, providing details of the massacres themselves as well as important contextual information (see Table 4.1). All interviews were tape-recorded, translated to Spanish when necessary, and transcribed. Forensic investigation reports also exist for the massacres in question, confirming their occurrence.[60]

The first three massacres in this sample were carried out in the municipality of Rabinal in December 1981 and January 1982. In all three villages, Achí Indian men and boys were selected according to lists, tortured and assassinated in very similar if not identical circumstances. Witnesses from one of the communities further detailed two additional massacres carried out by government forces in their village. In these five separate incidents approximately 10 per cent of the communities' estimated total population was killed. Death was often imparted by indigenous militiamen who were forced to sever their victims' ears, noses and lips before bludgeoning or garrotting them to death while armed soldiers looked on. To the extent that these killings annihilated a small part of an Indian group in the absence of an intent to destroy the entire group, they would seem to conform to what the truth commission and scholars have respectively referred to as selective or genocidal massacres.[61]

In terms of such crimes against humanity as persecution or extermination, the first three massacres in the sample appear to be systematic in that they were all carried out in the same manner and, in one community, repeated on three occasions in an eight-week period. Furthermore, the killing of these men was clearly intentional, perpetrators taking the time to gather members of the community, select their victims, torture and kill them, later disposing of their bodies in wells or mass graves. In other words, the massacres in question were neither fortuitous nor accidental. Finally, the cross-referencing of available secondary sources indicates the occurrence of over 40 massacres in the single indigenous municipality of Rabinal, indicating their widespread nature in the region between 1980 and 1983.[62]

Genocide and legal studies also draw our attention to the victims' status within their respective communities when assessing the overall impact of their demise.[63] One witness who had been the secretary of his community's development committee for 20 years said it had been "the health promoters who died, the catechists, the elders, the education promoters, ... all those who knew something, those who taught, those who contributed to the community". Another survivor remembered that government forces had killed "all the auxiliary mayors, delegates, healers, health promoters, and catechists".[64] What seems clear is that these selective or genocidal massacres targeted male individuals for their leadership capabilities or potential, thereby undermining the communities' livelihood and very existence.

Crisis, change and continuity

The three massacres described above, as well as an additional seven in the sample of 21, all took place under the military government of General Romeo Lucas Garcia, a man the *Washington Post* referred to at the time as the "bloodiest leader ruling in the hemisphere". [65] A military coup on 23 March 1982 brought the general's four-year reign to an abrupt end. Reasons for Lucas's downfall include Guatemala's growing international isolation because of rampant corruption and human rights violations. The country's foreign exchange reserves practically vanished under Lucas and international institutions refused to renew the country's outstanding loans. [66] Internally, the government lost support from the private sector, and illicit enrichment at the top of the military hierarchy at the expense of arms procurements had reportedly demoralised young officers and soldiers who were bitterly fighting and dying in the field. [67] "Our country," admitted a general, "was on the verge of collapse." [68]

In the social scientific and legal literature, crisis and war are two recurring factors that are believed to be conducive to genocide. [69] According to rapidly changing or worsening contextual considerations, scholars have concluded that genocidal intent can develop ad hoc and that there need not exist a plan or blueprint indicating how to go about destroying certain categories of people. [70] Though the intention at the outset may not have been the destruction of a protected human group, it may become the goal later on as events unfold in the context of war. [71] In this sense, genocide is very much a dynamic process and scholars have explained, for instance, that ethnocide (the destruction of a people's culture) can escalate into genocide (the physical destruction of a people) when the former is successfully resisted by indigenous populations. Genocide can then de-escalate once indigenous resistance has been overcome. [72]

The March 1982 coup brought Brigadier General José Efraín Ríos Montt to power as the head of a military triumvirate. Upon taking power, the junta suspended the constitution, dissolved the legislative congress, and ruled by decree. A 14-point proclamation defined the military government's priorities, four of which referred specifically to the nation in crisis. [73] In April, a National Security and Development Plan placed all public services under military control, making counterinsurgency the government's number one priority. [74] In June, Ríos Montt named himself president of the republic and commander in chief of the armed forces. [75] By then, the *New York Times* was reporting on the contents of mass graves unearthed in the department of Quiché, including the remains of Indian women and children. According to one Western European diplomat quoted at the time, Indians were "systematically being destroyed as a group". [76]

Building upon its 1981 counterinsurgency operations, the Guatemalan army launched its Victoria 82 (Victory 82) campaign plan on 1 July. Its main

Table 4.1 First-person accounts of 21 massacres carried out by state security forces in the Indigenous highlands of Guatemala, December 1981 to October 1982

Name of village, hamlet or estate	Municipality	Department	Ethnic group	Date of massacre
1 Panacal	Rabinal	Baja Verapaz	Achí	04.12.81
2 Pichec	Rabinal	Baja Verapaz	Achí	02.01.82
3 Chichupac	Rabinal	Baja Verapaz	Achí	08.01.82
4 Pacoj	San Martín Jilotepeque	Chimaltenango	Cackchiquel	12.02.82
5 Santa María Tzeja	Ixcán	Quiché	Quiché	13.02.82
6 Xix	San Gaspar Chajúl	Quiché	Quiché	16.02.82
7 Río Negro	Rabinal	Baja Verapaz	Achí	13.03.82
8 Cuarto Pueblo	Ixcán	Quiché	Various	14.03.82
9 San José Río Negro	Cobán	Alta Verapaz	Keqchí	17.03.82
10 Ilom	San Gaspar Chajúl	Quiché	Ixil	23.03.82
				23.03.82
11 La Plazuela	San Martín Jilotepeque	Chimaltenango	Cackchiquel	17.04.82
12 Puente Alto	Barillas	Huehuetenango	Kanjobal	07.07.82
13 Petanac	San Mateo Ixtatán	Huehuetenango	Chúj	14.07.82
14 Finca San Francisco	Nentón	Huehuetenango	Chúj	17.07.82
15 Plan de Sánchez	Rabinal	Baja Verapaz	Achí	18.07.82
16 Rancho Bejuco	El Chol	Baja Verapaz	Achí	29.07.82
17 San Francisco Javier	Santa María Nebaj	Quiché	Ixil	15.08.82
18 Vivitz	Santa María Nebaj	Quiché	Ixil	10.09.82
19 Agua Fría	Chicaman	Quiché	Achí	14.09.82
20 Chipastor	San Martín Jilotepeque	Chimaltenango	Cackchiquel	22.09.82
21 Santa Anita las Canoas	San Martín Jilotepeque	Chimaltenango	Cackchiquel	14.10.82

Notes
1 Five members of the community of Panacal were killed on 3 December 1981 in addition to the 47 killed during the 4 December 1981 massacre for a total of 52 victims.
2 The first massacre in Pichec occurred on 1 November 1981, when 32 men were killed; the second occurred on 22 November 1981 when 30 men were killed; and 35 men lost their lives on 2 January 1982, for a total of 97 victims.
3 Thirty-three members of the community of Xix were assassinated in two separate incidents before the 16 February 1982 massacre in which the 18 people who had not fled the community as soldiers erupted were killed, for a total of 51 victims.
4 Villagers from Río Negro were massacred on five separate occasions: seven members of the community were killed by military police on 4 March 1980; 55 men, nine children, and nine women were massacred in the neighbouring village of Xococ on 13 February 1982; on 13 March 1982, 177 women and children were killed; on 14 May 1982, 84 survivors who had sought refuge in Los Encuentros were massacred by the military and 15 women were taken away in a helicopter and never seen again. Finally, on 14 September 1982, 35 orphans from Río Negro, entrusted to the community of Agua Fría, were massacred along with most of that village's population. An estimated total of 391 people from Río Negro lost their lives in these massacres.

First-person accounts	Women	Men	Estimated population (1981–2)	Estimated killed in massacre	Estimated survived	Estimated death toll (%)	Part of population escaped prior to massacre	Rapes committed during massacre	Community razed to the ground
Military government of General Romeo Lucas García in power since July 1978									
2	1	1	720	52[1]	668	7			
2	1	1	450	97[2]	353	22			
8	3	5	650	32	618	5			•
6	2	4	330	48	282	15		•	
5	0	5	715	23	692	3	•	•	•
2	0	2	600	51[3]	549	9	•		•
6	4	2	1,100	391[4]	709	36		•	•
11	2	9	600	343	257	57		•	•
5	3	2	n.d.	93	n.d.	n.d.	•		•
5	0	5	1,600	173[5]	1,427	11			•
A military junta headed by General José Efraín Ríos Montt comes to power									
4	2	2	450	150[6]	300	33	•	•	•
2	0	2	400	350	50	88		•	•
8	3	5	100	84	16	84		•	•
5	0	5	365	350	15	96		•	•
14	4	10	300	268	20	89		•	•
4	2	2	30	25	5	83		•	
5	0	5	240	20	220	8	•		•
4	1	3	100	17	83	17	•		•
3	1	2	120	97	23	81	•		•
3	2	1	360	5	355	1	•		
3	1	2	2,000	44[7]	1,956	2			
107	**32**	**75**	**11,230**	**2,713**		**23.3[8]**	33%	48%	71%

5 Twenty-eight men from Ilom were killed by soldiers and civil patrollers prior to the massacre, including 16 who were taken away on 15 January 1982 and never seen again. On 23 March 1982 the army killed 85 boys and men aged between 14 and 60. Another 60 children are said to have perished from disease and hunger in the months following the massacre. Subtracting ten men killed by guerrillas, 173 deaths can be imputed to state forces.

6 Soldiers returned to La Plazuela over a three-month period killing an estimated 150 members of the community.

7 Thirty people were reportedly assassinated in Santa Anita las Canoas before 14 October 1982 when an additional 14 people were killed, for a total of 44 victims.

8 The death toll figure was obtained in the following manner: of the estimated 2,713 victims of the 21 massacres under consideration, the 93 from San José Río Negro were subtracted since no figure was found as to the community's estimated population in 1981–2. The total estimated population of 11,230 was then divided by 2,620 for a total percentile death toll of 23.3%.

objective was to continue with the elimination of armed subversives and their alleged local support throughout the Indian highlands. Of particular interest to military strategists were organisations working with the general population, such as church groups, unions and cooperatives,[77] as well as the growing number of indigenous refugees pouring across the Mexican border with their accounts of indiscriminate killing and destruction.[78] In terms of human displacement, the press reported 2,000 refugees a week making their way into Mexico in February, the number climbing to about 5,000 by the third week of July.[79]

The military offensive under Ríos Montt called for an increase in the number of troops deployed throughout the highlands and northern lowlands. Organised into 30 light infantry companies, 5,300 additional troops were deployed among pre-existing units and three new mobile strike forces. Of interest are some of the troops' ethnic origins: Victoria 82 called for the transfer to the indigenous highlands of soldiers from Guatemala City and the predominantly non-indigenous eastern departments of Zacapa, Jutiapa, Izabal, as well as Escuintla on the Pacific coast.[80] According to Robert Carmack, 15,000 to 20,000 soldiers were said to occupy the sole highland department of Quiché where over half of the 626 documented massacres attributed to the army by the Guatemalan truth commission were perpetrated.[81] If Jennifer Schirmer's estimates are correct, the monthly death toll in Guatemala rose significantly at the time, from 800 under Lucas García, to over 6,000 under General Rios Montt.[82]

Intent, *dolus specialis* and inference

Approximately 11,230 people lived in the 21 Indian communities I studied. Of that estimated total, some 2,713 inhabitants were killed in massacres, for an average death toll of 23.3 per cent. In 100 per cent of cases witnesses identified government soldiers and paramilitary forces as the perpetrators. In the first three massacres in the sample, discussed previously, young and elderly men were selected from lists, tortured and killed. Starting in February 1982, a month *before* General Ríos Montt came to power, the remaining massacres in the sample indicate a change in the army's *modus operandi*. From that moment onward government forces indiscriminately attacked men, women and children in 14 of the 18 remaining communities. In the same number of cases, entire communities were set ablaze and completely destroyed. Perpetrators tortured and mutilated victims in 15 out of 18 cases, women and young girls being raped systematically between March and August 1982.[83]

Killing rates in the communities under consideration ranged from 3 to 57 per cent of their estimated total population, before March 1982, climbing to 83 and 96 per cent by July.[84] At that time a US reporter interviewed three infantrymen in the town of Cunen, department of Quiché. The soldiers were asked how they were instructed to act if women and children were present when they raided a village suspected of harbouring guerrillas. One soldier responded that the order was to shoot them all. "Practically all of them are guerrillas," he said, "so the order is to attack everybody alike."[85] And so Indians were attacked as communities, and Indian women often bore the brunt of the army's violence. According to Jan Perlin, "the systematic, public, massive and graphic perpetration of sexual violence" against Indian women betrayed the army's intent to destroy individual members of their communities, as well as the social ties and group foundations that bound them together.[86]

According to Helen Fein, "intent or purposeful action ... is not the same in law or everyday language as either motive or function". "*For what purpose*," she writes, "is different from *why*, or *for what motive*" an act is committed. In this way, genocide is purposeful or deliberate as opposed to unintentional.[87] The legal definitional criterion for genocide is therefore intent, not motive, and intent is what distinguishes genocide from a crime against humanity like persecution or extermination.[88] As a subjective element of the crime of genocide, intent is twofold, taking into account the criminal intent required for the underlying offence, and "the intent to destroy in whole or in part" a protected group as such. This second intent is an aggravated criminal intention or *dolus specialis*, and demands that the perpetrator clearly seek to produce the act charged.[89]

In the absence of such direct evidence as formal confessions from perpetrators or the original written orders regarding the destruction of a human group, genocidal intent can be inferred or constructed from perpetrator actions, statements and, in some cases, even circumstantial evidence.[90] From a social-scientific point of view, Helen Fein draws our attention to a perpetrator's "pattern of repeated ... purposeful action" from which we can infer the intent to eliminate a protected human group. In other words, how perpetrators organise and carry out the killing of their victims can shed considerable light on their intent, that is, the actual purpose of their actions.[91]

A comparative analysis

Based on the first-person accounts at my disposal, I studied 170 comparative elements in 21 cases of massacre. The objective of the exercise was to determine and analyse recurring patterns, if any, in the way these massacres were carried out. If a comparative element was present in at least 15 of the 21 cases under consideration it was believed to be indicative of deliberation and planning. Although the sample at hand represented only 5 per cent of the estimated number of massacres committed by government forces between June 1981 and December 1982,[92] it did indicate patterns of repeated and purposeful action relevant to our understanding of a typical highland massacre in 1982.[93]

By then the communities in the sample were all known to the military because of previous visits by soldiers or other forms of surveillance. On the day the massacres took place, perpetrators arrived on foot early so as to gather a maximum number of villagers in their homes. Access to the communities was controlled or blocked, soldiers carrying out house-to-house searches and gathering community members in one place. Victims were then immobilised using ropes, rendered completely defenceless, to be tortured and mutilated. When the killings began, firearms were always used and victims were both men and women, young and old. Victims' bodies were often left where they fell, to be preyed upon by animals or otherwise desecrated. Following the killings, victims' homes were pillaged, their most intimate belongings stolen or destroyed. Finally, their simple dwellings, built with great effort with materials often carried over kilometres of mountain paths, were set ablaze and the communities utterly destroyed.[94]

Comparative elements in this study also allowed for a better understanding of what happened to survivors who managed to escape these initial massacres. It stands to reason that if perpetrators intended to destroy a protected group, they would continue to attack its members even if their communities and means of sustenance had been destroyed. Such persecution after the fact would also belie the often repeated contention that the army's sole or primary purpose had been to destroy the guerrillas' alleged social base of support. Once highland Indian communities had been razed and a majority of inhabitants killed, there would have been nothing left to support the insurgents and therefore no need to continue killing dispersed survivors. Yet that's exactly what transpired, soldiers killing fleeing Indians from the air and on the ground, for days, weeks and even months after the initial massacres. In terms of repeated, purposeful action, it is also worth mentioning that nine of the 21 communities under consideration were the targets of multiple killings, one community – Río Negro, Rabinal – having been subjected to five separate massacres before finally being razed to the ground.[95]

Living like wild animals, eating roots and bark, many fleeing Indians did not survive. Even if they managed to escape army bullets, men, women and children continued to die from sickness, exhaustion or hunger – in other words, from conditions, according to the United Nations Genocide Convention, calculated to bring about their physical destruction. Furthermore, attacks against survivors not only occurred inside Guatemala, but also took place across an international border. Human rights organisations are said to have documented as many as 60 separate Guatemalan army incursions directed against fleeing refugees in Mexico between 1982 and 1984.[96] The truth commission, for its part, documented five massacres committed in Mexico in 1982 and 1983.[97] Additional massacres like these, carried out in a foreign country against displaced populations, indicate the extremes to which the Guatemalan army was willing to go in order to track and kill people who had already escaped one or even numerous attempts to destroy their communities. These subsequent killings beyond Guatemala's borders clearly allude to the perpetrators' genocidal intentions.

In terms of the Genocide Convention, legal opinion has interpreted the expression "in whole or in part" to mean "in whole or in *substantial* part", in quantitative and qualitative terms. The International Law Commission in 1996 found that although it was not necessary "to achieve the complete annihilation of a group from every corner of the globe," the crime of genocide required "the intention to [physically] destroy at least a substantial part of a particular group".[98] In this sense, the International Criminal Tribunal for the Former Yugoslavia (ICTY) found that the selective killing of Bosnian Muslim men and boys in Srebrenica in 1995 could be considered genocide because the intent was to target the group's very existence. Furthermore, the perpetrators considered the killings in Srebrenica sufficient to annihilate the Muslim group as a distinct entity in the restricted geographical area in question. Previously, the International Criminal Tribunal for Rwanda (ICTR) had convicted Jean-Paul Akayesu of genocide in 1998 for inflicting serious bodily and mental harm on the Tutsi living within the confines of a single Rwandan commune.[99]

Death tolls were not possible to establish for all the regions where massacres in this study took place, and such research and analysis needs to be pursued in the future. In the single municipality of Rabinal, however, the truth commission estimated that 20 per cent of the population had been killed by government forces between 1981 and 1982, the commission considering all victims civilian non-combatants.[100] The commission also estimated that government troops provoked the total or partial destruction of between 70 and 90 per cent of all Ixil Indian communities in Quiché department, estimating a death toll of between 15.5 and 18 per cent of the total Ixil population, depending on the census data.[101] Though I would tend to agree with Leo Kuper that it is "quite repugnant to weigh the number of deaths which would accord significance in terms of the [UN Genocide] Convention",[102] such figures in Guatemala, when considered in light of extensive population displacements, would seem to indicate that killings were carried out with the intent to destroy a "substantial part" of indigenous communities and the ethnic groups to which they belonged. In light of the aforementioned rulings by the ICTR and ICTY, such regionally focused human destruction would therefore constitute genocide.

Why? For what motive?

The question remains, however, as to why groups of highland Indians were destroyed in the first place. And why, then, only *in part*? Why, in fact, would the Guatemalan government commit genocide against a population that has ostensibly constituted the country's prime source of wealth since the sixteenth century? Have Indian communities not been a dependable and renewable source of cheap, seasonal labour, indispensable to the country's agriculturally based export economy? Part of the answer to these questions lies in the Central American economic context of the late 1970s and early 1980s, a time of economic recession, rising fuel costs and, more importantly, falling agricultural commodity prices on world markets. The Guatemalan economy was reeling at the time and unemployment and underemployment in the highlands were rampant.[103] If there was ever an appropriate time to wreak exemplary forms of violence against what should have been a subservient labour force, turning to alternative forms of cooperative community development, trade unionism, or possibly armed insurrection, the early 1980s was certainly such a time.

Another part of the answer lies in the fact that it would not be the first time in Guatemala's history that violence, including massacres, would be used to quell Indian resistance and bring survivors into the fold. Thinking ahead to brighter economic times, it was undoubtedly important to teach the Indians a lesson once and for all (in contemporary terms). The Indians' importance as rural labourers also meant that, despite high unemployment, only part of the Indian population could be destroyed without jeopardising labour supplies in times of economic recovery. The military's strategy was presumably to eradicate a tangible threat to the status quo and make the repetition of such a threat in the future as hard as possible.[104]

By destroying Indian communities as such, the military also destroyed their proven capacity to organise and take part in unions, cooperatives and any other means of independent local development. As one survivor explained:

> with the cooperative and more cooperatives we sought ways so people wouldn't have to work on the coast: with cattle-raising projects, a fishing cooperative, people could dedicate their efforts to their own work, but then everything, all the ideas, ... all the *campesino* groups and their attempts to organise themselves were destroyed.[105]

Such wanton destruction not only resulted in the obliteration of Indian aspirations and the reformist means taken to achieve them in many regions of the Guatemalan highlands; it also undermined Indian agency by annihilating one if not two generations of outspoken and dedicated Indian leaders as well as the rural communities from which they had painstakingly emerged. In this sense, we can better understand why Indian communities were targeted and destroyed by the Guatemalan army in 1982, and how the army's pattern of repeated and purposeful actions throughout the highlands betrayed its genocidal intentions.

Finally, on the theoretical continuum of induced Indian metamorphosis in Guatemala, from *ladinisation* and what Alexander Hinton has called "the annihilation of difference", to outright physical extermination, there seems to be little or no room for Indian agency. Any form of viable local development that could somehow benefit the vast majority of Indian farmers in the country, including the acquisition of an adequate land base from which to prosper, has always been perceived with suspicion if not outright aversion by non-Indian authorities. In the twentieth century, this seems to have been especially true if such initiatives somehow undermined agricultural exports, large landholdings or the planters' recurrent dependency on Indian migratory labour. Today, in terms of justice for the aggrieved, it is also worth noting – and it is quite indicative of the Indians' fate in Guatemala – that not a single military or government official has been brought to justice for the atrocities committed in the early 1980s, despite serious efforts by sectors of Guatemala's civil society to do so. Such resounding and officially sanctioned impunity may very well be part and parcel of what Daniel Feierstein has provocatively termed *genocidal social practices* elsewhere in Latin America.[106] Here, again, students of Guatemala will not be surprised to find yet another indicator of historical continuity.

Notes and references

1 Quoted in J. Schirmer, "The Guatemalan Military Project: An Interview with Gen. Héctor Gramajo", *Harvard International Review* 13, spring 1991, p. 11.
2 M. J. MacLeod, *Spanish Central America: A Socioeconomic History, 1520–1720*, Berkeley: University of California Press, 1973, pp. 229–30, 291, 308–9. On colonial Indian labour see also W. L. Sherman, *Forced Native Labor in Sixteenth-Century Central America*, Lincoln: University of Nebraska Press, 1979; G. Lovell, *Conquest and Survival in Colonial Guatemala: A Historical Geography of the Cuchumatán Highlands, 1500–1821*, Montreal: McGill-Queen's University Press, 1985; and S. Martínez Peláez, *La patria del criollo. Ensayo de interpetración de la realidad colonial guatemalteca*, 13th edn, México: Ediciones en Marcha, 1994. Since independence, see also J. C. Cambranes, *Café y campesinos. Los orígenes de la economía de plantación moderna en Guatemala, 1853–1897*, 2nd edn, Madrid: Editoral Catriel, 1996.
3 D. McCreery, *Rural Guatemala, 1760–1940*, Stanford, CA: Stanford University Press, 1994, p. 86.
4 L. Cardoza y Aragón, *Miguel Ángel Asturias. Casi Novela*, Guatemala: Biblioteca Era, 1991, p. 56.
5 G. Grandin, *The Blood of Guatemala: A History of Race and Nation*, Durham, NC: Duke University Press, 2000, pp. 228–9; I. A. Velásquez, *La pequeña burguesía indígena comercial de Guatemala. Desigualdades de clase, raza y género*, Guatemala: Cholsamaj, 2002.
6 P. Centeno, "¿Quienes son los pueblos indígenas y dónde están?" in V. Á. Aragón (ed.), *El rostro indígena de la pobreza*, Guatemala: Facultad Latinoamericana de Ciencias Sociales (FLACSO), 2003, p. 240.
7 R. Stavenhagen, *Los pueblos indígenas y sus derechos*, México: UNESCO, 2008, pp. 23–38, 80, 86, 150.
8 McCreery, *Rural Guatemala*, pp. 172–9.
9 Ibid., pp. 9, 51, 239–40, 247; C. Lutz, *Santiago de Guatemala, 1541–1773: City, Caste and the Colonial Experience*, Norman: University of Oklahoma Press, 1994, p. 162; J. F. Cifuentes, "Apreciación de Asuntos Civiles (G-5) para el área Ixil", *Revista Militar* 27, September–December 1982, p. 46.
10 J. L. Cruz Salazar, "El Ejército en el contexto social", *Revista Militar* 17, July–September 1978, pp. 47, 49.
11 Hector Alejandro Gramajo Morales quoted in J. Schirmer, *The Guatemalan Military Project: A Violence Called Democracy*, Philadelphia: University of Pennsylvania Press, 1998, p. 114.
12 Radio Televisión Guatemala, 0400 GMT, 2 September 1982, as quoted in G. Black, N. Stoltz Chinchilla and M. Jamail, *Garrison Guatemala*, New York: Monthly Review Press, 1984, pp. 131, 143 n. 42.
13 Cifuentes, "Apreciación de Asuntos Civiles", pp. 44, 46. On the army's study of indigenous communities see also Oficina de Derechos Humanos del Arzobispado de Guatemala (ODHAG), *Guatemala: nunca más*, Guatemala: ODHAG, 1998, vol. 2, pp. 113, 120, 142.
14 H. A. Gramajo Morales, *De la guerra . . . a la guerra: la difícil transición política en Guatemala*, Guatemala: Fondo de Cultura Editorial, 1995, p. 196.
15 M. E. Casaús Arzú, *Guatemala: linaje y racismo*, San José: Facultad Latinoamericana de Ciencias Sociales (FLACSO), 1995, pp. 177–80, 187, 190–1, 194, 201–10, 274–6.
16 V. Perera, *Unfinished Conquest: The Guatemalan Tragedy*, Berkeley: University of California Press, 1993, p. 45.
17 Prominent primary and secondary sources on US intervention in Guatemala include R. Immerman, *The CIA in Guatemala: The Foreign Policy of Intervention*, Austin:

University of Texas Press, 1982; P. Gleijeses, *Shattered Hope: The Guatemalan Revolution and the United States, 1944–1954*, Princeton, NJ: Princeton University Press, 1991; N. Cullather, *Secret History: The CIA's Classified Account of its Operations in Guatemala 1952–1954*, Stanford, CA: Stanford University Press, 1999; S. M. Streeter, *Managing the Counterrevolution: The United States and Guatemala, 1954–1961*, Athens, OH: University Center for International Studies, 2000; W. Z. Slany (ed.), *Foreign Relations of the United States, 1952–1954*, Volume IV: *The American Republics Guatemala Compilation*, Washington, DC: United States Government Printing Office, 1983; and D. S. Patterson (ed.), *Retrospective Volume of the Foreign Relations of the United States, 1952–1954: Guatemala*, Washington, DC: United States Government Printing Office, 2003. Multiple US primary sources are also available online at www.gwu.edu/~nsarchiv/; and www.foia.cia.gov/ (accessed September 2008).

18 H. Rosada-Granados, *Soldados en el poder: proyecto militar in Guatemala (1944–1990)*, San José: Fundapen/University of Utrecht, The Netherlands, 1999, p. 250; P. Ball, P. Kobrak and H. F. Spirer, *State Violence in Guatemala, 1960–1996: A Quantitative Reflection*, Washington, DC: American Association for the Advancement of Science, Science and Human Rights Program, and the International Center for Human Rights Research, 1999, p. 13; G. Grandin, *The Last Colonial Massacre: Latin America in the Cold War*, Chicago: University of Chicago Press, 2004, p. 91.

19 S. H. Davis, "Introduction: Sowing the Seeds of Violence," in R. M. Carmack (ed.), *Harvest of Violence: The Maya Indians and the Guatemalan Crisis*, Norman: University of Oklahoma Press, 1992, p. 24; Black *et al.*, *Garrison Guatemala*, pp. 103–4; Gramajo Morales, *De la guerra ... a la guerra*, p. 154; Rosada-Granados, *Soldados en el poder*, pp. 152–4.

20 R. Bonner, "The Mayan War God in Under New Management", *New York Times*, 14 March 1982, sec. 4, p. 4; Comisión para el Esclarecimiento Histórico (CEH), *Guatemala, memoria del silencio*, Guatemala: United Nations Operations Systems (UNOPS), 1999, vol. 4: p. 264.

21 A. Valencia Tobar, "Conferencia dictada por el general Alvaro Valencia Tobar al Cuerpo de Comando del Caribe", *Revista Militar* 24, September–December 1981, p. 111.

22 Cifuentes, "Apreciación de Asuntos Civiles", pp. 27–8.

23 CEH, *Memoria del silencio*, vol. 6: pp. 13–23; Fundación de Antropología Forense de Guatemala (FAFG), *Informe de la Fundación de Antropología Forense de Guatemala: Cuatro casos paradigmáticos solicitados por la Comisión para el Esclarecimiento Histórico de Guatemala*, Guatemala: Serviprensa, 2000, pp. 34–48.

24 Central Intelligence Agency, "Guatemalan Soldiers Kill Civilians in Cocob", April 1981. Online, available at: www.gwu.edu/~nsarchiv/NSAEBB/NSAEBB11/ docs/12–01.htm (accessed 29 January 2004).

25 Central Intelligence Agency, "Counterinsurgency Operations in El Quiché", February 1982, Online, available at: www.gwu.edu/~nsarchiv/NSAEBB/NSAEBB11/ docs/14–01.htm (accessed 29 January 2004).

26 Davis, "Sowing the Seeds of Violence", pp. 16, 21. See a significant study on the matter by S. H. Davis and J. Hodson, *Witness to Political Violence in Guatemala: The Suppression of a Rural Development Movement*, Washington, DC: Oxfam America, 1982.

27 Ibid., p. 20.

28 R. M. Carmack, "The Story of Santa Cruz Quiché", in R. M. Carmack (ed.), *Harvest of Violence: The Maya Indians and the Guatemalan Crisis*, Norman: University of Oklahoma Press, 1992, p. 50.

29 L. Sandoval Villeda, *Estructura agraria y nuevo regimen constitucional*, Guatemala: Asociación de Investigación y Estudios Sociales (ASIES), 1987, p. 43; R. Cardona Recinos, "Caracterización del trabajo temporero en la agricultura", *Perspectiva: Ciencia, Arte, Tecnología* 1, 1983, pp. 17–19.

30 J. M. Paige, *Agrarian Revolution: Social Movements and Export Agriculture in the Underdeveloped World*, New York: Macmillan, 1975, p. 361.

31 Davis, "Sowing the Seeds of Violence", p. 20; Black *et al.*, *Garrison Guatemala*, p. 97; Carmack, "The Story of Santa Cruz", p. 52.

32 Black *et al.*, *Garrison Guatemala*, pp. 95–6; V. Sanford, *Buried Secrets: Truth and Human Rights in Guatemala*, New York: Palgrave Macmillan, 2003, pp. 55–6, 62–6; CEH, *Memoria del silencio*, vol. 6: pp. 13–23; FAFG, *Cuatro casos paradigmáticos*, pp. 34–48.

33 Davis, "Sowing the Seeds of Violence", p. 22.

34 Ball *et al.*, *State Violence in Guatemala*, p. 23; CEH, *Memoria del silencio*, vol. 6: pp. 163–82.

35 Carmack, "The Story of Santa Cruz", pp. 53–4.

36 Davis, "Sowing the Seeds of Violence", p. 20.

37 Black *et al.*, *Garrison Guatemala*, p. 100.

38 M. McClintock, *The American Connection*, Volume Two: *State Terror and Popular Resistance in Guatemala*, London: Zed Books, 1985, pp. 219–20.

39 Ball *et al.*, *State Violence in Guatemala*, pp. 26–7; CEH, *Memoria del silencio*, vol. 1: p. 197; vol. 3: pp. 298 n. 835, 301. The Guatemalan army has never provided a written copy of its 1981 campaign plan. Efforts to find such a copy have been thus far unsuccessful.

40 McClintock, *American Connection*, pp. 220, 227. According to Black *et al.*, *Garrison Guatemala*, p. 135, Benedicto Lucas trained at France's St-Cyr military academy and saw French counterinsurgency techniques applied in Algeria. See also Redacción, "La CIA implica a Benedicto Lucas en masacres", *El Periódico*, 4 May 2000, pp. 1, 4; and L. Jenkins, "Strong Force Used to Maintain Support; Guatemala Seeks to Pacify Indians", *Washington Post*, 7 March 1982, p. A1.

41 McClintock, *American Connection*, p. 226; Black *et al.*, *Garrison Guatemala*, p. 151; Grandin, *Last Colonial Massacre*, pp. 188, 278 nn. 71–2; A. Riding, "Guatemala Votes but It Hardly Seems to Matter", *New York Times*, 7 March 1982, sec. 4, p. 4.

42 McClintock, *American Connection*, p. 220; Black *et al.*, *Garrison Guatemala*, p. 120; Gramajo, *De la guerra . . . a la guerra*, p. 156.

43 Davis, "Sowing the Seeds of Violence", p. 22.

44 Black *et al.*, *Garrison Guatemala*, p. 120.

45 McClintock, *American Connection*, p. 226.

46 Riding, "Guatemala Votes", sec. 4, p. 4.

47 Carmack, "The Story of Santa Cruz", p. 61.

48 Ball *et al.*, *State Violence in Guatemala*, p. 26; Gramajo, *De la guerra. . . a la guerra*, p. 156; Rosada-Granados, *Soldados en el poder*, pp. 160–1; CEH, *Memoria del silencio*, vol. 2: pp. 48–51.

49 "El Ejército dará armas a los campesinos para su defensa", *Prensa Libre*, 19 November 1981, p. 1; "Ejército entrena campesinos para la defensa de los departamentos", *Prensa Libre*, 21 November 1981, p. 66.

50 K. Dill, "Violencia Estadista (1981–1984): El caso del pueblo Achí de Rabinal", unpublished manuscript, 2003, p. 24.

51 M. Drouin, "To the Last Seed: Atrocity Crimes and the Genocidal Continuum in Guatemala, 1978–1984", unpublished MA thesis, Concordia University, 2006, pp. 100, 105, 110, 183, 249–51. On the imposed change of local authorities by the Guatemalan army in indigenous communities, see also ODHAG, *Guatemala: nunca más*, vol. 1: pp. 100–1, 101 n. 1, 107–11, 114, 118–21, 126–7, 131–3, 257, 278–80; vol. 2: pp. 113–29, 135–6, 141. On the Guatemalan army's ethnic composition and *ladino* officer corps, see S. Bastos, *Etnicidad y fuerzas armadas en Guatemala. Unas ideas para el debate*, Guatemala: Facultad Latinoamericana de Ciencias Sociales (FLACSO), 2004.

52 Jenkins, "Strong Force Used to Maintain Support", p. A1.
53 Procuraduría de los Derechos Humanos (PDH), *Los Comités de Defensa Civil en Guatemala*, Guatemala: PDH, 1994; CEH, *Memoria del silencio*, vol. 2: pp. 496–8; vol. 4: p. 264; Drouin, "To the Last Seed", p. 250; ODHAG, *Guatemala: nunca más*, vol. 1: pp. 119, 120; vol. 2: pp. 124, 126, 136, 169–70.
54 G. A. Castañeda, "La Guatemalidad [y] la autodefensa civil", *Revista Militar* 27, September–December 1982, pp. 6–13.
55 Dill, "Violencia estadista", pp. 21–3; H. Fein, *Accounting for Genocide: National Responses and Jewish Victimization during the Holocaust*, New York: Free Press, 1979, p. 4.
56 W. Schabas, *Genocide in International Law*, Cambridge: Cambridge University Press, 2000, p. 240; L. Kuper, *Genocide: Its Political Use in the Twentieth Century*, New Haven, CT: Yale University Press, 1981, pp. 10, 16, 66.
57 H. Fein, "Genocide: A Sociological Perspective", *Current Sociology* 38, 1990, pp. 12, 18–9, 79. Chalk and Jonassohn also used the term to describe cases of "one-sided mass killing" in which there was no intent to destroy an entire group, or in which only a small part of a group was actually killed. They also use the term for cases bordering on genocide and ethnocide in which part of the victim group is killed "in order to terrorize the remainder into giving up their separate identity or their opposition to the perpetrator group or both". See Frank Chalk and Kurt Jonassohn, *The History and Sociology of Genocide: Analysis and Case Studies*, New Haven, CT: Yale University Press, 1990, p. 26.
58 CEH, *Memoria del silencio*, vol. 1: pp. 72–3; vol. 2: p. 15, 318; vol. 3: pp. 256, 417–23; vol. 5: pp. 21, 43, 48–51, 100.
59 Ibid., vol. 2: pp. 253–5; vol. 3: pp. 250–6.
60 Drouin, "To the Last Seed", pp. 112–13, 123–8.
61 Ibid., pp. 145–9, 246, 261–2.
62 CEH, *Memoria del silencio*, vol. 3: p. 377; Bert Janssens (ed.), *Oj K'aslik Estamos Vivos. Recuperación de la memoria histórica de Rabinal, 1944–1996*, Guatemala: Museo Comunitario Rabinal Achi, 2003, pp. 164–5; Equipo de Antropología Forense de Guatemala (EAFG), *Las masacres de Rabinal: Estudio histórico antropológico de las masacres de Plan de Sánchez, Chichupac y Río Negro*, 2nd edn, Guatemala: EAFG, 1997, p. 175.
63 International Criminal Tribunal for the Former Yugoslavia (ICTY), "Prosecutor vs. Radislav Krstic, Judgement", The Hague, 19 April 2004, paragraph 587.
64 Quoted and referenced in Drouin, "To the Last Seed", pp. 147–8. See also ODHAG, *Guatemala: nunca más*, vol. 1: pp. 109–10.
65 Editorial Desk, "Hands Off Guatemala", *Washington Post*, 24 January 1982, p. D6.
66 L. Jenkins, "Guatemalan Officers, Civilians Press Junta for Prompt Elections", *Washington Post*, 26 March 1982, p. A24; D. Oberdorfer, "After the Killing Stops; Guatemala's New Leaders Still Face Vast Problems", *Washington Post*, 18 April 1982, p. B1.
67 McClintock, *American Connection*, pp. 224–5; Black *et al.*, *Garrison Guatemala*, pp. 55, 120.
68 Schirmer, *Guatemalan Military Project*, pp. 18–20.
69 Fein, "A Sociological Perspective", pp. 71–2; M. I. Midlarsky, *The Killing Trap: Genocide in the Twentieth Century*, Cambridge: Cambridge University Press, 2005, pp. 67, 103, 104, 105–7, 369, 375, 381, 382; A. L. Hinton, *Why Did They Kill? Cambodia in the Shadow of Genocide*, Berkeley: University of California Press, 2005, pp. 29, 126, 282; T. Akçam, *A Shameful Act: The Armenian Genocide and the Question of Turkish Responsibility*, New York: Metropolitan Books, 2006, pp. 8, 74, 84, 86–7; S. Straus, *The Order of Genocide: Race, Power, and War in Rwanda*, Ithaca, NY: Cornell University Press, 2006, pp. 7, 87, 97, 224, 226; M. Shaw, *What is Genocide?* Malden, MA: Polity Press, 2007, pp. 34–6, 111–12, 129, 131, 145–9, 154.

70 D. Bloxham, "Bureaucracy and Genocide", paper presented at the Genocides: Forms, Causes and Consequences conference, Berlin, 13–15 January 2005, p. 16; T. Zwann, "On the Aetiology and Genesis of Genocide and other Mass Crimes Targeting Specific Groups", report presented to the Office of the Prosecutor of the International Criminal Tribunal for the Former Yugoslavia, Amsterdam: Centre for Holocaust and Genocide Studies, University of Amsterdam/Royal Netherlands Academy of Arts and Sciences, November 2003, pp. 23–4.

71 ICTY, "Prosecutor vs. Krstic", paragraphs 572, 711.

72 A. D. Moses, "Conceptual Blockages and Definitional Dilemmas in the 'Racial Century': Genocides of Indigenous Peoples and the Holocaust", *Patterns of Prejudice* 36, October 2002, p. 27; Chalk and Jonassohn, *History and Sociology of Genocide*, pp. 26, 195, 203; A. L. Hinton (ed.), *Annihilating Difference: The Anthropology of Genocide*, Berkeley: University of California Press, 2002, pp. 29–30.

73 L. Jenkins, "Decree Rule Begun in Guatemala; Leaders of Coup Drop Mention of Election Goals", *Washington Post*, 25 March 1982, p. A1; Inter-American Commission on Human Rights (IACHR), *Report on the Situation of Human Rights in the Republic of Guatemala*, Washington, DC: IACHR, 5 October 1983, introduction, pp. 4–5.

74 Black *et al.*, *Garrison Guatemala*, p. 125; CEH, *Memoria del silencio*, vol. 3: pp. 298–301.

75 UPI, "Guatemalan Assumes Sole Power, Ousting Other Members of Junta", *New York Times*, 10 June 1982, p. A8; Black *et al.*, *Garrison Guatemala*, p. 124.

76 R. Bonner, "Some Rights Gains Seen in Guatemala", *New York Times*, 3 June 1982, p. A9; R. Bonner, "Giving is No Picnic in Guatemala", *New York Times*, 6 June 1982, sec. 4, p. 2.

77 Ejército de Guatemala, Plan de Campaña "Victoria 82" 3-"M". 000007, Guatemala, [25 June 1982]. From photocopy of numbered typescript copy, II. Propósito: A. Propósito General: 2, 3; IV. Misión, p. 1, 2; Anexo "B" (Inteligencia) a la 0/0 No. 001 (Plan Victoria), II. EEI y ONI: A. EEI: 1, f; 2, c; 5, p. 17; Anexo "H" (Ordenes Permanentes para el Desarrollo de Operaciones Contrasubversivas) al Plan de Campaña "Victoria 82," D. Táctica a Utilizar, 104, p. 48.

78 See, for example, R. Chavira, "Guatemalan Refugees: They Talk of Death; Refugees Describe Terror in Guatemala; Guatemalan Human Rights Record Seen Improved, US Considers Resuming Aid", *San Diego Union*, 5 May 1982, pp. 1, 6.

79 See M. Simon, "Guatemalan Indians Crowd into Mexico to Escape Widening War", *Washington Post*, 19 February 1982, p. A23; and "Escapan a México en 4 días 3 mil Guatemaltecos", *El Excelsior*, 23 July 1982, p. 9. Inside Guatemala, an estimated 500,000 to 1.5 million people were displaced by the conflict, representing about 20 per cent of the country's estimated 7 million inhabitants at the time. See Paula Worby, *Lessons Learned from UNHCR's Involvement in the Guatemalan Refugee Repatriation and Reintegration Program (1987–1999)*, United Nation's High Commission for Refugees: Regional Bureau for the Americas, and Evaluation and Policy Analysis Unit, December 1999, p. 3.

80 Ejército de Guatemala, "Plan de Campaña 'Victoria 82'", VII. Distribución de las compañías de fusileros de la movilización parcial, p. 6; VIII. Misiones Específicas: B. Brigada Militar "Guardia de Honor": 4, 5, p. 6; C. Brigada Militar "Mariscal Zavala": 4, p. 7; 13. Brigada Militar "GMLB", Quetzaltenago: 5, p. 7; E. Brigada Militar "CGRC", Zacapa: 3, p. 8; F. Brigada Militar "GLGL", Poptún, El Petén: 3, p. 8; G. Zona Militar "MGS", Huhuetenarigo: 3, p. 8; 1. Zona Militar "GASM", Jutiapa: 3, 4, p. 9; 3. Zona Militar "GMGG", Puerto Barrios, Izabal: 2, p. 9; K. Base Militar T.P. "GFC", Puerto San José, Escuintla: 7, pp. 9–10; N. Agrupamiento Táctico de Seguridad de la FAG [Fuerzas Áreas Guatemaltecas]: 4, 5, p. 10; 0. Fuerza Área Guatemalteca: 1, 2, 3, 4, 5; Anexo "K" (Organización de la Fuerza de Tarea "Quirigua") al Plan de Campaña "Victoria 82," p. 51. Task forces explicitly

mentioned by name in the campaign plan, at pp. 11–12, are "Gumarcaj" Task Force, Santa Cruz del Quiché; "Iximché" Task Force, Chimaltenango; "Tigre" Task Force, Playa Grande, Ixcán.

81 Carmack, "The Story of Santa Cruz", p. 61; CEH, *Memoria del silencio*, vol. 3: p. 519.
82 Schirmer, *Guatemalan Military Project*, pp. 1, 18.
83 Drouin, "To the Last Seed", pp. 281–2, 286–7, 290.
84 Ibid., p. 246.
85 J. Dinges, "Guatemala Organizing Peasant Antirebel Units", *Washington Post*, 19 July 1982, p. A1.
86 J. Perlin, "The Guatemalan Historical Clarification Commission finds Genocide", *ILSA Journal of International and Comparative Law* 6, Spring 2000, pp. 408–9. On gender specific violence directed against indigenous women, see also ODHAG, *Guatemala: nunca más*, vol. 1: pp. 108–9, 203–18.
87 Fein, "A Sociological Perspective", pp. 19–20, 53.
88 International Criminal Tribunal for Rwanda (ICTR), "Prosecutor vs. Jean-Paul Akayesu, Judgement case no. ICTR 96–4-T", Arusha, Tanzania, 2 September 1998, paragraph 568; United Nations, "Report of the International Commission of Inquiry on Darfur to the United Nations Secretary-General," Geneva, 25 January 2005, paragraphs 513–22.
89 ICTR, "Prosecutor vs. Akayesu", paragraphs 498, 518; UN, "Commission of Inquiry on Darfur", paragraph 491.
90 International Criminal Tribunal for Rwanda (ICTR), "Prosecutor vs. Clément Kayishema and Obed Ruzindana, case no. ICTR-95-I-T, Judgement", Arusha, Tanzania, 21 May 1999, paragraph 93; Moses, "Conceptual Blockages", p. 29.
91 Fein, "A Sociological Perspective", p. 25; UN "Commission of Inquiry on Darfur", paragraph 502. See also J. Sémelin, *Purifier et détruire. Usages politiques des massacres et génocides*, Paris: Seuil, 2005, p. 348.
92 CEH, *Memoria del silencio*, vol. 3: p. 298.
93 Drouin, "To the Last Seed," pp. 173, 247–74.
94 Ibid., pp. 172–6.
95 Ibid., pp. 176–83, 236 n. 5. Four of the five massacres perpetrated in Río Negro took place in a six-month period in 1982.
96 D. Earle, "Mayas Aiding Mayas: Guatemalan Refugees in Chiapas, Mexico", in R. Carmack (ed.), *Harvest of Violence: The Maya Indians and the Guatemalan Crisis*, Norman: University of Oklahoma Press, 1992, p. 263; See also B. Manz, *Refugees of a Hidden War: The Aftermath of Counterinsurgency in Guatemala*, New York: State University of New York Press, 1988, pp. 148, 151; and ODHAG, *Guatemala: nunca más*, vol. 1: pp. 155–6, 158, 159.
97 CEH, *Memoria del silencio*, vol. 3: pp. 256, 519.
98 ICTR, "Prosecutor vs. Kayishema and Ruzindana", paragraph 96; ICTY, "Prosecutor vs. Krstic", paragraph 586.
99 As discussed in ICTY, "Prosecutor vs. Krstic," paragraphs 582–4, 590.
100 CEH, *Memoria del silencio*, vol. 3: pp. 360–3, 377.
101 Ibid., vol. 3: pp. 327, 345, 359, 420. For his part, David Stoll has estimated that 15 per cent of the Ixil Indian population died as a result of the army's counterinsurgency campaign in Quiché department. See D. Stoll, *Between Two Armies in the Ixil Towns of Guatemala*, New York: Colombia University Press, 1993, pp. 5, 228–33.
102 Kuper, *Genocide: Its Political Use*, pp. 31–2.
103 L. Schöultz, "Guatemala: Social Change and Political Conflict", in M. Diskin (ed.), *Trouble in Our Backyard: Central America and the United States in the Eighties*, New York: Pantheon Books, 1983, p. 180; Banco de Guatemala, Departamento de Estadísticas Económicas, Sección de Cuentas Nacionales, *Guatemala, cuentas nacionales: estadísticas globales y sectoriales, periodo 1980–1993*, Guatemala:

Banco de Guatemala, December 1994, pp. 7, 24, 26, 34, 59, 66, 72, 136; Black *et al.*, *Garrison Guatemala*, pp. 27, 41, 117–18.

104 R. Adams, "Conclusions: What Can We Know About the Harvest of Violence?" in R. Carmack (ed.), *Harvest of Violence: The Maya Indians and the Guatemalan Crisis*, Norman: University of Oklahoma Press, 1992, p. 288.

105 Quoted in Drouin, "To the Last Seed", p. 200.

106 Daniel Feierstein, *El genocidio como práctica social. Entre el nazismo y la experiencia argentina*, Buenos Aires: Fondo de Cultura Económica, 2007.

Part II
The mechanisms of violence

5 "Industrial repression" and Operation Condor in Latin America

J. Patrice McSherry[1]

During the Cold War hundreds of thousands of Latin Americans were tortured, abducted, or killed by right-wing military regimes as part of the US-led anticommunist crusade. Often they had been branded as "subversives" for their political ideas or activities rather than any involvement in armed groups (although clearly, persons accused of illegal acts are also due a fair trial under law). In Guatemala alone a savage counterinsurgency military killed some 200,000 persons, largely indigenous Maya, in horrific mass murders. In Argentina some 30,000 "disappeared" during the military dictatorship of 1976–83; under the regime of Pinochet in Chile some 3,000 were killed, and tens of thousands more suffered cruel torture. In Uruguay, although the number of persons murdered was fewer, tens of thousands were brutally tortured. Military squadrons in several countries seized hundreds of children from their parents and gave them to military or police families. Should such systematic, politically motivated violence and extermination be considered genocide?

This chapter examines that question, particularly considering the targeted repression of political leaders and social activists by Operation Condor, a transnational organization that was a component of the broader state violence. Condor was a top-secret operations and intelligence system organized by the South American militaries to unify and extend their "dirty war" campaigns across the entire continent and beyond. The Condor system focused on exiles who had fled their own countries and used extralegal methods to eliminate them: cross-border abductions and illegal transfers ("renditions") to their countries of origin; torture; murder; political assassination.

The Condor system employed a highly sophisticated apparatus of command, control, and intelligence in the counterinsurgency wars against leftist and progressive forces. Operation Condor also had the covert support of the US government. Washington provided Condor with military intelligence and training, financial assistance, advanced computers, sophisticated tracking technology, and access to the continental telecommunications system housed in the Panama Canal Zone.

It is important to understand the significance of Condor as a crucial component of the larger, continental counterinsurgency regime. While the militaries carried out massive repression within their own countries, the transnational

Condor system acted to silence individuals and groups that had escaped the dictatorships and prevent them from organizing politically or influencing public opinion outside of their own countries. Some of Condor's targets were armed insurgents, but many were grassroots-level social or political activists, unionists, or student leaders; others were prominent pro-democracy figures. The Condor apparatus assassinated former Chilean minister Orlando Letelier, for example, who was living in Washington, DC, and who was a prominent critic of the Pinochet regime in Chile. The transnational Condor system thus impeded the possibility that such leaders could carry out effective work from safer havens outside their own countries by denying them sanctuary worldwide. Second, Condor combined the efforts of six to eight South American military states in covert intelligence operations across a vast geographical area, with the secret sponsorship of Washington, creating a powerful and lethally effective system of political persecution. Condor was, in essence, the transnational arm of the dictatorships of Argentina, Bolivia, Brazil, Chile, Paraguay, and Uruguay, with Peru and Ecuador in less central roles.

Condor operations consisted of three levels. The first was mutual cooperation among the military intelligence services, to coordinate political surveillance of targeted dissidents and exchange intelligence information. The second was covert action, usually cross-border "hunter-killer" operations as well as other forms of offensive unconventional warfare. The third and most secret level was Condor's assassination capability, known as "Phase III." Under Phase III, special teams of assassins from member countries were formed to travel worldwide to eliminate "subversive enemies." Phase III was aimed at key political leaders who could organize and lead pro-democracy movements against the military regimes.

The question of genocide

The evidence suggests that the regime of state repression, and Condor in particular, exemplified *intent to destroy*, a crucial element of genocide. Condor was a central part of a meticulously planned and executed system to eliminate opponents of the dictatorships, annihilate leftist, socialist, dissident, and nationalist ideology, and terrorize broader societies. The Condor apparatus was based on premeditated planning by both national and international elites, on national security ideology that targeted "internal enemies," and on psychological warfare mechanisms to instill fear and dread in society.[2] Moreover, some of the military states went beyond eliminating militants and activists to also attack their families, friends, and social and professional networks, and indeed, entire social sectors considered to be "subversive," producing massive violence that touched every part of society. Yet under the letter of the Genocide Convention, these crimes did not constitute genocide because they targeted *political* human groups.

As Daniel Feierstein has argued,[3] why should groups murdered for their political beliefs be treated differently than, say, groups characterized by their religious ideology under the Genocide Convention? He contends that the crime of genocide should be defined by the nature of the mass destruction carried out, not by the identity of its victims (see also his chapter in this book). I have argued in previous work that during the Cold War, military states in Latin America carried out "industrial repression" – planned, methodical, prolonged, and deadly campaigns of massive disappearance, torture, and murder – much like the Nazis did during the Holocaust, although the sheer numbers were larger in Europe. The Latin American military states set up extensive new state and parastatal apparatuses to carry out their "dirty wars": clandestine infrastructures including secret prisons, fleets of unmarked cars and unregistered aircraft, unofficial cemeteries, secure communications systems, and other parallel structures funded by "black budgets." Specialized units were formed and trained in new methods and technologies of repression, and they reported to top commanders outside the normal chains of command. The parallel forces created by the counterinsurgency militaries included the clandestine groups, secret intelligence organizations, death squads, "task forces," and civilian informant networks acting covertly on behalf of the state. That is, the state greatly expanded its machinery for carrying out large-scale political violence, or what I have termed industrial repression. The concept builds upon Omer Bartov's notion of industrial killing. He describes such killing, which first emerged in World War I, as "the mechanized, impersonal, and sustained mass destruction of human beings, organized and sustained by states."[4] I extend Bartov's concept to capture the mass, systematic, state-organized repression carried out as part of counterinsurgency operations during this era in Latin America.

Key elements of the massive torture and killing in Latin America during the Cold War do seem to correspond to the Convention's definition of genocide. In a number of the national security states, military dictatorships went beyond selective anti-guerrilla campaigns. The regimes implemented messianic plans to completely remake their states and societies and change the mentality of their people (as both the Chilean and the Argentine juntas explicitly stated). Not only were whole social sectors targeted; the regimes dismantled constitutional institutions and criminalized a broad range of activities and ideas that challenged the military worldview. A key aim of these states was to depoliticize and demobilize politically active groups and social movements of workers, students, peasants, and intellectuals, which were identified as "internal enemies." The militaries acted, essentially, to quash democratic pressures from below. Thus, their objectives went far beyond eliminating "communists." The violence of the era has long been identified as state terror, and a number of studies have used that analytical lens.[5] This chapter is a beginning exploration of the question of whether that repression should be characterized as genocide.

In Argentina, Chile, Uruguay, and elsewhere, judges conducting human rights trials in recent years have seriously considered the issue of genocide. There have been unprecedented advances in the region in holding "dirty war" commanders and operatives accountable for crimes committed in the 1970s. Until recently, state-enforced impunity had shielded the perpetrators of the horrors of the "dirty wars." But the human rights abuses and state crimes of the Cold War era resurfaced as a burning public issue, especially after the 1998 arrest of former Chilean dictator Augusto Pinochet in England. Spanish judge Baltasar Garzón, who ordered the arrest, originally charged Pinochet with the crime of genocide.

In Guatemala, a United Nations-appointed Commission for Historical Clarification concluded in its 1999 report, "Memory of Silence," that the army's extreme violence against Maya groups in four regions of the country had constituted genocide.[6] In 2006 an Argentine court sentenced former Buenos Aires deputy police chief, Miguel Etchecolatz, to life imprisonment for human rights crimes. Significantly, the court described the "dirty war" in Argentina as genocide, arguing that the combination of disappearances, seizure of babies and children, rape, torture, and murder constituted a systematic plan to exterminate political dissenters. In another case in Argentina, a federal court convicted a Catholic priest, Christian von Wernich, who had been a chaplain to the security forces, of torture and kidnapping in October 2007. The judges declared his acts "akin to genocide." In late 2007 Italian judicial authorities issued arrest warrants for 140 Condor commanders and operatives in seven South American countries for crimes committed within the Condor framework.

In 1944 a Polish Jewish legal scholar named Raphael Lemkin had introduced the term "genocide" in a book on Axis rule, defining it as the systematic destruction of a targeted group by the state. Influenced by Lemkin and by the horrors of the Holocaust, the United Nations General Assembly, in its first session in 1946, issued Resolution 96 (I), which declared genocide to be

> a denial of the right of existence of entire human groups, as homicide is the denial of the right to live to individual human beings; such denial of the right of existence shocks the conscience of mankind, results in great losses to humanity in the form of cultural and other contributions represented by these human groups, and is contrary to moral law and to the spirit and aims of the United Nations. Many instances of such crimes of genocide have occurred when racial, religious, political and other groups have been destroyed, entirely or in part.[7]

Thus, political communities were originally included as groups that had been subject to genocide.

In 1948 the United Nations, after lengthy debate, concluded the Convention on the Prevention and Punishment of the Crime of Genocide (CPPCG), defining genocide in Article 2 as

> any of the following acts committed with intent to destroy, in whole or in part, a national, ethnical, racial or religious group, as such: (a) Killing members of the group; (b) Causing serious bodily or mental harm to members of the group; (c) Deliberately inflicting on the group conditions of life calculated to bring about its physical destruction in whole or in part; (d) Imposing measures intended to prevent births within the group; (e) Forcibly transferring children of the group to another group.[8]

Thus genocide was established as an international crime with a broad scope. Genocide could take place even without mass killings, if other, non-lethal acts were carried out to destroy the human group. Conspiracy to commit genocide was also established as a crime. The Convention imposed the standard of "intent to destroy, in whole or in part" the targeted group; but annihilation of the *entire* group was not required to define the act as genocide.[9] Political groups, however, were omitted as communities to be protected from genocide. A number of states had insisted on the removal of political groups during the UN debates, fearing language that was overly broad.[10]

The treaty entered into force in 1951. The USSR ratified in 1954 and the United States in 1986 (with a long list of reservations). Conservative senators (including Jesse Helms), backed by right-wing organizations such as the Liberty Lobby, had launched strong lobbying efforts to resist ratification for 35 years, arguing that the US could be prosecuted under the treaty for segregation, for the lynching of blacks and/or for the treatment of Native Americans, or for US acts in Korea or Vietnam during those wars.[11] In 1988 Congress finally passed legislation making genocide a crime under US law.

The Cold War and the "countersubversive struggle" in Latin America

In the early 1970s the Latin American counterinsurgency militaries of Argentina, Bolivia, Brazil, Chile, Paraguay, and Uruguay, with the backing of the US government, formed the prototype of Operation Condor, a yet-unnamed program of coordinated, continental abductions, "renditions," and assassinations. The military dictatorships targeted "internal enemies" and "subversives" for destruction under a national security doctrine in which the ends justified the means. These elastic categories came to encompass large sectors of society, which faced torture and death. Under Operation Condor, people who had gone into exile – often protected by United Nations refugee status – were kidnapped, tortured and killed in allied countries or illegally transferred to their home countries to be executed. Hundreds, or thousands, of such persons – the number still has not been finally determined – were abducted, tortured, and murdered in Condor operations.

Washington's Cold War anticommunist foreign policy paradigm led to "black world" counterinsurgency methods and operations that employed covert action, sabotage, and terror to combat perceived enemies. Determined to preserve and expand its hegemony as well as counter the challenge from the Soviet Union and various leftist forces in the Third World,[12] the US government undertook hundreds of covert operations worldwide, many of which used illegal and antidemocratic methods, to pursue its global interests. Despite its stance as the democratic superpower, and the opposition of important sectors of the US public and Congress, Washington allied itself with right-wing sectors in the developing world and strengthened military, security, and intelligence forces as key allies in the anticommunist crusade. Many of Condor's components – cross-border joint operations, regional intelligence sharing and planning, and extralegal methods – were rooted in earlier inter-American "countersubversive" plans and organizations, forged at the School of the Americas (SOA), the Conferences of American Armies, and elsewhere. Thus, Condor cannot be separated from the US-led counterinsurgency regime in the Americas.[13]

US leaders had long regarded Latin America as their "backyard," an important US market and source of raw materials and a crucial geopolitical territory. As labor, students, and peasants, among other social sectors, became more active in the 1950s and 1960s, demanding new rights and a fairer distribution of economic resources and political power, Washington grew increasingly concerned. Many Latin Americans were inspired by rising Third World nationalism and by the 1959 Cuban revolution and its promise of equality and social justice. Thousands of people joined movements and organizations that were struggling to end generations of political and social exclusion. At the same time, prominent Latin American leaders and intellectuals began to draw links between underdevelopment in their countries and neocolonial practices by the major Western states. Progressives and nationalists called for social, economic, and political reform. Militant social movements emerged and new elected leaders such as João Goulart in Brazil and Salvador Allende in Chile moved to build more egalitarian political and socioeconomic orders.

Witnessing the rising social mobilization in Latin America, Washington and its allies acted to defeat or neutralize the new progressive forces. The US government and its anticommunist partners in the region feared that "communism" was spreading. But ironically, many of these new movements were not communist, but rather nationalist, leftist, socialist, or radically democratic, fighting to represent the voiceless and the marginalized. Latin American unionists fought to maintain or improve standards of living, throw off the power of oligarchic owners or subservient leaders, strengthen labor rights, and influence public policy. Students demonstrated against the US presence in Vietnam and Latin America and against imperialism. Peasant movements agitated for a voice in land disputes and for agrarian reform to restructure the vast land holdings of the oligarchies. Under national security doctrine, all of these social sectors were considered potentially, or actually, subversive.

A tide of military coups swept Latin America in the 1960s and 1970s, and military dictatorships were established, usually with US backing. The counterinsurgency militaries rejected not only leftism, socialism, and communism, but also liberal democracy, union organizing, and civil and political liberties in general, which were seen as opening the door to "subversion." Moreover, the militaries and their US sponsors considered brutal, extralegal methods to be legitimate and necessary in a total war against subversion. Many regimes used death squads and other parallel forces against their political adversaries and made up death lists of hundreds of people; there is evidence that Condor intelligence commanders jointly discussed who should be eliminated. What ensued was an onslaught of state-directed bloodshed and terror across most of Latin America.

Operation Condor as a secret abduction-assassination system

Under Phases I and II of the Condor system the military regimes agreed secretly to systematically monitor one another's exiles, allow foreign intelligence commandos to operate on their soil, and cooperate in various ways to facilitate the "countersubversive" struggle. The associated militaries sent multinational death squads to allied countries, spreading the anticommunist "dirty wars" across Latin America and beyond. A Uruguayan Condor squad carried out numerous operations in Argentina from a base in Orletti Motors, for example, an abandoned auto repair shop in Buenos Aires, which was under the operational control of the Argentine First Army Corps and the intelligence apparatus SIDE.

Under Phase III, leading opposition figures were targeted. Constitutionalist Chilean general Carlos Prats, who had opposed the 1973 military coup in Chile, and his wife Sofía Cuthbert, were murdered in a massive car bombing in Buenos Aires in 1974 (more on this case follows). Chilean Christian Democrat leader Bernardo Leighton and his wife, Ana Fresno, were shot by Condor agents in Rome in 1975; they survived, but were permanently disabled. Orlando Letelier of Chile, Juan José Torres of Bolivia, and Zelmar Michelini and Hector Gutiérrez Ruiz of Uruguay were all assassinated by Operation Condor in 1976. Letelier and a US aide died in a powerful car bombing on the streets of Washington, DC. Former Brazilian president João Goulart died of an apparent heart attack the same year, and in 2008 new testimony emerged to suggest that this, too, was a Condor assassination. After the 1964 coup in Brazil, Goulart had joined forces with another former president to organize a broad-based movement to reinstate democracy. The military regime banned it, and Goulart went into exile in Uruguay. The Brazilian military closely followed his movements, in conjunction with Uruguayan and Argentine intelligence organizations, for years.[14] Any potential, perceived, or actual critics of the dictatorships – former government functionaries, party leaders, social activists, priests and nuns, unionists, students and teachers, as well as guerrillas – were subject to persecution, torture, and death by the regimes and by Condor.

In 2008 a former Uruguayan police intelligence agent named Mario Barreiro Neira – in prison for arms trafficking and other crimes – claimed that Goulart had been poisoned and that he (Barreiro) had been involved in the assassination. Goulart died while he was in Argentina. He had just been given a clean bill of health by his doctors. The Brazilian and Argentine militaries refused to permit an autopsy. In 2001, many years after the democratic transition, the Brazilian parliament conducted an investigation, but was unable to determine conclusively whether Goulart had been assassinated. The family always believed that he had been.[15] Barreiro said that the crime had been ordered by the Brazilian military dictator at the time, with the encouragement of the Central Intelligence Agency, and that a CIA officer had participated in a planning meeting.[16] The involvement of Uruguayan paramilitaries, under Brazilian orders, operating covertly in Argentina with CIA support would clearly fit the profile of a Condor crime. The government of Brazil admitted Barreiro's testimony as valid in early 2008 and launched a new investigation.

The Condor prototype appears in 1973

Condor was officially constituted during a secret summit in Santiago in November 1975, when the name "Condor" was adopted and the system was institutionalized in a foundational document. Military representatives created formal organizational structures and adopted a set of security procedures for covert intelligence operations at that meeting.[17] But the intelligence-operations prototype had actually been functioning since 1973, when cross-border disappearances and assassinations by multinational task forces began to occur. In that year, for example, a Bolivian named Jorge Ríos Dalenz was detained-disappeared in Santiago in an operation coordinated by Bolivia and Chile. Ríos had been a leader of the Movement of the Revolutionary Left in Bolivia until Hugo Banzer's 1971 coup. He moved to Chile and lived there quietly until the September 1973 coup in Chile, when he was kidnapped by a military commando. In another case in November 1973, four armed men, two in military uniform, abducted former Bolivian interior minister Jorge Gallardo Losada from his home in Santiago, where he had lived since 1971. He had served under nationalist president Juan José Torres – a Condor victim in 1976. Gallardo was transported to Bolivia and then to Argentina at a time when all aircraft traffic was tightly controlled by the Chilean junta. In another 1973 case, Brazilian police operating in Argentina abducted Joaquim Pires Cerveira and João Batista Rita, two Brazilians exiled in Buenos Aires.[18]

The wave of disappearances accelerated in 1974. In March, four Uruguayans, refugees in Argentina under UN protection, were detained, and in May they were illegally transferred to Uruguay. After the UN high commissioner for refugees intervened they were allowed to go into exile in other countries. On September 12, five other Uruguayans were abducted from their homes in Buenos Aires by men later identified as Uruguayan police. Their families were unable to locate them despite repeated pleas to Argentine authorities. On October 14, two were released, and they took refuge in Sweden. The bodies of the other three, disfigured by torture, were discovered later that month. The two refugees in Sweden subsequently described the tortures used against them and said that they had been imprisoned among the bodies of those who had already died. They identified a Uruguayan policeman, Hugo Campos Hermida, as one of their torturers. Campos Hermida became notorious in Uruguay for his role in Condor operations, as he was identified by numerous survivors as one of the interrogators and torturers in Orletti Motors. Campos Hermida had been trained by the CIA, and in 1970 had received a State Department scholarship to attend intelligence courses in Washington, DC, at the International Police Academy (IPA).[19] He became a member of the so-called Death Squad in Uruguay, and eventually participated in the Uruguayan hunter-killer squad that operated in Argentina within the Condor framework. Campos Hermida represented the organic linkages among CIA training, police death squads, and Condor.[20]

A number of declassified US documents include detailed accounts of the inner workings of the Condor system. Several confirm that the Condor prototype began operations in the 1973–4 period. One declassified CIA cable discussed the joint Chilean-Argentine surveillance operation against Carlos Prats, the former Chilean army commander who had opposed the coup against Salvador Allende. He had left Chile with his wife in 1973 to live in Buenos Aires. Shortly thereafter, the CIA cable reported that Chilean general Arellano Stark had

> left Santiago on a special mission … [to] discuss with the [Argentine] military any [WORD DELETED] they have regarding the activities of General Carlos Prats…. Arellano will also attempt to gain an agreement whereby the Argentines maintain scrutiny over Prats and regularly inform the Chileans of his activities.[21]

This sort of binational surveillance operation had been encouraged by CIA officers in Uruguay and Brazil previously, and was one of the functions (Phase I) of Operation Condor. Manuel Contreras, commander of the Gestapo-like Chilean DINA (Directorate of National Intelligence) and a CIA asset, crisscrossed the South American region in 1974 and 1975 to set up similar covert intelligence networks. Prats and his wife were murdered in an enormous car bombing on September 30, 1974. Their official security protection (provided by the Argentine army and police) was absent at the time.

The Prats assassinations were carried out by a multinational squad consisting of agents of DINA and members of the fascist Argentine group Milicia (an outgrowth of the death squad Triple A), with the complicity of the Argentine army and police. They were the first major assassinations committed by the as-yet-unnamed Condor prototype. One of the conspirators was US expatriate and trained assassin Michael Townley, who later admitted his role. Another was a far-right Chilean operative named Enrique Arancibia Clavel, who was also implicated in the assassination of General René Schneider, the constitutionalist predecessor of Prats as chief of the Chilean army. Arancibia Clavel had organized a Condor network in Buenos Aires under the orders of DINA Foreign Department commander Raúl Eduardo Iturriaga Neumann.[22] Arancibia carried out surveillance of Prats before the assassination and also tortured Chilean exiles in secret Argentine detention centers.[23] In November 2000, an Argentine court convicted Arancibia for his role in the Prats assassinations (however, he was released in a controversial decision in 2007). In July 2008 a Chilean court sentenced Contreras to two life sentences for the double assassinations, and Pedro Espinoza, another Condor/DINA commander, received 40 years for planning the crime.

Several other declassified US documents report a key meeting in Buenos Aires of security officers from five of the six Condor countries in February 1974, in which they discussed the systematic coordination of cross-border operations – the essence of Condor. A top-secret CIA *National Intelligence Daily* of June 23, 1976, released in 2000, stated:

> In early 1974, security officials from Argentina, Chile, Uruguay, Paraguay, and Bolivia met in Buenos Aires to prepare coordinated actions against

subversive targets. [5 LINES EXCISED] Since then [3 LINES EXCISED] the Argentines have conducted joint countersubversive operations with the Chileans and with the Uruguayans.[24]

This crucial CIA report confirmed that the Condor apparatus was already multi-national and already carrying out coordinated operations in early 1974. A declassified State Department document added more data:

in March 1974, [Argentine president Juan] Perón authorized the Argentine Federal Police and the Argentine intelligence to cooperate with Chilean intelligence in apprehending Chilean left-wing extremists in exile in Argentina. Similar arrangements had also been made with the security services of Bolivia, Uruguay, and Brazil. This cooperation among security forces apparently includes permission for foreign officials to operate within Argentina, against their exiled nationals.... This authority allegedly includes arrest of such exiles and transfer to the home country without recourse to legal procedures.[25]

In another case, Paraguayan educator Martín Almada was seized in Paraguay in November 1974 by combined commando forces. He testified that Paraguayans, accompanied by other South American officers, interrogated and tortured him, again showing that multinational Condor interrogations were operational in 1974. By that year, increasingly visible cross-border terror operations carried out by shadowy squadrons were causing panic among exile communities. The accumulated evidence provides overwhelming confirmation that Condor's most essential feature – its cross-border "hunter-killer" operations against political enemies – began in 1973 and was fully functional by 1974, long before the program was officially constituted as Operation Condor in 1975.

Condor targeting of political activists

Condor operations escalated in the period between 1975 and 1978. In March 1977 five young people from Uruguay and Argentina were detained in Paraguay in an emblematic Condor abduction. This case involved Condor units from Argentina, Uruguay, and Paraguay. The five (José Nell, Alejandro José Logoluso, Dora Marta Landi Gil, Nelson Rodolfo Santana, and Gustavo Insaurralde) were seized by Paraguayan police, interrogated and tortured by Paraguayan, Argentine, and Uruguayan intelligence personnel, illegally transferred from Paraguay to Argentina, and "disappeared" there. Uruguayan Nelson Santana was a leader of FUNSA, the tire workers union, and Gustavo Insaurralde was a unionist with the Uruguayan Teachers' Federation. Both were also members of Partido por la Victoria del Pueblo (PVP), a militant, but not a guerrilla, organization. The PVP was involved in organizing among unionists and other sectors to oppose the dictatorship. Insaurralde had traveled to Paraguay in hopes of transiting to Sweden to join his pregnant wife, and both had hoped to establish a route to Europe for others facing repression.[26] All five permanently disappeared.

Paraguayan authorities reported that they were freed, and the Argentine junta consistently denied responsibility. But a survivor of an Argentine secret detention-torture center called Club Atlético reported having seen Insaurralde there. Moreover, in 1977 Insaurralde's wife wrote to the archbishop of Asunción to ask for his help in locating her husband. He responded that Insaurralde had been transferred in an Argentine military plane to Buenos Aires and then he alone had been sent to Montevideo. His wife denounced the disappearance before the Organization of American States and Amnesty International at the time,[27] to no avail.

Official documents found in the Paraguayan Police Archives in 1992 confirmed that on May 16, 1977 the Paraguayan security forces had delivered the five to an Argentine intelligence unit (including an army intelligence officer and a navy officer from the infamous Navy Mechanics School, ESMA). They were flown in an Argentine navy plane to Buenos Aires, where they disappeared. The Paraguayan police report included their photos and fingerprints and the names of the Argentine officers who took them.

Documents discovered more recently in Paraguay showed that Uruguayan colonel Carlos Calcagno – a graduate of the School of the Americas, as were other Condor operatives – had been in Asunción to interrogate and torture the Uruguayans, alongside notorious Paraguayan police torturers and Condor operatives Pastor Coronel and Benito Guanes. The military report included intelligence documents on the political histories of Santana and Insaurralde and interrogation data provided by officers of the Paraguayan and Uruguayan security forces.[28]

The cases of Insaurralde and Santana as well as FUNSA leader León Duarte, who also disappeared in Argentina in 1976, were under consideration in April 2007 in a Uruguayan trial. (And in fact, one lawyer asked for the extradition of Henry Kissinger to question him about his involvement in Condor.) In March 2007 Sergio López Burgos (one of the survivors of Operation Condor) Duarte's son, and members of FUNSA had brought a denunciation before the Uruguayan court investigating secret Condor flights between Buenos Aires and Montevideo in the 1970s. During the trial, on April 14, a former political prisoner testified that when he had been imprisoned in a Uruguayan military garrison in 1976, he heard a voice cry out that he was León Duarte, that he had been illegally transferred from Argentina and that the military was going to execute him and all the others from the clandestine Condor flight.[29] This was the first information indicating that Duarte and others actually had been brought alive to Uruguay after disappearing in Argentina. The remains of Duarte, Insaurralde, and Santana have never been found. Neither has the body of Gerardo Gatti, leader of the Graphic Workers Union and a PVP member, who was also illegally abducted in Argentina and tortured in Orletti at around the same time. These crimes highlighted Condor's targeting of union leaders.

Evidence of US involvement in Condor

The 1975 disappearance of Chilean Jorge Isaac Fuentes Alarcón revealed a clandestine US role in Condor operations. Paraguayan security agents captured Fuentes, a sociologist and member of the radical group MIR, in May 1975, as he crossed the border from Argentina into Paraguay. Decades later, declassified US documents showed that the US legal attaché in the embassy in Buenos Aires had informed the Chilean military in writing of the capture and interrogation of Fuentes and listed the names and addresses of three individuals living in the United States whose names had been in Fuentes's possession. The memo stated that the FBI was conducting investigations of the three in the United States.[30]

In typical Condor coordination, several Chilean DINA officers, including the notorious Marcelo Moren Brito, traveled to Asunción to interrogate Fuentes and to "render" him to Chile. Chile's Truth and Reconciliation Commission later reported that the capture of Fuentes was a collaborative effort by Argentine intelligence services, personnel of the US embassy in Buenos Aires, and Paraguayan police. Fuentes was brought to Villa Grimaldi, the infamous secret DINA detention center in Santiago, where he was seen by other prisoners. Fuentes, ruthlessly tortured with beatings and electric shocks,[31] did not survive.

The legal attaché's letter, among others uncovered in recent years, demonstrate that US officials and agencies were cooperating with the military dictatorships, sharing intelligence, and acting as partners in Condor operations. Indeed, declassified documents make clear Washington's knowledge and awareness of Condor's extralegal abductions and of its assassination capability. One 1976 Defense Intelligence Agency (DIA) report stated, for example, that a Condor assassination unit was "structured much like a US Special Forces Team," and in matter-of-fact language described Condor's "joint counterinsurgency operations" to "eliminate Marxist terrorist activities."[32] The documents leave little doubt that Condor was a top-secret component of US-led counterinsurgency campaigns.

A declassified 1978 cable shed further light on the magnitude of US involvement with Condor. Ambassador to Paraguay Robert White authored the cable to Secretary of State Cyrus Vance, reporting on a meeting requested by the commander of Paraguay's armed forces, General Alejandro Fretes Dávalos. Fretes told White that Condor officers were utilizing the US telecommunications network housed in a US facility in the Panama Canal Zone.[33] According to Fretes, intelligence chiefs from Brazil, Argentina, Chile, Bolivia, Paraguay, and Uruguay employed "an encrypted system within the US telecommunications net[work]," which covered all of Latin America, to "coordinate intelligence information." White drew the connection to Operation Condor in his report and advised the Carter administration to reconsider the arrangement. He never received a response.

Clearly, Fretes was revealing direct, covert US sponsorship of the Condor system. US officials were placing at the disposal of Operation Condor the top-secret, secure communications channel for US surveillance of the continent and for inter-American operational coordination. Condor's intelligence and tracking capacities would be greatly expanded through such a powerful technological system, and Condor covert operations made more lethal and more effective. Moreover, US officers could monitor and keep track of Condor communications and operations through the system. Despite the former DIA commander's carefully formulated half-denial in 2001,[34] it is inconceivable that any foreign officer or military group could make use of the secure US telecommunications system without the deep knowledge, collaboration, and engagement of top US military and intelligence officials. Moreover, such covert collaboration indicated that high-level officials in Washington – it remains unclear who – considered Condor to be an operation that served US interests.

Conclusion

Did the massive crimes carried out by the Latin American military states, including those of Operation Condor, qualify as genocide? To reiterate, Condor should be seen as an integral piece of the larger regime of state violence and terror aimed at political dissidents and social groups during that era. The Condor system was part of a broad continental strategy to crush political and social opposition to the dictatorships. There are a number of elements that would seem to support the conclusion that this organized destruction was, in fact, genocidal.

The national security states conducted well-planned and orchestrated operations to repress and destroy large communities, considered potentially or actually subversive, throughout the region. Condor was an organized, coordinated system focused on the elimination of key individuals and groups that had escaped the dictatorships of their own countries. The Condor system operated with formal command structures and well-equipped operations centers in each member country. Condor operations, and the larger campaigns of state terrorism, reflected intent to destroy. The violence was not isolated, random, or sporadic. It was planned, coordinated, and executed with military discipline, and guided by ideological categorizations of large groups of people. While clearly each Condor country exhibited different levels of mass and selective violence against their populations, there were similar methods, operations, and torture techniques shared and used across the region as part of a hemispheric strategy.

Many of the practices used by the military states seem to fit the stipulations of the Genocide Convention:

> *Killing members of the group.* The military states, and Condor, targeted individuals and groups based on their political or social ideology and activity; some were insurgents, but many were not. Phase III targeted prominent pro-democracy leaders. The sheer size of the populations subjected to industrial repression – hundreds of thousands "disappeared," tortured, and killed – lends weight to the argument that genocide was committed.
> *Causing serious bodily or mental harm to members of the group.* The coordinated campaigns of disappearance, torture, and killing subjected societies as a whole, and politically leftist or socially active persons in particular, to

bodily trauma and psychological torture as well as death, or the threat of death. Military terror atomized and traumatized society. The overwhelming presence of the terrorist state created fear, dissolved social networks, and paralyzed collective political action. In some countries, meetings of any kind (including birthday parties) required state permission. Many people saw neighbors' homes ransacked or neighbors dragged away by armed squadrons of men in civilian clothes. Apart from a small sector of the population that was considered politically loyal, people from all social sectors were suspected of actual or potential subversion.

Deliberately inflicting conditions of life calculated to destroy a group. Throughout Latin America large sectors of society were dehumanized, threatened, and vilified by the state and its security forces, making daily life unendurable. The state, especially its intelligence apparatus, deeply penetrated society and obliterated the rights of all its inhabitants. In Argentina, Uruguay, Guatemala, and elsewhere, paramilitary units that "disappeared" persons also expropriated their property and stole their possessions. In several countries entire families were destroyed through killing or disappearance. The overarching atmosphere of stress and fear contributed to severe conditions of life for large populations living under state terror.

Imposing measures intended to prevent births within the group. It can be argued that sexual torture and rape, which were rampant in the secret torture centers, pertain to this clause.

Forcibly transferring children of the group to another group. This practice took place in Argentina and Uruguay in the 1970s and in El Salvador and Guatemala in the 1980s. The purpose of baby-trafficking was not only to torment the surviving families but also to give military and police families the task of preventing children from growing up to be "subversives."

It is indisputable that the mass killing and repression of the Cold War era caused "great losses to humanity in the form of cultural and other contributions represented by these human groups" and that the human rights atrocities carried out were "contrary to moral law and to the spirit and aims of the United Nations" (Resolution 96 (I) of 1946).

The Convention's current language erases from the strictures of international law the wide-scale, organized destruction of hundreds of thousands of people if they are identified as a "political group." Given the scale of the carnage in Latin America (and elsewhere) by states determined to crush internal opposition, this is a serious omission. The national security states acted above the law and violated the most basic civilized values. Without international sanctions and clear prohibitions, what is to prevent states from again using massive violence and crimes against humanity to secure their own power and impose exclusionary, tyrannical regimes?

The survivors of the "dirty wars" in Latin America have vowed, "Never again!" A compelling argument can be made that to honor that cry, to acknowledge the bloodshed and loss of human life in the recent past, and to prevent future state-sponsored and politically motivated extermination of large human groups, the international community should broaden the Convention's protections to encompass politically identified communities.[35] To do so would represent a momentous advance for the developing system of international law, and for humanity.

Notes and references

1 Many thanks to Raúl Molina Mejía and Marcia Esparza for their comments on earlier drafts.
2 See my book, J. P. McSherry, *Predatory States: Operation Condor and Covert War in Latin America*, Lanham, MD: Rowman & Littlefield Publishers, 2005. Scott Straus uses similar concepts in his book, S. Straus, *The Order of Genocide*, Ithaca, NY: Cornell University Press, 2006.
3 Daniel Feierstein, "Political Violence in Argentina and Its Genocidal Characteristics," *Journal of Genocide Research* 8, 2, 2006, pp. 149–68.
4 O. Bartov, "Industrial Killing: World War I, The Holocaust, and Representation," paper presented at Rutgers University, New Jersey, March 1997. Online, available at: http://muweb.millersville.edu/~holo-con/bartov.html (accessed March 14, 2008); See also O. Bartov, *Murder in Our Midst: The Holocaust, Industrial Killing, and Representation*, New York: Oxford University Press, 1996.
5 See, for example, B. B. Campbell and A. D. Brenner (eds), *Death Squads in Global Perspective: Murder with Deniability*, New York: St Martin's Press, 2000; M. McClintock, "American Doctrine and Counterinsurgent State Terror," in A. George (ed.), *Western State Terrorism*, New York: Routledge, 1991, pp. 121–54; McSherry, *Predatory States*; C. Menjívar and N. Rodríguez (eds), *When States Kill: Latin America, the US, and Technologies of Terror*, Austin, TX: University of Texas Press, 2005; M. Stohl and G. Lopez (eds), *Dependence, Development, and State Repression*, Stamford, CT: Greenwood Press, 1989; M. Stohl and G. Lopez, *Terrible beyond Endurance? The Foreign Policy of State Terrorism*, Stamford, CT: Greenwood Press, 1988; M. Stohl and G. Lopez, *Government Violence and Repression*, Stamford, CT: Greenwood Press, 1986; T. Wright, *State Terrorism in Latin America: Chile, Argentina, and International Human Rights*, Lanham, MD: Rowman & Littlefield, 2007.
6 The 1954 CIA-orchestrated overthrow of democratically elected president Jacobo Arbenz began four decades of bloody military rule in Guatemala. CIA officer Howard Hunt, a key participant, described the CIA's 1954 strategy this way:

> I suppose the example that I can best turn to, although I rather hate to, is [that] what we wanted to do was to have a terror campaign: to terrify Arbenz particularly, terrify his troops, much as the German Stuka bombers terrified the population of Holland, Belgium and Poland ... and just rendered everybody paralyzed.

As presented on CNN series *The Cold War*, Episode 18, "Backyard," 1998.
7 United Nations General Assembly, Resolution 96 (I), 11 December 1946, *The Crime of Genocide*.
8 United Nations Convention on the Prevention and Punishment of the Crime of Genocide, United Nations General Assembly Resolution 260 A (III), 9 December 1948 (entry into force January 12, 1951; approved and proposed for signature and ratification or accession in accordance with article XIII), Office of the United Nations High Commission for Human Rights.
9 K. Mundorff, "Other Peoples' Children: A Textual and Contextual Interpretation of the Genocide Convention, Article 2 (E)," *Harvard International Law Journal* 50, 1 (2009), pp. 61–127; see also http://science.jrank.org/pages/9497/Genocide-Genocide-

Convention.html on the Genocide Convention; Genocide Watch at www.genocide-watch.org.

10 See, for example, L. J. LeBlanc, *The United States and the Genocide Convention*, Durham, NC: Duke University Press, 1991, pp. 27–8 and Chapter 4.

11 People for the American Way Foundation, "UN-dermined: The Right's Disdain for the UN and International Treaties: The Genocide Convention and the International Criminal Court." Online, available at: www.pfaw.org/pfaw/general/default.aspx?oid=19033 (accessed November 17, 2007); and "The Genocide Convention." Online, available at: http.science.jrank.org/pages/9497/Genocide-Genocide-Convention. html (accessed December 7, 2007).

12 Michael McClintock has written extensively on this issue as has this author. See McClintock, "American Doctrine and Counterinsurgent State Terror"; M. McClintock, *Instruments of Statecraft: US Guerrilla Warfare, Counterinsurgency, Counter-terrorism, 1940–1990*, New York: Pantheon Books, 1992. One representative 1963 US document on Cuba stated, for example, that "our ultimate objective with respect to Cuba is the overthrow of the Castro/communist regime and its replacement by one compatible with the objectives of the US.".... Memorandum from the Coordinator of Cuban Affairs to the Executive Committee of the National Security Council, no. 272, January 24, 1963. For an eye-opening document detailing US plans to destroy Cuba, see Department of State, "Memorandum for the Record 286, Secret, Eyes Only," prepared by T. A. Parrott, Washington, January 11, 1962, in *Foreign Relations of the United States 1961–1962*, vol. X, *Cuba, 1961–62*, in which military and CIA officers discuss preemptive military, economic, political, and covert actions to "help the Cubans overthrow the communist regime from within Cuba and institute a new government with which the United States can live in peace."

13 For a relevant study see Menjívar and Rodríguez (eds) *When States Kill*.

14 "Goulart era vigilado por 'servicios' del Ejército, la Policía, Narcóticos y el SID," *La República*, October 3, 2008. Online, available at: www.larepublica.com.uy/politica/333972-goulart-era-vigilado-por-servicios-del-ejercito-la-policia-narcoticos-y-el-sid (accessed March 6, 2008); ANSA, "João Goulart fue espiado en Montevideo," *El Pais Digital*, February 16, 2008. Online, available at: www.elpais.com.uy/08/02/16/ultmo_330497.asp (accessed February 28, 2008); and R. Rodríguez, "Los archivos de la dictadura de Brasil registran todo lo ocurrido en Uruguay," *La República*, August 21, 2007.

15 For example, see "Asesinato por encargo del Gobierno Militar," *La República*, January 27, 2008, quoting a son of the Brazilian leader.

16 This agent had made similar statements to Róger Rodríguez of *La República* in 2002. Uruguayan press reports identified the CIA officer and said he had been involved in the 1954 overthrow of Arbenz as well as the destabilization of the Allende government in Chile, and was the CIA station chief in Uruguay in 1976. Representative articles include R. Rodríguez, "El ejecutivo, el Parlamento y la Justicia de Brasil investigan muerte de João Goulart," *La República*, May 14, 2008; "Brasil: Operacion Cóndor." Online, available at: www.pepitorias.blogspot.com January 31, 2008 (accessed March 4, 2008); "Testigo implica a la CIA en su versión de crimen de Goulart," *La República*, January 28, 2008.

17 The Condor founding document was discovered in Chile in 1999 and was reprinted in *Posdata* (Uruguay). "Acta Fundacional del Plan Cóndor: Uruguay Propusó el Nombre en Homenaje a los Anfitriones Chilenos," *Posdata*, June 18, 1999, pp. 19–20.

18 Cerveira was a former Brazilian army officer who opposed the dictatorship, and Rita was a student.

19 "Campos Hermida y Castiglioni fueron entrenados en 'inteligencia' en EEUU," *La Hora*, December 30, 1986.

20 For research on the links among US military and police training programs, inter-American counterinsurgency strategies, right-wing Uruguayan death squads, and the

Condor system, see my article J. P. McSherry, "Death Squads as Parallel Forces: Uruguay, Operation Condor, and the United States," *Journal of Third World Studies* 24, 1, Spring 2007, pp. 13–52 (translated and published as "Escuadrones de la muerte como fuerzas paralelas: Uruguay, Operación Cóndor y los Estados Unidos" in Ediciones de la Banda Oriental, *Cuadernos de la Historia Reciente 3*, Montevideo: Uruguay, September 2007, pp. 111–34).

21 The date is illegible on the document itself and the State Department document index gives the date as November 1974; however, this is impossible since Prats was assassinated in September 1974. CIA Directorate of Operations, secret report of November 27, 1973, title blacked out. Online, available at: http:foia.state.gov.

22 M. González, "Confirman que el ejército de Pinochet mató a Prats," *Clarín*, October 5, 2000; J. Escalante, "Los pagos de la DINA para matar a Prats," *La Nación*, February 7, 2005; "Caso Prats: dictan nuevo procesamiento y documento revela como la DINA vigiló al general," *La Nación*, June 22, 2007.

23 "Procesan a Enrique Arancibia Clavel por caso de torturas en Argentina," *Primera Línea*, August 20, 2002.

24 CIA, *National Intelligence Daily* (Top Secret), June 23, 1976. Another CIA document mentioned in passing that "cooperation between the respective intelligence/security agencies had existed for some time – perhaps as early as February 1974," but then asserted that Condor was not formalized until May 1976, an inaccurate statement.

25 C. M. Cerna, "Summary of Argentine Law and Practice on Terrorism," in M. E. Andersen, *Dossier Secreto: Argentina's Desaparecidos and the Myth of the "Dirty War,"* Boulder, CO: Westview, 1993, pp. 108. See also H. Verbitsky, "El Vuelo del Cóndor," *Página/12*, January 28, 1996; and M. Bonasso, *El presidente que no fue: Los archivos ocultos del peronismo*, Buenos Aires: Planeta, 2002, p. 819.

26 R. Rodríguez, "Denuncian al Goyo y al coronel Calcagno por desaparición de Santana y Inzaurralde," *La República*, April 1, 2007.

27 Rodríguez, "Denuncian al Goyo."

28 Rodríguez, "Denuncian al Goyo."

29 R. Rodríguez, "Soy León Duarte," *La República*, April 15, 2007.

30 National Security Archive, document 30–01 of 1975. Online, available at: www.gwu.edu/nsarchive/NSAEBB/NSAEBB8/ch30–01.htm (accessed March 30, 2008).

31 Comisión Nacional de Verdad y Reconciliación, *Informe Rettig*, Santiago: Chilean Government and Ediciones del Ornitorrinco, 1991, pp. 595–6; CODEPU, *Más allá de las fronteras: Estudios sobre las personas ejecutadas o desaparecidas fuera de Chile, 1973–1990*, Santiago: LOM Ediciones, 1996, pp. 78–83; Instituto Cono Sur, "Jorge Fuentes Alarcón, Víctima del Cóndor," August 12, 2001, in *Resumen nro. 385*; "Las preguntas que el juez Guzmán tiene para Pinochet," *La Nación*, September 25, 2004.

32 Defense Intelligence Agency (DIA), "Special Operations Forces," Washington, DC: US Army, Defense Intelligence Agency (DIA), October 1, 1976.

33 R. White, cable to Secretary of State, October 13, 1978. Online, available at: http:foia.state.gov/documents/StateChile3/000058FD.pdf (accessed February 2, 2008). See also D. J. Schemo, "New Files Tie US to Deaths of Latin Leftists in 1970s," *New York Times*, March 6, 2001. This author discovered this cable during her research on Condor.

34 He said that "if such an arrangement existed on an institutional basis, I would have known about it, and I did not then and do not now," but added, "that such an arrangement could have been made locally on an ad hoc basis is not beyond the realm of probability." Schemo, "New Files."

35 The mass killings of political enemies also occurred in Indonesia in 1965 and under the Pol Pot regime in Cambodia. D. Luban makes a persuasive argument for revisiting the Convention in his "Calling Genocide by Its Rightful Name: Lemkin's Word, Darfur, and the UN Report," *Chicago Journal of International Law*, 7, 1, summer, 2006. Online, available at: http://papers.ssrn.com/sol3/papers.cfm?abstract_id=903009 (accessed June 4, 2008).

6 The United States and torture

Lessons from Latin America

Jennifer K. Harbury

Even a cursory review of United States covert operations in Latin America makes certain conclusions inescapable. Witness statements and official records have long confirmed that the US participated in the violent coups that wracked the hemisphere, from Chile and Uruguay to Brazil to Central America.[1] The evidence also confirms that the US closely collaborated with the repressive military regimes that rose to power during those coups.[2] This reality hardly comes as news, especially to those who suffered the consequences. However, many US leaders now shrug off the events as matters of ancient history, requiring no reforms or reparations. This constitutes grave error. In the archives of the past lie inconvenient truths about the nature and scope of US participation in torture itself. Those truths, in turn, are crucial to a proper analysis of US torture practices today in the "war against terror." Without that analysis, the global community cannot salvage its much-eroded legal network of human rights protections. If and when that network collapses, we risk unprecedented chaos.

The truth is that the US intelligence networks, in particular the Central Intelligence Agency (CIA), have spent decades developing certain torture techniques and other counterinsurgency methods, such as forcible disappearances, and teaching and practicing them in Latin America. In short, the CIA has long engaged in torture and other grave human rights crimes in the absence of any national security threat of any kind. The real motivation has always been the protection of US financial interests. Such interests, in turn, are inextricably intertwined with those of the wealthy oligarchies of South and Central America.

The conjoined financial concerns have lead to devastating results, not only in terms of the final body counts, but also the obstruction of fundamental socioeconomic reforms long taken for granted by the citizens of other nations. The Latin American landed gentry or oligarchy classes are for the most part composed of the descendants of the conquistadors and other light-skinned Europeans. Their wealth and power are deeply rooted in, and utterly dependent upon, preservation of the skewed and near-feudal distribution of land and resources established in the early colonial era. The descendents of the first citizens of the hemisphere, the indigenous peoples, and the slaves dragged westwards from Africa, have been left to survive, if at all, as de facto serfs.[3] Their terrible sufferings, from starvation, lack of basic medical care, and the denial of a survivable minimum wage, have been repeatedly documented. Yet time and again their efforts to gain even minimal rights and protections have been crushed by the frightened oligarchies and their hired armies. Worse yet, as US corporations invested in the rich lands and natural resources of these countries, the convergence of financial interests brought with it the CIA and US military power.[4]

These powerful partners have long used the same strategies to deal with the defiant working classes, as well as any supportive dissidents or progressive leaders from the churches, unions, or universities. Such groups have been openly and systematically hunted and "eliminated" in the most brutal of ways. General Pinochet's grisly use of the Chilean National Stadium is but one illustration. The El Mozote massacre in El Salvador is yet another, not to mention the 660 Mayan villages massacred in Guatemala. Throughout Latin America, de facto genocide was routinely utilized. The target group was always the same; all persons challenging the antiquated socio-economic status quo, whatever their race or social class might be.

Full genocide was, of course, impractical. There must be survivors to work the mines and harvest the crops. However, those survivors must prefer to watch their children starve rather than seek a living wage. Hence the true role of torture. Intelligence experts have long agreed that a human being enduring torture will say anything at all.[5] The purpose is not to acquire information, but rather, to terrorize the population into submission. Hence the mutilated bodies of the victims in Latin America were left in town squares, busy roadways, and other public places, clear warnings to all others of the price of defiance. Systematic torture is but a tool of systematic terror, and has long been used as counterpart to the de facto genocide needed to halt the growing cries for reforms.

These truths have always been fiercely denied. US officials have been repeatedly forced to admit CIA participation in the violent *coups d'état*, and to the provision of equipment and funding to the most brutal of military regimes. However, those same officials have long built a firewall around the issue of any direct involvement in torture, insisting instead that the US has merely sought to "professionalize" the troops in question, and to promote democracy in their homelands. Various justifications have been proffered, such as the threat of communism and the war against drugs. However, collaboration in torture or other human rights violations has always been flatly denied. That line in the sand, of course, marks the boundary between questionable political decisions and crimes against humanity.

It was only after the tragic events of September 11, 2001 that this official position began to change. From the outset, leaders of the Bush administration made it clear that harsh methods would be used in dealing with Al-Qaeda and its sympathizers.[6] Slowly but surely, however, the hunt for Osama Bin Laden gave way to a war for the oil pipelines in Iraq and Iran. In the name of the "war against terror," the Geneva Conventions were declared inapplicable, and even a bit naïve.[7] Yet in the aftermath of the Abu Ghraib scandal, President Bush himself rushed to declare the torture methods depicted in the grim photographs to be immoral and "un-American," the isolated acts of a few poorly trained soldiers. As proof mounted that these were widely utilized techniques and had been ordered from above, the official story changed again. The techniques were declared to be harsh, admittedly, yet somehow less than torture. In the alternative, it was claimed that the practice of torture was somehow justified by the unprecedented national security threat posed by Al-Qaeda.

It is the purpose of this chapter to delve more deeply into the extent of US torture practices of the past in Latin America. Are the methods now in fact the same as the ones that have always been taught and utilized by the US, in the absence of any security risks? What is their true impact on democratization and international security? Has the failure of the global community to properly deal with this reality lead to the human rights crisis we face today? What are the long-term consequences?

Survivors' stories: same CIA, same methods

As the grim photographs from Abu Ghraib flashed across television screens around the world, most people in the United States responded with predictable shock and outrage. There were some, however, who sensed only chilling recognition. As the survivors of torture from Latin America gathered to discuss the news, their collective experience gave a crucial perspective to the scandal. They had all suffered precisely the same "interrogation methods," and in many cases, an American agent had been present in their secret prison cells. The following examples are key to an accurate understanding of the ongoing human rights debate today. In some cases, names have been changed in order to protect the survivor and his or her family.

Many ask why it took so long for these testimonies to be revealed. The sad truth of course, is that most of the victims did not survive to speak. Worse yet, perhaps, is that the fact that few survivors were ever asked about US participation, and those who did speak out were simply not believed. In the highly politicized era of Presidents Ronald Reagan and George H. W. Bush, those who sought to reveal the true extent of United States involvement were dismissed, rather ironically, as "unobjective." Survivors were branded as mentally unsound. Human rights organizations and scholars faced serious consequences, from funding cuts to FBI harassment.[8] Given these harsh realities, it is perhaps unsurprising that self-censorship crept into many circles. It was only after learning of the CIA's direct involvement in the torture and murder of my husband in Guatemala[9] (see below), and working closely with Sister Dianna Ortiz[10] that I began to ask questions. One by one the survivors began to answer.[11]

Water-boarding

This CIA interrogation method has received much-needed scrutiny, yet remains poorly understood in the US today. It has been used on a number of the current high-value detainees, including Khaled Sheikh Mohammed.[12] Our intelligence leaders tell us that the technique consists of placing a cloth over the victim's head, then pouring water over his face until "he thinks he is going to drown." This sounds rather innocuous. Attorney General Michael Mukasey was hardly alone when he claimed to be uncertain as to whether the method constitutes torture.[13] It sounds far less innocuous when described by the survivors.

"O"

"O" was a member of the resistance forces in Guatemala in 1988, when he was captured alive by the Guatemalan military, secretly detained, and severely tortured. At one point during his ordeal, he was subjected to three consecutive sessions of water-boarding. He was bound and seized by several interrogators, who plunged him head first into a large vat of water, keeping his face well under the surface. He struggled to hold his breath, but finally the cold water rushed into his nose and mouth, causing a searing pain in his head. He thought his eardrums would burst and he was choking terribly. He urinated against his will. Finally he lost consciousness. When he awoke he was on the floor, with an interrogator reviving him. A few minutes later, he was submerged again, with the same results.

> Later, an obvious North American was ushered into the room. His captors treated him with great respect and obeyed all of his orders. The man had a clear American accent and was tall with fair coloring. He questioned "O" at length about Cuba, demanded some photographs. Despite "O" 's frightening physical condition, the man did nothing to halt the torture, or report the situation to the police or an appropriate international forum. Instead he simply left "O" to his fate.[14]

(Ines, see below, suffered the same technique in Honduras.)

Dogs

One of the most horrifying photographs of the Abu Ghraib prisoners depicts a naked man cowering in fear as a ferocious dog leaps towards him. A second image shows him bleeding on the floor, a smiling guard about to sew up his wounds. Initially, government spokespersons insisted that this was an isolated incident, but after many divulgations to the contrary, it became clear that the use of frightening dogs is a standard interrogation technique,[15] and is widely used by US intelligence agents in Iraq, Afghanistan, and elsewhere.

Sister Dianna Ortiz

Sister Dianna was a young US citizen nun sent to serve in Guatemala. She spent several years in a small Mayan town, teaching elementary students. In 1989 she began to receive terrifying death threats, but decided to remain with her children. In November, she was abducted by the security forces and taken to the basement of the Politécnica in Guatemala City. There she was gang-raped and tortured, suffering more than 100 cigarette burns to her back alone. She was also attacked by a terrifying dog, an experience she cannot bear to remember, much less talk about. To this day the bark of a dog, no matter how distant, will cause her to weep and run for shelter.

In the midst of her ordeal, a tall fair man entered the room, speaking Spanish, but with a heavy American accent. He was angry, telling her captors that she was a US citizen and that there was already uproar over her disappearance. He ordered them to dress her and hand her over to him. They answered "Yes, Boss" and obeyed. He told Sister Dianna he was taking her to friends at the embassy, but she leaped from the jeep and ran for her life. The State Department later insisted that no such man could be working for the US government. Instead, official spokespersons strongly implied that she was mentally unstable and did not really know what had happened to her. Years later, a photograph was found of a CIA agent then in Guatemala. The face strongly resembled the police sketch of the man described by Sister Dianna.[16]

A terrifying dog was also used on Ines in Honduras, when she was secretly detained and tortured by members of Battalion 316, with the collaboration of a CIA agent. See below.

Sensory assaults and stress positions

In the midst of the Abu Ghraib scandal, a list of frightening techniques personally authorized by then Secretary of State Donald Rumsfeld was declassified. At the bottom of the list is his hand-written comment, noting that since he himself stands for eight hours or more a day, why should not the detainees?[17] Of course Mr Rumsfeld has the advantage of being permitted to move about during the day, and is not forced to remain in one fixed position. When a detainee is forced to stand stock still for long periods of time his feet and legs begin to swell terribly, causing excruciating pain, and, if the session is too prolonged, kidney damage.

Herbert Anaya, El Salvador[18]

Herbert Anaya was a renowned human rights leader in El Salvador who well understood that he would not survive the war. In 1987, he was seized by military agents in broad daylight and dragged away from his screaming children. He promptly became one of the *desaparecidos* in El Salvador, with the authorities insisting that they had no information as to his whereabouts. Eventually a relative with military connections informed his wife Mirna that he was being held in the basement of the much feared Policia de Hacienda station. She promptly sent her attorney to the building. The lawyer was first met at the door by a Salvadoran police officer, who explained that he would have to get authorization. After a few moments, a US military advisor came to the door and said that access would be granted, but that the man would have to wait for a while. At last the attorney was brought into a small room where he found Anaya, alive but exhausted and pale, sitting in a chair with a large blanket covering his lap. He had been forced to stand for so long that the police were unable to get his shoes back onto his feet. They had covered his swollen limbs so that the lawyer could not witness his condition. Herbert was later released and returned to his office to continue working for human rights. He was shot to death at his home a year later as he prepared his children for school.[19]

John Walker Lindh, American Taliban[20]

Not long after the United States engaged in combat activities in Afghanistan, Afghan General Abdul Rashid Dostum negotiated the surrender of a large number of Taliban soldiers in a remote region of the country. They were packed like sardines into large metal shipping containers on the back of trucks, and transported to another prison. Unfortunately they were given no water, and no air holes were cut into the containers. It is estimated that more than 1,000 of them died, slowly suffocating and going mad in the heat, during the mass transport now known as the Caravan of Death.[21] They were literally baked. Although the CIA and other US intelligence agents were working closely with Dostum, all denied any involvement in or knowledge of the events, insisting that the use of the hot containers was an old torture technique of the Afghan warlords. Not long afterwards, word quickly spread that the detainees in Iraq were being held in hot metal shipping containers, and that John Walker Lindh, the young American Taliban, had also been placed in just such a shipping container by his CIA interrogators.

Not surprisingly, this technique has a long history within the US intelligence networks. Colonel Anne Wright, a military officer and attorney, was with the US forces during the invasion of Grenada. At one point she was horrified to find a number of prisoners suffering in metal containers positioned directly in the fierce sunlight. Shocked, she harshly reprimanded the soldiers and ordered the prisoners released immediately.[22] Until the "war against terror," she had assumed that the incident was a matter of a few poorly trained military policemen. As she witnessed the war efforts unfurl in Afghanistan and Iraq, she resigned from the military after some 30 years of service, and has never returned.

"Inez"[23]

Inez was a young university student in Honduras in 1983 when she and a friend were violently abducted and secretly detained by members of Battalion 316, a notorious Honduran military unit known for its death squad activities. Remarkably, she survived a gamut of torture techniques that would have broken the strongest marine. She too suffered water-boarding that left her naked and unconscious on the floor and she too was subjected to terrifying dog attacks. She also endured what are now coyly known as "stress positions." At one point her hands and feet were tied behind her and she was suspended from the ceiling for hours, in the helicopter position. When asked if this was stressful, she responded that her shoulders were permanently damaged.

Inez also suffered the short shackling technique used in Guantanamo. As reported in declassified FBI files, recalcitrant prisoners were taken to a special cell, stripped naked, and left with their hands and feet chained tightly to the floor, leaving them bent in a painful position. The temperature rose and fell. Blinding strobe lights flashed in their faces, and ever-changing blasting music thundered into their ears throughout the night. They were given no toilet privileges, food, or water. The next morning the FBI agents found their prisoners lying limp on the floor in pools of excrement. Some could not walk. One had pulled the hair out of his head.[24] These techniques had long been banned as torture by the United Nations.

Ines suffered just such combined sensory assaults. She was bound and left blindfolded on the floor with ever-changing temperatures. Icy water was dashed into her face every few minutes, and a loud crashing sound like a jackhammer sounded off and on all night, close to her head. She received no food or toilet privileges. She remembers these combined techniques, together with the constant threats against her family, as the worst of all her suffering.

Ines also reported that an obvious American, known as Mr Mike, came repeatedly to her detention center to discuss information with the torturers, and to give advice. He saw her predicament but did nothing to help her. He reported nothing to the police, the courts, or even her family. One of her torturers later fled to Canada and confessed all, confirming that Mr Mike was a CIA agent. Eventually the CIA itself admitted that Mr Mike not only existed but was their own agent.[25]

"Dr X"

"Dr X" was a young physician in El Salvador who also suffered from stress positions. He was abducted by the Salvadoran army in 1982 and severely tortured. One of his most frightening memories is of hanging from the ceiling by his bound hands, his feet barely touching the floor, a sharpened stake placed into the opening of his rectum. Every time he tried to ease the pain in his hands by putting more weight on his feet, he was impaled. In the room was a North American, laughing.[26]

Electrical shocks

The man on the box

Few of us will forget the now iconic image of the hooded man standing on a box in Abu Ghraib prison, long electrical wires hanging from his hands and genitals. The man was warned not to move his raised arms, and he tried to comply. After an agonizing period of time his hands slipped downwards and he was blown of the box by the ensuing and violent electrical shock.

Once again we were told that this was the bizarre invention of a young soldier trying to amuse himself on a late evening shift. Intelligence experts from around the world tell us a different story. The technique was immediately recognized as a well developed and long utilized interrogation method. It is known as the Vietnam Position, because that is where it originated.[27]

"David"

David was a young student in the 1960s in Guatemala. He and a young friend were walking the streets of the capital when they were seized by soldiers and thrown into a moving vehicle. Both were severely tortured. During one session, David was bound to a special metal chair and given severe electrical shocks, which even today make him weep to describe. A tall fair man with a heavy American accent was present, instructing the torturer to place the wires at certain places in David's mouth and across his body, in order to maximize the pain.[28]

Marcos Arruda

During this time period, Dan Mitreone was becoming notorious for teaching electrical shock torture in both Brazil and Uruguay.[29] Marcos Arruda, a young student in Brazil, was one of the victims. Arrested in 1970, he was given electrical shocks to the toes, genitals, belly, ears, and mouth until he went into convulsions. There were Americans in the secret prison at the time.[30]

Ghost prisoners

The grim image of a battered man, dead and packed in ice at the Abu Ghraib prison, speaks volumes to many of us. The man was a prisoner of the CIA, and was apparently beaten to death during his interrogation sessions. No one knew his name, because the CIA agents were holding him secretly, and had forbidden the soldiers to properly register him. His whereabouts were never reported to his family members or to the Red Cross. After his death, an IV was placed in his arm so that he would appear to be unconscious. His corpse was smuggled out of the prison and buried in an unidentified location.

Who was this man? Are his family members searching for him, desperate to know if he is dead or alive, in need of care or comfort? How many of these ghost prisoners exist? What have we done with them?[31]

The concept of ghost prisoners, of course, is hardly new. In Latin America they are known as the *desaparecidos* or disappeared, and their ranks are vast indeed. From the Mothers of the Plaza de Mayo in Argentina to the members of the Grupo de Apoyo Mutuo in Guatemala, surviving loved ones still struggle to learn the truth about these vanished human beings and to recover their remains. The scars run deep. In Argentina, the Grandmothers still search for grandchildren born in secret cells and sold into adoption. Indeed the official practices of "disappearances" or ghost prisoners have been declared a form of psychological torture, not only of the prisoners themselves, but of their families as well.

US Department of State officials, quickly echoed by military and intelligence spokespersons, have long declared this cruel practice to be a local phenomenon, the natural result of a "violent culture." Additional funding was needed to "professionalize" the local troops and police and to teach them the "American way" of doing things. As with torture, any link between US agents and the disappearances was fiercely denied. As with torture, the denial was false.

"Everardo"

The case of Efraín Bámaca Velásquez, or Comandante Everardo, is hardly unique. Rather, it is merely typical of what became a day-to-day occurrence in Latin America during the "dirty wars." However, it is instructive with regards to the many resulting official US admissions.

A Mayan villager who rose to the highest ranks of the resistance movement in Guatemala, Everardo was captured by the army in 1992. He had survived some 17 years of combat, and given his rank, he possessed voluminous and crucial information. He became a long-term prisoner of the G-2, or military intelligence officers, who decided to fake his death in order to evade international human rights outcry. He was secretly detained, and tortured repeatedly for the next three years. He was also held in a full body cast so that he could not escape. Despite everything, he never gave true information, instead leading one platoon into a fierce ambush. His captors, frustrated, eventually ordered his extrajudicial execution. Although there are many versions of his death, the most credible are that he was either thrown from a helicopter or dismembered and scattered across a sugarcane field.[32]

Throughout his captivity, desperate efforts were made to save his life. The US ambassador and CIA spokespersons reported to all inquiries from his US citizen wife, the US Congress, the UN and the OAS, that they had no information about the case. In 1995 official disclosures revealed that Everardo had been tortured and killed by Guatemalan intelligence officers working as paid CIA informants or "assets." The CIA had known of his detention and torture and fully informed the embassy during the first week of his capture. CIA officials continued to pay the torturers for information about Mr Bámaca, and some 350 other secret prisoners, for the next three years and pass the information on to the State Department. By the time the truth was told, all were dead.

A fundamental question: why?

The human rights history of Latin America alone presents a clear, albeit grim, picture of the long-term participation of the United States in the secret detention and torture of civilian dissidents and prisoners of war. That history is echoed in other regions as well where the CIA advised and even led coups and counterinsurgency campaigns, such as Vietnam, the Philippines and Iran. The interrogation techniques used today are nothing new. As the above testimonies indicate, the techniques were designed by the CIA over many decades, then taught and utilized wherever US intelligence agents deemed them useful. The damage inflicted on the prisoners, their families, and their communities were both permanent and profound. Those of us who choose to live in the United States and enjoy its privileges thus face a disturbing question. Why?

As discussed above, the answer appears to be simple enough. Greed is the common denominator, the factor linking every CIA-backed coup. The case of Guatemala is a particularly useful example, given the startling historical parallels to the situation in Iraq during the US presidency of George W. Bush.

Guatemala has always faced severe societal divisions and unrest. Some 80 percent of the population is comprised of the indigenous Mayan people, yet a tiny minority of European descent owns virtually all of the land. Since there is little national industry, the landless face a life of near starvation. From 1944 through 1954 the Guatemalan people enjoyed what they fondly remember as the "Ten Years of Spring." President Arevalo was popularly elected in 1944 and began a series of basic reforms to alleviate poverty and introduce basic democratic rights. He was followed by President Jacobo Arbenz who continued these efforts. Recognizing the urgent need for land reform, he sponsored a limited program applying only to the largest landowners, and only to unused acreage. The government purchased the land at the value declared on the owners' tax forms, then sold it at low monthly rates to peasant cooperatives. President Arbenz began with his own landholdings, and the program immediately flourished.[33]

Sadly, one of the largest landowners in Guatemala was the United Fruit Company, which had vastly understated the value of its holdings on its tax returns. When portions of its land were purchased, company leaders flew to Washington DC and cried communism.[34] The response was swift. In 1954 the CIA organized a rag-tag group of army dissidents and carried out a military coup, forcing Arbenz into exile, and resulting in a bloodbath of frightening proportions. In an eerie sneak preview of later US "war against terror" policies in Iraq, Washington then decided to make Guatemala a "showcase of democracy," pouring funding into the country in order to exhibit the superiority of the capitalist model.[35] The project failed miserably. A 35-year civil war ensued, the army carried out a campaign of genocide against the Mayans, and the society remains devastated even today.

Although Arbenz was gone, the genie had escaped the bottle. The reform movement had taken on a life of its own. Church leaders worked with fledgling peasant cooperatives, rural health projects, and literacy campaigns. Unions took root in the city as well as the countryside. Perhaps most importantly, the Mayan civil rights movement grew powerful. The army, together with the CIA, responded with a terrifying 35-year counterinsurgency campaign that earned Guatemala the title of worst human rights violator in the hemisphere. Priests were shot to death in their churches, unions were decimated, and the universities lost their most gifted members to marauding death squads. Miss Guatemala, a beauty queen suspected of subversion, was left hacked to death on a main roadway. The Mayans, as always, were the hardest hit.[36]

And so it continued for decades. The devastating consequences to the people of Guatemala are described in the *Memoria del Silencio* report by the United Nations.[37] Some 200,000 people were either murdered or disappeared, a toll higher than Chile, Argentina, and El Salvador combined. More than 94 percent of these killings were carried out by the Guatemalan military. The civilian institutions remain paralyzed. Throughout the country, the scars and trauma remain only too evident, with people distrustful of their neighbors and fearful of community affairs.

This grim history is hardly unique. Rather, it is the history of the hemisphere, from the rich farmlands of El Salvador and Honduras, to Panama with its priceless canal, to the mines and natural resources of Brazil and Chile.

As for Iraq, it would seem that the people of the United States are working towards the same results. US economic interests, this time in oil, are only too obvious. George W. Bush, during his first campaign for the presidency, promised that he would return to Iraq to "finish what his father had started." This was long before the attack on the World Trade Center, and of course it is widely believed that the Bush family fortune, much like that of Bush's Vice-President Dick Cheney's family, has roots in petroleum sales. As the US public later learned, there were never weapons of mass destruction in Iraq, any more than there was a communist threat in Guatemala. Osama Bin Laden and his Al-Qaeda troops were never there. The true motive of the US government in sending its young soldiers into a brutal war is simply the protection of US economic interests.

Money. This has always been the true interest behind US policies. The emotional slogans about preventing communist takeovers, fighting the drug wars, protecting democracy, and now, engaging in the "war against terror," in the end are only masks for extraordinary national greed. Such stirring words make the actions appear justified, necessary, even heroic.

Yet we who choose to live in the United States must beware of false appearances. In the end we are what we do. Ours is a nation grown soft on excess, with a standard of living unheard of in almost all other societies. We citizens care little about the true costs to others of our exorbitant lifestyles; the peasant working the banana plantations for less than a dollar a day, the unhealthy child in the sweatshops, the Iraqi civilians dead at the roadsides. We accept these sacrifices as our due. Worse yet, we accept the suffering of persons of color as inevitable, as realities which, albeit sad, do not require any sacrifices on our part. We turn a blind eye to the fact that we ourselves are the cause of such suffering. Are we our brothers' keepers? According to our American values, clearly not.

In the end however, we must answer for the campaigns of torture and brutality carried out in our names and for our benefit. If we remain silent, then we are complicit.

Notes and references

1 See, generally, S. Schlesinger and S. Kinzer, *Bitter Fruit: The Untold Story of the American Coup in Guatemala*, New York: Doubleday, 1982; A. J. Langguth, *Hidden Terrors: The Truth About US Police Operations in Latin America*, New York: Pantheon Books, 1978 (on Brazil and Uruguay); J. K. Harbury, *Truth, Torture and the American Way: The History and Consequences of US Involvement in Torture*, Boston: Beacon Press, 2005.

2 Comisión para el Esclarecimiento Histórico (CEH), *Guatemala: memoria del silencio*, Guatemala City: United Nations Office for Project Services, 1999; P. Kornbluh, *The Pinochet File: A Declassified Dossier on Atrocity and Accountability*, New York: New Press, 2003 (on Chile); G. Cohn and G. Thompson, "Unearthed: Fatal Secrets," *Baltimore Sun*, June 11–18, 1995 (on Honduras).

3 T. Barry and D. Preusch, *The Central America Fact Book*, New York: Grove Press, 1986; J. Handy, *Gift of the Devil: A History of Guatemala*, Boston: South End Press, 1984; J. G. Carney, *To Be a Christian Is To Be a Revolutionary: The Autobiography of Father James Guadalupe Carney*, New York: Harper & Row, 1987 (on Honduras).

4 See, for example, the role of the United Fruit Company in Guatemala: Schlesinger and Kinzer, *Bitter Fruit*.

5 See, for example, the case of Saddam Saleh Aboud, who was tortured by US troops in Abu Ghraib, and "confessed" that he was Osama Bin Laden in disguise. He was later released for lack of evidence. I. Fisher, "Iraqi Tells of Abuse, from Ridicule to Rape Threat," *New York Times*, New York, May 14, 2004. See also comments of US interrogator Don Dzagulones, cited in J. Conroy, *Unspeakable Acts, Ordinary People: The Dynamics of Torture*, New York: Knopf, 2000, p. 113; Harbury, *Truth, Torture and the American Way*, pp. 161–5.

6 Harbury, *Truth, Torture and the American Way*, pp. 20–5; and official documents cited therein.

7 A. Gonzalez, "Decision re Application of the Geneva Convention on Prisoners of War to the Conflict with Al-Qaeda and the Taliban," Memorandum to the President, January 25, 2002, set forth in K. Greenberg, J. Dratel, and A. Lewis, *The Torture Papers: The Road to Abu Ghraib*, New York: Cambridge University Press, 2005.

8 W. King, "An FBI Inquiry Fed by Informer Emerges in Analysis of Documents," *New York Times*, February 13, 1988.

9 J. Harbury, *Searching for Everardo*, New York: Warner Books, 1996. Efraín Bámaca Velásquez was secretly detained and tortured for nearly three years by Guatemalan intelligence officers on CIA payroll, with the full knowledge and approval of the CIA. See also, Harbury, *Truth, Torture and the American Way*, pp. 56–65; and documents cited therein.

10 D. Ortiz, with P. Davis, *The Blindfold's Eyes: My Journey from Torture to Truth*, New York: Orbis Books, 2002. Sister Dianna was severely tortured in Guatemala until an American agent entered her cell and demanded her release to him because she was a US citizen.

11 A number of survivors were either friends or relatives of Central American refugees I had known for many years. They contacted me after the national publicity about my husband's murder. I also reached out to human rights organizations in Latin America, who quickly responded either about their members or about their own grim experiences. With the great generosity of the Radcliffe Institute of Advanced Studies, I was able to comb the vast archives at Harvard University, to locate still other cases. I travelled as necessary to meet with the survivors in person, interviewing them for several hours, and sharing my written accounts with them to review for any inaccuracies. Most remain in close contact with me today, and have participated in joint efforts to inform human rights organizations, members of Congress, and the United Nations, about the true extent of US involvement in torture.

12 J. Risen, D. Johnson, and N. Lewis, "Harsh CIA Methods Cited in Top Qaeda Interrogation," *New York Times*, New York, May 13, 2004, p. A1, cited in Harbury, *Truth, Torture and the American Way*, pp. 14–15.
13 D. Eggen, "Mukasey Losing Democrats' Backing," *Washington Post*, October 31, 2007.
14 J. Harbury, Personal interviews of "O," 1996, 1998, and 2006.
15 D. Jehl and E. Schmitt, "The Reach of War: Abuse; Dogs and Other Harsh Tactics Linked to Military Intelligence," *New York Times*, May 22, 2004.
16 Harbury, *Truth, Torture and the American Way*, pp. 69–70.
17 J. Diamond, "Rumsfeld OK'd Harsh Treatment," *USA Today*, June 22, 2004.
18 Personal communication with Judge Mirna Perla Anaya, widow of Herbert Anaya, November 2003.
19 Harbury, *Truth, Torture and the American Way*, pp. 74–6.
20 Ibid, pp. 4–6, citing Proffer of Facts, *US v. Lindh*.
21 B. Deghanpisheh, J. Barry, and R. Gutman, "The Death Convoy of Afghanistan," *Newsweek*, August 26, 2002, pp. 22–30.
22 Personal communication with Anne Wright, July 2005.
23 Harbury, *Truth, Torture and the American Way*, pp. 87–9; citing Cohn and Thompson, "Unearthed."
24 C. Leoning, "Further Detainee Abuse Alleged," *Washington Post*, December 26, 2004; N. Lewis, "Broad Use of Harsh Tactics Is Described at Cuba Base," *New York Times*, October 17, 2004.
25 Cohn and Thompson, "Unearthed."
26 J. Harbury, interviews of "Dr X," 2005.
27 J. Barry, M. Hirsch, and M. Issikoff, "The Roots of Torture," *Newsweek*, May 24, 2004.
28 Personal communication with "David," 2005.
29 Langguth, *Hidden Terrors*; M. H. Cosculluela, *Pasaporte 11333: ocho años con la CIA*, Havana: Editorial de Ciencias Sociales, 1978.
30 Personal communication with Marcos Arruda, 2005; see Langguth, *Hidden Terrors*, pp. 208–16.
31 Harbury, *Truth, Torture and the American Way*, citing J. Risen and D. Johnson, "Photos of the Dead May Indicate Graver Abuses," *New York Times*, May 7, 2004; E. Schmitt, "Four Navy Commandos Are Charged with Abuse," *New York Times*, September 4, 2004; D. Priest and J. Stephens, "The Road to Abu Ghraib," *Washington Post*, May 11, 2004.
32 Harbury, *Searching for Everardo*.
33 Schlesinger and Kinzer, *Bitter Fruit*, pp. 54–60.
34 See generally, Schlesinger and Kinzer, *Bitter Fruit*, pp. 66–77.
35 Ibid, pp. 233–4.
36 See generally Handy, *Gift of the Devil*.
37 CEH, *Guatemala*.

7 State violence and repression in Rosario during the Argentine dictatorship, 1976–83[1]

Gabriela Aguila

Latin American history in the twentieth century has been strongly marked by the constant presence of the armed forces in political life, be it through *coups d'état*, dictatorships, or exceptional regimes. Virtually none of the countries in the area has been exempt from these experiences. They have been one of the characteristic features of these political systems, which bluntly showed their difficulties in consolidating democratic and stable political orders. But although dictatorships were not a new phenomenon in Latin America, the military governments that settled themselves between the 1960s and the 1970s – in particular in Brazil, Chile, Uruguay, and Argentina – exhibited new features which were distinct from those of other authoritarian regimes, in terms of both their strategies and practices, and of the deep changes they introduced in their respective national histories.[2]

Throughout the decade of 1970 the Latin American Southern Cone was the setting for the bloodiest military dictatorship the region experienced.[3] It was marked, as they all were, by far-reaching repressive processes which included murders and disappearances, concentration camps, prisons, and exile. Mass extermination and institutionalized terror became the preferred practices military states used, to establish order in the face of intense social and political mobilizations which characterized nations of the region, and which had their roots in the 1960s.[4] Traditional political parties' inability to contain the social unrest, together with the advance of left-wing forces of different types, served as the states' motivation for the modernization of the armed forces that were in charge of implementing a systematic repressive strategy, the fundamental ideological support of which was the so-called Doctrine of National Security.

The traditional language of the Cold War, which focused on the anti-communist fight, articulated a logic of defense of a "national security" threatened by an "internal enemy" who was present, according to this conception, in all the areas and sectors of society, and who had to be fought by means of "unconventional" methods. And although the first to suffer the repression were the sectors which had mobilized during the period preceding the dictatorships, state terror spread over the whole of society.

It was in this context of the settlement of a new type of military dictatorships in the South Cone that the Argentine *coup d'état* took place. The political-institutional crisis of the Peronist government (1973–6) was due to multiple factors, including a rising inflationary spiral which had deteriorated the economic situation and real salaries, the lack of representativeness and credibility of the traditional political parties, and an increasing political and social mobilization which had characterized the previous years and had several actors: the labor movement, the guerrilla organizations, the left. The ruling party, with an increasingly small mandate, thanks both to pressures from social organizations and discontent from the right wing, was resolved by a new irruption of the armed forces onto the political scene.

On March 24, 1976, the armed forces began what would be the last of the military dictatorships in Argentina in the twentieth century. The overthrow of the debilitated government of María Estela (also known as Isabel) Martínez de Perón began the self-proclaimed Process of National Reorganization, the tragic extension of a succession of *coups d'état* and extraordinary military regimes that had marked the national political history for more than 50 years.

The *coup d'état* led by Lieutenant Jorge Rafael Videla at first appeared to be similar to one of the cyclical interruptions of the constitutional order that the country had experienced since 1930. However, it soon became evident that the armed forces had set more ambitious objectives, completely taking over the control of the state with the purpose of restructuring the economic, social, and political organization which had been in effect in previous decades.

Such restructuring intentions included the implementation of a new economic model with the following goals: guaranteeing the investment and reproduction of capital under conditions of a new capitalism formed at an international level and favoring the wealthiest economic groups; the reorganization of the operation of the state, limiting the ability of citizens to intervene; and, in particular, a dramatic reduction in the strong influence that unions had acquired both inside and outside the workplace. Goals for the military included transforming the prevailing political system by restricting the centrality of party organizations and, above all, bringing a dramatic and definitive end to the social and political mobilization which had increased remarkably in the early years of the 1970s.[5]

For the military that took power in March 1976, setting in motion such a project of comprehensive transformation required the initial reestablishment of order. From our viewpoint, this aspect – predominantly associated with the use of social and political terror – acquires a substantive character, as it both became a requisite for and accompanied the deployment of the military project objectives: the reformulation of the accumulation and development model; the resolution of the bourgeois domination crisis; the establishment of an authoritarian and stable political order; the shaping of a disciplined, immobilized, and fragmented society. In this sense, the use of violence was the preliminary and founding condition of the more comprehensive program designed and implemented by the Argentine military.

The armed forces made its central objective the defeat of "subversion," a label it used to categorize activities of all those characterized as "enemies" of the system.[6] It assumed a role as the incarnation of the "national essence," the mission of which was to "cure" a society in danger of dismemberment. To this end it deployed a complex repressive machinery, within the framework of combat, the nature of which was strictly warlike. Thus military intervention in the "war" against "subversion" became, at the same time, the supreme objective and one of the main sources for legitimization of the regime.[7]

In addition, the military state deployed a set of mechanisms of social discipline, the intention of which was to modify individual and collective values and practices, and which covered all the spheres of the state–society relationship, ranging from education to the mass media. However, this organization, which was imposed from the top by the military regime over a mostly silent society, relied not only on terror but also on the existence – particularly visible in its early stages – of social and political support of the regime.

Without overlooking the fact that the dictatorship implemented a political and social project on a national scale and a repressive strategy which covered the entire territory, in this study we will analyze the particular case of the city of Rosario,[8] focusing on the connection between the practices in which the dictatorship engaged in carrying out genocide, and their effects on the society as a whole. In addition to exploring the particulars of the repression at a local level, and analyzing some social behaviors which marked this period, this inquiry also articulates the continuity between this complex phase of recent history and the present, which is confirmed in the persistent marks that the military dictatorship has left on the individual and collective memory(ies) of people living in the city.

The modalities of the repression[9]

Although the repressive actions had begun well before the *coup d'état*, and were tolerated and protected by the constitutional government and connected to the activities of the para-police bands of the Anti-Communist Argentine Alliance (the Triple A) in the realms of politics, unions, and education,[10] such actions reached much greater proportions with the *coup* of March 1976. The armed forces took over command and responsibility for carrying out repressive actions, coordinating the activities of the security bodies at a national level[11] and replacing the "Triple A's" selective repression with the efficient machinery of the terrorist state. Within this new framework, the modality of repression included a double system supported by state power, in which a facade of legality[12] was combined with the clandestine or paralegal activities of "task forces."

The repressive work implemented since the *coup d'état* had specific characteristics: it was designed, coordinated and executed by the armed forces and counted on the active participation of other repressive forces (including the federal or provincial police); it was marked by a fundamentally clandestine or "paralegal" nature, characterized by the work of the "task groups" and the existence of clandestine detention centers; it incorporated the systematic use of torture on prisoners, kidnapping, shootings, and disappearances, as well as the appropriation of minors born in captivity, and common crimes. It was led by a relentless logic which delimited the annihilation of the political-military organizations' militants as well as their superficial structures as an objective, but also included a touch of chance, as it pursued – and eventually eliminated – people with no political relevance.

Repressive practice followed a territorial scheme represented by dividing the forces into army corps (1st, 2nd, 3rd, 4th, 5th), each of them responsible for a system of clandestine detention centers scattered throughout the entire nation, and task forces with different areas of operation.[13] In the particular case of the 2nd Corps, whose headquarters were in the city of Rosario, the provincial police and penitentiary forces had been placed under the "operational control" of the command of that army corps since late 1975, with the objective of repressing "subversion."[14] After 1975 repressive activities became more intense and included the detention of militants, "rake" operations in manufacturing areas (which meant the control of the population and eventually massive detentions), and control over the university and the urban front in general. Prisons began to increase their populations, and improvised detention centers began to appear at military buildings, police stations, and at the police headquarters in Rosario.

In September 1975, Lieutenant General Genaro Díaz Bessone assumed leadership of the 2nd Corps. In October 1976, after his appointment to lead the national planning ministry, the military command was transferred to Lieutenant General Leopoldo Fortunato Galtieri until, in 1979, changes higher up in the armed forces led him to more senior assignments.[15] In early March 1976, Commander of the Gendarmerie Agustín Feced was appointed as chief of police of Regional Unit II. Feced would play a central role in the design and execution of the repression within the scope of the 2nd Corps.[16]

From that moment on, the police and military forces were reorganized and re-coordinated, and task forces began their activities, the main objective of which was to carry out repressive actions. These forces were formed by members of the police and/or military forces, and included the participation of some civilians. In several cases, their members had already been part of semi-official clandestine groups. They learned to use nicknames or false names and disguises. In several cases, they had already been part of semi-official clandestine groups such as Triple A, where they had acquired experience in the "counterinsurgency fight" by committing kidnappings, murders, and criminal activities. These gangs or brigades generally operated in civilian clothing and on some occasions used vehicles without visible identification. They were also in charge of kidnapping, murdering, torturing and/or "disappearing" people or corpses, as well as actions such as the looting of raided homes. Within the new context the military regime provided police and military intelligence services for the task of locating those individuals or groups they targeted for eradication, many of whom had already been detected and followed since the beginning of the 1970s.

Potential victims of the repression were designated by reference to their militant activities or to some degree of connection with what police and intelligence jargon called "gangs of subversive criminals" or "gangs of terrorist criminals," mainly formed by political-military organizations which operated at the regional level and included legal divisions or "surface" structures at the neighborhood, union, and educational levels.[17]

However, the scope of the category of "subversive criminal" was as broad as it was blurry, and was made to include both the militants of guerrilla organizations and the members of other movements, generally of a left-wing nature, who carried out their activities in the city or in nearby towns. A person was a "subversive criminal" because he or she was "active" in student centers, in neighborhoods, or in the internal commissions of labor unions, or because he or she was found to participate in what the intelligence services called "insurgent activities," political acts such as painting slogans, throwing leaflets on the street, or simply possessing or reading a publication of those organizations.

Once the target was detected, the task forces began their activities, usually in conjunction with officers from various police or military forces, which consisted of breaking into homes and/or arrests – usually brutal – of individuals or groups who were transferred to police buildings or clandestine detention centers operating in the area.[18] Additionally, in many cases these operations ended with the public street execution of some of the victims.[19]

Together with the task groups, clandestine detention centers formed the core of repressive activities. They began to operate fully by 1976, and were improvised at police or military buildings or at homes or country estates which were assigned for such purposes.[20] Their main functions were to provide places for obtaining information, especially by means of torture,[21] and to temporarily confine detainees. Those who arrived at the centers were blindfolded and tied, were subjected to sessions of torture, and were kept under subhuman conditions, until the torturers "completed" the task of extracting information.

The time of detention was as arbitrary as it was variable. It could include transfers to more than one camp; and detainees were subjected to the most aberrant methods of torture, with no defense against oppressors who exercised brutal and absolute power within the confines of the premises. They dehumanized their victims, instilling feelings of defeat and terror until, finally, police or military authorities decided their fates.[22] The concentration camps of the Argentine dictatorship could be horrific places of transit towards death or disappearance or, in cases in which detainees gained recognition or legal status, could represent steps towards conviction and a sentence of several years in prison.

The local press, very slowly, as months went by, began to report some episodes by transcribing the communications of the 2nd Corps. These accounts, along with police reports, described police operations and home raids and the consequent discoveries of weapons, explosives, documentation or print materials, or armed confrontations between "subversive criminals" and "legal forces." Only occasionally did the accounts identify the bodies, which invariably belonged to the "subversives." The reconstruction of many of these events showed that such confrontations were actually executions of unarmed persons who, after having been imprisoned at the clandestine detention centers where they had been tortured, were murdered and thrown into the street, to be subsequently transferred to the city morgues and buried, on many occasions as unidentified corpses in unmarked graves in different public cemeteries in Rosario and other small cities.[23]

Although in some cases the corpses could be identified and handed over to their families, the "disappearance" of persons was one of the strategies used by the repressive forces of the 2nd Corps. The majority of those kept at detention centers remained classified for some time as "disappeared" or "unrecognized." The police and military forces adopted systematic denial, or, alternatively, the release of succinct reports which indicated that these persons had been quickly released and claimed that their final destination was unknown.

On the other hand, many of those who escaped death were then placed in the hands of the National Executive Power as political prisoners, and in some cases were subjected to court martial proceedings which were held at the command headquarters of the 2nd Corps. In other cases, criminal charges were brought in the federal court, generally for the violation of laws against subversive activities, and victims were sentenced to several years in prison.

By 1977, as a result of the fierceness of the repression, it had become evident that the armed organizations had entirely lost their operational capacity. Constant public statements made by military leaders, claiming that they had "left subversion with no leaders,"[24] did not stop the detentions and the raids coordinated by so-called "legal forces."

The several hundreds of "disappeared" and the thousands of detainees who went through the clandestine centers or the prisons of the 2nd Corps formed a heterogeneous group. It was made up not only of militants who were mostly young men and women with different degrees of responsibility and involvement in various political organizations, but also of people who had been detained because they were neighbors, relatives, or friends of those whom the police and military forces persecuted. On many occasions those targeted were accused of not reporting, or of hiding, "subversive criminals." For the repressive forces, it was not only about persecuting militants or eliminating political organizations, but also about destroying social, political, and family networks, extending the persecution to the "accomplices," and attempting to wipe out the social and political movement to which they belonged.[25]

From a more general perspective, it was not only insurgent groups but also the entire society that was the target of the repressive onslaught implemented by security organizations; and so streets, schools and universities, labor unions, and areas of citizens' private lives became the battlefields of this conflict. Workers suffered a hard onslaught as a result of both physical coercion and the individual and collective terror, which seriously affected their capacity to respond and significantly reduced the activity of labor unions.[26] This "disciplinary" action was combined with a corporate offensive within the labor sphere to undermine working conditions. Workers' uncertainty due to the threat of dismissals, and the undoing of all the labor movement's achievements, engendered an outlook dominated by fear.

After the *coup d'état*, a series of measures for the restriction of labor union activities was set in motion.[27] The government took control of the most important unions, with the result that those sectors which had shown the highest level of activity during the preceding period significantly reduced their presence in the political and union scene. This happened to the unions of the northern area of

Gran Rosario and to the large industrial labor unions. In addition, union leadership was affected by freezing union activity. The local General Labor Confederation and a handful of unions remained under the control of the military until the early years of the 1980s.

The repression was also aimed at the educational system and, in particular, at the university, which was the stronghold of the so-called "ideologists of subversion."[28] It resulted not only in the persecution and disappearance of teachers and students, but also in the control of educational content, the introduction of strict disciplinary measures for students, and the eradication of political activities from campuses. Also, in addition to the brutal action of the repressive squads resulting in death and disappearances mostly of young people, a systematic offensive was carried out over the society as a whole and, in particular, against young people in their social spheres, especially reflected in the demonization of evening activities and the imposition of reactionary values which had an impact on the everyday lives of these age groups.[29]

In 1978, the municipality coined the slogan "Rosario: a clean city, a healthy city, an educated city" and Captain Augusto F. Cristiani, head of the city council, sought to promote this image.[30] He had the enthusiastic support of the so-called "representative" sectors of the community, and his image was the visible face of the state terror imposed after March 1976. The success of the repressive strategy was measured, in those early years, by the nearly complete absence of opposition and the widespread apathy of the citizens of Rosario. The silence was only broken spasmodically with the nationalist impetus provided by the government, such as in 1978, when Rosario became one of the venues for the Football World Cup Championship.

Secretary of State Henry Kissinger arrived in Argentina to attend the World Cup, alongside the junta military leaders. Kissinger's warm welcome took place in the context of efforts made by top military commanders to stress to their distinguished visitor the many similarities between the US and Argentina, especially with regards to doctrines of anticommunism and the Cold War in the country. Kissinger's visit also took place in the context of widespread torture and the implementation of concentration camps. More than anything, however, Kissinger's presence in Argentina demonstrated the full support of the US to Argentina's reorganization process.[31]

Individual and collective memory(ies) of the dictatorship

It is no news to say that the *coup d'état* of March 1976 met with the approval or indifference of the majority of Argentine society; the city of Rosario was no exception. The military coup was the last stage of along process of the alienation of society from the political order, and the degradation of state power. A crisis of representation by traditional parties, intensified by the *crescendo* of violence, marked the 1973–6 period. The diagnosis that the armed forces perceived "subversion" as the main threat, and that they could implement drastic solutions in order to eradicate it, found a significant social base of support.

The absence of conflicting voices – an absence which was particularly visible in the first stages of the dictatorship – was the result, to a large extent, of the vote of confidence that significant sectors gave to the military government, together with the active collaboration of political leaders, members of corporate organizations, ecclesiastical sectors, and the media.[32] The analysis of the bloodiest dictatorship in the entire Argentine history must take into consideration this complex equation built on terror and social support, without forgetting the fact that there were different degrees of responsibility and collaboration and that, in spite of the omnipresence of state terror and authoritarianism, there were different forms of resistance.[33]

Although a large percentage of the repressive activities were carried out clandestinely and, supposedly, away from public view, it is impossible to deny the fact that many people were witnesses of these events. The most important detention center in Rosario, the Information Service, was located right in the middle of the city center, surrounded by private homes, a place where thousands of citizens passed by every day. Many of the other detention centers were located within the urban perimeter or in nearby towns, and some were rented out by their owners to the security organizations.

Moreover, although most of the procedures carried out by the repressive forces were performed at night or in the early morning, others took place in broad daylight, generally with the mobilization of many officers both in civilian clothes and in uniforms, with a remarkable display of firepower (assault vehicles, long weapons, tanks, etc.). Streets were blocked, homes were raided, and neighbors were alerted so that they could stay in their homes. Common practices included stealing belongings or partially destroying the houses of the detainees, threatening neighbors or the passers-by who were watching the procedures and were forced to act as "witnesses," and even detaining some of those passers-by. This ostentatious repression was an integral part of the atmosphere of terror implemented by the dictatorship.

The concept of the "internal enemy" which repressive forces used promoted the image of a society which was entirely affected, in all its areas, by the activities of "subversion." It cast a cloak of suspicion over the behaviors of the inhabitants, as the repressors themselves repeatedly urged citizens to "report extremist elements," thus effectively spreading a stereotype of "subversive" criminals which encouraged the prejudices of the community and had the open objective of engaging the participation of the society in that fight. The dictatorship established an oppressive atmosphere in which denunciation and suspicion became widespread, while a largely silent and/or indifferent society acted as if nothing was happening. Yet, they saw or knew vaguely of the raids, kidnappings, and disappearances which the security forces perpetrated. It would be interesting to ask ourselves whether the family and social silence which was imposed as a widespread behavior represented the best expression of an indulgent (complicit?) society, an indispensable index of the state terror and its efficacy.

Members of human rights organizations began to break the society's silence after 1978, supported by the international repercussions of the reports surfacing regarding the brutal violations of people's rights and integrity committed in Argentina. For several years, however, Argentine society refused to accept that the reports and the international condemnation had grounds which were more solid than what the executors and legitimators of that macabre plan were willing to admit.[34]

Only in 1982, with the end of the Malvinas/Falklands War, when social and political discontent was beginning to be expressed, did the reports of the human rights organizations have an impact. Finally, the city became willing to listen, when their long and, until then, lonely fight became articulated, in conjunction with the claims of other social and political sectors, accompanying the accelerated disintegration of the military regime.

The end of the dictatorship and the lifting of the veil which had concealed the character and features of the repression was followed by the systematic construction of mechanisms of concealment and denial, expressed in the "theory of the two demons" or the laws of impunity,[35] which partially explain why the murderers and their collaborators are still walking the streets of the city, and why many of those who legitimated the dictatorship still hold important positions of power in politics, in the media, or in local and provincial corporate associations. Nevertheless, during the post-dictatorial years, the human rights organizations continued, both in the national sphere and in Rosario city, with their incessant struggle for truth and justice, questioning the intent to close that past and the state's refusal to penalize the lese humanity crimes perpetrated during the dictatorship.

Generally speaking, the situation of the city of Rosario is not so different from that of the rest of the country, in that there are no clear and systematic policies for the preservation of the memory of the dictatorship. This is true also of the places associated with the repression, such as command headquarters of the 2nd Corps, or the police station, scenes of disputes which illustrate the enormous difficulties facing those seeking to preserve memories of the dictatorship's actions in the city.[36] Only in a few cases is there a will to preserve those locations by turning them into places where the horrors that the society of Rosario experienced during the military dictatorship can be remembered. It is important to mention that in those cases which have been solved positively, the fundamental reason has been the action and decisions of human rights organizations, of sectors which are sensitive to the need for this type of vindication, and of some news media.

Moreover, some of the cases aimed at finding the "historical truth" about repression within the command of the 2nd Corps have been opened only in the last few years, after the abolition of the laws of impunity. As happened in other cities in Argentina, in recent years, court cases that had been closed since the mid-1980s have been re-opened. Likewise, other cases in which human rights violations are being investigated have been initiated or reactivated, making possible the imputation and, in very few cases, the conviction of the perpetrators. In Rosario's federal courts, the so called "Feced Cause" is one of them: the most important and voluminous file in which crimes perpetrated by the repressive forces in the sphere of the 2nd Army Corps and the south of the province are investigated. There are also others related to clandestine centers that operated in the area. On top of that there is the identification of bone remains of missing people by forensic anthropologists and, through this, the clarification of some of the dynamics of the repressive action.[37] In addition, there is the implementation, in more recent times, of a state human rights policy which contrasts strongly with the one that dominated in almost the last two decades of democratic governments.

There is no doubt that the retrieval of these places, the promotion of the "trials for truth," and the historical investigations play a particularly central role in confronting the systematic construction of obscurity which has characterized Argentina in the last few decades. However, the road ahead is still extremely long. The retrieval of individual and collective memories of the dictatorship requires the convergence of many efforts, efforts which have often been fragmented. It is necessary to confront the silence of those who have been accomplices, by opening debates which have remained closed down for more than two decades. It is essential for this society to decide, once and for all, to face its past of extreme suppression. Only in this way will these tasks of remembering be able, not only to settle a traumatic past, but also to build a social order which is more fair, equal, and democratic, and which under no circumstances can be based on silence, lies, and oblivion.

Notes and references

1 This chapter is a broadened version of the text published as "Dictatorship, Society and Genocide in Argentina: Repression in Rosario, 1976–1983," *Journal of Genocide Research* 8, 2, 2006, pp. 169–90.
2 For a characterization of these "new" dictatorships see I. Cheresky and J. Chonchol (eds), *Crisis y transformación de los regímenes autoritarios*, Buenos Aires: Eudeba, 1985; M. Garretón, "Repensando las transiciones democráticas en América Latina," *Revista Nueva Sociedad* 148, 1997, pp. 20–9; W. Ansaldi, "*Matriuskas* de terror: Algunos elementos para analizar la dictadura Argentina dentro de las dictaduras del Cono Sur," in A. Pucciarelli (ed.), *Empresarios, tecnócratas y militares: La trama corporativa de la última dictadura*, Buenos Aires: Siglo XXI, 2004, pp. 27–51.
3 Although in Brazil the *coup d'état* had taken place in 1964, the new type of military dictatorships became consolidated in the area in the 1970s; these dictatorships included Chile (1973), Uruguay (1973), and Argentina (1976). This does not imply ignoring the significant differences observed among these regimes, including different phases, economic strategies or the implementation of state repression. For an approach to some of these problems see P. Weiss Fagen, "Repression and State Security," in J. Corradi, P. Weiss Fagen, and M. Garretón (eds), *Fear at the Edge: State Terror and Resistance in Latin America*, Berkeley and Los Angeles: University of California Press, 1992, pp. 39–71.
4 In Latin America, the Cuban revolution (1959) was undoubtedly the fundamental, though not exclusive, activator of processes of social and political radicalization. This experience opened the possibility of social revolution in the subcontinent, and at the same time it generated a profound crisis within the traditional left wing. Its correlate was the emergence of the "new left" which placed in the center of the political imagery the need to take over power and which, among its expressions, included the generation of guerrilla organizations which vindicated the armed methods and the

"theory of the focus," supported by theoretical formulations of a fundamentally Guevarist origin.

5 The well-known and repeatedly quoted statement of General Saint Jean, formulated in 1977 as regards the Argentine dictatorship, harshly illustrates the magnitude of the repressive project: "First we will kill all the subversive criminals, then we will kill their collaborators, then their supporters, then those who remain indifferent, and then we will kill those who are undecided."

6 The word "subversion" had a scope which was as broad as it was diffuse. The Argentine military used it to define those who had to be "eradicated" from society through repression, particularly the militants from the political organizations of the armed and non-armed left groups, the union leaders, and the social organizations or the "ideologists," which included intellectuals and university teachers, as well as the victims' relatives and friends. Strictly speaking, the direct use of violence – repression – was selective: beyond the objectives and the scope of the military project, not all the inhabitants, nor society as a whole, shared that character nor were directly affected by the actions of the security forces.

7 The context which preceded the settlement of the regime can hardly be presented as a war. What happened in Argentina after 1975–6 was not a confrontation between belligerent armies, nor can it be characterized as a "civil war," but as a deployment of a brutal repression implemented and embodied by a state that monopolized the uses of "legitimate violence," whatever their modalities, over political-military groups which had lost, by 1976, a good deal of their operational capacity. In relation to this topic see D. Feierstein, *El genocidio como práctica social: Entre el nazismo y la experiencia Argentina*, Buenos Aires: Fondo de Cultura Económica, 2007, pp. 275 ff.

8 Rosario is one of the three most important cities in the country due to its demographic and economic significance, which turned it into a center of regional development with a leading importance at a national level (particularly due to the industrial strip of Gran Rosario, one of the areas with the highest concentrations of factories in the country). It is interesting to point out that, just as happens with other historical issues and problems, studies on the Argentine dictatorship have not yet incorporated the regional dimension, confining themselves to transferring the experience of Buenos Aires to the entirety of the territory. In this sense, although there are some peculiarities at regional and local scale, what happened in Rosario does not differ in a significant way from what could be observed in the large cities of the country and, in general, in the national territory as a whole, both in terms of the organization of political and military power or the social and economic strategies implemented by the dictatorship and the modalities in the use of state repression and terror.

9 The terms violence, terror, or repression have been indistinctly used to define the actions realized by the military state and the repressive forces. However, we have decided to sharpen their use here. When we refer to the use of physical violence (and this includes persecution, imprisonment, kidnapping, murder and/or people's disappearance) we will use the term repression, as terror (both political and social) involved not only the use of physical violence, but also of other modalities which go beyond this strict use.

10 By 1975 the Peronist government had already started up a series of regulations and decrees that configured the new legal framework for the implementation of the repressive strategy that would be expanded after March 24. In October that year Decree No. 2722 was passed, where it was stipulated as follows: "To execute the military and security operations necessary with the object of annihilating the actions of the subversive elements in all the territory of the country." The territorial scheme represented by the division into army corps was completed with the demarcation of zones, subzones, and areas.

11 Which included the contacts and the coordination of repressive actions with neighboring dictatorships, just as it happened with the Plan Cóndor, a counterinsurgency

operation organized by the governments of Chile, Argentina, Bolivia, Brazil, Paraguay, and Uruguay, with the objective of exchanging information, watching, kidnapping, and murdering opponents from any of these countries and handing them over to their corresponding governments. See M. Robin, *Escuadrones de la muerte: La escuela francesa*, Buenos Aires: Sudamericana, 2005.

12 With this objective, a group of laws which facilitated the repressive activities was set in motion; among others, Law No. 21264, which punished with up to ten years of prison those who "publicly, and by any means, promote collective violence and/or cause a breach of peace"; Law No. 21460 which established that the armed forces would investigate subversive crimes; Law No. 21461 which constituted special courts martial for subversive activities, etc.

13 Without excluding the disputes among the forces (army, provincial police, etc.) or the possible alteration of this "order," in general each task force used a certain clandestine detention center and, probably, certain practices to dispose of the bodies (for example, warehouse locations). See D. Olmo, "Reconstruir desde restos y fragmentos: El uso de los archivos policiales en la antropología forense en Argentina," in L. Da Silva Catela and E. Jelin (eds), *Los archivos de la represión: Documentos, memoria y verdad*, Buenos Aires: Siglo XXI, 2002, pp. 179–94.

14 Provincial Law No. 7753, published on the *Boletín Oficial*, July 1, 1976.

15 In 1981, Lieutenant General Galtieri was appointed as commander-in-chief of the army and he assumed the leadership of the National Executive Power, replacing Lieutenant General Eduardo Viola who had also acted as head of the 2nd Corps of the army before 1976; a significant coincidence in the career of two of the main leaders of the dictatorship, but also, probably, a sign of the military importance of such an assignment.

16 Agustín Feced had been chief of police of Rosario at the beginning of the 1970s under the previous dictatorship, and he opened the "antisubversive fight" in the city with the creation of the Antisubversive Service of Rosario (Servicio Antisubversivo de Rosario – SAR). This role was extended and intensified with his return as head of the police in 1976, as is shown by the central role that repression played in the actions of the Information Service of the police, which Feced commanded. This service ran the most important clandestine detention center at their headquarters and was the most active task force in the area. In the early months of 1978, Feced left the police command, according to some testimonies, because of the questions raised by his brutal and criminal methods within military circles.

17 In 1970, a group of armed organizations appeared in Argentina; these organizations came from the Peronist and Marxist spheres, and they placed themselves in the center of the political scene. They all developed mass organizations with work, legal, and labor union divisions, and youth and student groups. From the beginning of the decade the Partido Revolucionario de los Trabajadores (Workers' Revolutionary Party) and its armed division, the Ejército Revolucionario del Pueblo PRT-ERP (People's Revolutionary Army), of a Marxist background, carried out significant activity within the city of Rosario. After 1973–4, the Montoneros – the political military organization of the Peronist left-wing – became the most influential organization to attract militants from other spheres of Peronism as well as youth groups, and had considerable penetration in workers' groups, neighborhoods, schools, and universities.

18 The most important of which was the Information Service of the provincial police, located in the basement of the police headquarters. The other detention centers which were recognized were La Calamita (in Granadero Baigorria,) the Quinta de Funes, Battalion 121, the "Domingo Matheu" weapon factory, the Command of the 2nd Corps of the army, the Magnasco Technical School, La Intermedia (in Timbúes) and the weapon factory of Fray Luis Beltrán. Recently, at least three more buildings have been identified which acted as detention centers in the area.

19 See note 22.

20 In the particular case of the 2nd Corps and, in general in the Argentine case, there was no construction of concentration or extermination camps specifically for such purposes, as in Nazi Germany; they used buildings which already existed and which had been used for other purposes, or where the space was shared with other divisions, for example, police stations or military facilities.

21 The detection of the victims by the military and police intelligence services was supported, to a large extent, by information obtained by torture or, as happened in the Information Service, through the simple collaboration of some detainees.

22 In this regard, see the significant text by P. Calveiro, *Poder y desaparición: Los campos de concentración en la Argentina*, Buenos Aires: Colihue, 1998; who focuses her analysis on the experiences of detainees in three detention centers located in Buenos Aires and Córdoba.

23 One of the forms of physical elimination which was widely used in Rosario city in the early years of the dictatorship was the fake "confrontation." The security forces would describe attacks or ambushes by alleged subversives in which invariably they died, hiding the fact that they had been kidnapped, put in clandestine detention centers, and then murdered. These "confrontations" were neatly recorded, both in terms of the settings and the writing of the police and military reports, and were often reproduced in the local and national press. An example took place in December 1976, when seven supposedly *montonero* militants who had been kidnapped in different procedures were executed in the town of Ibarlucea. The report of the 2nd Corps stated that a "confrontation" had taken place after an attempted takeover of the town's police station. Subsequent testimonies determined that reports of such a confrontation had been forged by the police and military forces who had supposedly taken part in it. A similar documented case was the so-called "Los Surgentes massacre" in October 1976, when four men and three women were transferred from the police headquarters and executed in the town of that name in Cordoba, and their bodies were subsequently found by inhabitants of the area. The city of Rosario and some neighboring towns were also the scene of similar procedures between 1976 and 1978.

24 See, for example, the press conference called by the military junta before national and foreign media, *La Capital*, April 20, 1977.

25 Being married to a "subversive criminal" or having a relative with such a label used to be reason enough for detention or even disappearance. The footsteps of the repression, on many occasions, followed the course of a social fabric formed by family networks (boyfriends and girlfriends, husbands and wives, brothers and sisters, parents, brothers- and sisters-in-law,) or by relationships of friendship, schoolmates or workmates. For the case of Chile, see A. García Castro, "¿Quiénes son? Los desparecidos en la trama política chilena (1973–2000),"in B. Groppo and P. Flier (eds), *La imposibilidad del Olvido: Recorridos de la memoria en Argentina, Chile y Uruguay*, La Plata: Al Margen, 2001, pp. 195–208.

26 A few months after the *coup d'état*, the general minister of labor Horacio Liendo analyzed the labor situation before 1976, translating the thinking of the armed force toward workers and their organizations:

> The relationships between businessmen and workers were distorted by the preeminence of one sector over the other and by the absence of responsibility and representation of the leaderships of the union and corporate entities. ... The outbursts were so manifest, and the union functions were exercised in such a coarse manner, that it became necessary to review the applicable guidelines and legislation as regards both sectors. ... This situation favored the subversive aggression that the country was already suffering. ... Factory 'soviets' appeared, who destroyed the foundations of the labor union structure, due to the incompetence, incapacity and immorality of its leaders.
>
> (*La Capital*, September 16, 1976)

27 Among them, the suspension of the right to go on strike (Law No. 21261), the prohibition of political activity by union groups, the control of labor union funds and union social care funds, the prohibition of direct action measures (Law No. 21400), the elimination of union jurisdiction (Law No. 21263), a new labor contract system and, in November 1979, the Law of Professional Associations (Law No. 22105).

28 General Acdel Vilas, commander of the 5th Corps of the army, with headquarters in Bahía Blanca, explained within this context the thinking of the armed forces as regards the university:

> The fight against subversion ... has so far been carried out against the visible head, which is the subversive criminal, but not against the ideologist, who generates, trains and shapes this new type of criminals.... These ideologists, who are inserted into every field, are poisoning young people from university classrooms to secondary schools, and if we do not unmask and break down this criminal-generating machine, the infiltration will be complete ... we cannot be content with eradicating, annihilating, or eliminating the result of this process of infiltration; we must knock down and destroy the resources which nourish, train, and indoctrinate the subversive criminals, and their source is at the university and secondary schools. Until we manage to clean up the educational system ... and until the teacher is a man with Christian thinking and ideology, we cannot achieve victory in this fight to which we are all committed.
>
> (*La Capital*, August 5, 1976)

29 Shortly after the *coup d'état*, Rosario began a moralizing campaign in nightclubs carried out by the police forces commanded by Agustín Feced which, in the opinion of the main newspaper of the city, "receives the highest praise and support from our population" and "is thus addressing an old concern of all the representative groups and institutions of citizens" (*La Capital*, May 29, 1976). This "task of cleaning-up of habits" promoted by the provincial and municipal government, the declared objective of which was the "defense of our children" and which included night raids every weekend and a wide range of actions of the police "public morality" section became the necessary complement of the "fight against subversion."

30 A little over a month after the coup, the military assigned Captain A. F. Cristiani to the position of head of the municipal government. Cristiani became, for five years (1976–81), the visible face of the dictatorship in the city.

31 Even though the US backing of Argentina's military dictatorship constitutes a fact, there remains a gap in the study of US–Argentina's relationship during the Cold War era.

32 While the "legal forces" were beginning to execute their sinister plan of social and political terror, the Catholic Church, the editorials of the city's main newspaper, national celebrations, and military acts became passionate forums of the most intense justification of the repression and legitimization of the new social order imposed on the country and the city by the dictatorship. In this regard, see G. Aguila, "El terrorismo de estado sobre Rosario, 1976–1983," in A. Pla (ed.), *Rosario en la historia: De 1930 a nuestros días*, Rosario: UNR, 2000, pp. 121–221.

33 Although until 1981, the spheres of resistance were almost insignificant and many of them chose external and internal exile, social discontent was expressed in the few gaps left open by the dictatorship: the fight for human rights, certain cultural circles, or the spheres of private life. This situation was modified between 1982 and 1983, when the growing discredit of the dictatorship provided the social and political opposition with broader resonance and new contents and players.

34 Within this framework, the military government strove to fight a battle both internally and internationally against what they had called the "anti-Argentine campaign," hoping to restore, with that slogan, the support which significant sectors of the society had given to the regime up to that moment, and which was beginning to crack. The

campaign deployed through the news media produced the desired effect: a majority of Argentine society preferred to continue to embrace the junta's slogan which dictated that the rights of Argentinean people were respected. At the same time, visits made by representatives of international human rights organizations were received, in general, with hostility or indifference by the junta and society – with the exception of the mothers and relatives of the disappeared persons who demanded answers.

35 The "theory of the two demons," formulated during the first stages of the constitutional government of Raúl Alfonsín (1983–9), stated that the dictatorship was the result of the confrontation between two bands with equal responsibilities, and that both the "excesses" and the punishments should be distributed in an equitable manner. This is associated with the notion of a society which is a "victim" and innocent as regards the excesses of the conflicting bands. On the other hand, it is also associated with the idea that subordinates were only obeying orders. While in the early years of democracy it was accompanied by the work of the National Commission on the Disappearance of Persons (Comisión Nacional sobre la Desaparición de Personas – CONADEP) and the trial of the military juntas, its most resounding expression was the design of a specific legal machinery (the laws of *Punto Final* and *Obediencia debida*) which, together with pardons, have ensured the impunity of the majority of the repressors to this date.

36 These aspects have been covered in G. Aguila, "Dictadura, memoria(s) e historia: El conflictivo contrapunto entre las memorias de la dictadura en Rosario," *Prohistoria* 11, Rosario, 2007, pp. 91–106.

37 See Equipo Argentino de Antropología Forense, *Annual Report 2005, Informe anual del Equipo Argentino de Antropología Forense*, Buenos Aires and New York: EAAF, 2005.

8 US–Colombian relations in the 1980s

Political violence and the onset of the Unión Patriótica genocide

Andrei Gómez-Suárez

It is commonplace to say that Colombia is facing one of the longest armed conflicts to date (1964–2009). Today, Colombia has the second largest number of internally displaced people after Darfur, some four million, and one of the worst human rights records documented.[1] This "new war," to use Kaldor's term,[2] in which the distinctions between private/public, international/national, and combatant/civilian are blurred, has attracted the scholarly interest of political scientists and international relations and conflict studies scholars alike.[3] What is not common, however, is to find scholars discussing the occurrence of genocide in Colombia. As I have argued elsewhere,[4] however, genocide happened and is still ongoing today. Between 1985 and 2002, an entire political party, the Unión Patriótica (UP), was annihilated in the midst of the 40-year Colombian armed conflict.

The UP was a political front bringing together the Communist Party and other leftist and centrist political forces. It was the product of the Uribe Agreements between the Fuerzas Armadas Revolucionarias de Colombia (FARC), a Marxist-Leninist oriented guerrilla movement, and the Colombian government in 1984. Although the UP was thought of as the means for the FARC to demobilize, the year itself seemed not to be the right moment for such a strategy. In fact, the UP was set up at a time of adverse conditions. Internationally, Reagan was carrying out his campaign against communism in order to defy the belief that the United States' hegemony was declining.[5] In Colombia itself, the counterinsurgency campaign led by the Colombian government had stepped up since 1981 when the army, drug traffickers, and governmental officials established a paramilitary group based in the Middle Magdalena Valley in order to defeat various guerrilla groups. This, together with the FARC's own new (1982) strategy of government takeover, which meant a rise in kidnapping for ransom and ever more harassment of landowners and other sectors of the population in order to increase their finances, resulted in a degenerate war in which all the actors increasingly targeted non-combatants as a means of winning the war. In spite of these conditions, the UP was publicly launched in May 1985.

According to some UP survivors, the assassination of civilians involved in the UP process started even before the official launch.[6] It is estimated that, since 1985, between 3,000 and 5,000 of its members have been assassinated, hundreds have been disappeared, thousands displaced and many others rejected their UP affiliation so as to survive the violence.[7] Over the last 20 years or so, different genocidal practices have brought down the social and political power of the UP resulting in its annihilation. Cepeda[8] suggests that the UP genocide occurred in three phases: first, the weakening of organizational structures (1984–92), then, the *coup de grâce* phase that normalized its destruction (1992–2002), and finally, although the UP formally ceased to exist in Colombian politics in 2002 due to a lack of affiliates and support in the polls, the last stage is the destruction of the survivors which is, according to Cepeda, still ongoing today.

This chapter is an attempt to explore some dynamics within the first period of the UP genocide. Given that the first stage of the genocide developed along with the international turmoil of the unexpected end of the Cold War, which saw, in the early 1980s, the re-emergence of the US crusade against communism, I pay special attention to the role that US–Colombian relations played in the development of the genocide. This analysis, I believe, demonstrates Grandin's assertion that "the conception of democracy now being prescribed as the most effective weapon in the war on terrorism is itself largely, at least in Latin America, a product of terror."[9]

I develop the analysis to complement a new line of research that is emerging in genocide studies, which attempts to overcome the shortcomings of mainstream genocide scholars. Following Shaw,[10] I see genocide as a particular form of warfare against the social power of civilian groups, which usually takes place in the midst of a broader conflict.[11] This "external" relation of genocide with war brings my analysis closer to Bloxham's[12] study of the Armenian genocide, which sees genocide as not only the result of domestic forces but also the product of geopolitical tensions; this is precisely the case in Cold War Latin American geopolitics. The analysis is structured in two parts. First I explore how US foreign policy's representations of Colombia interacted with domestic factors, creating an environment for the destruction of the UP to happen. In the second part I turn to study the domestic developments that brought about the perpetrators of the UP genocide, the discourses that legitimated the destruction, and the way in which these discourses interplayed with international dynamics in the occurrence of the genocide.

US foreign policy towards Colombia during the 1980s

Since the 1980s US foreign policy towards Colombia has relied on two "scripts"[13] of the country. On the one hand, Colombia is described as the most stable democracy in Latin America, on the other hand, it is depicted as a dangerous place in which insurgency and drug trafficking have brought into being a terrorist threat, namely "narco-guerrillas." These two scripts of course do not just reveal reality; they also help to create reality. This creation of reality through mere representations rather than through raw events has brought about what O'Tuathail calls "the principle of hyperreality" in foreign policy.[14] That is to say that scripts structure ways of seeing reality, admitting "only certain political possibilities as ways of responding to that 'reality.'" The result, then, is "a persuasive story designed to explain the messy complexity of events in a simple fashion." The principle of hyperreality, accordingly, "reached a grand apotheosis in the Reagan years."

After 1978, US presidents Jimmy Carter and Ronald Reagan both saw Colombia as the perfect ally in South America in spite of the sharp increase in human rights violations during the presidency of Julio Cesar Turbay Ayala (1978–82). During Turbay's term in office, the "Security Statute" was issued,[15] a decree "which gave greater authority and autonomy to the military, identified new, vaguely defined crimes such as 'disturbing public order,' and restricted press freedom."[16] This resulted in thousands of arbitrary detentions.[17] Colombia, however, was depicted by both US administrations as one of the few democracies in the western hemisphere, fighting the "war on drugs" and, therefore, was rewarded during these years "with $16 million in additional antidrug assistance."[18] Nevertheless, by 1982, when President Belisario Betancur assumed power, drug traffickers had thoroughly permeated social, economic, and political circles in Colombian society. Furthermore, dangerous alliances between drug traffickers, governmental officials, and the army were proliferating in different regions of the country in order to fight guerrilla groups.[19] Vice-President George Bush (Snr) and President Reagan visited Colombia in August and December 1982 respectively. They "scripted" Colombia as a free society which, according to Reagan, had a "profound tradition of law and liberty"[20] but was endangered by insurgency movements; according to Bush, it was hence necessary that "the United States build a military base in Colombia to monitor the country's insurgents."[21]

By 1985, the principle of hyperreality that shaped Reagan's foreign policy encouraged alliances between the CIA, the Contras in Nicaragua, Noriega in Panama, and the Medellín Cartel in Colombia,[22] among others; such alliances were to be made public years later when the investigation into the Iran–Contra scandal was carried out. In early 1989 the US Senate Subcommittee on Terrorism, Narcotics, and International Operations published the *Drug, Law Enforcement and Foreign Relations* report (hereafter Kerry Report) demonstrating how during Reagan's war against communism in Central America the drug cartels had consolidated, posing "a continuing threat to national security at home and abroad."[23] Nevertheless, the report also used the common scripts of Colombia in describing the country as "the oldest democracy in Latin America" threatened by the alliance between drug traffickers and guerrillas. According to them, for example, the "M-19 had become an enforcement mechanism of the [Medellín] Cartel, using its soldiers to protect narcotics shipments and intimidate the Colombian government."[24]

The raw events that these representations of Colombia did not tell is that Amnesty International (AI) visited Colombia in 1988 and found that assassinations of political activists were taking place along with the "systematic extermination" of the Unión Patriótica. According to the report, paramilitary groups, such as MAS (Death to Kidnappers), were not the only perpetrators; alongside them, high-rank officers of the Colombian armed forces and drug traffickers had orchestrated paramilitary actions and many government officials had colluded with them. The day after the report was published, the minister of defense, Gen. Rafael Samudio Molina, stated against AI's claims that the armed forces only acted in defense of Colombia's "democratic" institutions; most civil servants afterwards followed suit to support the general's claims and disregarded the findings of the report.[25] The US foreign policy scripts of Colombia undoubtedly were largely created by the interaction of Colombian and American elites dominating the governments of both countries. In the reproduction of this interplay of representations, then, the reality of the "dirty war" and the UP genocide was overshadowed by the hyperreal *oldest democracy* threatened by hyperreal *narco-guerrillas*.

The administration of George Bush Snr was aware of allegations about the large number of human rights violations. Nevertheless, according to Human Rights Watch's (HRW) report, *Colombia's Killer Network: The Military–Paramilitary Partnership and the United States*, "from 1989 to 1993, the State Department issued thirty-nine licenses to US firms to export small arms to Colombia, for a total value of $643,785."[26] Although arms transfers were legitimated through the need to protect an old democracy, the transfers themselves were part of the US security strategy for the western hemisphere. The important role that arms transfers played in the Cold War US foreign policy is demonstrated by Blanton:

> During the Cold War, US arms transfers were … both an instrument of influence and an indicator of US political support…. The United States thus exported arms to friendly and often regionally dominant governments – democracies and non-democracies alike – that voiced opposition to communism…. Therefore, during the Cold War years, human rights and democracy were likely overshadowed by traditional security concerns.[27]

However, with the Cold War finally "over," the communist threat was supposedly replaced by the drug threat, thus arms transfers were bound together with Bush's "Andean Initiative, a five-year, $2.2 billion plan designed to heighten the United States' war on drugs."[28]

The rise of arms transfers since 1989, though, was also the result of a shift in Colombian politics. In late 1987, due to the deadlock in the peace process, the decision was made by the FARC to return to fighting a war against the state. This had reinforced the central government's counterinsurgent discourse, opening the space for a new intelligence strategy to fight the insurgency. In 1990, within the framework of the Andean Initiative, the US government formed an advisory commission of CIA and Pentagon officials to develop a set of national security recommendations for Colombia's Ministry of Defense. As a result, the Colombian government issued Order 200–05/91, which was a plan to better combat "escalating terrorism by armed subversion."[29]

HRW demonstrates how, through Order 200–05/91, paramilitary groups were incorporated into the armed forces' intelligence apparatus in order to carry out surveillance of opposition political leaders and attacks on "dangerous" individuals selected by the army's high command.[30] The consolidation of this military intelligence network resulted in the proliferation of massacres against the UP in different regions of Colombia, such as Meta, Arauca, Casanare, and Urabá. From 1992 to 2002, then, what I have called a "perpetrator bloc," of armed forces, drug traffickers, governmental officials, paramilitary and so-called self-defense groups,[31] carried out the second stage of the UP genocide. Throughout those years, US foreign policy continued using the same scripts about Colombia: a *democracy* threatened by a *narco-guerrilla*. After September 11, 2001, however, these scripts merged under another grand apotheosis of the principle of hyper-reality: George W. Bush's "war on terror."[32] These periods need to be analysed elsewhere. For the time being, I turn to discuss the complex dynamics in which the UP genocide developed in its first stage.

The institutionalization of a complex web of violent relations in 1980s Colombia

Colombia was, at the turn of the 1980s, in a state of political and social turmoil. Although 1978 had marked the end of the "transition" of the Frente Nacional,[33] public and government positions were still shared equally and exclusively between the traditional parties: liberal and conservative. Yet, instead of addressing the crisis of legitimacy that the political system was facing, President Turbay turned a blind eye towards the possibility of reforming it, opting rather to align forces with the Carter administration in an attempt to tackle the buoyant narcotics industry.[34] During the previous administration, drug trafficking had proliferated, in part because

> The very abundance of foreign exchange on the black market [had] induced the Central Bank to become involved in the laundering business itself.... Thus, in 1975 the Central Bank [had] opened a so-called "sinister window" through which it could buy foreign exchange with no questions asked, a practice which was [only] eliminated in 1983.[35]

Turbay's foreign policy against narcotics was designed to match his counterinsurgency strategy. He thought that, "a clear, tough and repressive policy would effectively resolve the problems and restore public order."[36] In so doing, Turbay resorted, as all the administrations before him had done since 1947, to article 121 of the 1886 constitution, which gave him special powers to introduce a "state of siege" in case of social unrest. Thus, Colombia, as many analysts contend, was during most of the twentieth century in "an almost permanent state of siege."[37]

The military repression, during the Turbay administration, however, did not resolve the counterinsurgency threat nor did it stop the consolidation of the narcotics business. On the contrary, according to Pearce, "for the first time guerrilla movements were articulating the people's real preoccupations ... there was a good deal of sympathy for them"[38] and drug traffickers were moving towards a strategy of military and political consolidation in different regions of the country. The former began to materialize in 1981 when Jorge Luis Ochoa Vásquez, together with other 223 drug barons, created the MAS paramilitary group. [39]

In 1982, President Betancur moved from the outset of his administration to distance himself from the Reagan administration and to develop a more independent Colombian foreign policy. He called Colombia to join the Non-Aligned Movement and created alongside Mexico, Venezuela, and Panama the Contadora Group as a counterbalance to "the Reagan administration's hardline policies in Central America."[40] Betancur's shift in foreign policy reflected the changes he was to implement in domestic politics in order to "confront the regime's deepening legitimacy crisis and the problem of continuing political violence."[41] Once in office, he opened up negotiations with various rebel groups and proposed a package of political reforms, among which, the most ambitious one was the popular election of mayors. Notwithstanding President Betancur's new policies, Colombia continued steadily to fall into the worst socio-political and humanitarian crisis. This was so because of (1) the strengthening of drug trafficking cartels, which developed a twofold strategy of regional power consolidation: politicization and militarization; (2) a weak and inefficient judicial system, which allowed extremely high levels of impunity; and (3) the collusion between various social groups (such as military institutions, political entrepreneurs, and government officials) and paramilitary and so-called self-defense groups, which resulted in a "dirty war" characterized by what Guerrero[42] has rightly called "a counterinsurgency war delegated to private actors" and within which the UP genocide occurred.

The reason why the Medellín Cartel became by the mid-1980s one of the most powerful transnational criminal organizations is, bluntly, that during the Reagan administration, as Bagley put it, "the struggle against communist expansion has always been given diplomatic priority over the war against drugs."[43] This was demonstrated by the 1989 Kerry Report, which points out precisely that the strengthening of the Medellín Cartel between 1984 and 1986 was related to the fact that

> the supply network of the Contras was used by drug trafficking organisations, and elements of the Contras themselves knowingly received financial and material assistance from drug traffickers. In each case, one or another agency of the US government had information regarding the involvement.[44]

Thanks to the transnational consolidation of the drug cartels in which evidently the US government participated, drug traffickers acquired an economic power capable of having a major impact on Colombia's social and political institutions. At the level of everyday life, the expansion of the underground economy brought Colombian society into what Thoumi[45] called a "dishonesty trap." In such a situation, a weak judicial system could only get weaker. At the macro-socio-political level, "the narcotraffic was an armed instrument of political and social intolerance"[46] that allowed the assassination of thousands of civilians, and once the Uribe Agreements were signed, it contributed to the genocidal campaign against the UP in various regions of Colombia, such as the Middle Magdalena Valley and Urabá.

The involvement of drug traffickers in the armed conflict meant not only that they established an underground economy but also that they saw themselves as an actor that could influence the structure of the state itself, which, according to González et al.,[47] was at the time still under construction. New landowners in colonization regions, drug traffickers, and FARC became contenders. In search of territorial control, the landowners and traffickers needed a military force to confront the FARC. The first step towards the consolidation of their military strategy was the creation of the MAS which, according to the Kerry Report, was on the advice of a US government official to the members of the Medellín Cartel. This would explain, in Guerrero's view,[48] the organic nexus between the Nicaraguan Contras and the proliferation of paramilitary groups that took place throughout the 1980s in Colombia. Hence, drug traffickers not only attempted to control the whole paramilitary structure in the Middle Magdalena Valley, but they were one of the "private financiers" of the "dirty war" that provided paramilitary groups with a larger budget, better arms, and more mercenaries.

This privatization of the war allowed the expansion of a "narco-paramilitary campaign" against Cordoba and Urabá, where drug barons had become big landowners.[49] Their battle against the FARC allowed the flourishing of their particular political identity, which opposed social movements demanding social reforms and defended the "liberal-capitalist" system. Both the militarization and politicization of drug traffickers coincided with the armed forces' counterinsurgency tactics and the regional elites' reaction to the guerrillas' harassment.[50] This proved to be fatal for the UP; it had to be destroyed not only because it had been created by the FARC, but also because it was seen as one of those social movements. Thus, drug traffickers such as Fabio Ochoa, Pablo Escobar, Fidel Castaño, Gilberto Molina, Víctor Carranza, and Gonzalo Rodríguez Gacha, actively participated in the genocidal campaign against the UP.[51]

The armed forces colluded with drug traffickers in part because some of its high-rank officers, such as General Manuel José Bonett Locarno and Colonel Luis Bernardo Urbina Sánchez, continued to be trained in counterinsurgency operations at the School of the Americas (SOA). Even more telling is that Colombia was one of the "three counties [that throughout the 1980s] increased ... [officers'] enrolment several fold."[52] This training, as Gill has demonstrated,[53] was "shaped by the geopolitical field of force in which the United States define[d] its national interests and security concerns." As the Reagan doctrine was fighting communists – "an enormous elastic category that could accommodate almost any critic of the status quo"[54] – throughout the Third World during the 1980s, Colombian officers trained at SOA went back to the country to fight the "internal enemy." The US National Security Doctrine (NSD) had provided them with the rationale and the courses at SOA with the tactics for fighting "communists" internally.

Thus, whilst President Betancur strived to negotiate peace with the FARC, senior armed forces commanders impeded the materialization of the Uribe Agreements. This contradiction within the establishment was never resolved. Throughout the 1980s, the SOA-trained Colombian military officers managed regional intelligence networks, which "cultivated relations with paramilitary groups [and sometimes] ... worked temporarily with the paramilitaries,"[55] just as happened on August 15 and 16, 1987, when paramilitaries and army intelligence agents, under the orders of Urbina Sánchez, murdered Alvaro Garcés Parra, one of the 23 UP mayors elected in 1986.[56] Thousands of assassinations and hundreds of massacres of members of the UP and other social organizations show that SOA played a central role in exporting a particular geopolitical discourse (that represented Colombia's insurgency as a threat to peace and security in the western hemisphere)[57] which entangled with local understandings and produced hyperreal threats, shaping local practices of dealing with the social unrest evident across Colombian society.

Reading the justification of perpetrators' actions and the large number of academic works discussing the armed conflict in Colombia and the destruction of the UP,[58] the accepted explanation for the destruction of the UP seems to be: *La combinación de todas las formas de lucha* (the combination of all forms of struggle). During the first two years when FARC and the Colombian government were still holding peace talks, military officers within the "perpetrator bloc" justified the violent campaign against the UP on the ground that the group was the political arm of the FARC which, in their view, had designed, along with the Communist Party, a secret plan of power takeover. This assumption was to be reinforced in 1987, when the FARC went back to wage war against the state. At this stage, paramilitary leaders within the perpetrator bloc justified the destruction of the UP by arguing that they were killing guerrilla fighters dressed as civilians.[59] Scholars' accounts of these episodes have relied on the perpetrators' representation of the conflict which, instead of depicting raw events, allowed them to wage war on the UP. According to Pizarro,[60] for instance, FARC's and the Communist Party's ambiguity of waging war and doing politics, represented in *la combinación de todas las formas de lucha*, continued to inform their strategy in the peace talks; this served as the motive for the perpetrators to wage war on the UP.

The same thesis is supported by Dudley[61] who argues that the UP was only a part of a master plan to open up political space for the FARC. *La combinación de todas las formas de lucha* is a discursive practice that in my view requires further research. Although Giraldo[62] analyzes the transformation of the UP's discursive practices, which in his view started a radical transformation in 1989, it is necessary to further study the way perpetrators appropriated them to carry out the annihilation of the group. Suffice to say, for the time being, that interviews with UP leaders show that the group itself had began to distance itself from the FARC in 1987. By 1988, this was evident in the consolidation of a new national government board of the UP that regarded political dialogue between FARC and the Colombian government as the only way to overcome the armed conflict.[63]

UP political speeches and attitudes did not convince governmental and military officials within the perpetrator bloc. In the prelude of the geopolitical victory of capitalism over communism, there was no space for a political group product of *la combinación de todas las formas de lucha*. The "dirty war" against any social movement was well under way by then; it was only a matter of finishing off the UP within it.

The political death toll in 1980s Colombia is well over 10,000.[64] Within this campaign of assassinations, albeit underinvestigated and generally regarded as less systematic than the Argentinian case and which deserves to be investigated under Feierstein's[65] perspective of genocide as a social practice, the UP death toll approximately accounted for about 20 percent of the total.[66] The pattern of the actions that demonstrate that UP victims were selected only because of their membership is explicit in three of the most bloody plans against the group between 1985 and 1991: Operación Cóndor (1985), the Plan Baile Rojo (1986), and the Plan Esmeralda (1988). The first two campaigns attempted "to undermine the national governing board of the party and to murder or disappear those members elected to public offices," whereas the last sought "to destroy the grassroots of the party in Meta and Caquetá."[67] Operación Cóndor had an immediate effect in the UP; according to one of its leaders "more than three hundred UP members had already been assassinated, and the party hadn't even had its first anniversary."[68]

By the time President Betancur left office in 1986, his two most ambitious projects were under way. On the one hand, FARC had renewed the commitment to continue peace talks with the new president Virgilio Barco; on the other hand, a new constitutional reform was to enable the first democratic elections of mayors in 1988. However, as a strategy to transit towards a more open political system, the decision was taken by the central government to give 23 mayoralties to the UP in towns where the party had become the dominant political force in the 1986 municipal assembly elections. Between late 1986 and early 1988, 46 UP members acting as mayors or town councillors or competing for these positions were murdered; the violent campaign against UP candidates, as Gaitán recognizes,[69] was particularly vicious in the months before the first democratic elections of mayors. In all, as Dudley remarks, "the tally of UP dead reached five hundred in the first two years of the party's existence."[70]

Alongside this murderous campaign in which some UP parliamentarians had been shot down, the assassination of UP president Jaime Pardo Leal in October 1987 demonstrated that nobody would escape the violence deployed by the various actors forming the perpetrator bloc. In 1988, when the Plan Esmeralda began to be deployed in earnest, massacres were not only a common practice in the Middle Magdalena Valley and Meta, but they were proliferating towards Cordoba and Urabá.[71] The Segovia massacre, one of the best-documented episodes[72] was to become the benchmark of the genocidal campaign: the killing of anyone who was associated with the UP, including women, children, and the elderly. This campaign left a clear message floating about Colombian society: "the UP had to disappear, or the people would suffer."[73]

It was not the genocidal campaign against the UP that led President Barco to issue Decree 1194, which declared paramilitary groups illegal in 1989. Rather, it was the imminent danger that the violence deployed by these groups represented for the survival of the Colombian establishment. Paramilitary groups had given the confidence drug traffickers needed to declare a war against the state in order to disrupt the extradition treaty that in 1984 had been put into force again. By 1989 drug traffickers' terrorist actions had created a regime of terror not only in the peripheral regions where their standing armies patrolled, but also in the cities. Although the military-paramilitary strategy had weakened the power of the FARC in some regions, Colombian civil institutions seemed incapable of assuring the monopoly of violence. Barco's attempt to bring to an end the "counterinsurgency war delegated to private actors" did not however prosper. The alliances between governmental officials, armed forces, drug traffickers, and paramilitary leaders had become engrained across the country.

The genocidal campaign against the UP also continued. In March 1990, Bernardo Jaramillo, the last UP presidential candidate, was assassinated; this marked the end of the group's political power at the national level. Many people withdrew from the party and the decision was taken by the UP not to present a candidate for the 1990 presidential elections. Notwithstanding, the destruction of the few members that remained did not halt; it concentrated in the regions in which UP members still retained some social and political power, namely Urabá, Casanare, Arauca, and Meta.

Under President Cesar Gaviria (1990–4), Decree 1194 remained in place, though the links between the armed forces and paramilitaries became institutionalized under the defense ministry's Order 200–05/91. The US government, as mentioned earlier, participated in this process through forming an advisory commission to develop the set of recommendations that the Colombian government adopted in order to redesign its intelligence strategy. Order 200–05/91, in the words of HRW,

> laid the groundwork for continuing an illegal, covert partnership between the military and paramilitaries ... Although the term "paramilitaries" is not used in the order, the document lays out a system similar to the one present under the name of MAS and its military patrons in the Middle Magdalena ... the order provided a blueprint for: a secret network that relied on paramilitaries not only for intelligence, but to carry out murder.[74]

This was to become the pattern of paramilitary action throughout the 1990s. This alliance was not only responsible for an increase in the killing of civilians but, as the Plan Golpe de Gracia (1992) and Plan Retorno (1993) demonstrate, this alliance was responsible for the continuation of the genocidal campaign against the UP. The covert operations between military and paramilitaries against the UP made possible the participation of state institutions in the destruction of the group. However, the government has not taken responsibility because it is argued that the UP was trapped in the war between paramilitary groups and the

FARC. Although Romero[75] carried out excellent research on the evolution of paramilitary groups from 1982 to 2003, further investigation is needed regarding the war that the ACCU (United Self-defense of Cordoba and Urabá) and the AUC (United Self-defense of Colombia) and many other paramilitary groups before them waged against the UP. What must be said in order to close the analysis of this first period of the UP genocide is that in 1991, the transformation in the army's intelligence strategy brought about by order 200–05/91 enabled the last stage of the process of concentration of coercion that paramilitary leaders had begun in the Middle Magdalena Valley years before. Therefore, 1991 is the turning-point that marks the transition from the first period of the UP genocide, in which different groups gathered together to destroy the UP without a cohesive apparatus that integrated their actions, to the second period of the genocidal campaign, in which a more hierarchical type of perpetrator carried out the destruction of the last remnants of the UP.

Conclusion

Genocide is usually studied from a domestic perspective. What I have tried to show here is that although the criminal responsibility lies only on the perpetrators, international relations matter. In the case of the destruction of the UP in Colombia, some representations that underpinned US foreign policy were disastrous for the group. The destruction of the UP during the last years of the Cold War was possible due to the anti-communist geopolitical indoctrination of Colombian militaries trained at the School of the Americas. These discourses merged with local representations flourishing in the armed conflict, creating a fertile field for genocide to happen. US economic and military support to Colombia and the misrepresentation of the threat that guerrilla groups represented for the security of the hemisphere, allowed drug traffickers to consolidate a military apparatus capable of destabilizing the country and carry out, together with the Colombian armed forces, government officials, and mercenaries, the UP genocide. These alliances generated a socio-political turmoil within which the judicial system was incapable of prosecuting criminals.

The US fortified the widespread impunity in the country by providing packages of military aid to Colombia thus allowing the persecution of social movements and the destruction of the UP. US foreign policy did not take action to make the Colombian institutions involved in these crimes accountable to justice; instead, the realist approach that dominated US foreign policy advised the Colombian government to implement the counterinsurgency measures which were responsible for the paramilitary expansion of the 1990s. This paramilitary expansion carried on with the violence against the UP in the peripheries and brought about the annihilation of the group through massacres and displacement. Put simply, US–Colombian relations were the backdrop against which paramilitary groups, armed forces, governmental officials, and regional elites created genocidal traps in which the UP perished. The need today is to uncover such traps in order for Colombia to transit from war to peace, or at least to begin the process.

Notes and references

1 United Nations Refugee Agency (UNCHR), *Refugees by Numbers*, Geneva: Edition, Media Relations and Public Information Service, 2006.
2 M. Kaldor, *New and Old Wars*, Cambridge: Polity Press, 1999.
3 J. Pearce, *Colombia Inside the Labyrinth*, London: Latin American Bureau, 1990; D. Pécaut, *Guerra contra la sociedad*, Bogotá, Espasa Hoy, 2001.
4 A. Gómez-Suárez, "Perpetrator Blocs, Genocidal Mentalities, and Geographies: The Destruction of the Union Patriotica in Colombia and Its Lessons for Genocide Studies," *Journal of Genocide Research* 9, 4, 2007, pp. 635–60; A. Gómez-Suárez, "Bloques perpetradores y mentalidades genocidas: El caso de la destrucción de la Unión Patriótica en Colombia," *Revista de Estudios sobre Genocidio* 1, 2, 2008, pp. 42–55.
5 K. Oye, "International Systems Structure and American Foreign Policy," in K. Oye, R. Lieber and D. Rothchild, *Eagle Defiant: United States Foreign Policy in the 1980s*, Boston: Little, Brown and Company, 1983.
6 These statements are part of a documentary filmed by Yesid Campos with UP survivors called *El Baile Rojo* (2003).
7 J. Quiroga, "La Unión Patriótica: El exterminio de una esperanza," in *Memorias: Seminario Taller. Grupo de trabajo que propende por la búsqueda de una solución amistosa en el caso de la Unión Patriótica que se adelanta ante la Comisión Interamericana de Derechos Humanos*, Bogotá: Procuraduría General de la Nación – Embajada de Suiza, 2003.
8 I. Cepeda, "Genocidio político: El caso de la Unión Patriótica en Colombia," *Revista Cetil* 2, 2006, pp. 101–12.
9 C. Grandin, *The Last Colonial Massacre: Latin America in the Cold War*, Chicago: Chicago University Press, 2004.
10 M. Shaw, *What is Genocide?* Cambridge: Polity Press, 2007.
11 M. Shaw, *War and Genocide*, Cambridge: Polity Press, 2003.
12 D. Bloxham, *The Great Game of Genocide: Imperialism, Nationalism, and the Destruction of the Ottoman Armenian*, Oxford: Oxford University Press, 2007.
13 I borrow this term from O'Tuathail's analysis of US foreign policy towards South Africa. According to him a script is "a set of representations, a collection of descriptions, scenarios and attributes which are deemed relevant and appropriate to defining a place in foreign policy." G. O'Tuathail, "Foreign Policy and the Hyperreal: The Reagan Administration and the Scripting of 'South Africa,'" in T. Barnes, and J. Duncan, *Writing Worlds: Discourse, Text and Metaphor in the Representation of Landscape*, London: Routledge, 1992, p. 156.
14 Ibid., p. 157.
15 According to one Colombian scholar, Amnesty International carried out an investigation that showed how human rights violations had increased due to the actions of military officers acting under the Decree 1923. See F. Leal, *Estado y politica en Colombia*, Bogotá: Siglo Veintiuno Editores, 1984, p. 270.
16 M. Shifter, and R. Stillerman "US Human Rights Policy Toward Colombia," in D. Lian-Fenton *Implementing US Human Rights Policy*, Washington: USIP Press Books, 2004, pp. 334–5.
17 Pearce, *Colombia Inside the Labyrinth*, p. 232.
18 Shifter, and Stillerman "US Human Rights Policy Toward Colombia," p. 335.
19 M. Romero, "Élites regionales, identidades y paramilitares en el Sinú," in R. Peñaranda and J. Guerrero *De las armas a la política*, Bogotá: Tercer Mundo Editores-IEPRI, 1999.
20 See Reagan's complete speech: www.reagan.utexas.edu/archives/speeches/1982/120382d.htm (accessed on March 28, 2008).
21 Shifter and Stillerman, "US Human Rights Policy Toward Colombia," p. 336.

22 The complex relationship between drug cartels and the Contras is discussed on pp. 36–61 of US Senate, Committee on Foreign Relations, Subcommittee on Terrorism, Narcotics, and International Operations [Kerry Report], *Drug, Law Enforcement and Foreign Policy*, Washington: US Government Printing Office. 1989.
23 Ibid., p. iv.
24 Ibid., pp. 25, 28.
25 W. Ramírez, "Amnistía Internacional: Ese incomodo visitante," *Análisis Político* 1988, p. 4.
26 Human Right Watch Online, available at: www.hrw.org/reports/1996/killer6. htm#313th (accessed on March 28, 2008).
27 S. L. Blanton, "Foreign Policy in Transition? Human Rights, Democracy, and US Arms Exports," *International Studies Quarterly* 49, 2005, pp. 648–9.
28 Shifter and Stillerman, "US Human Rights Policy Toward Colombia," p. 338.
29 Human Rights Watch. Online, available at: www.hrw.org/reports/1996/killer3.htm (accessed on March 28, 2008).
30 This strategy is translated by HRW directly from the original document, which can be accessed online at www.hrw.org/reports/1996/killerapendixa.htm (accessed on March 28, 2008).
31 Gómez-Suárez, "Perpetrator Blocs," pp. 641–5.
32 An insightful analysis about US influence on the dynamics of the armed conflict is developed by Rojas. According to her, "the US has played a central role in the changing dynamics of the Colombian armed conflict by confusing a counternarcotics war with a counterinsurgency war in one single strategy, today identified as the war on terrorism" (my translation). D. Rojas, "Estados Unidos y la guerra en Colombia," in F. Gutierrez, M. Wills, and G. Sanchez (eds), *Nuestra guerra sin nombre: Transformaciones del conflicto en Colombia*, Bogotá: Grupo Editorial Norma, 2007, p. 41.
33 The Frente National was a political agreement signed between the leaders of the liberal and conservative parties in 1957. According to this, they were to share power for the next 16 years.
34 According to Tokatlián, due to quiet diplomacy on the drug issue, President Turbay implemented three changes in the political system: he signed the Treaty of Extradition (1979), drafted a Mutual Legal Assistance Treaty (1980), and instituted a vast program to eradicate marijuana. In return, between 1979 and 1981, Colombia received airplanes, communications and other operational materials, and more than $25 million in security assistance. See J. Tokatlián, "National Security and Drugs: Their Impact on Colombian–US Relations," *Journal of Interamerican Studies and World Affairs* 30, 1, 1988, p. 143.
35 F. Thoumi, "Some Implications of the Growth of the Underground Economy in Colombia," *Journal of Interamerican Studies and World Affairs* 29, 2, 1987, p. 41.
36 Tokatlián, "National Security and Drugs," p. 44.
37 Pearce, *Colombia Inside the Labyrinth*.
38 Ibid, p. 174.
39 J. Guerrero, "La sobrepolitización del narcotráfico en Colombia en los años ochenta y sus interferencias en los procesos de paz," in R. Peñaranda, and J. Guerrero *De las armas a la política*, Bogotá: Tercer Mundo Editores-IEPRI, 1999, pp. 247.
40 M. Bagley, and J. Tokatlián "Colombia Foreign Policy in the 1980s: The Search for Leverage," *Journal of Interamerican Studies and World Affairs* 27, 3, 1985, p. 41.
41 Ibid., p. 35.
42 Guerrero, "La sobrepolitización del narcotráfico," p. 245 (my translation).
43 M. Bagley, "The New Hundred Years War? US National Security and the War on Drugs in Latin America," *Journal of Interamerican Studies and World Affairs* 30, 1, 1988, p. 169.
44 Kerry Report, p. 36.
45 Thoumi, "Some Implications of the Growth of the Underground Economy," p. 48.

46 Guerrero, 'La sobrepolitización del narcotráfico," 1999, p. 222.
47 F. González, I. Bolívar, and T. Vázquez, *Violencia política en Colombia: De la nación fragmentada a la construcción del estado*, Bogotá: Cinep, 2004.
48 Guerrero, "La sobrepolitización del narcotráfico," p. 238.
49 A. Reyes, "Paramilitares en Colombia: Contexto, aliados y consecuencias," *Análisis Político* 12, January/April 1991.
50 Romero, "Élites regionales," p. 177.
51 See S. Dudley, *Walking Ghosts: Murder and Guerrilla Politics in Colombia*, New York: Routledge, 2004, p. 98.
52 L. Gill, *The School of the Americas: Military Training and Political Violence in the Americas*, Durham, NC: Duke University Press, 2004, p. 83.
53 Ibid., p. 9.
54 Ibid., p. 10.
55 Ibid., pp. xv–xvi.
56 For an account of military participation in the plot see www1.umn.edu/humanrts/cases/1%5E94col.htm (accessed on April 1, 2008).
57 It is calculated that by 1992 half of Colombian officers trained at SOA were responsible for gross human right violations (World Organisation Against Torture quoted in Gill, *The School of the Americas*, p. 137).
58 See Dudley, *Walking Ghosts*; González *et al.*, *Violencia política*; C. Ortíz, *Urabá: Pulsiones de vida y desafíos de muerte*, Bogotá: La Carreta Social, 2007; E. Pizarro, "Las terceras fuerzas en Colombia hoy: Entre la fragmentación y la impotencia," in R. Peñaranda and J. Guerrero *De las armas a la política*, Bogotá: Tercer Mundo Editores-IEPRI, 1999.
59 See Castaño's statements in M. Aranguren, *Mi confesión: Carlos Castaño revela sus secretos*, Bogotá: Oveja Negra, 2001, p. 98.
60 Pizarro "Las terceras fuerzas," p. 310.
61 Dudley, *Walking Ghosts*, pp. 95–7.
62 F. Giraldo, *Democracia y discurso político en la Unión Patriótica*, Bogotá: CEJA 2001.
63 M. Harnecker, *Entrevista con la nueva izquierda*, Managua: Editorial Colombia Nueva Ltd, 1989, pp. 29–43.
64 Pearce, *Colombia Inside the Labyrinth*, p. 232.
65 D. Feierstein, *El genocidio como práctica social: Entre el Nazismo y la experiencia Argentina*, Buenos Aires: Fondo de Cultura Económica, 2007.
66 This percentage varies depending on the sources. I rely on victims' statistics. Due to the high levels of impunity, the number of UP members assassinated is not known. See M. Cepeda and C. Girón, "La segregación de las víctimas de la violencia política," in A. Rettberg, *Entre el Perdón y el Paredón: Preguntas y Dilemas de la Justicia Transicional*, Bogota: Uniandes-CESO-IDRC, 2005.
67 Matta quoted in Cepeda and Girón, "La segregación," p. 274, my translation.
68 Herrera quoted in Dudley, *Walking Ghosts*, p. 93.
69 P. Gaitán, "Primera elección popular de Alcaldes: Expectativas y frustraciones," *Análisis Político*, 1988, p. 4.
70 Dudley, *Walking Ghosts*, p. 103.
71 Romero, "Élites regionales," p. 201; A. Ramírez, *Urabá: Los inciertos confines de una crisi*, Bogotá: Planeta, 1997, pp. 126–34.
72 See Dudley, *Walking Ghosts*, pp. 124–6.
73 Gómez-Suárez, "Perpetrators Blocs," p. 641.
74 Human Rights Watch. Online, available. at: www.hrw.org/reports/1996/killer3.htm (accessed on April 1, 2008). UNCHR, *Refugees by Numbers*.
75 M. Romero, *Paramilitares y autodefensas 1982–2003*, Bogotá: IEPRI, 2003.

Part III

The aftermath of state violence and genocide

9 Political violence, justice, and reconciliation in Latin America[1]

Ernesto Verdeja

Over the past 25 years, Latin America has confronted human rights violations in the context of highly constrained democratic transitions. These transitions had common features: the region had been a battlefield in the Cold War, a situation exacerbated by the success of the Cuban revolution and greater US intervention to stave off the spread of communism; Latin American military officers trained in the US and returned to their countries steeped in "National Security Doctrines" that privileged military stewardship above democratic politics; domestic leftist movements and revolutionary groups further polarized politics; and, economic uncertainty and weak political institutions paved the way for the rise of reactionary right-wing regimes. This chapter explores several important Latin American responses to legacies of human rights abuses that occurred in this context. For lack of space, I will look at only four cases – Argentina, Chile, Guatemala, and Peru – which have moved away from violent or otherwise authoritarian rule toward democracy, however imperfectly. Part I presents several normative goods that are necessary, I believe, to secure justice and reconciliation, and follows this with a discussion of institutions and strategies that may promote them (truth commissions, apologies, reparations schemes, trials, and others). Part II discusses several case studies in light of these norms.

Part I Normative concerns

When societies emerge from massive violence or war, they must face the difficult challenge of how to confront the past. Should they seek accountability for perpetrators, even if prosecutions may destabilize a fragile democratic regime, or focus instead on the needs of victims? Is it better to avoid any reckoning with past abuses, and simply "move on"? And what of reconciliation? What does it mean to reconcile a society that has been shattered by terrible abuse and violence? We should start, perhaps, with a consideration of the normative goals that transitional societies seek, with an understanding that under certain conditions these goals may be in conflict with one another.

Transitional societies often seek to secure a number of normative ends which are considered necessary to establishing a morally just peace. *Truth-telling* is crucial, for without knowledge of what actually happened it is impossible to address the legacies of violence or develop the necessary social trust for social regeneration. Holding perpetrators *accountable* is also important, as victims are unlikely to accept perpetrators who have not been punished.[2] Knowledge of wrongs is intimately tied to *victim acknowledgment,* underscoring the importance of inscribing narratives of past atrocity with the manifest recognition of the individuals and communities who suffered. Recognizing victims can serve several functions, including restoring their sense of dignity and self-worth, as well as contributing to and informing broader historical memory by complementing the work of formal historical projects. Establishing the *rule of law* is a common goal. A commitment to the rule of law means that the successor regime has agreed to reform relevant state institutions responsible for past crimes and provide the necessary mechanisms of accountability and oversight to ensure that individual rights will be respected. Finally, *reconciliation* – broadly understood as a normative shift from dehumanization, estrangement, and distrust to a notion of *respect* for others, including (most importantly) enemies – is necessary, if renewed violence is to be avoided.

While these may be worthy normative goods, they do not always work together; indeed, too much accountability in fragile circumstances can risk a political backlash, while victim recognition and truth-telling in the context of amnesties may only serve to further embitter survivors who see no possibility of securing justice. We should keep these concerns in mind as we consider the practical measures available to promote these normative goals.

How are these goals pursued? What are the institutional mechanisms available to transitional societies seeking reconciliation and justice? The answers are varied, depending partly on the transition and the constraints on incoming elites, the strength of civil society, and the role of external actors, such as the US.[3] Latin American transitions differ in important ways, but we can identify several general factors that affected each transition.

One is the nature of the violence. In the Southern Cone in particular, authoritarian regimes terrorized prone publics. While guerrilla groups existed in Argentina, Brazil, Chile, and Uruguay, they were minor threats to military rule, and in some cases were largely vanquished before state terror became acute. Elsewhere, there were significant leftist insurgencies, such as in El Salvador, Guatemala, and Peru (the last being nominally democratic during the first part of the civil war). The conflicts engulfed entire communities, often indigenous, and devastated the social landscape. While in all of these cases violence created a climate of fear, the violence in Central America (particularly Guatemala) was proportionally much higher than in the rest of Latin America, and was accompanied by the destruction of material infrastructure and cultural bonds. Consequently, the type and scope of the violence affect the necessary forms of social repair.

The mode of transition between regimes is also important. Most Latin American transitions were "pacted": incoming elites negotiated the terms of the transfer of power with outgoing leaders, in the process providing some concessions.[4] There were amnesties in Argentina, Brazil, Chile, El Salvador, Guatemala, Nicaragua, Peru, and Uruguay. Negotiated transitions differ, however, based on the relative strength of the actors. In Chile, Pinochet left office with significant political power, including control over the military, a favorable constitution, and amnesty, and only since his 1998 detention in Britain did his power begin to wane. In Argentina, the military was weaker during the transition, though it enjoyed impunity until relatively recently, when the amnesty was decisively overturned and prosecutions resumed. Undoubtedly, civil society's ability to pressure elites shapes justice and reparative measures.[5]

Third, the international context matters. Elites watched how neighboring Latin American countries, such as Argentina, dealt with their respective transitions and they attempted to learn lessons from those experiences. Perhaps the most important international actor, however, has been the US. Because of its support for abusive regimes throughout the region, the US has played a disproportionate role in transitional politics. With the end of the Cold War, American administrations have publicly supported a democratic (and free market) Latin America, but US intelligence services have continued to withhold incriminating evidence linking them to some of the region's most notorious perpetrators. This has severely hampered domestic prosecutions, strengthened impunity, and distorted understandings of the past.

With these factors in mind, we can consider a number of transitional justice mechanisms. A popular mechanism has been the *truth commission*, a temporary official institution investigating abuses in a specific country over a delimited period of time, producing a public record of violations and responsibility.[6] Truth commissions contribute to truth-telling by providing an account of the past based on available evidence, countering, to some extent, existing misrepresentations and lies. In Peru, the commission worked closely with civil society to provide spaces (*audiencias*) where victims, bystanders and perpetrators could publicly tell their stories and experiences, thereby contributing to victim acknowledgment. Commissions occasionally make recommendations for reparations and institutional reform of security forces and the judiciary.

Prosecutions normally play a central role in transitional justice, though given the constraints of most Latin American transitions, they are often limited or altogether absent, at least until well after the handover of power. Advocates argue that trials secure some degree of individual accountability for the greatest perpetrators and also promote the rule of law by curbing impunity and limiting authoritarian enclaves. Some countries have also begun *reparations* programs for victims.[7] The types of reparations vary widely, and may include financial compensation for torture or murder, restitution of stolen or destroyed property, and medical as well as psychological support for trauma, among other initiatives. *Official apologies* have become more popular, serving as important symbolic gestures of atonement and signaling to the entire society the importance of recognizing the wrongness of past actions and the rights of victims.[8]

Part II The cases

These transitional justice mechanisms have been used across Latin America, though to differing effect. This section sketches the transitions in four cases:

Argentina, Chile, Guatemala, and Peru. A more comprehensive account would include El Salvador, Honduras, Nicaragua, Uruguay, Brazil, and Colombia, at the very least, but this brief presentation provides a snapshot of the various responses to the past in Latin America, as well as the continued challenges these societies face.

Argentina

Argentina has a long history of military rule, but the juntas ruling from 1976 to 1983 were particularly violent, carrying out a terrifying "anti-subversive" campaign against alleged communists and leftists, resulting in the disappearances of between 10,000 and 30,000 persons. Under a radical National Security Doctrine and with explicit backing from the US, thousands were detained, tortured and killed, with many victims buried in clandestine graves or thrown into the sea.[9] After several years of economic and political failures and a humiliating defeat in the Malvinas/Falkands War, the military transferred power to civilian rule through a carefully negotiated transition. Newly installed President Raúl Alfonsín established the National Commission on the Disappeared (CONADEP) in 1983 to investigate human rights abuses committed by the military. Nongovernmental organizations (NGOs) had pushed for a stronger commission with the right to compel information from violators and originally opposed CONADEP, though most eventually supported the commission's work. Unsurprisingly, the commission was strongly opposed by the military.

CONADEP held no public hearings, but it collected 7,000 statements from individuals and eventually tallied 8,960 disappearances in its final report *Nunca Más* (*Never Again*), though this is now considered too low.[10] Argentina also provided substantial reparations for victims through a series of laws. Families of the disappeared and killed received $220,000 in state bonds,[11] and reparations were given to those who were imprisoned without trial or temporarily disappeared (i.e., where the state denied their detention). Congress also created a legal category, "forcibly disappeared," allowing families to process wills and close estates while still recognizing the possibility of the victim's reappearance.[12] In 1990, the government eliminated mandatory military service for children of the disappeared (though it is now a volunteer service), and passed legislation for housing credits and other material compensation for children of the disappeared. In 2004, reparations were extended to children of the disappeared who were kidnapped by military families.

The history of Argentina's human rights trials has been more complex. Alfonsín placed limited pressure on the military, identifying some officers for prosecution while encouraging the armed forces to clean house internally. In June 1985 several former junta members were tried and found guilty. Rather than bring closure to the past, however, the trial created greater unrest in the armed forces, particularly among junior officers. Increased military hostility culminated in new amnesty laws: the 1986 Ley de Punto Final or "full stop" law, which put a short deadline on bringing charges against alleged perpetrators, and the 1987 Ley de

Obediencia Debida, or "due obedience" law, which gave officers and soldiers legal protection if they could prove that they were "merely following orders" in committing atrocities. From the mid-1980s through 1990 several small but spectacular military uprisings dampened government interest in trials, though civil society groups like the Madres de Plaza de Mayo continued bringing attention to ongoing impunity. Carlos Menem, successor to Alfonsín, pardoned several convicted junta members and military officers, attempting to draw a dramatic line between the past and future. Nevertheless, interest in prosecutions resurfaced in 1998, when courts ruled that the pardons did not cover kidnappings of children of the disappeared, which constituted ongoing crimes. In March 2001, a federal judge ruled the full stop and due obedience laws unconstitutional, allowing for a number of human rights cases to proceed through the courts.[13]

. Over the past several years, the judiciary has begun pursuing offenders.[14] In 2006, former senior police official Miguel Etchecolatz was tried and found guilty of murder, kidnapping, and torture in a highly publicized case where the court ruled that the final years of the dictatorship had constituted "genocide."[15] Several former junta members lost many of their earlier legal protections, leaving open the possibility that they would serve out their entire life sentences handed down in 1985. Chaplin Christian von Wernich's prosecution in 2007 illuminated the Catholic Church's complicity in abuses,[16] a connection long known but nevertheless strongly denied by the Church.[17]

While Argentina originally preferred to pursue truth-telling and reparations, the past several years have witnessed a return to prosecutions for major offenders, many of whom no longer enjoy the protection or clout they once had. However, the full extent of US involvement with the juntas is still unclear; significant evidence showing American support for the vicious "dirty war" emerged in 2002, with the US State Department's release of thousands of classified documents from the era, but more documentation remains classified.[18] Nevertheless, the past is no longer hidden to the public, and the military no longer commands the respect and fear it once did.

Chile

Between 1973 and 1990, Chile suffered under a military junta led by General Augusto Pinochet. On September 11, 1973, with explicit US support, the military overthrew the leftist, democratically elected President Salvador Allende and immediately began the systematic persecution of members of his government, union leaders, and others who were considered supporters of the old government. Tens of thousands were imprisoned and tortured, and thousands were murdered.

The transition from authoritarian to civilian rule was highly constrained. The incoming government, a group of socialists and Christian Democrats called the Concertación, faced a 1978 amnesty and a constitution that provided the armed forces with significant financial and institutional autonomy and military influence in the Senate.

Because perpetrators could not be prosecuted, incoming President Patricio Aylwin established a Truth and Reconciliation Commission shortly after taking office in 1990. The commission was tasked with investigating "disappearances after arrest, executions, and torture leading to death committed by government agents or people in their service, as well as kidnappings and attempts on the life of persons carried out by private citizens for political reasons."[19] It did not investigate torture cases which did not result in death, though the number of torture victims is in the tens of thousands, and possibly low hundreds of thousands. Like Argentina's CONADEP, Chile's commission did not hold public hearings, but rather collected massive amounts of documentation on the "dirty war," as well as private depositions from victims and in a few cases, members of the military who spoke to commission members anonymously. Characteristically, the military actively opposed the commission, and its lack of subpoena power made it difficult for commission members to acquire information from the armed forces.

The commission's final report, completed in February 1991, catalogued nearly 3,000 disappearances and identified torture centers and military and police units involved in violations. The report held that over 95 percent of violations were committed by the state, undermining the claim that the armed forces were involved in an "internal war."[20] President Aylwin formally presented the final report several weeks later in a ceremony held in Santiago's national sports stadium, where the armed forces had detained and abused civilians in the early days of the coup. Speaking in his official capacity, Aylwin issued an apology and begged for forgiveness from victims and asked the nation to reflect on the violence brought on by military rule.[21] The report spent only a brief period in the headlines, however, for shortly after its publication a conservative senator was assassinated, and the right was able to return to a discourse of law and order and sideline discussions about human rights. For several years afterwards, there was little public discussion of past violations.[22]

Nevertheless, the government did provide reparations for the families of the killed and disappeared through the establishment of a National Corporation of Reparation and Reconciliation. Those families receive a monthly stipend of approximately $480 for life, as well as medical and psychological support. Children of the disappeared receive educational support, and those who were dismissed from government employment for political reasons have had their pensions reinstated, with lost years included. The government has also created a number of "memory sites," such as the former torture center Villa Grimaldi, to provide symbolic recognition of victims.

Chile's defining transitional justice development was the arrest of Pinochet in London in October 1998 on a warrant issued by a Spanish judge. The dictator spent nearly a year and a half in detention, and while he was eventually released on the specious grounds of ill-health, the case reanimated justice efforts in Chile and strengthened universal jurisdiction for serious human rights abuses.[23] In the following years in Chile, the amnesty law was weakened and a number of indictments were brought against human rights violators, including charges of torture against Pinochet himself in 2006 (he died shortly afterwards). By that year, over

100 military and police officials had been found guilty for disappearances, extra-judicial killings and torture, and over 30 generals of the armed forces and police had faced or were facing trial.[24]

Most attention has been on violations within Chile committed by Chileans, though there has been interest in investigating the role of the United States in the coup[25] and US support for international intelligence operations. Declassified CIA and State Department documents show close relations between the US and the junta, well after human rights violations were known in Washington.[26] In partic-ular, Operation Condor, a multinational Latin American intelligence program that targeted thousands of civilians across several countries, has come under stricter scrutiny since the transition.[27] This wider focus has provided a broader understanding of the complex relations between South American dictatorships and the United States, contextualizing the repression in the Southern Cone within the ongoing Cold War. Unfortunately, while these relations are well known in Latin America, in the US they receive little sustained attention.

In many respects, Chile has achieved remarkable results in its ongoing efforts to confront the past. While the military is still a powerful institution, many of the old guard supporters of Pinochet are no longer in power, and the repression of the "dirty war" years can no longer be denied. Nevertheless, Chile remains a divided nation, with significant portions of the population still supporting the coup and the violence it unleashed.

Guatemala

Guatemala's civil war between the leftist Unidad Revolucionaria Nacional Gua-temalteca (URNG) and the US-backed government took the lives of 200,000 people. The majority of the deaths have been attributed to government forces, which carried out particularly vicious attacks in the 1980s including large-scale massacres of indigenous peoples and the entire destruction of rural villages.[28] The war came to an end through a series of UN-mediated peace negotiations in the mid-1990s.[29]

The peace negotiations resulted in a commitment to establish a UN-backed truth commission. The commission, known as the Historical Clarification Com-mission (CEH), was put forth as a viable alternative to prosecutions, which were impossible given the political climate at the time of transition.[30] Civil society groups organized through the Assembly of Civil Society had been extremely active in the transition and welcomed the CEH as an important mechanism for shedding light on past abuses and recognizing the rights and dignity of victims, though support thinned noticeably after it emerged that some of the commis-sion's powers would be strictly curtailed, including its right to name individual perpetrators in its final report. Nevertheless, the CEH amassed significant docu-mentary and testimonial evidence of human rights violations. It also successfully petitioned the US government for thousands of files related to the civil war, which proved pivotal in outlining Guatemala's military command structures and the responsibility of different units for atrocities. Furthermore, it brought attention to the role and responsibility of the US in the conflict, situating the civil war in the context of Cold War proxy battles between the superpowers.[31]

The CEH's final report, released in 1999, was an important step in Guatemala's reckoning with its past.[32] Released in a moving ceremony attended by thousands, the report provided a nuanced account of Guatemala's history of peasant exploitation, tracing the dynamics of repression and marginalization since the country's early years. Its reading of the civil war detailed massive human rights abuses by state security forces, and concluded that "agents of the state of Guatemala, within the framework of counterinsurgency operations carried out between 1981 and 1983, committed acts of genocide against groups of Mayan people."[33] The commission recommended reparations for victims and institutional reform of the judiciary and state security agencies, though there has been little progress on these fronts.

Civil society actors have played a particularly important role in post-conflict Guatemala.[34] The Catholic Church's Human Rights Office established its own investigative project called Recovery of Historical Memory (REMHI), which sent interviewers into remote rural villages to take testimonies from victims. Organized through local church groups, the interviews resulted in a remarkable portrait of the civil war told in the words of the people who suffered through it.[35] Its report *Nunca Más* reinforced the findings of the CEH and gave greater moral support to Maya claims for repair and restitution. Its findings were sufficiently dramatic that the main force behind REMHI, Catholic Bishop Juan José Gerardi, was bludgeoned to death days after the report was released.

US involvement in the Central American wars has been well documented, thanks largely to the role played by Guatemalan human rights groups working closely with US and international NGOs. Since the Peace Accords in 1996, significant evidence has emerged of US logistical and financial support for Guatemala's military during the conflict, as well as American training of some of the most violent Guatemalan officers.[36] As recognition of American complicity, then President Bill Clinton apologized in 1999 for US support of anti-democratic forces in Guatemala, though the apology was evasive and in any case received little attention in the US.[37]

Over the past decade, justice has moved slowly in Guatemala. There has been little success in prosecuting human rights violators, and in December 2007 Guatemala's Constitutional Court refused to extradite former dictator Efraín Rios Montt and other officials to Spain to stand trial for genocide and crimes against humanity (indeed, he still exerts substantial political power at home).[38] There have been practically no reparations for the Mayan community, and while in 2004 the government formally recognized responsibility for the 1990 murder of human rights activist Myrna Mack (after pressure from the Inter-American Court of Human Rights),[39] security forces still commit human rights abuses and enjoy little accountability or oversight. Weak democratic institutions, continued impunity in the security forces, and little practical victim support mean that reconciliation in Guatemala is still far off.

Peru

Peru's 20-year civil war (1980–2000) between the state and two armed leftist groups, the Sendero Luminoso (SL) and the Movimiento Revolucionario Túpac Amaru (MRTA), resulted in the deaths of approximately 69,000 people and displaced and harmed tens of thousands more. The conflict largely ended under the rule of the democratically elected, increasingly dictatorial President Alberto Fujimori (1990–2000) who, following a 1992 "auto-coup," closed Congress, purged the courts, and passed a number of radical anti-terrorism laws and an amnesty for security forces, and permitted them to carry out disappearances and torture. State institutions were left weakened and corrupt and the security forces enjoyed widespread impunity for human rights violations. President Fujimori fled to Japan in 2000 as secret videotapes emerged of his powerful advisor, Vladimiro Montesinos, bribing politicians and military leaders. As a first step in responding to the legacy of civil war, an interim government established a truth commission in 2001.

While there was originally significant public support for prosecuting corrupt officials, there was markedly less interest in pursuing human rights violators. Peru's Truth and Reconciliation Commission (CVR), tasked with investigating the causes, effects, and responsibility of the civil war, initially met skepticism and opposition from across the political spectrum. Nevertheless, a well-organized human rights movement operating under the umbrella group Coordinadora Nacional de Derechos Humanos launched a major political and media campaign to investigate abuses, and the commission succeeded in capitalizing on this renewed support. The commission was the first in Latin America to hold public hearings and permit victims to speak about their experiences at length. Between public hearings and private interviews, it collected nearly 17,000 testimonies throughout the country[40] and identified 4,600 mass graves, inspecting 2,200 of them.[41]

The final report was published in 2003. It documented widespread abuses amounting to crimes against humanity, including massacres, disappearances, rape, torture, and the destruction of entire communities. The report held the SL responsible for the majority of deaths and disappearances, with the armed forces and police responsible for most of the remainder. The CVR found that preexisting racial and gender discrimination exacerbated the violence, and noted that the majority of the victims were indigenous peoples, even though they constitute a minority of the population.[42] Furthermore, the commission recommended a comprehensive reparations program; reparations legislation was passed in 2005 and recently 250 rural communities received collective reparations.[43] Nevertheless, exactly who qualifies as a victim has been a topic of heated debate, as evident when the Inter-American Court of Human Rights ruled that family members of SL guerrillas who were massacred in prison have a right to reparations.[44]

In an effort to complement accountability measures, the commission's findings and evidence were forwarded to the Public Ministry for criminal investigation. The CVR recommended further investigation in 43 cases, and prosecution in over a hundred others.[45] A 2001 decision by the Inter-American Court of Human Rights ruling the 1995 amnesty in violation of international law made this possible. Because many insurgents were tried during the civil war, most of the recent prosecutions are against the security forces, though rebels have been retried due to the lack of impartiality of earlier military trials. While prosecutions have been relatively slow, members of the Colina Group, one of the most notorious government death squads, have been convicted for violations, as well as some members of SL. Most importantly, Fujimori was found guilty of corruption and human rights abuses.[46]

While the US did not provide as extensive military and logistical support to Fujimori as it did to its Central American allies, the extent of direct US support is still unknown, largely because relatively few relevant cables and documents have been released publicly. Unlike earlier US efforts regarding Guatemala and El Salvador to release records related to those civil wars, Washington has largely refrained from providing substantial support to Peru's CVR or human rights prosecutors.

The prospects for reconciliation in Peru remain uncertain. While the CVR had a marked impact on the public understanding of the war, there seems little sustained interest in investigating violations. It is unclear whether renewed focus on Fujimori will promote public reflection on the legacies of the conflict.

Conclusion

Latin America still struggles with its past. Some countries have seen real, if limited, successes in fighting impunity and uncovering abuses, while others have barely confronted the consequences of massive violations. This chapter has only sketched some of the responses in a handful of cases, but even this relatively brief discussion highlights the varied ways that societies have reckoned with repression, and the real obstacles to reconciliation that still exist. Argentina and Chile have made significant advances in reckoning with past abuses, though this has been possible only with the erosion of military power (more so in Argentina than Chile) and a strong democratic commitment to reasserting the rule of law. While reparations policies were enacted relatively early in both countries, prosecutions occurred much later. Peru's confrontation with its past has been somewhat mixed. The truth commission's widely circulated findings, combined with broad support from the human rights community, has put the suffering of indigenous peoples squarely in public debate, but the country has been more concerned with investigating corruption scandals than human rights violations. Guatemala has accomplished the least in terms of transitional justice and reconciliation. Old authoritarian enclaves still persist, and rampant impunity of the armed forces and police, a corrupt judiciary, and continued exploitation and marginalization of the indigenous population hamper significant change. Both truth commission reports helped raise awareness of the atrocities committed during the war, but perpetrators and their supporters can still thwart justice efforts.

We can make several general observations: first, that transitional societies often seek several moral ends, including a reasonably accurate description of past atrocities, accountability for the most egregious violators, some form of victim acknowledgment and reparation, and the establishment of the rule of law. Whether and how these goals are met depend on the context of the transition and the relative power of the actors involved, but meaningful reconciliation is unlikely if past atrocities are denied, perpetrators continue to enjoy impunity, and victims are ignored and live in fear and poverty. Second, particular institutional devices, such as truth commissions, trials, apologies, reparations programs, and institutional reform, can further some of these goals, though their success requires more than technical expertise; it also necessitates support from civil society and democratic elites as well as weakened authoritarian enclaves. Where the military and their supporters still exercise significant power, the promises of reconciliation and justice may not come to fruition and the legacies of past violence will carry over into the future. Third, international actors such as the US are important to the prospects of justice. While Washington has often publicly encouraged curbing impunity and reinstalling the rule of law, US intelligence agencies have provided important information only grudgingly, and many details of US involvement in the "dirty wars" of Latin America remain unknown.

The challenges to reintegrating survivors, securing accountability, remembering the past, and promoting democratic practices are significant. Whether Latin America will succeed in overcoming these challenges remains to be seen.

Notes and references

1 Special thanks to Marcia Esparza and anonymous reviewers for their helpful comments and suggestions.
2 C. Nino, *Juicio al Mal Absoluto*, Buenos Aires: Ariel, 2006.
3 G. Gill, *The Dynamics of Democratization: Elites, Civil Society and the Transition Process*, Basingstoke: Macmillan Press, 2001.
4 J. Zalaquett, "Balancing Ethical Imperatives and Political Constraints: The Dilemma of New Democracies Confronting Past Human Rights Violations," *Hastings Law Journal* 43, 6, 2002, pp. 1425–38.
5 L. Castro Leiva and A. Pagden, "Civil Society and the Fate of Modern Republics of Latin America," in in S. Kaviraj and K. Sunil (eds), *Civil Society: History and Possibilities*, Cambridge: Cambridge University Press, 2001, pp. 179–203.
6 P. Hayner, *Unspeakable Truths: Confronting State Terror and Atrocity*, London: Routlege, 2001.
7 P. De Greiff, (ed.), *The Handbook of Reparations*, Oxford: Oxford University Press, 2006; E. Verdeja, "Reparations in Democratic Transitions," *Res Publica* 12, 2, June 2006, pp. 115–36.
8 Elazar Barkan, and Alexander Karn (eds), *Taking Wrongs Seriously: Apologies and Reconciliation*, Stanford, CA: Stanford University Press, 2006.
9 H. Verbitsky, *The Flight: Confessions of an Argentine Dirty Warrior*, New York: New Press, 1996.
10 Argentine National Commission on the Disappeared *Nunca Más: Report of the Argentine National Commission on the Disappeared*, New York: Farrar Straus & Giroux, 1986.

11 Argentina, Law No. 24,411 (1994).
12 Argentina, Law No. 24,321 (1994).
13 *La Nación*, March 8, 2001, p. 1.
14 C. Acuña, "Transitional Justice in Argentina and Chile: A Never-ending Story?" in J. Elster, (ed.), *Retribution and Reparation in the Transition to Democracy*, Cambridge: Cambridge University Press, 2006, pp. 209–15.
15 *La Nación*, September 19, 2006, p. 1.
16 BBC Online, "'Dirty War' Priest gets Life Term," October 10, 2007. Online, available at: http://news.bbc.co.uk/2/hi/americas/7035294.stm (accessed on January 21, 2008).
17 Mark Osiel, *Mass Atrocity, Evil and Hannah Arendt: Criminal Consciousness in Argentina's Dirty War*, New Haven, CT: Yale University Press, 2002.
18 National Security Archive, "State Department Opens Files on Argentina's Dirty War" (August 20, 2002). Online, available at: www.gwu.edu/~nsarchiv/NSAEBB/NSAEBB73/press.htm (accessed on July 25, 2008).
19 Chile, "Decree Establishing the National Commission on Truth and Reconciliation," Supreme Decree No. 355, April 25, 1990, reprinted in N. Kritz, (ed.), *Transitional Justice: How Emerging Democracies Reckon with Former Regimes*, Washington, DC, United States Institute of Peace, 3, 1995, p. 102.
20 Chile, *Informe de la Comisión Nacional de Verdad y Reconciliación*, Santiago, Ministerio del Interior de la República de Chile, 1991, vol. 1, p. 15.
21 Patricio Aylwin, "Chile: Statement by President Aylwin on the Report of the National Commission on Truth and Reconciliation," in N. Kritz (ed.), *Transitional Justice: How Emerging Democracies Reckon with Former Regimes*, Washington, DC: United States Institute of Peace Press, 1995, pp. 171–2.
22 T. Moulian, *Chile actual: Anatomía de un mito*, Santiago: LOM ARCIS, 1998.
23 Christiane Wilke, "A Particular Universality: Universal Jurisdiction for Crimes against Humanity in Domestic Courts" *Constellations* 12/1, 2005, pp. 83–102.
24 Human Rights Watch "Pinochet Held on Torture Charges," *Human Rights News* (October 31, 2006).
25 Peter Kornbluh, *The Pinochet File*, New York: New Press, 2004.
26 Central Intelligence Agency, "CIA Activities in Chile" (September 19, 2000). Online, available at: www.gwu.edu/~nsarchiv/news/20000919/index.html (accessed on July 22, 2008).
27 John Dinges, *The Condor Years*, New York: New Press, 2004.
28 Victor Montejo, *Testimony: Death of a Guatemalan Village*, Willimantic CT: Curbstone Press, 1987.
29 S. Jonas, *Of Centaurs and Doves: Guatemala's Peace Processes*, Boulder, CO: Westview Press, 2000.
30 United Nations, "Acuerdo sobre el establecimiento para el esclarecimiento histórico de las violaciones a los derechos humanos y los hechos de violencia que han causado sufrimientos a la población guatemalteca," UN Doc. A/48/954/S/1994/751 (June 23, 1994).
31 US government documents and cables available at National Security Archive, "The Guatemalan Military: What the US Files Reveal," 2 vols. (June 1, 2000), Online, available at: www.gwu.edu/~nsarchiv/NSAEBB/NSAEBB32/index.html (accessed on July 10, 2008).
32 Comisión para el Esclarecimiento Histórico, Guatemala, *Informe final: Memoria del silencio* (1999). Available http://shr.aaas.org/guatemala/ceh/mds/spanish/. Accessed January 10, 2008.
33 Comisión para el Esclarecimiento Histórico, "Conclusiones y recomendaciones," in ibid. para. 122.
34 K. B. Warren, *Indigenous Movements and Their Critics: Pan-Mayan Activism in Guatemala*, Princeton, NJ: Princeton University Press, 1998.

35 Proyecto Interdiocesano Recuperación de la Memoria Histórica *Guatemala: Nunca más* , 4 vols, Guatemala City: Archdiocese of Guatemala, 1999.
36 L. Gill, *School of the Americas: Military Training and Political Violence in the Americas*, Durham, NC: Duke University Press, 2004.
37 Mark Gibney and Erik Roxstrom, "The Status of State Apologies," *Human Rights Quarterly* 23, 4, 2001, pp. 911–39.
38 BBC, "Spain Seeks Guatemalan Ex-Rulers," December 23, 2007. Online, available at: http://news.bbc.co.uk/2/hi/americas/6205327.stm (accessed on January 25, 2008).
39 Human Rights Watch, "State: Government Recognizes Role in Political Killing," *Human Rights News*, April 22, 2004.
40 Peru, *Informe Final de la Comisión de la Verdad y Reconciliación de Perú*, 9 vols, Lima: Comisión de la Verdad y Reconciliacíon, 2003, p. 40. Online, available at: www.cverdad.org.pe/ifinal/index.php accessed (accessed on January 13, 2008).
41 Peru, *Informe Final*, vol. VIII, appendix 2, "El proceso de exhumación de fosas."
42 Peru, *Informe Final*, vol. I, ch. 3 "Los rostros y perfiles de la violencia," 45.
43 "Entregan reparaciones colectivas a 250 comunidades," *Enlace Nacional*, November 22, 2007. Online, available at: http://enlacenacional.com/2007/11/22/entregan-reparaciones-colectivas-a-250-comunidades/ (accessed on January 23, 2008).
44 "Perú pide a la CIDH que no lo obligue a pagar reparación a Sendero Luminoso," *El Comercio*, January 2, 2008. Online, available at: www.elcomercioperu.com.pe/ediciononline/HTML/2008–01–02/Peru-pide-CiDH-que-no-lo-obligue-pagar-reparacion-Sendero-Luminoso.html (accessed January 23, 2008).
45 L. Laplante, "The Peruvian Truth Commission's Historical Memory Project" *Journal of Human Rights* 6, 2007, p. 443.
46 "Minuto a minuto: juicio contra Alberto Fujimori," *El Comercio*, December 10, 2007. Online, available at: www.elcomercioperu.com.pe/ediciononline/HTML/2007–12–10/minuto-minuto-juicio-contra-alberto-fujimori.html (accessed on January 24, 2008).

10 Vicious legacies?

State violence(s) in Argentina[1]

Guillermina S. Seri

> The military, who did they send first? The police...
> Who went to the forefront? The police.
> Who kicked out the houses' front doors to enter? The police.
> Who were the ones who "marked" places? The police. The police...
> > Police commissioner, Argentina, 2003

What are the legacies of genocidal violence? Argentina hardly resembles what it was in the period after March 24, 1976 when the military dictatorship of El Proceso[2] made 30,000 people "disappear." Three decades later, democratic institutions have proven resilient and, after Congress annulled laws preventing trials for past state atrocities,[3] more than 200 such lawsuits, out of an anticipated thousand, are under way. For the first time, the word *genocide* has gained legal currency. Ex-police chief Miguel Etchecolatz and Catholic priest and former chaplain Christian von Wernich have been sentenced for crimes committed "in the framework of the genocide that took place in Argentina between 1976 and 1983."[4] As time passes, genocide becomes a term and a part of history that is more readily acceptable, as is the case with the former generals Antonio Domingo Bussi and Luciano Benjamín Menéndez. Their indictment brings light to and characterizes the state's killings, which were designed in September 1975 as a "final solution."[5] However, ongoing judicial prosecutions do not prevent the past from mentally and physically haunting Argentines. On September 17, 2006, Julio López, a key witness in Etchecolatz's case, *disappeared.* And just as his absence has allowed us a glimpse into the shadows of state terror, other witnesses have been threatened, and ESMA[6] torturer Héctor Febres died from cyanide before being sentenced. Meanwhile, CORREPI, the Coordinator against Police and Institutional Repression, reports less visible, albeit extended, arbitrary killings by members of the police and the security forces. In fact, CORREPI has documented the deaths of 2,334 harmless individuals since the return of democracy in 1983.[7] The victims, overwhelmingly male, poor, and young – including children – were killed in the street just because of their appearance, or died in deplorably overpopulated prisons, or while locked away in police stations.[8] Even though the total numbers are unknown, this data shows that, in Argentina, state violence has not ended but has become diffuse. Puzzlingly, more than one third of these deaths, 847, occurred under the government of Néstor Kirchner, a president who made human rights a priority. Are deaths by the police a continuation of El Proceso or do they call for a more extended genealogy?

This essay interrogates Argentina's violent palimpsest in its endogenous, structural, and transnational roots, focusing on the legacies of the genocidal violence of El Proceso in current forms of state violence. Similarities and continuities between violent practices connected to the state, performed by its different specialized organs and developing at a different pace, find a decisive link in policing. Julio Simón, Etchecolatz, and Von Wernich, the first condemned in recent trials, were part of *la bonaerense*, the police of the Buenos Aires province. In the 1970s, police officers constituted the largest group of perpetrators after the army. In fact, the genocidal violence of El Proceso took the form of a police operation advanced by what Julie Taylor appropriately characterizes as a police dictatorship.[9] As Taylor observes, the decades after El Proceso gave a free rein to state terror, it "now openly stalks the Argentine streets as the *gatillo fácil*,"[10] the police trigger-happy eagerness to use deadly force. Furthering this analysis, I draw here on the transcripts of about 70 tape interviews with members of the police and public security officers from eight different Argentine districts collected between 2001 and 2007, on documents, and on secondary data, to explore the bonds between past genocidal violence and current police violence.

Acknowledging the specificity of genocide should not prevent us from recognizing how regular police techniques of collecting information and identifying, arresting, and interrogating individuals, all central to maintaining order in liberal democracies, are also key elements in the organization and implementation of massacres by the state. Modern states consist of relatively autonomous and self-preserving administrative, military, and police apparatuses coordinated by an executive in a "Janus faced structure" of internal and transnational alliances.[11] States trust policing to professionalized officers and, in varying degrees, also to intelligence and military agents and private bodies. One of the main aspects involved in policing is law enforcement. The other is maintaining public order, which Argentine police officers refer to as prevention and describe as comprising "everything," from giving street directions to detaining suspicious individuals.

Approximately 170,000 police officers watch the lives and property of almost 40 million Argentines. The country's "effort of police" comprises one federal and 23 provincial civilian forces, plus two militarized bodies, the gendarmerie and the prefecture, which patrol borders, ports, and airports. By law, the Argentine military performs police functions only exceptionally, yet the increasing presence of the security forces controlling street protests amounts to militarizing policing. Throughout history, Argentines have endured domestically "the hostilities that citizens of other states experience mainly in the area of foreign relations."[12] As one commissioner observes, the problems with the police in Argentina are not just "a consequence of the military regime of 1976, or 1983; we verify them throughout history."[13] In fact, Argentina exhibits a solid tradition of elite association with the police, the military, and irregular forces in eliminating "internal threats."[14] After the beginning of the twentieth century, immigrants were received with strict residence laws, deportations, and violence. In 1909, the police killed close to a hundred strikers in Buenos Aires. Helped by Liga Patriótica paramilitaries, the number of dead escalated to several hundred in 1919, and the military executed hundreds more in Patagonia in 1921. Torture became systematic in police stations after the 1930 military coup and the introduction of the *picana* (electric prod) in 1934.[15] The foundational violence of the Argentine state against indigenous peoples, *gauchos* – traditional nomadic cowboys – and provincial *caudillos*, would reappear targeting immigrants, political subversives in the 1970s, and now "criminals."

Patriotic traditions notwithstanding, El Proceso materialized a wave of Cold War state terror with a conservative death toll estimate of 22 million.[16] Mounted on a shadow state apparatus outside the law, Cold War violence mixed police techniques used to track individuals with the military might to destroy them as internal enemies. Focusing on examining the police links between the terror of El Proceso and current forms of state violence in Argentina, in this essay I also interrogate the role of foreign actors and transnational networks in perpetuating clandestine state apparatus. Overall, I contend, Argentina illustrates the always latent genocidal potential within state power.

During the Argentinean genocide: El Proceso as a police operation

In 1977, at a press conference, President General Jorge Rafael Videla told journalists that the thousands of people they were asking for were neither dead nor alive, but just *disappeared*. Like its Kafkaesque reference, El Proceso offered the experience of a totalitarian police state that sent people to death for no apparent reason, other than having books or ideas judged dangerous. It was the way the dictatorship protected what Judith Filc calls the "great Argentine family" from subversion,[17] an enemy that a Rosario police chief qualified as non-Argentine,[18] and priests such as von Wernich or generals such as Camps considered as "non-persons." For the dominant Catholic-nationalist military faction, subversion grew everywhere, surreptitiously and ontologically, undermining "Christian and Western values" and natural patriarchal hierarchies.[19] Along these lines, Argentine crusaders judged themselves "the West's moral reserve" or "the extreme West."[20]

Subversives were likened to a pest or cancer corroding the Christian and Western state. Thus, Videla's Chancellor Guzzeti justified right-wing terrorism as the "antibodies" necessary to prevent "microbes" from eating up society's "entrails," which inexorably called for "surgical" solutions. Yet far from being clean and tidy, the state's scalpels were *grupos de tareas*, paramilitary squads mixing military and police personnel with common criminals. Exercising the broadest discretionary power regarding life and death, they kidnapped, tortured, murdered, and stole babies and property, supported by the police authorities freeing zones for them by not responding to calls. Those defined as "subversives" – university students and professors, teenagers, schoolteachers, factory workers, journalists, entire families, grassroots religious activists, and even military children – were taken to clandestine centers of detention[21] or makeshift death camps in public buildings or private homes. Surrounded by extreme cruelty, pain, blood, filth, and death, life in these detention centers alternated between the routine of torture and the terrifying transfers indicating executions or twisted surreal scenes such as perpetrators offering a Christmas banquet to prisoners before killing them. Most who did not die during torture sessions were executed or thrown alive from planes into the sea. Very few survived. Frequently, those who did survive had to face an official denial of any atrocities. Rare occasions when the truth lay bare felt no less surreal, as when the Buenos Aires' military governor announced that after subversives were dealt with, their their "collaborators," "sympathizers," the "indifferent" and "the timid" would also be killed[22] Like von Wernich, many other priests comforted the torturers.[23]

It is often overlooked that terror started before the coup, through right-wing paramilitary squads such as the Argentine Anticommunist Alliance (Triple A) created in 1973 and 19 other groups operating between 1970 and 1975.[24] The Triple A, for example, organized by ex-police officer and Perón's main aide Jose López Rega and by Commissioner General Alberto Villar, which integrated civilians and police and military personnel, murdered an estimated 700 to 2,500 people.[25] Tolerated by Perón, the organization linked Argentines to police, intelligence, and military agents throughout the Americas. The Triple A dissolved after the coup as its members joined *grupos de tareas*, the first of which was joined by the federal police.

Officially, repression began in February 1975, when President Isabel Perón set the Operativo Independencia in Tucumán to "annihilate the action" of guerrillas. In a few months, police and security forces were subordinated to the army, a council of internal security coordinated repression with provincial authorities, and future Videla minister General Albano Harguindeguy headed the federal police. Soon after the coup, military officers led all police forces. Yet beyond a militarization of the police, there was "*un transvasamiento*," or exchange, one commissioner observed,[26] through which the police became subordinated to the military and the military learned from the police how to individualize and chase subversives, an essential aspect of El Proceso's terror.

Not only did the military use the police "as cheap labor for their worst activities,"[27] but such a war could not have been fought without the police, who, as one of my interviewees highlights, knew "how to operate in the terrain of a neighborhood."[28] Thus, argues this commissioner, when Argentina in the 1970s confronted "subversion, terrorism," since "the military man does not know how to move in an urban setting," but "the police officer does," the military sent the police to the front lines of "the war against subversion." Although many policemen died, he observes, it was the military that got the "big screen" and were deemed "heroes" for having "defeated and banished subversion and terrorism from our country."

State terror, especially manifested in genocide, generally must take the form of a police operation. The state claim to the monopoly of violence identified by Max Weber is no less important than its control of the *means of legibility* discussed by James Scott,[29] which make the lives of individuals transparent and governable. The conjunction of violence and information endows the state with an extraordinary power, which allows benign uses but contains a genocidal potential. Both legibility and violence meet in the exercise of policing. Supported by state force, police officers have discretion to decide whether and how to intervene. Ultimately, their decisions are authorized by the state until successfully questioned in a court of law. If fusing information, law, and violence makes the police "ghostly," as Walter Benjamin puts it, and a potentially totalitarian power, these nightmarish possibilities materialized in El Proceso.

As fictional Colonel Mathieu explains to his subordinates in *The Battle of Algiers*, even if they despise police work, "the police method," including traditional techniques of identifying, arresting, and interrogating individuals, is key in identifying, localizing, interrogating; in this context, this becomes a euphemism for torture, and eventually the elimination of internal enemies. The image of police work as dirty but essential is popular in Argentina. It lies behind Luis Abelardo Patti's rejection of involving the military in policing as the police and security forces have "already covered themselves with mud."[30] It emerges in former Colonel Seineldín's understanding of policing as the combating of "internal diseases" of the nation or of "microorganisms" that rot from the inside. As their "daily combat against Evil" surrounded by "filth" exposes the police to "contagion" and "contamination,"[31] Seineldín judges it wise to have generals and colonels head police forces.

In any event, El Proceso did not give police officers the choice not to get "contaminated." Not many had the courage to leave the force, the luck to survive, and the honor to be called back by democratic authorities.[32] Members of the police reluctant to collaborate with the "war against subversion," or who knew "too much," were themselves frequently murdered. This was the fate of Inspector Carlos María Aristegui, who was never seen again after receiving families and giving them information about their missing, disappeared, or murdered relatives. Others, such as Juan Sirnio, were murdered for refusing to torture, or for being suspected guerrilla sympathizers, or for getting caught in the battles between military, police, and intelligence forces.[33] The state blamed these deaths on subversives. A significant number of police officers remain missing today.[34]

The aftermath of genocide: police violence, the underbelly of a *rioplatense* leviathan

Rodrigo Corzo borrowed his father's car to go visit his girlfriend. While he was driving through Villa Tesei, in Greater Buenos Aires, two patrol officers judged him suspicious and decided to follow his car. Crossing a bridge, one of the police officers pulled out his gun and shot at Rodrigo while he continued driving. The bullet, entering him from behind, killed him. The police planted a gun on the body to fake a shoot-out. This occurred on June 28, 2003. In another blatant case of police abuse, on October 6, 2007, in Rosario, Diego Blanco, 29, was found dead, hanging in his cell soon after his detention. If one has to trust official police and prison reports, too many individuals detained for identification or misdemeanors seem to feel an urge to commit suicide by hanging right after entering police stations in Argentina.

From newspaper records, the Center for Social and Legal Studies (CELS) counts 2,753 deaths by the police between 1996 and 2006 in the Buenos Aires metropolitan area alone. Forty nine percent of the 2,334 victims recorded by CORREPI nationwide were under 25, most of them poor males living in "difficult" neighborhoods. More than half of the deaths were "trigger-happy" killings, and one third occurred in police stations and prisons, frequently after torture. In 2001, a "death squadron" operating in the north of the Greater Buenos Aires came to light. Two of its victims, "Piti" Burgos, 16, and "Monito" Galván, 14, were found dead, gagged, with their hands tied, just a few hours after being picked up by a Tigre police patrol car. The same death squadron murdered 16-year-old Angel Fabián Blanco.

Like the federal police, most provincial police forces have enjoyed the prerogative of arresting individuals and groups preventively. In 1953, Perón's Code of Police Justice exempted police officers from civilian jurisdiction.[35] Organized by President Justo after 1932, political policing expanded under Perón, as the federal police's "Special Section" infiltrated and crushed political, cultural, and civic organizations, using such tactics as *disappearing*.[36] After its creation in 1946, SIDE, the centralized organism of intelligence, has not ceased expanding under successive presidents.[37]

As bad as this sounds, no inherent "police culture" should be blamed. Indeed, the organization of policing in modern Argentina deliberately excluded its own civic traditions, which emerged from its early decades of "intense institutional experimentation."[38] Losses include the institution of civilian commissioners represented by Hipólito Irigoyen, Argentina's first democratic president in 1916. Purging any civilian and republican roots through waves of professionalization, Argentine elites brought their police closer to the military through a repertoire of authoritarianism, secrecy, isolation, and harassment and criminalization of the poor. The police were also alienated from civilian life. Only certain categories of people gained access to *political* forms of government, while most of the poor remained governed through *police*. After the 1990s neoliberal restructuring, testimonies of the poor reveal that this is still the case.

"Support your police: beat yourself up." This graffiti, in Barrio Paraná XX, in Entre Ríos, makes one smile only until one learns about the brutal police beatings and threats targeting teenage boys in order to contain them within their neighborhoods. "As prisons can't take more people," a frustrated father explains, the police turn the houses of the poor into *de facto* prisons for their children.[39] In contrast to the shantytowns built by migrant industrial workers in the 1950s and the 1960s, excluded Argentines "are neither employed nor mobilized," Javier Auyero observes,[40] nor are their children permitted to look for opportunities in a country with a GINI index close to 0.50. Warehousing, ostracizing, and ghettoizing the socially vulnerable in "hyper-shantytowns"[41] accompanies their identification as a new internal threat.

Evoking the treatment of "subversives" in Argentina, President Menem in 1998 bluntly chose the language of El Proceso to securitize criminal suspects by defining crime as "a new modality in the field of subversion." Helped by media-amplified fear of crime, *mano dura* arguments gained ground in the 1990s, preaching "maximum violence to show efficacy in terms of the quantity of the dead and people in prison"[42] and dismissing due process as a formality, notes León Arslanián. These views led to sound electoral victories of El Proceso figures now indicted, such as Patti in the Buenos Aires province or Bussi in Tucumán. With the promise of "filling criminals with bullets," rightist Carlos Ruckauf became governor of Buenos Aires in 1999.

Even the politically mobilized did not escape violence. Detained for an alleged misdemeanor, Cristian Ibáñez, a *piquetero* from Jujuy, was found dead by hanging in his cell on October 2, 2003. As people marched to protest his death, the police killed Marcelo Cuéllar, Cristian's friend. The cold-blooded street executions of Maximiliano Kosteki and Dario Santillán in a *piquetero* protest on June 26, 2002, in Puente Pueyrredón, Buenos Aires, and the murder of Carlos Fuentealba, a schoolteacher and union leader, on April 5, 2007, in Neuquén, are well documented. The hundreds wounded in Puente Pueyrredón and other protests are not. CORREPI has identified 51 community leaders and activists killed by the police and the security forces in Argentina since 1995. Most of the killers were underpaid, undertrained, underclass police subordinate personnel.

> We *are* the Governor. We are the Governor's "Godfather." Do you know the novel? The Godfather is involved in everything. In good things, in bad things, in little affairs, in big issues. We are the Godfather of the Governor ... For what would the Governor do without the police?[43]

Members of provincial police forces are responsible for 66 percent of the deaths documented by CORREPI, a reminder of the role of provincial state apparatus as an authoritarian reservoir in Argentina. Even if it is against the law, most provincial police forces perform political policing. An entire illegal economy flourishes supported by police complicity with gaming, prostitution, robberies, extortive kidnappings, drug, car, and human trafficking, or by supplying guns and "freeing zones." Like *bonaerense* Iván Esteban Penida, 34, officially killed by "criminals" until his parents declared that he had been "executed" for denouncing his chief's misconduct, decent, law-abiding police officers face murder if they report inside crimes. Contributing to "the illegal financing of politics,"[44] police criminal activities make many politicians tolerant.

Such dense entanglements came to light in Santiago del Estero after the *disappearances* of Leila Nazar, 22, and Patricia Villalba, 25, in 2003 unveiled a clandestine police apparatus linking politicians, the police, and El Proceso perpetrators. Leila's body had been dismembered and the parts hidden in a place called La Dársena, near the provincial capital, as were those of her friend Patricia, tortured and murdered soon afterwards. The investigation led to Antonio Musa Azar, a retired police commissioner close to *caudillo* Carlos Juárez since 1973. Neither El Proceso nor the return of democracy interrupted Musa Azar's career. Identified as responsible for at least 23 *disappearances* before and after the 1976 coup, he benefited from pardon laws. In 1993, he was put in charge of public security.

Musa Azar's *grupo de tareas* had carried out political murders, extortive kidnappings, and drug and human trafficking, and had terrorized peasants. But his private zoo where animals were fed with human remains was the most horrendous discovery of all. The federal intervention set up prosecutions of Musa Azar and state officers, including multi-time governor Juárez and his wife and ex-governor Nina, and designated a new state Supreme Court. Forty thousand records of political policing were disclosed.

Extreme yet not exceptional, La Dársena links layers of state violence replicating regionally. Police association with the military, death squads, and organized crime are proving hard to dismantle also in the Buenos Aires province. In 1998, *Juicio a las Juntas*[45] judge and former minister of justice León Arslanián launched an ambitious reform of *la bonaerense*, with 48,000 agents at the time. Forced to resign after an "insecurity" counterattack made crimes skyrocket, Arslanián was called back in 2004 once *mano dura* policies proved unable to protect anybody. Among the 4,000 police officers fired by the minister, at least 400 suspected of participating in El Proceso's *grupos de tareas* were investigated for the *disappearance* of López.[46]

"The quicker you succeed the better"; *El Amigo Americano*

"We wish the new government well. We wish it will succeed. We will do what we can to help it succeed." These were the words of Secretary of State Henry Kissinger as he expressed his support for the Argentine Chancellor Admiral Guzzetti in 1976. Despite being informed about El Proceso's paramilitary squads, the American advised Argentines to act *fast*: "If there are things that have to be done, you should do them quickly ... before Congress gets back" to avoid sanctions.[47] Guzzetti's reported "state of jubilation" concurs with Videla's perception that they had the US government's blessing; the period coincides with a peak of *disappearances* in Argentina. These dialogues expose the contours of the "US–Latin American interstate regime" of terror expanding through the Cold War years and its local impact.[48]

State clandestine apparatus support each other. Operation Condor, the "Cold War-era assassination program"[49] coordinated by the Argentine, Chilean, Uruguayan, Paraguayan, Bolivian and Brazilian militaries, and sponsored by the US, to track and kill subversives regardless of citizenship, crudely exposes such solidarity. Including Argentina's "most prolific assassins" on the CIA payroll does as well.[50] Aníbal Gordon was one of them. A common criminal and Nazi sympathizer turned intelligence agent, Gordon headed the Condor death camp Automotores Orletti where at least 300 people *disappeared*. At that time, he frequently visited the US embassy in Buenos Aires.[51]

As the US–Argentina anti-communist alliance deepened, Cold War depictions of "internal enemies" found a fertile ground in Argentine robust traditions of chasing compatriots. More than 4,000 Argentines were trained by the US between 1950 and 1979,[52] and more than 700 attended the School of the Americas, including El Proceso presidents Roberto Viola and Leopoldo Fortunato Galtieri. Their training focused on effective methods of intelligence gathering, interrogation techniques, urban zoning, and riot control. Counterinsurgency methods fused police, military, and paramilitary groups. Argentines learned also from the French who, like the Americans, provided "instructors, observers, and an enormous amount of literature," writes *bonaerense* military chief General Camps in *La Razón* in 1981. Many, like Triple A founder Villar, learned from both.[53]

In Argentina, the Office of Public Safety (OPS) never gained visibility as in Brazil and Uruguay after filmmaker Costa-Gavras immortalized its chief Dan Mitrione in the film *State of Siege* (France, 1972). OPS, created under President Kennedy to centralize foreign police assistance, was part of the Agency for International Development. Initially promoting institution building and economic development, the office shifted to counterinsurgency training and grew closer to the CIA.[54] In 1965, OPS assessed the Argentinean police's capabilities to confront subversion and lawless border zones.

Consistent with US legal guidelines, after the 1966 coup General Juan Carlos Onganía's defense law introduced the figure of the *internal enemy*, which facilitated brutal repression and transformed Argentina into a national security state. Despite police requests for training, and OPS willingness to provide it, military governments judged it unwise to have Americans training police officers in Argentina, and sent its students to the US instead. Eighty-three Argentine police officers and two high-ranking federal police intelligence agents received training between 1961 and 1973, mostly at the Washington International Police Academy.[55] Policemen were also trained under military programs. And after a short lapse of democratic rule in 1973, the country evolved into the Orwellian police state of El Proceso.

Decades of US military aid and training significantly contributed to Argentina's state terror. As Gareau[56] put it, "Washington is guilty of being an accessory before the fact." US government branches and offices acted semi-autonomously and contradictorily toward El Proceso. In April 1977, after visiting Argentina, Secretary for Human Rights Patricia Derian protested the "dangerous and double message" sent by the US. With many in the administration mocking human rights, Derian asked President Carter to enforce their instruction among "all branches of the armed forces … the CIA, the FBI and all other intelligence agencies," and to dismiss those who did not comply.[57] Meanwhile, American businesses and military-intelligence networks helped to neutralize the effect of economic and military bans passed by the US Congress.[58]

The military of El Proceso celebrated the Reagan administration, while Jeanne Kirkpatrick, US Ambassador to the UN, profusely supported President General Galtieri.[59] Cooperation with CIA-sponsored counterinsurgency in Central America started at the end of 1979, or perhaps earlier in 1976.[60] Argentines trained Contras in El Salvador, Guatemala, and Honduras, instructing more than 1,000 paramilitaries in Honduran territory alone.[61] Seineldín, who since his junior years defended irregular methods in view of the "coming" revolutionary war, joined the first commando unit trained by Americans, Los Halcones, and served as a paramilitary instructor in Argentina and Central America.[62]

OPS closed in 1975 after human rights scandals. The Drug Enforcement Administration (DEA) became its natural heir, absorbing its agents and resources.[63] Disclosure of SOA (School of Americas) torture manuals made the US government rename the school and move it to Fort Benning in Georgia. Concerned American citizens have persistently lobbied to have the school closed; still, its students constitute 1 percent of all foreign personnel trained by the US every year.[64] In the long run, Huggins shows, both in the US and abroad, citizen oversight of military and police forces was resisted through increasing fragmentation, decentralization, and secrecy, growing police autonomy, governmental loss of control of state force and its devolution to private groups such as death squads in Brazil. The CIA, DEA, FBI, Pentagon,[65] and private contractors handle training programs, which, despite including human rights courses and claiming to train police officers "for democracy,"[66] remain opaque and outside citizen scrutiny. "The strong militarization of the police," a *bonaerense* officer observes, is currently "expanding from the United States," with emphasis on drug trafficking, organized crime, and counterinsurgency. The 2004–5 annual report by the US Secretary of State to Congress includes military training of Argentinean police in "more effective counterterrorism initiatives." From the 12 officers listed in the Counterterrorism Fellowship Program in 2004, the number rose to 70 in 2005.

A transnational "matrix of 'authoritarian security' "[67] perpetuates the network of the Cold War years. Huggins, Haritos-Fatouros, and Zimbardo identify narratives of *professionalism* replacing Cold War arguments in Brazil as a rationale "to decide the acceptability, accessibility, or unacceptability of gross human rights violations."[68] It seems no different in Argentina, as in the following firsthand account echoing professionalist tropes:

> I, for example, joined the police under a military government, and now I am with the police under a democratic government. I think the police are apolitical. Tools may vary, but the job is the same ... I get paid to chase criminals and to solve crimes ... The tools I am given do not matter.[69]

Like many in the police who are afraid of their superiors as well as of revenge and purges by human rights groups and reformers, my interviewee thinks that, by being "apolitical," he protects his job. According to the times, it is implied, one may find him upholding and respecting the law and due process or not, sometimes chasing thieves, rapists, at other times "subversives," or poor teenagers. This police officer's understanding of professionalism and of being "apolitical" poses deeply disturbing possibilities for society.

Involving the direct governance of individuals and groups, policing overdetermines the political regime and the extension of citizen rights.[70] In Argentina, a democratic political regime coexists with parts of the state apparatus governed through other, antagonistic principles. Like many senior police and military officers, Etchecolatz defined himself as a participant in a war won militarily but lost politically. A better way of putting this, perhaps, is to say that, supported by domestic and transnational alliances, we are winning the battles regarding the political regime, while they still hold governing power through the state coercive apparatus.

"Democracy is coming now, but do not forget: we will always be here"

While violence is apparent in killings and genocide, and less visible in oppressive structures extending over time, Johan Galtung[71] notes that they relate in the same way an earthquake results from tectonic plates moving over a fault line. With a view of present and past violence in Argentina, the frightening words, quoted in the subheading above, of perpetrator Simon, now in prison, remind us that the state monopoly of violence and legibility identified by Weber and Scott looks like the tectonic plates evoked by Galtung. For what is genocide if not the conjunction of state legibility and violence in destroying a part of the people? This essay shows how the amalgam of information and violence in regular policing ambiguously informs benign as well as violent practices.

El Proceso genocidal policies are finally being given legal recognition. Leaders such as Videla, Harguindeguy, Bussi, Díaz Bessone, and dozens of top officers face trial for a number of crimes. Following Spain and France, Italy has indicted 140 Condor members from Argentina, Paraguay, Uruguay, and Bolivia. No US officers have been accused, even though "the names of US officials keep cropping up in key places and moments" from Condor documents[72] and judges from different countries may eventually call Henry Kissinger.

Yet what should we make of Argentina's piecemeal killings by the police and the security forces? Concerned with the "politics of naming," Mahmood Mamdani[73] invites us to resist privileging some victims and forms of state violence over others to avoid leaving some of them in the dark. This seems especially appropriate when confronting the microscopic but systematic killing of the young and poor by the police. While in the specific case of Argentina current forms of police violence exhibit legacies from El Proceso, considered in general this form of violence exposes the genocidal potential embedded in any modern state apparatus.

A semi-autonomous cluster of self-perpetuating bureaucratic apparatuses, the state endows street-level bureaucrats such as police officers with extraordinary prerogatives over life and death, with terrifying consequences that not even the consolidation of a political democracy seems able to prevent.

Notes and references

1 My special thanks to Juli.
2 El Proceso de Reorganización Nacional, literally "process of national reorganization," was the name adopted by the dictatorship arisen from a military coup that governed Argentina from 1976 to 1983.
3 The Full Stop Law (23493) set a deadline for presenting cases in court, and the Due Obedience Law (23521) excluded middle- and lower-ranking military, police officers, and intelligence agents from prosecution. In 1990, President Carlos Menem pardoned those in prison at the time.
4 M. J. Lucesole, "Condenaron a reclusión perpetua a Etchecolatz," *La Nación*, September 20, 2006. Online, available at: www.lanacion.com.ar/841991 (accessed September 20, 2008). Telam, National News Agency of Argentina, "Rotundo fallo: 'Von Wernich es un torturador y asesino'," *Perfil*, November 1, 2007. Online, available at: www.perfil.com/contenidos/2007/11/01/noticia_0071.html (accessed October 21, 2008).
5 D. C. Hodges, *Argentina's "Dirty War": An Intellectual Biography*, Austin, TX: University of Texas Press, 1991, p. 178.
6 ESMA, the Navy School of Mechanics in Buenos Aires, served as the largest concentration camp between 1976 and 1983.
7 CORREPI, *Boletín Informativo No. 458*, Buenos Aires, CORREPI, December 16, 2007. Online, available at: http://correpi.lahaine.org/articulo.php?p=836&more=1&c=1 (accessed September 18, 2008).
8 In the Buenos Aires province alone, four out of five detainees await trial and individuals held in police stations oscillate between 4,000 and 5,000.
9 J. Taylor, "A Juridical Frankenstein," in A. Sarat (ed.), *The Killing State*, Oxford: Oxford University Press, 1998, pp. 60–80.
10 Ibid, p. 66.
11 T. Skcopol, *States and Social Revolutions*, New York: Cambridge University Press, 1979, p. 31.
12 Hodges, *Argentina's "Dirty War,"* p. ix.
13 Personal interview, Buenos Aires, 2003.
14 L. Kalmanowiecki, "Policing the People, Building the State," in D. E. Davis and A. W. Pereira (eds), *Irregular Armed Forces and Their Role in Politics and State Formation*, New York: Cambridge University Press, 2003, pp. 209–231.
15 M. Ungar, *Elusive Reform: Democracy and the Rule of Law in Latin America*, Boulder, CO: Lynne Rienner, 2002, p. 73.
16 C. Tilly, "State-Incited Violence 1900–1999," *Political Power and Social Theory* 9, 1995, p. 161.
17 J. Filc, *Entre el parentesco y la política: Familia y dictadura, 1976–1983*, Buenos Aires: Biblos, 1997.
18 Hodges, *Argentina's "Dirty War,"* p. 182.
19 Ibid., p. 167; M. J. Osiel, "Constructing Subversion in Argentina's Dirty War," *Representations* 75, 2001, p. 158.
20 C. Escudé and A. Cisneros, "Capítulo 68: El regimen militar (1976–1983)," in C. Escudé and A. Cisneros (eds), *Historia de las relaciones exteriores argentinas*, Buenos Aires: Grupo Editor Latinoamericano, 2000. Online, available at: www.cema.edu.ar/ceieg/arg-rree/historia.htm (accessed November 12, 2008).
21 The last CONADEP update refers to 651 camps, *Clarín*, March 25, 2001.
22 I. Saint-Jean, "La dictadura del '76 al '83 en: Frases," Ministerio de Educación de la Nación Argentina, May 1977. Online, available at: www.me.gov.ar/efeme/24demarzo/frases.html (accessed November 3, 2008).
23 T. Rosenberg, *Children of Cain: Violence and the Violent in Latin America*, New York: Penguin, 1991, p. 124.

24 W. Heinz and H. Früling, *Determinants of Gross Human Rights Violations by State and State-sponsored Actors in Brazil, Uruguay, and Argentina*, Cambridge, MA: Martinus Nijhoff Publishers, 1999, p. 703.

25 Ibid., p. 703; J. P. McSherry, "Condor Figures," *NACLA Report on the Americas* 39, 1, 2005, p. 74; Hodges, *Argentina's "Dirty War,"* p. 175.

26 Personal interview, Argentina, 2003.

27 As quoted on: M. S. Hinton, *The State on the Streets: Police and Politics in Argentina and Brazil*, Boulder, CO: Lynne Rienner, p. 32.

28 Personal interview, Argentina, 2003.

29 J. Scott, *Seeing Like a State*, New Haven, CT: Yale University Press, 1998, p. 57.

30 Interview, Escobar, 2001. Patti, a politician and former *bonaerense* police subcommissioner, is known for his endorsement of tough *mano dura* policing; his career was interrupted after he was indicted for participating in "disappearances" in the 1970s.

31 After leading the last and bloody *carapintada* rebellion in 1990, former Colonel Seineldín, a Malvinas/Falklands War hero and a Catholic nationalist, spent 11 years in prison for sedition (personal interview, Campo de Mayo, August 2001).

32 Personal interview with police commissioner, Argentina, 2006.

33 E. M. Andersen, *La Policía*, Buenos Aires: Sudamericana, 2002, pp. 269, 278, 282.

34 Héctor José Rivera, Pedro Solís, Héctor Gustavo and Adolfo Agustín Ramírez, Eduardo Ernesto Sánchez, Rodolfo Segarra, Roque Núñez, Daniel Omar Martinicorena, Ricardo Fermín Albareda, Juan Mario Astorga, Wenceslao García, Enrique Victorio Heredia, Silvestre García, Juan Carlos Castro are just a few names included in *Nunca Más* and other reports.

35 Andersen, *La Policía*, p. 148.

36 L. Kalmanowiecki, "Origins and Applications of Political Policing in Argentina," *Latin American Perspectives*, 2000, 27, pp. 36–46.

37 G. Young, *SIDE: La Argentina secreta*, Buenos Aires: Planeta, 2006.

38 O. Barreneche, *Crime and the Administration of Justice in Buenos Aires 1785–1853*, Lincoln, NE: University of Nebraska Press, 2006, p. 114.

39 O. Quintana, "Lobo suelto, cordero atado," *El Colectivo*, 2007, 14.

40 J. Auyero, "The Hyper-Shantytown: Neo-liberal Violence(s) in the Argentine Slum," *Ethnography* 1, 1, 2000, p. 100.

41 Ibid.

42 Personal interview, Buenos Aires, 2001.

43 Personal interview, Argentina, 2003.

44 G. Palmieri (personal interview, Buenos Aires, 2001).

45 F. Harari, "Por que desapareció López?," *El Aromo* 32, October 2006, p. 2. Online, available at: www.razonyrevolucion.org.ar/textos/elaromo/secciones/Editorialpdf/aromo32editorial.pdf (accessed on November 13, 2008).

46 Under El Proceso military dictatorship (1976–83), the head of the government consisted of a junta, a tripartite formation integrated by the chiefs of the Argentine army, navy, and air force. *Juicio a las Juntas* was the historic trial ordered by President Raul Alfonsin (1983–9), from April to December, 2005, prosecuting the leaders of the dictatorship for their direct responsibility in thousands of cases of torture, murder, and forced *disappearances*.

47 Memorandum of conversation. Online, available at: www.gwu.edu/~nsarchiv/NSAEBB/NSAEBB133/19760610%20Memorandum%20of%20Conversation%20clean.pdf (accessed November 29, 2008).

48 C. Menjívar and N. Rodríguez, "New Responses to State Terror," in C. Menjívar and N. Rodríguez (eds), *When States Kill*, Austin, TX: University of Texas Press, 2005, pp. 335–46.

49 McSherry, "Condor Figures," pp. 42–4.

50 Andersen, *La Policía*, p. 292.

51 Young, *SIDE*, pp. 51–9.

52 F. Gareau, "Argentina's Dirty War," in F. Gareau (ed.), *State Terrorism and the United States*, London: Zed Books, 2004, p. 105.
53 J. P. McSherry, *Predatory States: Operation Condor and Covert War in Latin America*, Lanham, MD: Rowman & Littlefield, 2005, p. 74.
54 T. Lobe, *United States National Security Policy and Aid to the Thailand Police*, Monograph Series in World Affairs 14, 2, Denver, CO: University of Denver, 1977.
55 Heinz and Früling, *Determinants of Gross Human Rights Violations*, pp. 699–703.
56 Gareau, "Argentina's Dirty War," p. 107.
57 C. Osorio (assisted by K. Costar), *Electronic Briefing Book No. 104*, Washington, DC: National Security Archive, 2003.
58 Escudé and Cisneros, "Capítulo 68."
59 G. Grandin, "The Bloody 'Realism' of Jeanne Kirkpatrick, Mid-wife of the Neocons," *Counterpunch*, December 2006, pp. 9, 10.
60 Escudé and Cisneros, "Capítulo 68."
61 L. Valladares Lanza and S. Peacock, *In Search of Hidden Truths*, Tegucigalpa: Prografic, 1998. Online, available at: www.gwu.edu/~nsarchiv/latin_america/honduras/hidden_truths/hidden.htm (accessed on October 29, 2008).
62 D. Sheinin, "Finding an Alliance: Rethinking Argentine–United States Cold War Relations," *MACLAS Latin American Essays*, 2002, p. 16.
63 W. Blum, "Uruguay 1964–1970: Torture – as American as Apple Pie," in W. Blum (ed.), *Killing Hope: US Military and CIA Interventions since World War II*, Monroe, ME: Common Courage Press, 1995. Online, available at: http://members.aol.com/bblum6/uruguay.htm (accessed on October 28, 2008); McSherry, "Condor Figures," p. 75.
64 S. McCoy, "The Politics of Impunity: The Cold War, Trauma, Trials, and Reparations in Argentina and Chile," *Latin American Research Review* 42, 2005, p. 1.
65 Lobe, *United States National Security Policy*; M. Huggins, *Political Policing: The United States and Latin America*, Durham, NC: Duke University Press, 1998.
66 O. Marenin, "From IPA to ILEA: Change and Continuity in United States International Police Training Programs," *Police Quarterly* 1, 4, 1998, pp. 93–126.
67 C. Schneider, and P. Amar, "The Rise of Crime, Disorder and Authoritarian Policing: An Introductory Essay," *NACLA Report on the Americas* 37, 2, 2003, pp. 12–16.
68 M. K. Huggins, M. Haritos-Fatouros, and P. G. Zimbardo, *Violence Workers*, Berkeley, CA: University of California Press, 2002, p. 209.
69 Personal interview, Argentina, 2003.
70 Ungar, *Elusive Reform*, p. 63; S. P. Pinheiro, "Democracies Without Citizenship," *NACLA Report on the Americas* 30, 2, 1996, pp. 17–23.
71 J. Galtung, "Cultural Violence," *Journal of Peace Research* 27, 3, 1990, p. 292.
72 L. Carlsen, "The Bloody Legacy of Stroessner, Pinochet and Ríos Montt: Latin America's Archives of Terror," *Counterpunch*, October 25, 2003, n.p. Online, available at: www.counterpunch.org/carlsen10252003.html
73 M. Mamdani, "The Politics of Naming: Genocide, Civil War, Insurgency," *London Review of Books* 29, 5, March 8, 2007, p. 5.

11 Courageous soldiers (*valientes soldados*)

Politics of concealment in the aftermath of state violence in Chile[1]

Marcia Esparza

In 2003, President Michelle Bachelet, who at that time was Chile's Defense Secretary (2002–4), told a foreign newspaper of her hopes that the military's pacts of silence would be broken. Breaking the walls of military silence was essential for the victims and families of the Chilean military junta to finally leave behind a painful past.[2] Bachelet's call for the military to disclose information came 30 years after a bloody *coup d'état* overthrew socialist President Salvador Allende, thus inaugurating a long regime of terror under the command of General Augusto Pinochet (1973–90). Her pleas were also made after a decade of investigation by the Chilean Truth Commission (known as the Rettig Commission) when thousands of victims and survivors loaded with criminal evidence – that they themselves had collected over the long years of General Pinochet's regime – responded and mobilized to testify before the commission.[3]

To confront past crimes against humanity, truth and reconciliation commissions were set up in Latin America, in the aftermath of state violence and genocide in Argentina, Chile, Peru, and Guatemala, with the backing of the United States. These ad hoc commissions of inquiry are often praised as one of the most important transitional justice tools available for post-conflict or authoritarian societies.[4] They offer, the claim goes, a vehicle that a violence-ridden society needs in order to deal with a haunting past, where a political compromise can be achieved amongst contending forces. On the one hand, there are victims' groups who demand truth, memory, and justice, while on the other hand, there are those implicated in crimes who claim to have followed orders to serve the country and thus oppose any form of criminal accountability.

Another claim made on behalf of truth commissions' investigations is that they have the capacity to construct a historical "truth." But this claim is not entirely supported and serves as fodder for a growing disagreement among scholars. E. Daly has noted for example that,

> Perhaps the biggest problem with the truth is not that there are too many truths but rather that there is not enough truth. Often the truth that victims and others most want to hear is not the forensic truth, nor the historical or dialogic truth, but the psychological truth. Why did the perpetrators do this?[5]

In fact, for the most part, the reconstruction of the past has relied on testimonies drawn from victims, survivors, and human rights organizations keeping records of human rights allegations. These narratives, observers note, can be considered counter-hegemonic because they defy relentless official denial of responsibilities.[6]

Following Daly's observation of "not enough truth," this chapter examines the absence of perpetrators' testimonies provided to truth commissions and suggests that, in the Chilean case, state agents' refusal to collaborate with the Truth Commission can be explained by the army's politics of concealment. For the most part, their refusal to testify is often understood as part of their efforts to avoid criminal investigations.[7] But truth commissions do not have the legal power to prosecute human rights offenders and the evidence suggests that truth commissions do not lead to criminal investigations.[8] All this means that there are no legal repercussions for military officers and civilian collaborators who decide to come forward to testify. Moreover, across the board, testifying to the Commissions is voluntary and anonymous – no one is obliged to partake in this truth-telling. Considering these provisions, it might be worth considering perpetrators' collective silence.

I further argue that unwritten arrangements, these pacts of silence President Bachelet referred to, designed to cover up crimes committed to eliminate an "internal enemy," were already in place by the time the Chilean Truth Commission was set up in 1990. Through an examination of secret agents' testimonies I found in court files, I argue that these pacts of silence are fostered by a military culture that squashes independent and reflective thinking. Key aspects of this military culture are (a) norms of due obedience that state agents alleged to have followed, and (b) intra-group cohesion.

I primarily examine transcripts recorded at the murder trial of trade union leader Tucapel Jimenez in 1982 by the state's intelligence groups. While accounting for limitations faced when examining trial confessions, I conclude that court testimonies offer a glimpse into a relentless military culture that continues to shape people's confessions decades after the Chilean coup of 1973. I examine these overarching questions: Do military intelligence personnel express feelings of guilt or remorse? Do they use claims of due obedience and loyalty to the military institution? Did they question what they were ordered to do?

The Truth Commission in Chile: historical memory and silence

In Chile, the socialist elected President Patricio Aylwin ordered the creation of the Truth Commission in 1991, through Presidential Decree 3.591.[9] In so doing, Aylwin concluded that the nation could not wait for criminal courts to examine all human rights abuses committed during the military regime.[10] The courts were considered to be simply too ineffective and powerless to carry out exhaustive investigations of the thousands of petitions of habeas corpus opened during the dictatorship. A limited mandate made possible the investigation of crimes considered to be crimes against humanity: forced disappearances and extrajudicial executions and torture that resulted in death were included.

Few members of security forces came forward to testify to the Rettig Commission. One notable exception was the testimony provided by Luz Arce, a former member of the Socialist Party who, after being savagely tortured, became a collaborator with her own victimizers. Arce provided the commission with valuable information about the fates of detainees whom she had previously turned over to security forces, as well as details of the mechanisms of violence. Her confession illustrates that military personnel, perpetrators or accomplices, can in fact be compelled to break the walls of military silence after long years of secrecy and denials.[11] But was Arce's public disclosure of her ordeal first as a victim of and then as collaborator with the regime of General Pinochet the norm or the exception?[12]

In Latin America, for the most part, alleged perpetrators have stayed away from truth commissions.[13] In Argentina for example, the Comisión Nacional de Desaparición de Personas (CONADEP, the National Commission on the Disappeared) also made requests to the military to testify in order to clarify those tragic episodes that caused the disappearance of thousands of students and workers under the repressive military juntas (see Daniel Feierstein, Gabriela Aguila, and Ernesto Verdeja in this volume). These requests were met with refusal and denial.[14]

In Chile, General Augusto Pinochet's army also regarded the aims of the Truth Commission with suspicion. Requests made to the military to come forward and provide testimonies proved ineffective. The commission solicited approximately 160 testimonies from the military. Only two uniformed members of the military "showed readiness to provide statements"[15] and when they testified, they denied having any information of criminal acts, claiming that – due to bureaucratic procedures and military law – all documentation pertaining to detainees had been incinerated.

In an official response, military authorities contested the findings of the commission as one-dimensional and unreliable. President Aylwin asked the armed forces to acknowledge the suffering they had caused during the dictatorship. But far from recognizing any wrongdoings, General Pinochet remorselessly expressed his disagreement with the report and maintained that the army had saved the country from the communist menace.[16] For human rights activists and lawyers, Pinochet's death in 2006 led to the cracking of military agreements to keep silent over their personal responsibilities in human rights crimes. Yet when the Rettig Commission' Report was made public in 1991, Pinochet's refusal to acknowledge any responsibility for his commands to execute counter-terrorist strategies meant that the Rettig Commission could only provide partial truths.

Another effort designed to deal with the legacy of the Chilean military regime was the Mesa de Dialogo (Discussion Table), a human rights initiative involving member of the armed forces, the Church, and civil society. The initiative produced a report that was submitted to President Ricardo Lagos in 2001, containing the names of 180 people arrested between 1973 and 1976, along with 20 unidentified victims. The information stated that most of the victims had been thrown into the ocean and rivers in Chile. In spite of the army's recognition of human rights violations, the report was flawed because it included vague information that families and human rights organizations contested.[17] According to members of Corporacion de Defensa y Promocion de los Derechos del Pueblo, (CODEPU, Corporation for the Defense and Promotion of the Rights of the People), the report did not include the date of the arrest of the disappeared nor where the remains could be found, once again leaving families without enough information about the fate of their loved ones.[18]

In another more recent attempt to justify the army's role in state crimes within the Cold War context, General Cheyre acknowledged responsibility for crimes committed, yet he fell short of offering information on the whereabouts of the remains of the detained and disappeared.[19] According to scholars Norbert Lechner and Pedro Güell, the army's failure to offer a moral justification explaining their counterinsurgency operations reduced hopes for reconciliation between politically polarized sectors.[20]

By comparison, in Africa, where truth commissions have been warmly embraced, South Africa's Truth and Reconciliation Commission offers important lessons. Widely cited for its uniqueness in offering amnesty to perpetrators in exchange for full disclosure for crimes committed under apartheid, the commission nonetheless was a disappointment because few state agents came forward to testify.[21] There, according to the Amnesty Committee which was charged with reviewing over 7,000 amnesty petitions submitted for consideration, only 1,674 were accepted.[22] The remaining applications were rejected mainly because of "lack of political motive, late or defective applications, no guilt, personal gain or no full disclosure." Against the almost 40,000 testimonies provided by victims, observers have noted, "Many persons, it has to be said, simply did not come forward. They remain unknown."[23]

More importantly in the South African case, is the question of who came forward to testify. Few perpetrators (only 17 percent of the total) came from the earlier South African government and its security forces because "most security forces viewed the amnesty process with antipathy and 'deep suspicion' [as] ... many were angered by what they regarded as betrayal by former political masters, almost none of whom came forward."[24] Most amnesty applications came from the African National Congress which resisted the apartheid regime.

Criminal research, transcripts, a military culture and politics of concealment

Research investigating trials transcripts presents several dilemmas.[25] The most obvious one is the reliability of the confessions. How truthful can they be? This is particularly vexing in the context of criminal proceedings seeking to establish criminal responsibilities. Christopher Browning's classic study, *Ordinary Men: Reserve Police Battalion 101 and the Final Solution in Poland*, notes that studies relying on judicial interrogations offer conflicting "perspectives and memories"[26] and that people lie during court confessions to avoid prosecution. These narratives, as noted by Ronald L. Cohen, "are retrospective accounts, so one must acknowledge the possibility of faulty memory and biased reporting."[27] In her analysis of confessions perpetrators have made publicly in Argentina, Leigh A. Payne also notes, "Trials often produce confessional amnesia."[28]

Yet, regardless of their limitations, court files can be an immense help in understanding the broader psychological and ideological dynamics that shape state violence, in addition to documenting "what transpires in courts."[29] They offer a rich variety of written documentation: testimonies of alleged perpetrators, victims, witnesses, bystanders, and accomplices; medical examinations of victims; police records; and copies of decrees and newspaper articles from the Cold War period. Criminal proceedings also expose inter-agency cooperation between different intelligence and military units.

These transcripts correspond to criminal investigations against those accused of planning and executing the murder of 60-year-old trade union leader Tucapel Jiménez, on February 25, 1982.

Interestingly, while locating these files, I was often deterred from further investigation into the narratives of perpetrators by human rights lawyers representing victims and their families. Some of them scoffed at the idea of searching for judicial testimonies because it was often fruitless. "Perpetrators don't talk," I was hastily told. Others commented on the fact that most defendants had justified any wrongdoing because they were following orders, observations that dismiss the importance of digging into court files that might uncover perpetrators' "truth."

The murder trial of Tucapel Jimenez: unveiling politics of concealment

Tucapel Jimenez was assassinated on February 25, 1982 when two intelligence agents who, disguised as passengers, boarded the taxi Jiménez was driving. Hours later, his body was discovered with his throat slit, and also bearing multiple gunshot wounds, on the outskirts of Santiago. At the time of his execution, Jiménez was a prominent leader of the Asociación Nacional de Empleados Fiscales (ANEF, the National Association of Public Workers) and was unifying various anti-junta political sectors for a national general strike against the military regime. The trial sentenced retired Major Carlos Herrera to life imprisonment for the kidnapping and killing of Jimenez and of a civilian, a carpenter named Juan Alegria, who was murdered as a cover-up for Jimenez' killing.[30] The trial also established that a network of Pinochet's secret service were involved in illicit activities, such as the Dirección Nacional de Inteligencia (DINA, National Intelligence Directorate) and the Centro Nacional de Inteligencia (CNI, National Information Center).[31] DINA and CNI were Pinochet's intelligence services (operating at different time periods), with the capacity for centralized action, economic resources, and state-supported means of carrying out widespread human rights crimes.[32]

For over 17 years, investigation into the killing of Jimenez was stalled in the hands of Judge Sergio Valenzuela Patino. Human Rights Watch, addressing the slow proceedings in this homicide, and the massacre of another 12 alleged communist terrorists, noted "Court investigations into both crimes, although not subject to the amnesty law [2,191], were stalled for years by official disinformation, the protection of suspects, suppression of evidence, and judges' prevarication."[33] A verdict was issued in 2002, 20 years after the crime. Two themes emerge from the suspects' confessions that help us understand the role played by the military culture in shaping pacts of silence – due obedience and social cohesion.

Military culture and due obedience

If pacts of silence are sustained through the reproduction of a military culture, then it is necessary to address the role of culture in the socialization of military intelligence agents. Donna Winslow defines culture as "a social force that controls patterns of organizational behavior. It shapes members' cognitions and perceptions of meanings and realities. It provides affective energy for mobilization and identifies who belongs to the groups and who does not."[34] Military culture, accordingly, relies on patterns of group cohesion and solidarity, patriotism, courage, self-sacrifice, and above all, blind obedience to superiors' orders.[35] Military culture also relies on shared norms such as a hyper-masculinity and prejudice against women.[36]

The military's *raison d'être* is to socialize its cadres to follow orders and it does so in a social setting where ordinary people's minds are conditioned through training and social life that provides them with a new set of peers and networks. Anthropologist Leslie Gill has noted the role played by US military training (particularly at the former School of the Americas) in the indoctrination of Latin American officers with anticommunist rhetoric. Combat training on US soil involves teaching courses on torture techniques, teaching of songs, and granting favors to those who cooperate. She also notes how members of the armed forces typically reside in military housing and social life rests upon military networks.[37] Observers have noted that one of the purposes of the "militarization of the minds"[38] is to get people to "react without question or hesitation to institutional stimuli."[39] People subjected to this process learn not to question the consequences or significance of their actions, because the socialization of military values and obedience to superiors produces soldiers who do not "think for themselves."[40]

In the aftermath of World War II, international treaties and courts have rejected the defense of "just following orders." Crimes of obedience, under the guise of following orders, affirms Wolfendale, "can and does lead to horrific acts"[41] because obedience involves "suspending one's moral judgment and substituting another's judgment for one's own"[42] and thus following orders cannot be seen as a virtue.

The following confession by a former director (from January 1978 to July 1980) of the CNI reflects features of a military ethos. As he absolutely denies having any responsibility in planning the murder of Jimenez, in his testimony he declares that he was aware that there was interest in getting to know the world of unions, but this information he received as processed information, and as an intelligence report; and he was never told (or exposed to) the ways in which this information was obtained.

This intelligence collaborator acknowledges the espionage work he was assigned to carry out. However, his own assertion that he raised no questions about the methods used to extract information reflects that he in fact functioned as an automaton because he was convinced that he had a mission to fulfill at all costs, as dictated by the military's patriotic values. As Dan Bar-On has noted, "They [perpetrators] believe themselves to be moral people and who did what they did as a 'mission.'"[43]

This officer's lack of critical judgment might be explained by his prior military training, where adjustment to military life implies blindly following orders and involves the creation of inter-group social bonding.

In another testimony, a witness who had occupied several important posts (as former chief of public relations (1979–80) of the CNI and director of intelligence for the army testified that,

> In [the] different assignments that he was ordered to serve, he never knew of a possible special intelligence multiple-officer operation that took place in February 1982 that would carry out the physical elimination of Tucapel Jimenez Alfaro.

This witness fails to assume any responsibility for spying on Jimenez. More importantly, his testimony draws attention to how this agent claims to have followed due-obedience military norms ("he was ordered to serve"), which allows him to deny his presumed responsibility as an accomplice.

Another testimony from a former CNI director illustrates this lack of reflective judgment as he claims to have followed orders: "He is not authorized to tell what his specific tasks were unless they are authorized by his superior officers." This claim was also found in the study by Martha K Huggins *et al.* of Brazilian police torturers during Brazil's national security state (1964–85).[44] She noted that only one out of her 23 Brazilian security personnel interviewees recognized his wrongdoings. In their testimonies, most offer justifications that relate to their professionalism and loyalty to the armed forces. Thus, for them following orders is valued over critical judgment, as examined by Hannah Arendt in the trial of Adolf Eichmann.[45] As a result, their unified loyalty to the army serves to enhance the army's core values of due obedience.

Another former director of the CNI (July 1980–6) testifies:

> To obtain all the information various methods were used, open and closed sources, among them collaborators, and informants. People were followed, pictures were taken, audiotapes were made, telephones were wiretapped, and other surveillances were used as well. With regards to those people who

were public figures, only those political opponents to the regime were scrutinized, solely with the objective of preventing any [terrorist] actions, never to cause any harm to themselves or their families.

Although he acknowledges the spying on political opponents, this witness fails to remember the spying on Tucapel Jimenez. He notes,

> Within the techniques used to gather information, telephone eavesdropping was one of them. He does not remember having to follow Tucapel Jiménez, neither does he remember specific orders aimed at spying on Jiménez. He believes that personal initiatives account for trying to audiotape the meetings where Jiménez attended.

By claiming that personal initiatives can account for spying on political opponents, this witness camouflages institutional responsibility. At the same time, he notes that if spying on Jimenez indeed took place, this was the result of actions by only a few bad apples, and thus upholds the values the military professes.[46]

Two CNI covert agents also expressed no remorse for their actions, as they were following orders. One notes "he deems that his job performance was adequate, but that the government committed various mistakes, such as the detained-disappeared, and the case of Tucapel Jiménez, among others." A second former army officer and member of the CNI (1979) testified that his task was "limited to following orders to search for information, according to the orders given by his superior Col. Fernando Salazar."

Military culture and social cohesion

Social cohesion allows the military to inculcate group solidarity above individual concerns. This aspect of military culture is crucial for combat operations: soldiers need to rely on one another. Furthermore, as Donna Winslow explains, this interdependence and excessive group cohesion can result in the formation of informal or illegal networks.[47] But unlike Winslow's study of a Canadian peacekeeping operation, in which illegal networks were formed and hidden from higher officers, the cold-blooded murder of Jimenez took place in a political context of organized state violence and genocide. Thus, the formation of illegal networks was not a random event – rather, these networks were the result of well coordinated military strategies.

In another testimony, a witness who was said to have been in charge of the headquarters of regional units of the CNI declared,

> About controlling the flow of information throughout the entire country.... The information that passed through his domain was directly related to the political, the economic, the religious, the collegiate, and the investigations which had been carried out with respect to the movements of public sector and private sector employees.

Nevertheless, this witness does not remember,

> if he had come across an investigation of the Central Intelligence Agency whose purpose was to determine the possible responsibility of the CNI in the murder of Tucapel Jimenez; and if a person had accomplished the assassination, he would have been found out because he would have had to transmit the order to other units.

In this confession, this former intelligence agent resorts automatically to silence as a viable option offered to him by the institution because the opposite, hard truth finding, is not the norm within a context of impunity. As he claims not to remember any intelligence investigation regarding the assassination of Jiménez, his silence reinforces unity among his network to cover up their illicit activities – a similar finding noted in Payne's study of confessions in post-dictatorship in Brazil. Silence, comments Payne, reinforced unity in Brazil's military's own efforts at covering crimes committed.[48] Likewise, by claiming "not to remember," this agent's temporary amnesia has reinforced the Chilean army's brotherhood.

Silence for these security force agents, explains Edwin Chemerinsky in his study of corruption within police officers in Los Angeles, "is easier" than having to deal with contradictory explanations, or disagreements about their criminal actions with their fellow intelligence officers. In his study, Chemerinsky concluded that a military mentality has been embedded in the minds of police officers. In the same vein, this military state of mind accounts for an "unwritten silence" kept by intelligence officers about illegal activities, silence that helps them cover up their criminal responsibilities, further perpetuating the loyalty and trust within the group. Furthermore, Chemerinsky notes that this silence obeys a "simple rule – an officer does not provide adverse information against a fellow officer ... silence ... is easier than tangling with fellow cops."[49] Rather than pitting one against another, silence strengthens group bonding and becomes an enabler of even more illicit actions.

Instead of seeing perpetrators' silence as an individual's act to conceal their criminal complicity, their silence can be seen as a social construction that is rooted in the institutional complicity to safeguard the honor of the armed forces. As a result, pacts of silence maintained by the army contribute to the "general silencing,"[50] a collective amnesia that helps sustain a military memory that contains patriotic Cold War myths about the past.[51] This historical silence reveals larger patterns of concealment where military training and the assimilation of a military culture can turn ordinary people into torturers and killers, and thus can reveal dimensions of the banality of evil in this particular regional context.

Conclusion

Court testimonies of alleged perpetrators and their collaborators offer important insights into the forging of long-lasting and almost unbreakable pacts of silence between members of the army and their close civilian allies. Long-term ideologies of violence are not so easily dismantled even after peace negotiations and pacted transitions take place. This is the case in the context of judicial testimonies for the murder of union leader Tucapel Jimenez. Moreover, an analysis of pacts of silence in the aftermath of General Augusto Pinochet's regime exposes three pillars that sustain a military culture: a militarized mind, blind obedience and social cohesion.

The Chilean army's politics of concealment has continued to shape intra-military relations long after formal transition to electoral democracy. This can be noted in court testimonies drawn from a sample of retired Chilean military personnel. These men, mostly in their sixties or older, continue to express loyalty to the military institution. These unwritten pacts are agreements aimed not only at covering up active participation in crimes, but at preventing retired army officers from recognizing their involvement in state crimes. These unwritten agreements prevent Chilean military personnel from expressing remorse or feelings of culpability.

These pacts of silence, I argue, had long been in place at the time of the work of the Chilean Truth Commission in 1990, which can partly explain why perpetrators did not testify to the commission. In contradictory ways, truth commissions gave a voice to victims and survivors of state violence yet they failed to acknowledge that without perpetrators' testimonies, the official story of Chile's Pinochet regime remains incomplete.

The memories of former state agents are vital to understanding the larger processes of military training that socializes military personnel into following orders. There were no excesses, as General Augusto Pinochet's regime liked to claim: those involved in crime were trained to follow orders to conduct espionage tasks, to intercept phones, to follow victims, to torture them, and ultimately to kill them.

Notes and references

1 The author is grateful to John Jay College of Criminal Justice's Research Assistance Program for providing funds for translations and editing, and to anonymous reviewers for their insightful comments. The research is based on an analysis of pieces of various court transcripts I have gathered from various institutions and private individuals since 2007. I have omitted all names of the sources to safeguard their confidentiality. These transcripts are in the author's possession.

2 "Secretary of Defense, Michelle Bachelet calls for the armed forces to break their 'Pacts of Silence'" ("Bachelet llama a las FFAA a romper su "pacto de silencio"). *La Tercera*, Sección Política, September 3, 2003. Online, available at: www.cee-chile.org/resumen/chile/chi100–150/semchi102.htm#Anchor-5677 (accessed on March 19, 2009).

3 In another more recent episode, court minister Claudio Pavez denounced the existence of a pact of military silence implicated in the killing of the ex-Colonel, Gerardo Huber. As a result of this crime, Pavez charged various high-level officers belonging to the DINE – the Dirección de Inteligencia del Ejercito – among others.

4 P. B. Hayner, *Unspeakable Truths: Confronting State Terror and Atrocity. How Truth Commissions Around the World are Challenging the Past and Shaping the Future*, New York: Routledge, 2001.

5 E. Daly, "Truth Skepticism: An Inquiry into the Value of Truth in Times of Transition," *International Journal of Transitional Justice* 2, 1, 2008, p. 27.

6 S. Parker, "All Aboard the Truth Bandwagon: Our Fascination with Truth Commissions," *Antipoda, Revista de Antropologia y Arqueologia* 4 (Universidad de los Andes, Bogota, Colombia), January–June 2007, pp. 207–24.

7 My experience with the Guatemalan Truth Commission also bears on perpetrators' testimonies. It was only on one occasion that two members of a paramilitary group came to one of the branches of the commission and testified. They confessed to having participated in the execution of a village neighbor the army believed was a "communist guerrillero." In their crime, they had tied a rope around the victim and various pro-army community members pulled the rope until the victim died of suffocation. I asked them what made them come forward. They replied that they were now "new born Christian" and wanted to clean their souls.

8 Daly, "Truth Skepticism," pp. 23–41.

9 The commission only investigated political murders and torture resulting in death. Years later, in 2004, the National Commission on Political Imprisonment and Torture Report, known also as the Valech Report, concluded that out of the 30,000 people who came forward to testify, an estimated 28,000 had been subjected to unspeakable acts of torture. The report established that over 1,000 detention centers were established during the dictatorship. Most of the young males had been trade union members. R. Bacic and E. Stanley, "Dealing with Torture in Chile. Achievements and Shortcomings of the Valech Report." Online, available at: www.menschenrechte.org/beitraege/lateinamerika/Dealingwithtorture.htm (accessed on March 28, 2009). As with the Rettig Commission, no perpetrators were publicly identified and recorded testimonies are not public records.

10 Amongst its goals were (1) to establish as complete a picture as possible of those grave events, (2) to gather evidence that might make it possible to identity the victims by name and determine their fate or whereabouts. *Informe de la Comisión Nacional de Verdad y Reconciliación*, vols. I, II, III. Secretaría de Comunicación y Cultura. Ministerio Secretaría General de Gobierno. Santiago, February 1991.

11 See the remarkable research of L. A. Payne, *Unsettling Accounts. Neither Truth nor Reconciliation in Confessions of State Violence*, Durham, NC: Duke University Press, 2008.

12 Further insights into the world of collaborators are offered in Arce's autobiography. Her text stands today as a poignant reminder of how, after being savagely tortured, survivors were occasionally compelled to ally with their torturers and became collaborators. L. Arce, *The Inferno: A Story of Terror and Survival in Chile*, Madison, WI: University of Wisconsin Press, 2004.

13 For Greg Grandin, the work of truth commissions "moved their work out of the legal arena into the realms of ethics and emotions" and that they became an essential condition to consolidate neo-liberal economies. G. Grandin, "The Instruction of Great Catastrophe: Truth Commissions, National History." Online, available at: www.historycooperative.org/journals/ahr/110.1/grandin.html (accessed on January 6, 2009).

14 Hayner, *Unspeakable Truths.*

15 *Informe de la Comisión*, vol. I, p. 9.

16 Hayner, *Unspeakable Truths*, p. 37.

17 See Amnesty International, "Chile: 26 Years of Injustice and Impunity Must End." Online, available at: www.amnesty.org/en/library/info/AMR22/021/1999/en (accessed June 17, 2009).

18 See Viviana Uribe Tamblay, "Mesa de Dialogo: Un informe que desinforma," CODEPU, Separata Boletin No. 33, March 2001. Online, available at: www.codepu.cl/index.php?option=com_content&task=view&id=532&Itemid=43&lang=es (accessed on March 10, 2007).

19 General J. E. Cheyre. "Ejercito de Chile: El fin de una vision," *Estudios Publicos,*

pp. 505–8. Online, available at: www.cepchile.cl/dms/archivo_3480_1918/r97_cheyre_ejercito_chileno.pdf. (accessed March 19, 2009). Also, two generals, Patricio Campos (air force) and Jorge Molina Johnson (army) have been accused for the reports' shortcomings. See *Informe de Derechos Humanos del Primer Semestre de 2003*, Santiago: Arzobispado de Santiago, Fundacion Documentacion y Archivo de la Vicaridad. Online, available at: www.vicariadelasolidaridad.cl/index1.html (accessed on March 9, 2009).

20 N. Lechner and P. Guell, "Construccion social de las memorias en la transicion chilena." Online, available at: www.archivochile.com/Ceme/recup_memoria/ceme-memo0024.pdf (accessed on March 19, 2009).

21 D. Foster, P. Haupt, and M. de Beer. *The Theater of Violence: Narratives of Protagonists in the South African Conflict*, Oxford: James Currey Ltd., 2005.

22 Ibid.

23 Ibid., p. 13.

24 Ibid.

25 See Payne, *Unsettling Accounts*.

26 C. Browning, *Ordinary Men: Reserve Police Battalion 101 and the Final Solution in Poland*, New York: HarpersCollins, 1992, p. xviii.

27 R. L. Cohen, "Silencing Objections: Social Constructions of Indifference," *Journal of Human Rights* 1, 2, June 2002, pp. 187–206 at p. 198.

28 Payne, *Unsettling Accounts*, p. 244.

29 E. Faber and E. Rowland, *Trial Transcripts of the County of New York, 1883–1927: A Historical Introduction with an Index to the Microfilm Collection*, New York: John Jay Press, 1989.

30 Carlos Herrera Jimenez, the killer of Tucapel Jimenez, broke his silence in 2009. Sentenced to life in prison in 2002, Herrera Jimenez, ex-graduate from the former School of the Americas, revealed that Tucapel Jimenez had in fact been the fourth name in a death list after other prominent union leaders. *La Nacion*, Tema del Domingo, January 18–24, 2009, p. 18.

31 It is important to note that Minister Muñoz undertook the investigation in April 1999 after 17 years of unsuccessful work by Judge Sergio Valenzuela Patiño.

32 See Pablo Policzer's discussion of the CNI and DINA's political prerogatives. P. Policzer, *The Rise and Fall of Repression in Chile*, Notre Dame, IN: University of Notre Dame Press, 2009.

33 Human Rights Watch, "When Tyrants Tremble,." Online, available at: http://hrw.org/reports/1999/chile/Patrick-03.htm 12/28/07 (accessed on December 28, 2007).

34 D. Winslow, "Misplaced Loyalties: The Role of Military Culture in the Breakdown of Discipline in Two Peace Operations," Ross Ellis Memorial Lecture in Military and Strategic Studies, University of Calgary, January 21, 1999. Online, available at: http://cmss.ucalgary.ca/past/ellis (accessed on March 20, 2009).

35 J. Wolfendale, *Torture and the Military Profession*, Basingstoke: Palgrave Macmillan, 2007.

36 C. Enloe. *Maneuvers, The International Politics of Militarizing Women's Lives*, Berkeley, CA: University of California Press, 2000.

37 L. Gill, *The School of the Americas: Military Training and Political Violence in the Americas*, Durham, NC: Duke University Press, 2004. Penny Lernoux also notes that Course O-47, taught to Latin American militaries at the former US Army School of the Americas in the Panama Canal Zone, emphasized that subversion was not limited to armed insurrection, it can also include non-violent forms of actions. Psychological operations (PSYOPS) were also taught at the US army Institute for Military Assistance at Fort Bragg, North Carolina. P. Lernoux, *Cry of the People*, New York: Doubleday, 1980, pp. 180–1.

38 Wolfendale, *Torture and the Military*, p. 77.

39 Ibid., p. 79.

40 D. Bar-On, "The Psychology of Perpetrators." Online, available at: http://74.125.93. 104/search?q=cache:gUvk3tLVKTcJ:www.bgu.ac.il/~danbaron/Docs_Dan/genocidal %2520mentalities.doc+dan+bar+on+they+believe+themselves+to+be+moral+people &cd=1&hl=en&ct=clnk&gl=us&client=safarip. 4 (accessed on March 28, 2009).

41 M. I. Baro, *Writings for a Liberation Psychology*, London: Harvard University Press, 1994.

42 B. Hollingshead, "Adjustment to Military Life," *American Journal of Sociology* 51, 5, 1946, p. 441.

43 Ibid., p. 442.

44 M. K. Huggins, M. Haritos-Fatouros, and P. G. Zimbardo, *Violence Workers: Police Torturers and Murderers Reconstruct Brazilian Atrocities*, Berkeley, CA: University of California Press, 2002.

45 H. Arendt, *Eichmann in Jerusalem*, New York: Penguin Books, 2006.

46 In Argentina, retired vice-admiral Luis María Mendía, who was chief of naval operations from 1976 to 1979, accepted responsibility for the infamous "death flights," in which political prisoners were dumped alive into the sea, and said that those officers under his command, "fought with abnegation, courage, bravery, subordination and heroism during the eight years of war against subversive, terrorist organizations, and at no time did they go beyond the orders received from the chiefs of staff, which were faithfully followed." Marcela Valente, "Human Rights – Argentina: Reviving the Concept of Due Obedience," IPS Inter Press Service News Agency, February 2, 2007. Online, available at: http://ipsnews.net/news.asp?idnews=36422 (accessed on March 19, 2009).

47 Winslow, "Misplaced Loyalties."

48 Payne, *Unsettling Accounts*, pp. 173–95.

49 E. Chemerinsky, "An Independent Analysis of the Los Angeles Police Department's Board of Inquiry Report on the Rampart Scandal," pp. 574–5. Online, available at: http://eprints.law.duke.edu/archive/00001384/ (accessed on March 19, 2009).

50 M. R. Trouillot, *Silencing the Past. Power and the Production of History.* Boston: Beacon Press, 1995.

51 See V. Salvi, "Memoria y justificacion. Consecuencias de la auto-victimizacion del Ejercito Argentino," paper presented at the Second International Congress on Genocidal Practices, Buenos Aires, November 2007.

12 Bringing justice to Guatemala

The need to confront genocide and other crimes against humanity

Raúl Molina Mejía[1]

This chapter makes five arguments regarding the need to confront genocide and other crimes against humanity in Guatemala: first, genocide was perpetrated by the state of Guatemala during the internal armed conflict; second, the state has failed to comply with its commitments according to the UN Convention on the Prevention and Punishment of the Crime of Genocide, by failing to further investigate acts of genocide or bring to justice those people responsible; third, the judicial system has also failed in Guatemala with regard to human rights violations and crimes against humanity; fourth, the international community has not been able or willing to confront impunity for crimes against humanity in Guatemala; and five, the only way of bringing justice to Guatemala regarding the crime of genocide is through the establishment of a special international tribunal.

Several historians claim that Latin American indigenous peoples, among them the Maya descendants in Guatemala, suffered genocide at the hands of Portuguese and Spanish *conquistadores*. An analysis of measures taken by *criollos* against indigenous peoples during Guatemala's reform of 1871 could also lead to the conclusion that genocide and ethnocide took place with the introduction of capitalism and the forced displacement of rural indigenous communities. Both periods are open to debate and discussion. What is not open to discussion, however, is the genocide that was perpetrated by the state and its military and security forces against indigenous peoples in the 1980s, as a tool of counterinsurgency and a consequence of the National Security Doctrine and Cold War ideology, strategies and tactics.

The report presented by the UN-supported Comisión para el Esclarecimiento Histórico (CEH, Historical Clarification Commission),[2] *Guatemala: Memory of Silence*, in 1999 clearly demonstrated that genocide was perpetrated in Guatemala in a certain period and in specific localities. It declared very clearly the accountability of the state and its military and security forces in those acts of genocide. However, today, 12 years after the signature of the Firm and Lasting Peace Accord and nine years after the public presentation of the CEH report, nothing has been done in Guatemala to further investigate or prosecute genocide, the most heinous crime against humanity.

The chapter analyzes events in Guatemala in the 1970s and 1980s, demonstrating that, in fact, genocide went beyond the limited areas described by the

CEH and the period of time in question. The entire strategy applied by the armed forces from 1978 on was, indeed, genocidal, not only against indigenous peoples but also against ideological enemies. My argument is that repression against "the internal enemy" was also a type of genocide. This chapter also demonstrates that this crime cannot be judged in Guatemala, due to its weak and corrupt justice system, nor by the International Criminal Court, because the events took place before its creation. Therefore, the right approach for achieving justice is the creation of an ad hoc international tribunal. Guatemala has uncovered, so far, some important truths about the dark period of genocide, but it is still far from legal justice, compensation, and reparation.

Peace accords and historical memory

On December 29, 1996, the government of Guatemala and the Unidad Revolucionaria Nacional Guatemalteca (URNG, the Guatemalan National Revolutionary Unity) signed the Firm and Lasting Peace Agreement that put an end to the 34-year-old internal armed conflict. In the context of the Cold War between the West and the Soviet bloc and the application of the US-sponsored National Security Doctrine, 200,000 persons were killed or disappeared during the conflict, 93 percent of them by repressive actions of the Guatemalan state.

According to the findings of the CEH, most of the victims were civilians and 87 percent were Mayans. As indicated year after year since the early 1980s by the UN Commission on Human Rights, the Guatemala state was responsible for gross and systematic violations of human rights, *inter alia* extrajudicial executions, massacres, torture, and forced disappearances.

The CEH provides data about its investigations and estimates of human rights violations during the internal armed conflict, as well as its analysis of events, in *Guatemala: Memory of Silence*. Of particular importance is the reference it makes to the brutality of the military and paramilitary forces during the 626 massacres perpetrated throughout the country.

The CEH has noted particularly

> serious cruelty in many acts committed by agents of the state, especially members of the army, in their operations against Mayan communities. The counterinsurgency strategy not only led to violations of basic human rights, but also to the fact that these crimes were committed with particular cruelty, with massacres representing their archetypal form. In the majority of massacres there is evidence of multiple acts of savagery, which preceded, accompanied, or occurred after the deaths of the victims. Acts such as the killing of defenseless children, often by beating them against walls or throwing them alive into pits where the corpses of adults were later thrown; the amputation of limbs; the impaling of victims; the killing of persons by covering them in petrol and burning them alive; the extraction, in the presence of others, of the viscera of victims who were still alive; the confinement of people who had

been mortally tortured, in agony for days; the opening of the wombs of pregnant women, and other similarly atrocious acts, were not only actions of
extreme cruelty against the victims, but also morally degraded the perpetrators
and those who inspired, ordered, or tolerated these actions.[3]

The most important finding was clearly that genocide was perpetrated by the
state while carrying out its counterinsurgency operations. The CEH affirmed that
"agents of the State of Guatemala, within the framework of counterinsurgency
operations carried out between 1981 and 1983, committed acts of genocide
against groups of Mayan people who lived in the four regions analyzed."[4]

The commission reached this conclusion based on Article II of the UN Convention on the Prevention and Punishment of the Crime of Genocide. Members
of Mayan groups were killed (Article II.a), serious bodily or mental harm was
inflicted upon Mayan groups (Article II.b) and groups were deliberately subjected to living conditions calculated to bring about their physical destruction in
whole or in part (Article II.c). The conclusion was also based on the CEH's findings that all these acts were committed "with intent to destroy, in whole or in
part" groups identified by their common ethnicity (Article II, first paragraph).

In short, the commission based its assessment on the strict definition legally
applied for genocide. A significant portion of the crimes perpetrated by the state
from 1981 to 1983 in the four regions of Guatemala analyzed by the CEH were
undoubtedly acts of genocide. Nevertheless, a great number of crimes against
humanity and other serious violations of human rights took place in the rest of the
country for a span of 34 years, particularly between 1978 and 1984. Given that
these acts were designed to eliminate vast sectors of Guatemalan society, I maintain that such repressive actions were also part of a genocidal strategy and plan.

This chapter argues that fundamental justice should have been pursued in Guatemala soon after the signature of the 1996 Peace Agreement. Unfortunately, the
government abstained from taking any action, and the national judicial system by
itself was unwilling or incapable of initiating significant proceedings to prosecute
those responsible for war crimes, crimes against humanity, and other serious violations of human rights. Unlike the transitions to democracy in South America, no
effort has yet been made to set any trials in motion. Moreover, attempts to bring
several flagrant cases to international courts have also proved unsuccessful, creating a profound sense of impunity and contempt for the rule of law.

I have strongly posited for many years that the constant deterioration of the
Guatemalan state can be traced back to this total absence of justice – first,
because the judicial system was at the service of the national security state
during the armed conflict, and second, because no real effort has been made
since 1996 up to the present to correct the system. This situation is leading the
country to a condition of a "failed state." I have also argued that the constant
disintegration of society, now immersed in a climate of violence and terror, is
intrinsically linked to the impunity for human rights violations enjoyed by high-
ranking military and civil personnel of the successive Guatemalan governments.
The international community, which was very instrumental in the success of the

peace-seeking negotiations process, has a responsibility to act in Guatemala, in order to restore credibility to the system of justice and, especially, to prevent a recurrence of an internal armed conflict or a social explosion.

Examining the extent of genocide in Guatemala

The verdict of the CEH

It is not possible to argue against the powerful statement presented by the CEH in *Guatemala: Memory of Silence* which affirms:

> Based on the fundamental conclusion that genocide was committed, the CEH, in keeping with its mandate to present an objective judgment on the events of the internal armed confrontation, indicates that, without prejudice to the fact that the active subjects are the intellectual and material authors of the crimes in the acts of genocide committed in Guatemala, the State is also responsible, because the majority of these acts were the product of a policy pre-established by a command superior to the material perpetrators.
>
> (paragraph 112)

As the CEH points out, the state of Guatemala failed to comply with its obligation to investigate and punish acts of genocide committed in its territory, thus contravening the Convention on the Prevention and Punishment of the Crime of Genocide. Moreover, political responsibility rests as well with successive democratically elected governments, including the present one.

The general framework the CEH used for its analysis on the question of genocide in Guatemala is the following:

> genocide means any of the following acts committed with intent to destroy, in whole or in part, a national, ethnic, racial or religious group, as such:
>
> a   Killing members of the group;
> b   Causing serious bodily or mental harm to members of the group;
> c   Deliberately inflicting on the group conditions of life calculated to bring about its physical destruction in whole or in part;
> d   Imposing measures intended to prevent births within the group;
> e   Forcibly transferring children of the group to another group.

On this basis, the two fundamental elements of the crime are first, intentionality, and second, the fact that the acts committed include at least one of the five criteria cited above.

The CEH selected four geographical regions for study (Maya-Q'anjob'al and Maya-Chuj, in Barillas, Nentón and San Mateo Ixtatán in North Huehuetenango; Maya-Ixil, in Nebaj, Cotzal and Chajul, Quiché; Maya-K'iche' in Joyabaj, Zacualpa and Chiché, Quiché; and Maya-Achi in Rabinal, Baja Verapaz). It confirmed that between 1981 and 1983 the Army identified groups of the Mayan population as the internal enemy, considering them to be an actual or potential support base for the guerrillas, with respect to material sustenance, a source of recruits and a place to hide their members. In this way, the Army, inspired by the National Security Doctrine, defined a concept of internal enemy that went beyond guerrilla sympathisers, combatants or militants to include civilians from specific ethnic groups.[5]

In paragraphs 110 to 122 of its report, the CEH explained its rationale for the conclusion that genocide was perpetrated by the Guatemala state. First, the reiteration of destructive acts, which were directed systematically against Mayan groups, demonstrated that "the only common denominator for all the victims was the fact that they belonged to a specific ethnic group." The CEH points to the fact that these acts were committed "with intent to destroy, in whole or in part" these groups.

Among acts aimed at the destruction of Mayan groups, the CEH indicated that killings and massacres were of paramount importance, and added,

> In accordance with the testimonies and other elements of evidence collected, the CEH established that, both regular and special Army forces, as well as Civil Patrols and military commissioners, participated in massacres. The aim of the perpetrators was to kill the largest number of group members possible.
>
> (paragraph 112)

The CEH established that, as a component of the killings, the perpetrators

> systematically committed acts of extreme cruelty, including torture and other cruel, inhuman and degrading actions, the effect of which was to terrorize the population and destroy the foundations of social cohesion, particularly when people were forced to witness or execute these acts themselves. Many of the actions committed constituted "serious bodily or mental harm to members of the group."
>
> (paragraph 114)

Based on its investigation the CEH also proved that the killings, especially those that were indiscriminate massacres, were accompanied by the razing of villages. In the four regions investigated, people who escaped were also persecuted during their displacement. The CEH concluded that these acts constituted the "deliberate infliction on the group of conditions of life" that could bring about, and in several cases did bring about, "its physical destruction in whole or in part" (paragraph 116). For the execution of these acts, the national military structures were strictly coordinated, and they followed specific strategies and plans. The CEH examined the army plans for 1982 and 1983, and noted:

Military plan *Victory 82*, for example, established that "the mission is to annihilate the guerrillas and parallel organizations"; the military plan *Firmness 83–1* determined that the Army should support "their operations with a maximum of PAC members, in order to raze all collective works."

(paragraph 119)

Thus, the CEH concluded that the acts with the intent to destroy Mayan groups were not excesses by soldiers out of control or the result of decisions made in the moment of the attack by commanders in the ground, but rather acts that

obeyed a higher, strategically planned policy, manifested in actions which had a logical and coherent sequence ... The State chose to cause the greatest loss of human life among non-combatant civilians ... the State opted for the annihilation of those they identified as their enemy.

(paragraph 120)

The breadth and depth of genocide in Guatemala

A crucial question must now be asked: Was genocide in Guatemala limited to a particular regional territory – the four regions mentioned above – during a specific period of time (1981–3)? That was the set of conditions that the CEH could fully investigate and document during its limited existence, but the commission never said that these were the only existing sets of genocidal conditions in Guatemala. As a matter of fact, the commission affirmed in paragraph 123 of its report: "The CEH has information that similar acts occurred and were repeated in other regions inhabited by Mayan people."

A brief analysis of other sections of the CEH report illustrates that the four regions are but a sample of what happened in most of the Guatemalan territory and for a longer period of time. For instance, while affirming that state forces were responsible for 626 massacres,[6] the commission indicates that only half of them occurred between 1981 and 1983.[7] Moreover, according to two maps in the appendix of the CEH report, one of the linguistic communities of Guatemala and the other on the number of massacres by department, the four regions analyzed by the CEH occupied only a small part of three departments: Huehuetenango, where 88 massacres were perpetrated; El Quiché, where 344 took place; and Baja Verapaz, where 28 occurred. Testimonies by witnesses and survivors indicated that the methods applied by the army were the same in practically all the massacres. Army units would surround a particular village, gather the villagers at the center of the town, and separate men, women, and children. The second stage would be to kill all of them by various heinous ways. Finally, army units and civilian collaborators would set the dwellings on fire.

All these actions started well before 1981, although they were not as widespread. For example, I represented the National University of Guatemala in a commission established to investigate the massacre of Panzós, Izabal, which took place on May 29, 1978. According to our findings, in that town the mayor invited *campesinos* opposing constant invasion of their lands to come to a town-hall meeting in the central plaza. Before they came, army soldiers started to dig trenches around the plaza and install weapons. When the *campesinos* came to Panzós, without any sort of warning they were received with gunfire. More than 100 people died, including elders, women, and children. People were killed in a carefully planned, staged, and executed attack by the army against the civilian population. Moreover, that was not the first massacre of civilians. In Sansare, El Progreso, a few years before, the army had attacked *campesinos* and killed dozens of them. Additionally, the army perpetrated selective collective killings of Mayan people in the Western Highlands and the jungle in Ixcán between 1975 and 1980.[8]

A turning point was reached with the massacre at the Spanish embassy in Guatemala City on January 31, 1980. A group of *campesinos* from El Quiché, trade unionists, and university students peacefully occupied the embassy. They were calling on the international community to demand a halt to massacres against Mayan people in the Western Highlands. In flagrant violation of international law and human rights, security forces commanded by President Lucas García and his minister of interior, Donaldo Álvarez, acting against the express will of the Spanish ambassador, set the building on fire. Thirty-seven people burned to death. Only the ambassador escaped, and one *campesino*, Gregorio Yujá, temporarily survived. The *campesino* was, within hours, abducted from a hospital, tortured, and killed. His body was thrown on the National University's campus. With this action, the Guatemalan state trampled upon the rule of law and trespassed any limitations to its genocidal strategy. After this, massacres and scorched-earth operations erupted all over the country.

Clearly, acts of genocide not only occurred before and after the 1981–3 period, as previously explained, but they also took place all over Guatemala during at least five years. I propose four reasons for this conclusion. First, the National Security Doctrine that sustained the Victory 82 and Firmness 83–1 army plans was applied to the entire country, and not only to the four specific regions in the CEH report. That doctrine was firmly established in Guatemala with the military coup of 1963. The military plans of 1982 and 1983 were implemented nationwide and included massacres and scorched-earth campaigns in other areas of the departments of Huehuetenango, Quiché, and Baja Verapaz already mentioned, as well as in other fifteen departments throughout the entire country.

Second, the CEH clearly stated that according to the National Security Doctrine, during the armed confrontation the state's idea of the "internal enemy" became increasingly inclusive. Victims of army operations "included men, women and children of all social strata: workers, professionals, church members, politicians, peasants, students and academics; in ethnic terms, the vast majority were Mayans."[9] The CEH also concluded that the Mayan population was considered a collective enemy of the state: "Mayans as a group in several different parts of the country were identified by the Army as guerrilla allies."[10] In other words, this approach applied to the different areas where guerrilla forces were located, which encompassed practically half the country's territory.

Third, racism, which historically has been a significant factor encouraging genocide throughout history, has been embedded in Guatemala's society, particularly its ruling sectors, since the Spanish conquest in 1524. Marta Casaús, a Guatemalan political author, says that in those multiethnic and multicultural states where an ethnic minority or "a minimized ethnic majority" exists, like in Guatemala, and where racism is fundamental for the power structures, traditional practices, attitudes, and acts contribute to the perpetration of acts of genocide.[11] The CEH stated in paragraph 33 of its report:

> the undeniable existence of racism expressed repeatedly by the State as a doctrine of superiority, is a basic explanatory factor for the indiscriminate nature and particular brutality with which military operations were carried out against hundreds of Mayan communities in the west and north-west of the country.

And fourth, the evidence of the CEH regarding the actions taken by the state to attack and terrorize rural communities expands beyond the period 1981–3 and touches all parts of the country where the conflict took place. Massacres and other criminal acts were committed uniformly as a result of concrete army plans. The report stated:

> Mayan communities also became a military objective ... Militarization of the communities disturbed the cycle of celebrations and ceremonies ... Aggression was directed against elements of profound symbolic significance for the Mayan culture. The CEH gives special attention to the massive forced displacement of people, particularly Mayan population. Estimates of the number of displaced persons by massacres and devastation of villages go as high as one million, and because populations fled under persecution by the army and with scarce resources, a great number of children and elderly died.[12]

The CEH mentioned special attacks suffered by children and women, which is an intrinsic component of genocide: "the rape of women, during torture or before being murdered, was a common practice ... The majority of rape victims were Mayan women."[13]

Although these four reasons sustain my assessment regarding the extent of genocide in Guatemala, clearly an official statement or judicial sentence expanding the historic conclusion of the CEH cannot come from an individual alone. It should be up to a specific national or international body to make a ruling. In this sense, it was promising what Victoria Sanford, referring to the Inter-American Court of Human Rights' sentence on the massacre of Plan de Sánchez in Guatemala, wrote: "For the first time, a judicial sentence stated that there was genocide in Guatemala, and it assigned the responsibility for the 1982 massacre and genocide to the Guatemalan army."[14] However, a more comprehensive and definite assessment is certainly needed. Yet the Guatemalan state and the international community have failed to fully investigate all other acts of war in Guatemala between 1962 and 1996, as obligated under the UN Convention on the Prevention and Punishment of the Crime of Genocide and many other international instruments. For the international community this is a significant lapse, but for the successive governments of Guatemala from 1996 to the present this is also a most serious legal and moral failure.

Genocide as a process

The case of Guatemala is key in our interpretation of the term genocide and its application for the "dirty wars" in Latin America. In fact, there was a sustained effort by the dominant sectors in Guatemala, and in other parts of Latin America as well, to wipe out an entire segment of the population, based on an ill-conceived definition of "internal enemy" as portrayed in the National Security Doctrine. The "internal enemy" was defined in ideological terms, not necessarily as armed combatants, and included all those people holding alternative views to the established political and economic model. The internal enemy was targeted for elimination and destruction, or co-opted. In the war against the internal enemy, the military and elites accepted the metaphor that in order to eliminate the fish it was necessary to drain the water. That is, in order to eliminate the opposition they had to destroy potentially supportive populations. This formulation, in my view, is tantamount to genocide.

In the former Yugoslavia and Rwanda, genocidal acts were perpetrated mostly in a short period of time when armed people were allowed and/or mandated to go rampant to kill their enemies. In most cases, however, genocide has been a calculated process. Conditions have been carefully put into place and different steps have been followed. In the case of the Holocaust, for instance, the Nazi regime first acted against political opponents, particularly communists and socialists, who were killed or imprisoned. Then the regime promoted a series of measures to strip the Jewish population of their rights as citizens, as well as to deprive them of their national identity and property. Concentration in ghettos was the next step, before implementing the "final solution" approved by the Nazi leadership: the transfer of the Jewish people to concentration camps and their annihilation there.

A similar pattern can be seen in the case of Guatemala, when many sectors of society organized and mobilized to reconstruct the country after the 1976 earthquake. In 1978 a first stage of assassinations and forced disappearances of the social and political opposition began in a selective way. By the end of 1979 and early 1980 the campaign was transformed into a massive persecution of leaders and members of the social movement and opposing political parties. By 1981 a full campaign of massacres and scorched-earth tactics was in full swing in the rural areas of Guatemala. The scale of these campaigns in Guatemala has no parallel elsewhere in Latin America. One million people were forcibly displaced and 300,000 refugees fled to neighboring countries, mainly Mexico. The original repression, a component of counterinsurgency operations against revolutionary forces and a "dirty war" against persons and organizations opposing the military regime, became a genocidal campaign when large segments of the civilian population became a target. As General Héctor Gramajo, former head of the army, once said to journalists, the army was satisfied if for every ten persons eliminated, two were insurgents. That formulation fits the concept of genocide, in my view, because it means the deliberate, mass killing of innocent civilian populations for whatever purposes, be it in national or occupied territories by Germany during World War II, or recently in the Sudan or in the occupied Palestinian territories by Israel.

The concept of genocide as a process – to target a wide spectrum of the civilian population for incremental repression in order to eliminate real or perceived internal enemies – allows us also to see the "dirty wars" in Latin America as acts of genocide. With a few exceptions, there were no insurgencies in most of the region at the time the "dirty wars" were launched. Therefore, imprisonment, exile, torture, disappearance, and widespread killings were measures taken against civilian populations and not counterinsurgency operations (even if some of the victims might have been willing to take up arms). The idea of annihilating a sector of society was always present. This was further exemplified with the creation of Operation Condor, a system that extended beyond national borders to accomplish that objective. Often extrajudicial executions and disappearance rather than wholesale massacres seemed to suffice for exterminating the internal enemy. That "dirty war" approach was also used by the state in Guatemala as a complement to the massive repressive campaigns during 1978–85. As a matter of fact, they were also perpetrated during several months after the US-organized overthrow of Jacobo Árbenz in 1954, as well as during the repressive regimes led by Julio César Méndez Montenegro and Carlos Arana Osorio, from 1966 to 1974.

Confronting impunity in Guatemala after the signature of the Peace Accords

The search for truth and justice after 1996

Human rights defenders, including myself,[15] were very much aware of the threat of impunity in Guatemala long before the end of the peace-seeking negotiations process, and warned about the various forms of impunity that we would need to confront. A particular concern was not to buy peace through impunity for those who had been responsible for atrocities. Guatemalans were pleased by the fact that the Firm and Lasting Peace Agreement of December 1996 did not provide for any sort of amnesty or blanket impunity. However, we noted that the specific accord on the reintegration of URNG combatants to civilian life[16] had left a window open for legal impunity, not only for URNG members but also for members of the security forces carrying out some military actions. The National Reconciliation Law approved by Congress on December 18, 1996, further expanded that window of impunity.

While there was still some room for confronting impunity and seeking justice, the burden of opening the cases in the courts was left to the victims, their relatives, and those supporting them. Very few people were willing to try this avenue at that time, before the judicial system could be overhauled, democratized, and duly strengthened by constitutional amendments. Most victims, their relatives, and human rights organizations preferred to wait for the implementation of the Peace Accords, and particularly for the truth-seeking work of the CEH. It is important to note that the main issue blocking decisive action against impunity was fear, or what a colleague and I termed the political/psychological dimension of impunity.[17] Guatemalans felt that those who had abused power had been left untouched after the signature of the Peace Accords.

Many human rights defenders agree that the first step towards the elimination of impunity is determining the truth about past events. The CEH started its groundbreaking work in Guatemala in 1997, although it did so under the shadow of two constraining limitations contained in the pertinent peace agreement:[18] First, it could not name those people responsible for violations of human rights and acts of violence; and second, its findings could not be used as evidence for any legal case in Guatemalan courts. Because of these two limitations, the Catholic Church's Proyecto para la Recuperación de la Memoria Histórica (REMHI, Project for the Recovery of Historical Memory) had already begun its own countrywide investigation into acts of violence against the population, with no limits to its work.

On April 23, 1998, Bishop Juan Gerardi publicly presented the REMHI report: *Guatemala: Never More*. The report blamed both parties in the internal armed conflict, the state and the insurgency, for violence and human rights violations. However, that document made clear that the state, which had waged a "dirty war" against real and alleged opposition, was chiefly responsible for attacks on the civilian population during counterinsurgency operations. Two days later, in a well-calculated response, Monsignor Gerardi was bludgeoned to death at his residence in the San Sebastian parish.[19] In a wave of outrage, thousands of people marched in the streets to protest and demand investigation and punishment. Unfortunately, newly awakened fears also spread to every corner of the country. In the eyes of the population a horrendous politically motivated crime had again been perpetrated, and the report's affirmation "never more" had not lasted even three days. For the next few years, despite numerous legal and extralegal obstacles, the investigation and prosecution of those responsible for Monsignor Gerardi's murder became the main focus in the struggle against impunity. Today, more than 10 years after this crime, justice has only been partially obtained.[20]

On February 12, 1999, the CEH produced its final report, *Guatemala: Memory of Silence*. Experts in the field of truth-seeking efforts have pointed out that this report is the most profound set of findings on repressive operations ever produced in Latin America. The most general assessments of the report are certainly incontrovertible, and they provide the official account of the 34 years of internal armed conflict. Unfortunately, the government of Guatemala under

Presidents Álvaro Arzú, Alfonso Portillo, and Óscar Berger failed to follow up on the large majority of the important recommendations of the report. The political will to implement them has been completely absent, and as of this writing, President Álvaro Colom has made no governmental commitment to do so.

The defeat of constitutional reforms and other obstacles in the implementation of the Peace Accords

At the same time that the CEH was presenting its report, Congress was finalizing a set of constitutional reforms based on the 1996 Peace Accords, most of which derived from one specific agreement.[21] All the new provisions were crucial, especially the reform of the judicial system. The reforms adopted by Congress were put to the vote of the population in a national referendum that took place on May 17, 1999. However, forces opposed to the reforms launched a black propaganda campaign to sway the public, aiming particularly to instill fear among the *ladino* population. *Ladino* middle classes were told that the reforms would allow indigenous peoples to dominate. That, combined with the population's lack of real knowledge about the issues at stake, the electorate's lack of interest, and insufficient support by the government and allied political parties, led to rejection of the reforms by the voters. Not only was the judicial system left untouched but also the armed forces, responsible for genocide and other heinous crimes, kept its status as guardian of both external and internal security (mandated by the military-era constitution).

To make matters worse, in the 1999 general elections the Frente Republicano Guatemalteco (FRG), the right-wing party formed by former head of state General Efraín Ríos Montt, won a majority in Congress, and Alfonso Portillo, its candidate, was elected president. Foreseeing this event, just before the election Nobel Peace Prize laureate Rigoberta Menchú Tum had presented an accusation in Spain against Ríos Montt for the crime of genocide. For the next four years, however, Ríos Montt was President of Congress and enjoyed total immunity. As predicted, the Portillo administration (2000–3) did very little to investigate crimes from the era of the internal armed conflict. However, it did move in the direction of partially clarifying Bishop Gerardi's case. Nevertheless, in general both the government and the judicial system showed unwillingness or total incapacity to prosecute anyone accused of any crimes, particularly human rights crimes, whether perpetrated before or after the signature of the Peace Accords. It did not help at all that the Constitutional Court itself violated the letter and spirit of the 1985 constitution by allowing Ríos Montt to be a candidate for the presidency in 2003. The FRG was able to form a Constitutional Court that has permanently blocked efforts to overcome impunity.

By the 2003 general elections the country's security situation had dramatically deteriorated. Portillo's administration, deeply immersed in corruption and abuse of power, contributed to the overall travesty of justice by giving economic compensation to former members of the paramilitary civilian patrols (PAC). Some *patrullas de autodefensa civil*, used by the army to militarize society and augment their counterinsurgency forces, had been responsible for massacres and other serious violations of human rights during the internal armed conflict.[22]

Meanwhile, the government deferred compensation to the victims of those terrible acts. The government further failed to confront organized crime and gang activities. Lawlessness and acts of violence became the trademark of the FRG administration. In one incident, mobs took over a significant part of Guatemala City on "Black Tuesday" when the Constitutional Court was due to rule on Ríos Montt's candidacy for president. In a demonstration of force, thousands of FRG members and supporters, including members of Congress, surrounded several buildings and streets in various parts of the city to exert pressure on the courts in favor of Ríos Montt. Confronted with this new threat, the population finally reacted and punished the FRG in the elections. Ríos Montt finished a distant third for the presidency in 2003 and could not compete in the second round of elections.

Failures of the Guatemalan government regarding justice during the period 2004–8

Óscar Berger became president in January 2004, and he was expected to improve security, the rule of law, and justice. That did not happen. In fact, corruption became more pronounced. Both former President Serrano and former President Portillo, in Panama and Mexico respectively, enjoyed millions of dollars that they had embezzled from national funds, without firm action by the Guatemalan government. Governmental corruption grew, particularly affecting the judicial system. Violent crimes of all sorts proliferated, and the government lost control of the security situation. "Social cleansing," "femicide," and lynching became widespread, deepening the crisis of human rights in Guatemala. Although such violence seemed to be random, many victims were members of social movements or organizations striving for justice. Today, human rights defenders, honest journalists, prosecutors, judges, witnesses, and people seeking democratic change live under death threats and are targeted for violent action, including assassination. The climate of intimidation and fear has reached intolerable levels. Toward the end of Portillo's term, pressed by the alarming increase in violence, Guatemala's movement for human rights came together and asked the United Nations to create an international commission to investigate and dismantle illegal security groups and clandestine security structures involved with organized crime.[23] Although the UN secretary-general was willing to organize such a commission, both the Constitutional Court and Congress in Guatemala tried to block its formation. Only after careful and long negotiations did Guatemala finally accept the establishment of the UN-sponsored International Commission Against Impunity in Guatemala (CICIG) in 2007.

The commission's functions include determining the existence of illegal security groups and clandestine security structures, collaborating with the state in the dismantling of such groups and structures, promoting the investigation, criminal prosecution, and punishment of crimes committed by their members, and recommending to the state the adoption of public policies for eradicating such groups and structures and preventing their re-emergence. The commission's first annual report, entitled *One Year Later*, was issued in September 2008. Among its very relevant conclusions are the following:

> The dismantling of the illegal groups and clandestine structures entrenched in many public entities in Guatemala is the responsibility of the State. CICIG will continue to provide ... all the support and assistance it can offer to ensure that these groups and structures are finally eradicated ... In order to meet this objective, however, the State of Guatemala must ensure that all agents of the justice system who consistently strive for fairness in the administration of justice can operate freely and not in a climate of threats, pressures or even killings. Since the beginning of 2008 at least eight public officials in the areas of security and justice have been killed. All of them were working on or had information about high-impact cases.[24]

It is clear that progress in the struggle against embedded structures of violence is very slow.

Impunity in Guatemala in early 2009 remained as rampant as during the internal armed conflict, even for the most outrageous crimes. A paramount case was the assassination of three Salvadoran members of the Central American Parliament (PARLACEN) and their driver. On February 20, 2007, newspapers reported the discovery of four bodies by the highway from Guatemala to El Salvador. The police identified them as Eduardo D'Aubuisson, William Pichinte, and José Ramón González, members of PARLACEN, and their driver Gerald Napoleón Ramírez. All of them were members of the Alianza Republicana Nacional (ARENA), the right-wing political party in government in El Salvador. Authorities in both Guatemala and El Salvador were astonished and outraged. Two days later, four agents of Guatemala's National Civil Police (PNC) were arrested and accused of killing the Salvadorans. They were Luis Arturo Herrera López, head of the organized crime unit, and three others: José Adolfo Gutiérrez, Marvin Langen Escobar, and José Korki López. All were taken to a high-security prison, El Boquerón, in Cuilapa in the department of Santa Rosa. On February 25, the population was shocked again to learn that the four detainees had been killed inside the prison in a commando-like operation. The killers had passed through several security gates to perpetrate the crime and then left the facilities without anyone stopping them. Despite the fact that the Salvadoran government strongly demanded investigation and prosecution, and that the FBI was working on the investigation, this case has not advanced at all.

Impunity is even more systematic regarding lesser-known victims. During a conference in New York in early 2008, Guatemalan procurator for human rights Sergio Morales mentioned that only 2.63 percent of all cases of crimes against the right to life that the Office of the Public Ministry admits for consideration are finally convicted. That is, there is an impunity rate of 97.37 percent for crimes committed in Guatemala. This is a serious indictment of the justice system, con-

sidering that in the last five years more than 25,000[25] people have been assassinated (an average of 14 persons a day). Regarding this matter, the CICIG's
report states very strongly that

> a careful analysis of the convictions handed down shows that the justice sys-
> tem's effectiveness is at an unacceptably low level. While it is true that the
> Office of the Public Prosecutor and the National Civilian Police have the
> fundamental responsibility for investigation and criminal prosecution,
> judges are ultimately responsible for ensuring that the investigation is
> carried out effectively and in line with the requirements of due process, so
> that it will lead to a conviction where appropriate. This is the responsibility
> of the judiciary in a state governed by the rule of law.[26]

We can conclude, therefore, that 12 years after the signature of the Peace
Accords, the lack of justice has made Guatemala nearly a failed state. Impunity
reigns for recent crimes as well as for those politically motivated crimes perpetrated during the internal armed conflict. For that reason, special tribute must be
paid to the incredible efforts some people continue to make to pursue the truth:
from searching the newly found archives of the National Civil Police to digging
into clandestine graves to exhume victims of the conflict. Even more strenuous
are efforts to prosecute those people involved in terrible crimes in order to bring
about justice. Among those efforts, there are a few outstanding cases: the Gerardi
case; the Myrna Mack case (see below); the genocide charge against General
Ríos Montt and other high-ranking officers of the Guatemalan army; the massacre of Xamán; and a few other massacres.[27] In all these cases, after true legal
ordeals, justice has not yet been fully achieved.

International tribunals and cases from Guatemala

During the internal armed conflict, cases related to violations of human rights
were opened in several international venues. The most outstanding ones were
filed with the Inter-American Commission on Human Rights, some of which
reached the level of the Inter-American Court of Human Rights, and the UN
Working Group on Forced or Involuntary Disappearances.

The UN Working Group on Forced or Involuntary Disappearances, after
almost 30 years of compiling cases of forced disappearances in Guatemala, has
admitted for its consideration 3,155 cases. Human rights organizations in Guatemala have consistently stated that 45,000 disappearances took place between
1966, when the first case was reported, and 1996, when the Peace Accords were
signed. In any case the government of Guatemala and other sources have been
able to clarify the whereabouts of only 258 disappeared persons since January
1997. This shows that the Guatemalan state has failed to abide by its international commitments by not clarifying 2,899 outstanding claims presented to it by
the United Nations. This fact, by itself, should lead the International Criminal
Court (ICC) to start a preliminary proceeding regarding Guatemala, given the

fact that forced disappearances, as crimes against humanity, are part of its mandate, as well as the fact that any forced disappearance is an ongoing crime until the person is accounted for (whether the crime occurred after the ICC was established or not).

Some of the cases presented to the Inter-American system of human rights have been legally completed, mainly through agreements reached between the government of Guatemala and the plaintiffs. Although they have brought about moral and material compensation in most cases, legal accountability has not been brought because that aspect has been placed in the hands of the Guatemalan judicial system, which has been totally ineffective in this regard.

I briefly mention some cases:[28] The Inter-American Court of Human Rights, while promoting a settlement of the case between the state and the victims or their relatives, has unanimously mandated in all cases the application of all legal measures in Guatemala to guarantee full investigation of the cases, and prosecution and punishment of those responsible.

In the case of Efraín Bámaca, a disappeared guerrilla commander married to a US lawyer, the court unanimously decided

> that the State must locate the mortal remains of Efraín Bámaca Velásquez, disinter them in the presence of his widow and next of kin, and deliver them … that the State must investigate the facts that generated the violations of the American Convention on Human Rights and the Inter-American Convention to Prevent and Punish Torture in the instant case, identify and punish those responsible, and publicly divulge the results of the respective investigation.

No action has been taken by the state.

In the case of the White Panel, which involves the assassination of university students by security forces, the court unanimously decided:

> That the State of Guatemala must investigate the facts that generated the violations of the American Convention on Human Rights in this case, and identify and punish those responsible.

No action has been taken by the state.

In the case of Street Children, which involves the killing of street children by security forces, the court unanimously decided:

> That the State of Guatemala must investigate the facts of this case, identify and punish those responsible and adopt, in its domestic law, the provisions needed to ensure compliance with this obligation.

No action has been taken by the state.

In the case of Myrna Mack, who was killed in downtown Guatemala by an assassin, the court unanimously decided that the State must effectively investigate the facts of the instant case, with the aim of identifying, trying, and punishing all the direct perpetrators and accessories, and all others responsible for the extra-legal execution of Myrna Mack Chang, and for the cover-up of the extra-legal execution and other facts of the instant case, aside from the person who has already been punished for those facts; and that the results of the investigations must be made known to the public ... that the State must remove all de facto and legal obstacles and mechanisms that maintain impunity in the instant case, provide sufficient security measures to the judicial authorities, prosecutors, witnesses, legal operators, and to the next of kin of Myrna Mack Chang, and resort to all other means available to it so as to expedite the proceeding.

No action has been taken by the state.

In the case of Maritza Urrutia, who was abducted, tortured, and killed by state agents, the court unanimously decided

That the State shall investigate effectively the facts of this case, which resulted in the violations of the American Convention on Human Rights and non-compliance with the obligations of the Inter-American Convention to Prevent and Punish Torture; identify, prosecute and punish those responsible, and also publish the results of the respective investigations."

No action has been taken by the state.

Needless to say, other cases are in a similar situation. The only hope for legal justice for some Guatemalans lies now in the few cases that tribunals in other parts of the world have accepted. The most important is the case in the Spanish courts that was opened by Rigoberta Menchú Tum and other plaintiffs in 1999. The route has been difficult, but some progress has been achieved. The courts have issued an international warrant for several former high-ranking officials and army officers,[29] and asked the state of Guatemala to cooperate with extraditing some of them. Again, the most significant obstacle has been Guatemala's Constitutional Court, which recently opposed the extradition of General Ríos Montt. Since then, Ríos Montt was again elected member of Congress and enjoys immunity.

How to confront genocide and other crimes against humanity in Guatemala?

Clearly, confronting genocide and other crimes against humanity in Guatemala through the domestic judicial system will be a most difficult and slow process. Justice delayed is justice denied. Perpetrators and those who masterminded such heinous crimes would be long deceased. Therefore, the only viable route is through international tribunals. Nevertheless, although I highly value the extraordinary efforts made so far by Spanish courts, which may be eventually followed by courts in Italy, Belgium, and other places, the outcomes of the trials would not entirely satisfy the need for direct and substantial justice for the Guatemalan people, unless extraditions take place (a condition that so far has been prevented). It will not suffice to bring shame, apply economic sanctions, and produce travel constraints against perpetrators. These perpetrators deserve to go to jail for a significant period of time.

The question of enforced disappearances

Guatemala deserves a specific international tribunal. The ICC, for its part, should take on forced disappearances in Guatemala as a matter of immediate special concern, given its decision to include that crime within its mandate. In the same way as he recently did regarding crimes against humanity in Darfur, Luis Moreno Ocampo, the ICC's prosecutor, should act regarding the Guatemalan state, under the logic that no clarification has been made regarding thousands of cases of people disappeared already in the UN files. Those are outstanding crimes.

The latest report of the UN Working Group on Enforced or Involuntary Disappearances (A/HRC/7/2 of January 10, 2008) analyzes the case of Guatemala. The working group stated that it had transmitted 3,155 cases to the government, and of those, 79 cases were clarified on the basis of information provided by the source, and 177 cases on the basis of information provided by the government. The rest, 2,899 cases, remain outstanding. Furthermore, the working group expressed its concern about the suspension of investigations in disappearance cases and reminded the government of "its obligations to conduct thorough and impartial investigations for as long as the fate of the victim of enforced disappearance remains unclarified," in accordance with article 13, paragraph 6, of the UN declaration on the Protection of All Persons from Enforced Disappearance of December 18, 1982.

Unfortunately, in cases of torture and genocide, crimes against humanity also within the ICC's mandate, the ICC cannot pursue cases retroactively. In Guatemala these crimes were perpetrated before the creation of the ICC. However, many human rights experts argue that intrinsic to any forced disappearance is torture, not only for the victims directly abducted but also for their relatives, who must endure great psychological and emotional trauma while seeking their loved ones. Forensic data collected on remains of people who were "disappeared" for a long period of time and later found dead demonstrate that practically all those victims suffered physical torture. More recently, information obtained from "renditions" in the war on terror launched by the United States delineates a pattern showing that every person illegally captured went through an ordeal of physical and/or psychological torture. In this sense, for every ongoing forced disappearance, torture is ongoing as well.

In my view, although the ICC can and should prosecute the crimes of forced disappearance and related torture in the case of Guatemala, unfortunately the case of genocide, which was plainly demonstrated by the CEH, remains outside its jurisdiction because genocidal acts were halted before 1996. This means that the only possible way of properly dealing with genocide in Guatemala is by creating a Special Tribunal on Genocide in Guatemala.

A Special Tribunal on Genocide, other crimes against humanity, and war crimes

How would a tribunal for Guatemala compare with the tribunals in the former Yugoslavia and Rwanda? What lessons could be drawn from Darfur, Sudan, or the international tribunal for Cambodia? The fact is that no two situations are identical, but the international community has the obligation to find applicable proceedings to try outrageous acts instead of simply avoiding controversial political situations. My position is that we should draw all possible lessons from other cases, in order to guarantee the successful elimination of impunity for genocide, other crimes against humanity, and war crimes in Guatemala.

The International Criminal Tribunal for the former Yugoslavia was the first established under Chapter VII of the UN Charter in 1993.[30] According to the United Nations, this experience led to the creation of an independent system of law, the most modern law facilities in the world, and the establishment and consolidation of an effective victims and witnesses program. Stating that this tribunal has spearheaded the shift from impunity to accountability, which is a fundamental new approach, the web page for the International Criminal Tribunal for the former Yugoslavia (ICTY) declares:

> By holding individuals accountable regardless of their position, the ICTY's work has dismantled the tradition of impunity for war crimes and other serious violations of international law, particularly by individuals who held the most senior positions ... the question is no longer *whether* leaders should be held accountable, but rather *how* can they be called to account.[31]

Among the core achievements of the tribunal, along with establishing the facts and strengthening the rule of law, are bringing justice to thousands of victims and giving them a voice. Up to date, over 3,500 witnesses have testified in court, giving victims and witnesses and their communities the sense that they are involved in the peace-seeking process. We can only imagine the healing effect that a similar experience might have with indigenous communities all over Guatemala, who suffered the brunt of the repressive acts.

On November 8, 1994, the UN Security Council approved its resolution 955 (1994), which established "an international tribunal for the sole purpose of prosecuting persons responsible for genocide and other serious violations of international humanitarian law committed in the territory of Rwanda ... between January 1, 1994 and December 31, 1994." The Security Council adopted in the same act the Statute of the International Criminal Tribunal for Rwanda. Article 6 of this statute addresses individual criminal responsibility: "A person who planned, instigated, committed or otherwise aided and abetted in the planning, preparation or execution of a crime referred to in articles ... of the present

Statute, shall be individually responsible for the crime."[32] The more recent cases of Darfur and Cambodia present more complexities. Human rights defenders welcomed the decision made by Moreno Ocampo to indict the head of state of Sudan. Some experts in peacekeeping operations questioned the advisability of bringing charges against such a key political figure at a moment when peace-seeking negotiations were at a critical juncture. Others considered, however, that the decision helped move forward the dialogue seeking a political solution. Most human rights experts believe that justice cannot be held hostage to political considerations. In that sense, no matter what the political conditions are, it is time to make justice a priority for the state of Guatemala.

In the case of Cambodia, where the Khmer Rouge was accused of killing more than a million people during four years of terror from 1975 to 1979, political considerations blocked the establishment of a true special international criminal tribunal. A sort of a hybrid body was finally agreed upon. Although some analysts considered the decision a precedent to investigate events of the past, human rights groups questioned the potential work of courts that also included Cambodians. The Global Policy Forum stated, for example:

> Finally, on March 17, 2003, the United Nations reached a draft agreement with the Cambodian government for an international criminal tribunal to try former Khmer Rouge leaders … Under the agreement, the panel of judges will include a majority of Cambodians. Human rights groups argue that the government's ability to impose its will on these judges poses an unacceptable obstacle to justice. On the other hand, with many likely defendants over the age of 70, time is running out for justice to be served.[33]

The experiment in Cambodia is not exactly a special international criminal tribunal of the same kind as was implemented in Rwanda and the former Yugoslavia. Under the name of Extraordinary Chambers in the Courts of Cambodia (ECCC), this tribunal is part of the Cambodian court system with a special status: members of the staff, including prosecutors and judges, are drawn from both Cambodia and the international community.

The ECCC were set up to deal with the proceedings against senior Khmer Rouge leaders by mid-2008. The principal justifications for the trials included the fact that they would

> (a) provide accountability to the millions of Cambodians for the crimes of the Khmer Rouge; (b) have a deterrent effect…; (c) enhance people's understanding of justice and the rule of law; and (d) the jurisprudence and practices of the ECCC would be absorbed by the rest of the Cambodian system of justice.[34]

Regrettably, however, in his recent report to the Human Rights Council the Special Representative of the Secretary-general for Human Rights in Cambodia clearly stated: "The irregularities noted by the audit team were so numerous and of such magnitude that it recommended that, if its recommendations were not accepted, the United Nations should seriously consider withdrawing from the project."[35] Considering that the situation in Guatemala corresponds very much to the original assessment of the Cambodian judiciary made by a group of experts appointed in 1997 by the UN secretary-general – the group concluded that endemic corruption and political influence would make it impossible for Cambodian prosecutors, investigators and judges to be free from political pressure – the ECCC model would likely fail in Guatemala.

As we have seen, Guatemala is experimenting now with CICIG as an international commission to help the government confront impunity, mainly for crimes perpetrated since the signature of the Peace Accords. So far, the General Procurator's Office and the entire judicial system have demonstrated their incapacity to deal with the wave of criminal violence and the demand for justice. In other words, the model used in Cambodia would be totally ineffective in the case of Guatemala, because the justice system has proven to be such a failure. This fact reinforces our view that an international tribunal is the only option for Guatemala; no Guatemalan judges, prosecutors or investigators should be involved. Nothing prevents CICIG from preparing conditions for an eventual international tribunal; as a matter of fact, such an initiative could enhance CICIG's present work. But the present agreement between the United Nations and the Guatemalan state will expire soon, and a new mandate for CICIG is to be sought.

One of the objections that concerned parties may have to a new international tribunal is its cost. However, as noted by the ICTY, the expense of bringing to justice those most responsible for war crimes and strengthening the rule of law in the former Yugoslavia pales in comparison to the true costs of the crimes. Would it be too much to ask the same for Guatemala?

From theory to action: finding the international political will to bring justice to Guatemala

There are some clear conclusions to be drawn from this chapter. First, the international community is the key and indispensable component in the process of bringing justice to Guatemala and ending impunity for genocide and other crimes against humanity. Second, the Peace Accords, which were supposed to set in motion fundamental changes in Guatemalan state and society, have failed to produce an environment where justice could reign, due to their weak and incomplete implementation. Many of the provisions in the Accords, significant both in number and depth, have not been fully implemented or even considered.

Moreover, the set of recommendations contained in the CEH report was largely ignored, particularly those recommendations oriented to justice and reparation. I quote here some of the most important ones regarding justice. The CEH recommended:

> That the Government and the judiciary, in collaboration with civil society, initiate, as soon as possible, investigations regarding all known forced

disappearances. All available legal and material resources should be utilised to clarify the whereabouts of the disappeared and, in the case of death, to deliver the remains to the relatives. (Paragraph 22 of the part on recommendations)

That a commission should be established by the President of the Republic using his constitutional prerogative, to be under his immediate authority and supervision, and which will examine the conduct of the officers of the Army and of the various bodies of state security forces active during the period of the armed confrontation. (Paragraph 42 of the part on recommendations)

That the powers of the State fulfil, and demand fulfilment of, the Law of National Reconciliation, in all of its terms and in relation to the rest of Guatemalan law. Those crimes for whose commission liability is not extinguished by the said law, should be prosecuted, tried and punished, particularly following Article 8, "crimes of genocide, torture and forced disappearance," as well as those crimes that are not subject to prescription or that do not allow the extinction of criminal liability, in accordance with domestic law or international treaties ratified by Guatemala. (Paragraph 47 of the part on recommendations)

Third, human rights violations perpetrated in Guatemala during the internal armed conflict, once they were finally known, outraged the people of the world and the international community. For that reason, it was unconceivable in 1996, and even more so after the CEH report was issued in 1998, that legal or de facto impunity could be tolerated. That is why no pact was made to protect from prosecution any member of either side of the conflict, and the National Law of Reconciliation of 1997, although regrettably leaving some windows open, did not provide for immunity or impunity.

Fourth, the judicial system in Guatemala, which the CEH found to be extremely weak and responsible for de facto impunity, has not been restructured, renovated, or strengthened as mandated by the Peace Accords. On the contrary, during the years of the peace-seeking negotiations process it was infiltrated at all levels by personnel close to powerful people linked to military and political forces active in the conflict. Many of these people became involved in organized crime after the signature of the Accords, maintaining the same level of impunity they had enjoyed during the internal war. The judicial system failed to act, and was further debilitated by corruption and acts of intimidation. Thus far, the system has demonstrated itself to be absolutely incapable of prosecuting and punishing those responsible for serious violations of human rights both during and after the armed conflict.

With no legal recourse at home, tribunals in other countries have been of the outmost importance to the victims and human rights organizations. Justice-seeking actors believe that those bodies abroad should continue their proper consideration of the case of Guatemala. Sentences that impose shame on perpetrators, restrict their travel, or require monetary compensation to the victims, may further a sense of justice. However, we must also admit that the work of bodies abroad is not enough because they cannot bring to civil society the level of justice required by the magnitude of the crimes.

I believe that the ICC should participate in the case of Guatemala by prosecuting those responsible for ongoing crimes against humanity. This is the way that enforced or involuntary disappearances of the past are being considered in Argentina and elsewhere. The phenomenon of forced disappearance still directly affects tens of thousands of victims today. We must recall that there are 2,899 outstanding Guatemalan cases on file with the UN Working Group on Enforced or Involuntary Disappearances. Thousands of relatives of the victims still have no truth or justice. The participation of the ICC is even more crucial when one considers that forced disappearances were a key component of the genocidal campaign in Guatemala. It is time for the ICC to act strongly against the phenomenon of forced disappearance in order to eventually eradicate this scourge from the planet.

As in the cases of the former Yugoslavia and Rwanda, the Security Council should create a Special Tribunal on Genocide in Guatemala. The ICC and the special tribunal could work together in order to draw important new lessons about the dangers in doctrines of "national security" – or more recently "homeland security." Those doctrines led in Latin America to massive human rights atrocities. Both the ICC and the special tribunal could fully use the valuable information provided by the CEH in Guatemala, which regrettably cannot be used in Guatemalan courts.

This urgent action will not take place unless the necessary political will is mustered in the international community. It does not exist today, and not many efforts are being made to generate it. This book on genocide in Latin America is an initial fundamental step. How can we confront genocidal policies and actions in the rest of Latin America when the international community fails to address the clear-cut case of genocide in Guatemala?

The main question now is how to move from the present situation in the international community, marked by a lack of interest regarding Guatemala, to decisive action by international actors to create a special tribunal, on the one hand, and open a case at the ICC, on the other. Although a full strategy must be developed to move from theoretical concern to action, I propose following preliminary steps:

a   to strengthen the few cases that are open in Guatemala, confronting the constraining decisions of the Constitutional Court, and protecting victims, judges, and witnesses;

b   to demand a review of cases of all plaintiffs before the Inter-American system of human rights based on the lack of action by the Guatemalan state regarding legal criminal prosecution of the perpetrators;

c   to ask the UN Working Group on Enforced and Involuntary Disappearances to recommend that the UN Human Rights Council take concrete action regarding the question of the disappeared in Guatemala, based on the indifference the Guatemalan state has shown;

d   to promote a tribunal of conscience, a sort of a Permanent People's Tribunal, to analyze genocide and other crimes against humanity in Guatemala; and

e   to seek legal advice from particular academic institutions specializing in legal matters, and support from institutions that have accompanied important cases in other countries, such as Human Rights Watch, the Center for Justice and Accountability, and the International Center for Transitional Justice.

It is clear that demands for international justice action can only be presented at the ICC and the UN Security Council. Important questions must be dealt with, such as which actors should present the cases, under which conditions, and what the strategy should be. Evidently, a widespread public education and awareness campaign should be launched through the media and by other means from the very first stages. At the same time, a political campaign should be directed towards countries where justice-seeking actions have already been taken. Mutual solidarity is a fundamental element for success. Confronting the issue of genocide in Guatemala could be the cornerstone for a new architecture of justice in the entire Latin American region.

Some final conclusions

It is clear that genocide took place in Guatemala during its internal armed conflict. The Guatemalan Historical Commission (CEH) found evidence of that in four regions in the country from 1981 to 1983. I have tried to demonstrate that genocide took place beyond those four regions during a longer period of time. However, neither the Guatemalan state nor the international community has complied with the recommendation by the CEH to further investigate crimes against humanity during the internal armed conflict.

Genocide in Guatemala followed a deliberate process, which started with high levels of repression and then was transformed into a "dirty war" against persons and organizations identified as internal enemies. The moment the state included in this category large sectors of the civilian population – who were not involved in insurgency – the state's war crimes and crimes against humanity became genocide. A similar process, based on the National Security Doctrine, took place in other parts of Latin America. Repression in Latin America must be now reanalyzed under the framework of the Convention on the Prevention and Punishment of the Crime of Genocide.

Presently, there are no conditions for prosecuting perpetrators of genocide in Guatemala. There is an embedded impunity supported by fear and a failed judicial system. Existing international tribunals or tribunals in other countries do not seem to be able to provide the justice needed in Guatemala either. The International Criminal Court seems unable to take up cases of genocide in Guatemala, since the events took place before its creation. The only possible solution is, then, to establish a special tribunal.

This means that, in order to bring justice to Guatemala, those concerned must raise the consciousness and the will of both the international community and internal actors regarding the crime of genocide. This is a task that should not be left to Guatemalans alone. It must become a joint effort by all those who claim to stand for justice and peace all over the world. As in most human rights struggles, we must realize that actions in one place will always have an impact in others, and contribute to the collective reservoir of fairness and justice for all humankind.

Notes and references

1 The author thanks J. Patrice McSherry for her comments on an earlier version of this chapter.
2 With the assistance of the United Nations the CEH was established in 1997 based on the Agreement on the Establishment of the Commission to Clarify Past Human Rights Violations and Acts of Violence that Have Caused Guatemalan Population to Suffer, the accord signed by the Guatemalan government and the URNG on June 23, 1994.
3 The references to reports and resolutions of the United Nations and other international organizations are based on the paragraph number, given the fact that different editions of the same document have different page numbers. This quote is from paragraph 87 of the report by the CEH (Historical Clarification Commission), *Guatemala: Memory of Silence*. Paragraphs 80 to 146 are available online at: http://shr.aaas.org/guatemala/ceh/report/english/conc2.html.
4 CEH, *Guatemala: Memory*, paragrah 122.
5 CEH, *Guatemala: Memory*, paragraph 110.
6 CEH, *Guatemala: Memory*, paragraph 86.
7 CEH, *Guatemala: Memory*, paragraph 33. Paragraphs 1 to 79 are available online at http://shr.aaas.org/guatemala/ceh/report/english/conc1.html.
8 Ricardo Falla documented these repressive acts beginning on June 10, 1975. Ricardo Falla. *Masacres de la Selva, Ixcán, Guatemala (1975–1982)*. Editorial Universitaria, Universidad de San Carlos de Guatemala, 1993.
9 CEH Report. Paragraph 15.
10 CEH, *Guatemala: Memory*, paragraph 31.
11 Marta Elena Casaús Arzú, *Genocidio: ¿La maxima expresión del racismo en Guatemala?*, Guatemala: F&G Editores, 2008, p. 13. The expression "minimized ethnic majority" refers to the fact that, although indigenous peoples in Guatemala are a majority of the population, their treatment by ruling sectors is equivalent to treatment of marginalized ethnic minorities in other countries.
12 CEH, *Guatemala: Memory*, paragraphs 62, 66, and 67.
13 CEH, *Guatemala: Memory*, paragraph 91.
14 Reference to the sentence by the Inter-American Court of Human Rights on April 29, 2004. Victoria Sanford, *Guatemala: Del genocidio al feminicidio*, Guatemala: F&G Editores, 2008, pp. 22 and 23.
15 Raúl Molina Mejía, "The Struggle Against Impunity in Guatemala," *Social Justice* 26, 4, *Shadows of State Terrorism: Impunity in Latin America*, winter 1999, pp. 55–83.
16 Agreement on the Basis for the Legal Integration of URNG, December 12, 1996.
17 J. Patrice McSherry and Raúl Molina Mejía, "Confronting the Question of Justice in Guatemala," *Social Justice* 19, 3, fall 1992, pp. 1–28.
18 The agreement had been signed in Oslo in 1994, but entered in force together with the other agreements only on December 29, 1996.
19 Raúl Molina Mejía and J. Patrice McSherry, "Justice in the Gerardi Case: But Terror Continues," *NACLA Report on the Americas* 35, 1, July/August 2001, pp. 8–11.

20 Two army officers and a priest were found guilty of supporting and covering up the crime and are serving a sentence, but no person has ever been charged as intellectual and/or material author of the crime.
21 Agreement on Constitutional Reforms and Electoral Regime, 1996.
22 See CEH, *Guatemala: Memory*, paragraphs 50 and 88.
23 The United Nations and the government of Guatemala signed on January 7, 2004 the Agreement for the Establishment of a Commission for the Investigation of Illegal Groups and Clandestine Security Organizations in Guatemala (CICIACS), but Guatemalan Congress never ratified it.
24 First report by CICIG in September 2008, pp. 5, 6. Copy in English in possession of the author.
25 Figures provided by newspapers and human rights organizations for the period 2004–8 surpass 25,000 people killed.
26 CICIG, first report, p. 6.
27 Space constraints prevent a careful analysis here of these cases. As indicated before, in the Gerardi case no one has been accused for the material and intellectual authorship. In the Myrna Mack case, although a person was convicted, high-ranking officers who ordered the assassination were not even accused. The few massacres that have reached the tribunals have yet to provide real justice.
28 Inter-American Court of Human Rights, cases. Online, available at: www.worldlii. org/int/cases/IACHR/ Quotes are taken from the various cases.
29 Those under warrant are: former Generals Ríos Montt, Mejía Víctores, Fernando Lucas García, Benedicto Lucas García, Guevara Rodríguez, and Donaldo Álvarez, Germán Chupina and Pedro Arrendondo. Sanford,*Guatemala: Del genocidio al femi-nicidio*, p. 23.
30 The International Tribunal for the Prosecution of Persons Responsible for Serious Violations of International Humanitarian Law Committed in the Territory of the Former Yugoslavia since 1991, commonly referred to as the International Criminal Tribunal for the former Yugoslavia or ICTY, was established by resolution 827 (1993) of the UN Security Council of May 25, 1993.
31 ICTY. Online, available at: www.un.org/icty/glace-e/index.htm.
32 Resolution 955 (1994) of the Security Council of November 8, 1994.
33 Global Policy Forum. Online, available at: www.globalpolicy.org/intljustice/camindx. htm (accessed February 2. 2009).
34 Paragraph 75 of the Report of the Special Representative of the Secretary-General for Human Rights in Cambodia (A/HRC/7/42) of February 29, 2008.
35 Paragraph 85 of the report contained in document A/HRC/7/42.

Conclusions
Unfinished business – in search of the next agenda

Henry R. Huttenbach

Essentially, this anthology has sought to explain the rash of extreme post-independence violence that has wracked literally every Latin and Central American country in the latter half of the past century. In itself, this should come as no surprise, not even the ferocity and intensity of each instance. Both post-French Revolution Europe and postcolonial Africa and Asia have had similar eruptions that continue to this day. The underlying factors are two kinds of nationalism: (1) the nationalism that is aimed at consolidating the centralizing authority of dominant ethnic majority over a reluctant minority, and (2) the nationalism of an ethnic minority seeking to exit from the rule of a suppressive majority. Both cases are examples of state power versus elements of the populace. We need only point to the Third Reich and its war against the German Jews and to the Ibo attempt to establish their own state – Biafra – to be carved out of Nigeria. In both instances genocidal force of various degrees came into play.

It should, therefore, come as no surprise to learn how little is known when encountering the collective reality of the numerous internal wars suffered in the southern hemisphere. Not only are they insufficiently known and understood by the peoples within the region itself but they are almost totally ignored by scholars outside the region; things Latin American simply do not appear in the broader global context. The biases and ignorance of North American- and Euro-centrism vis-à-vis the lower hemisphere virtually exclude in-depth references to the chronic violence in this part of the world, as if it belonged to an entirely distinct category with no integral connection to 'mainstream' world history. It was to rectify this parochialism that this collection of case studies was originally conceived and assembled, both to serve as a modest beginning and to stimulate future efforts by helping to set an agenda. Three goals spring to mind.

The first is to encourage more scholarship on the part of native researchers. Their numbers are still too few to push aside all the inhibiting factors. The older ones suffer from continued paralyzing fear, the legacy of years of stifling intellectual suppression. In a very real sense these survivors are still prisoners of their authoritarian anti-democratic past. Understandably they feel unsure of the stability and reliability of the present post-dictatorial status quo. Living in fragile young democracies they are still prepared psychologically for a political setback and the inevitable accompanying retribution. What these courageous persons must do is to nurture a new unafraid generation for whom the past is indeed the past and to whom the present is not a threat. Their initial task is to further open the archives, some of which are still restricted.

Furthermore, they will have to connect with colleagues abroad. This partially entails financial support to invite counterparts and, in turn, to attend academic functions abroad. There is still a feeling of lack of confidence. A corollary of this theme is the need to engage in cooperative ventures to encourage comparative studies as a means to weave Latin America into the greater global contextual fabric. To date there is still too much marginalization. The very notion of viewing Latin American mass political violence through the prism of genocide remains a source of often-rancorous disputation on both sides of the Atlantic Ocean. Hence the need to incorporate Latin American studies of massacral killings into the already well-developed field of genocide studies. All this will require time and patience but not willful delay. That only plays into the hands of deniers.

Next, an element of confusion remains central to the study of state violence which targets the civilian population. It is the satisfactory definition of central terminology. One term is the notion of the state. Not what is the state? But who and what comprises the state and its component parts. In the context of quasi-civil wars, there are para-state organizations, some permanent, others of an ad hoc or ephemeral nature. The state is often structurally a fluid phenomenon, and not only in weak states; there are numerous agencies in the US government that are technically independent and yet behave as arms of the executive branch. More complicated is to pinpoint the population at large. Throughout the essays, to varying degrees, the term *el pueblo* is mentioned – a seemingly shifting concept whose meaning(s) ought not be taken for granted. The line dividing the population into *el pueblo* and others is a murky one, reflecting more the subjectivity of the user than reliance on objective criteria. The complexity of the term is reminiscent of the mixed role played by the loaded pre-Soviet Russian term *chrestianin* (peasant). By the end of the nineteenth century it had acquired sociological and psychological and political meanings not to mention the religious.

Finally, there is the dominating problem of outsider participation in the acts of violence. Specifically this comes down to the imperial role of the United States. The foreign policy of the United States made and still makes it an ubiquitous presence and often active player. The decisions taken in Washington constantly washed over its southern border into Latin and Central American affairs. So far, much of US academic assessment of its involvement "down south" is either partisan or blatantly polemical. Future investigations of each instance of mass violence must factor in accurately the part, if any, of the USA. To depoliticize academic studies of the US impact and render it purged of distractive prejudices vis-à-vis the events that suggest that it did indeed willfully contribute or lend support to genocidal behavior will be difficult. It will be a challenge to the compilers of future agendas.

Even as these thoughts are being written, the danger persists. Even as his new administration settles in, President Obama confronts a renewed challenge in

Peru. For some years already, lethal conflict has been festering in that country. Once again the peasant population, *el pueblo*(?), is trapped between the government's army and a well-armed rebel force: the goal is to get control of the lucrative cocaine drug trade. The same brutality reminiscent of the last round in Peru in 2000 – which killed over 70,000 people, mainly civilians – is rearing its head again. Entire villages are being destroyed, their inhabitants either killed outright forced to flee en masse. The intensity of the violence is clearly exterminational. How will the US respond? That is the key question; in the answer lies the future not only of Peru but of the entire hemisphere. The extreme polarization of the army and the forces of the Shining Path virtually guarantee major massacres with genocide potential. It is of the utmost urgency that this case be thoroughly studied and brought to the attention of lackadaisical policy-makers and the flaccid international community at large. The momentum for genocide prevention must not be squandered. As far as the villagers are concerned it may be too late already.

Selected bibliography

Actis, M. and Aldini, C. (eds), *Ese infierno. Conversaciones de cinco mujeres sobrevivientes de la ESMA*, Buenos Aires: Sudamericana, 2001.

Aguila, G., "Dictadura, memoria(s) e historia: El conflictivo contrapunto entre las memorias de la dictadura en Rosario," *Prohistoria* 11, 2007, pp. 91–106.

Akhavan, P., "The Crime of Genocide in the ICTR Jurisprudence," *Journal of International Criminal Justice* 3, 4, 2005, 992.

Andersen, M. E. (ed.), *Dossier Secreto: Argentina's* Desaparecidos *and the Myth of the "Dirty War,"* Boulder, CO: Westview, 1993.

Argentine National Commission on the Disappeared, *Nunca Más: Report of the Argentine National Commission on the Disappeared*, New York: Farrar Straus & Giroux, 1986.

Barreneche, O., *Crime and the Administration of Justice in Buenos Aires 1785–1853*, Lincoln, NE: University of Nebraska Press, 2006.

Barros, R. J, *Constitutionalism and Dictatorship: Pinochet, the Junta, and the 1980 Constitution*, Cambridge: Cambridge University Press, 2002.

Bartov, O., *Murder in Our Midst: The Holocaust, Industrial Killing, and Representation*, New York: Oxford University Press, 1996.

Bauman, Z., *Modernity and the Holocaust*, Ithaca, NY: Cornell University Press, 1989.

Black, G., Stoltz Chinchilla, N., and Jamail, M., *Garrison Guatemala*, New York: Monthly Review Press, 1984.

Black, J. K., *Sentinels of Empire: The United States and Latin American Militarism*, New York: Greenwood Press, 1986.

Boff, L. and Boff, C., *Introducing Liberation Theology*, New York: Orbis Books, 1998.

Calveiro, P., *Poder y desaparición. Los campos de concentración en Argentina*, Buenos Aires: Colihue, 1998.

Camacho, D. and Menjivar, R. (eds), *Los movimientos populares en America Latina*, Mexico, Siglo XXI Editores, 1989.

Campbell, B. B and Brenner, A. D. (eds), *Death Squads in Global Perspective: Murder with Deniability*, New York: St Martin's Press, 2000.

Chalk, F. R. and Jonassohn, K., *The History and Sociology of Genocide: Analyses and Case Studies*, New Haven, CT: Yale University Press, 1990.

Cockcroft,J., *Neighbors in Turmoil: Latin America*, New York: Harper & Row, 1989.

Comisión para el Esclarecimiento Histórico (CEH). *Guatemala: memoria del silencio*. 12 vols, Guatemala: United Nations Operations Systems (UNOPS), 1999.

Comisión Nacional sobre Prisión Política y Tortura, *Informe de la Comisión Nacional sobre Prisión Política y Tortura* (Valech Report), Santiago: Ministerio del Interior, 2004.

Comisión Nacional de Verdad y Reconciliación. *Informe Rettig: Informe de la Comisión Nacional de Verdad y Reconciliación*. Santiago: La Nación and Ediciones Ornitorrinco, 1991.

Comisión de la Verdad y Reconciliación de Perú, *Informe Final de la Comisión de la Verdad y Reconciliación de Perú*, 9 vols, Lima, 2003. Online, available at www. cverdad.org.pe/ifinal/index.php.

Corradi, J., Weiss Fagen, P. and Garretón, M. A., *Fear at the Edge. State Terror and Resistance in Latin America*, Berkeley, CA: University of California Press, 1992.

Cullather, N., *Secret History: The CIA's Classified Account of its Operations in Guatemala 1952–1954*, Stanford, CA: Stanford University Press, 1999.

Da Silva, L. C. and Jelin, E. (eds), *Los archivos de la represión: Documentos, memoria y verdad*, Buenos Aires: Siglo XXI, 2002.

Davis, D. E. and Pereira, A. W. (eds), *Irregular Armed Forces and Their Role in Politics and State Formation*, New York: Cambridge University Press, 2003.

De Brito, A. B., Gonzalez-Enriquez, C., and Aguilar, P. (eds), *The Politics of Memory: Transitional Justice in Democratizing Societies*, Oxford: Oxford University Press, 2001.

De Greiff, Pablo (ed.), *The Handbook of Reparations*, Oxford: Oxford University Press, 2006.

Dinges,J., *The Condor Years*, New York: The New Press, 2004/5.

Drouin, M. "To the Last Seed: Atrocity Crimes and the Genocidal Continuum in Guatemala, 1978–1984," unpublished MA thesis, Concordia University, Montreal, 2006.

Dudley, S., *Walking Ghosts: Murder and Guerrilla Politics in Colombia*, New York: Routledge, 2004.

Escalante Hidalgo, J., *La misión era matar: El juicio a la caravana Pinochet-Arellano*, Santiago: LOM Ediciones, 2000.

Esparza, M., "Post-War Guatemala: Long-Term Effects of Psychological and Ideological Militarization of the K'iche Mayans," *Journal of Genocide Research* 7, 3, 2005, pp. 377–91.

Feierstein, D., *El genocidio como práctica social. Entre el Nazismo y la experiencia argentina*, Buenos Aires: Fondo de Cultura Económica, 2007.

Feierstein, D., *Seis estudios sobre genocidio. Análisis de relaciones sociales: otredad, exclusión, exterminio*, Buenos Aires: Editores del Puerto, 2008.

Fein, H., *Accounting for Genocide: National Responses and Jewish Victimization during the Holocaust*, New York: Free Press, 1979.

Fein, H., *Genocide: A Sociological Perspective*, London: Sage, 1993.

Feitlowitz, M., *A Lexicon of Terror: Argentina and the Legacies of Torture*, New York: University Press, 1998.

Figueroa Ibarra, C., *Los que siempre estarán en ninguna parte. La desaparición forzada en Guatemala*, México: Instituto de Ciencias Sociales y Humanidades de la Benemérita Universidad Autónoma de Puebla, 1999.

Frazier, L. J., *Salt in the Sand: Memory, Violence, and the Nation-State in Chile, 1890 to the Present*, Durham, NC: Duke University Press, 2007.

Galeano,E., *Las venas abiertas de América Latina*, Montevideo: Ediciones del Chanchito, 1987.

Gareau, F. (ed.), *State Terrorism and the United States*, London: Zed Books, 2004.

Gill, L., *School of the Americas: Military Training and Political Violence in the Americas*, Durham, NC: Duke University Press, 2004.

Giraldo, F., *Democracia y discurso político en la Unión Patriótica*, Bogotá: CEJA 2001.

Gómez-Suárez, A., "Perpetrator Blocs, Genocidal Mentalities, and Geographies: The Destruction of the Union Patriotica in Colombia and Its Lessons for Genocide Studies," *Journal of Genocide Research* 9, 4, 2007, pp. 635–60.

Grandin, G., *Empire's Workshop. Latin America, the United States, and the Rise of the New Imperialism*, New York: Metropolitan Books, 2006.

Groppo, B. and Flier, P. (eds), *La imposibilidad del Olvido: Recorridos de la memoria en Argentina, Chile y Uruguay*, La Plata: Al Margen, 2001.

Handy, J., *Gift of the Devil: A History of Guatemala*, Boston: South End Press, 1984.

Harbury, J. K., *Truth, Torture and the American Way: The History and Consequences of US Involvement in Torture*, Boston: Beacon Press, 2005.

Harff, B. and Gurr, T., "Toward Empirical Theory of Genocides and Politicides," *International Studies Quarterly* 37, 3, 1988, pp. 359–71.

Hayner, P., *Unspeakable Truths: Confronting State Terror and Atrocity*, London: Routledge, 2001.

Heinz, W., and Früling, H., *Determinants of Gross Human Rights Violations by State and State-sponsored Actors in Brazil, Uruguay, and Argentina*, Cambridge, MA: Martinus Nijhoff Publishers, 1999.

Hinton, A. L. (ed.), *Annihilating Difference: The Anthropology of Genocide*, Berkeley, CA: University of California Press, 2002.

Hinton, M. S., *The State on the Streets: Police and Politics in Argentina and Brazil*, Boulder, CO: Lynne Rienner, 2006.

Holden, R. H., *Armies without Nations: Public Violence and State Formation in Central America, 1821–1960*, New York: Oxford University Press, 2004.

Holden, R. H. and Zolov, E., *Latin America and the United States: A Documentary History*, New York: Oxford University Press, 2000.

Huggins, M. K., Haritos-Fatouros, M., and Zimbardo, P. G., *Violence Workers*, Berkeley, CA: University of California Press, 2002.

Janssens, B. (ed.), *Oj K'aslik estamos vivos: Recuperación de la memoria histórica de Rabinal, 1944–1996*, Guatemala: Museo Comunitario Rabinal Achi, 2003.

Jonas, S., *Of Centaurs and Doves: Guatemala's Peace Processes*, Boulder, CO: Westview Press, 2000.

Kaldor, M., *New and Old Wars*, Cambridge: Polity Press, 1999.

Kiernan, B., *Blood and Soil: A World History of Genocide and Extermination from Sparta to Darfur*, New Haven, CT: Yale University Press, 2007.

Kletnicki, A., "Disappeared Children in Argentina: Genocidal Logic and Illegal Appropriation," *Journal of Genocide Research* 8, 2, 2006, pp. 181–90.

Kornbluh, P., *The Pinochet File: A Declassified Dossier on Atrocity and Accountability*, New York: New Press, 2003.

Kuper, L., *Genocide: Its Political Use in the 20th Century*, New Haven, CT: Yale University Press, 1981.

Leffler, M. P. and Painter, D. S., *Origins of the Cold War: An International History*, 2005.

Lemkin, R., *Axis Rule in Occupied Europe*, Washington, DC: Carnegie Endowment for International Peace, 1944.

Lernoux, P., *Cry of the People*, New York: Doubleday, 1980.

Levy, G., "Considerations on the Connections between Race, Politics, Economics and Genocide," *Journal of Genocide Research* 8, 2, 2006, pp. 137–48.

Loveman, B., *For La Patria: Politics and the Armed Forces in Latin America*, Wilmington, DE: SR Books, 1999.

McClintock, M., *The American Connection*, Volume Two: *State Terror and Popular Resistance in Guatemala*, London: Zed Books, 1985.

McCoy, K. E., "Trained to Torture? The Human Rights Effects of Military Training at the School of the Americas," *Latin American Perspectives* 32, 6, 2005, pp. 47–64.

McSherry, J. P., *Predatory States: Operation Condor and Covert War in Latin America*, Lanham, MD: Rowman & Littlefield Publishers, 2005.

Mamdani, M., *When Victims Become Killers: Colonialism, Nativism, and the Genocide in Rwanda*, Princeton, NJ: Princeton University Press, 2001.

Manz, B., *Refugees of a Hidden War: The Aftermath of Counterinsurgency in Guatemala*, Albany, NY: State University of New York Press, 1988.

Menjívar, C. and Rodríguez, N. (eds), *When States Kill: Latin America, the US, and Technologies of Terror*, Austin, TX: University of Texas Press, 2005.

Midlarsky, M. I., *The Killing Trap: Genocide in the Twentieth Century*, Cambridge: Cambridge University Press, 2005.

Mires, F., *La rebelion permanente, las revoluciones sociales en America Latina*. Mexico: Siglo XXI Editores, 1988.

Moulian, T., *Chile actual: Anatomía de un mito*, Santiago: LOM ARCIS, 1998.

National Security and International Affairs Division, *School of the Americas US Military Training for Latin American Countries*, Washington, DC: US General Accounting Office, 1996.

Nino, C., *Juicio al mal absoluto*, Buenos Aires: Ariel, 2006.

Nunn, F., *The Time of the Generals: Latin American Professional Militarism in World Perspective*, Lincoln, NE: University of Nebraska Press, 1992.

Oficina de Derechos Humanos del Arzobispado de Guatemala (ODHAG), *Guatemala: nunca más*, 4 vols, Guatemala: ODHAG, 1998.

Osiel, M., *Mass Atrocity, Evil and Hannah Arendt: Criminal Consciousness in Argentina's Dirty War*, New Haven, CT: Yale University Press, 2002.

Padilla, Ballesteros E., *La memoria y el olvido: Detenidos desaparecidos en Chile*, Santiago: Ediciones Orígenes, 1995.

Paoletti, A. (ed.), *Como los Nazis, como en Vietnam. Los Campos de Concentración en Argentina*, Buenos Aires: Asociación Madres de Plaza de Mayo, 1996.

Payne, L. A., *Unsettling Accounts. Neither Truth nor Reconciliation in Confessions of State Violence*, Durham, NC: Duke University Press, 2008.

Pearce, J., *Colombia Inside the Labyrinth*, London: Latin American Bureau, 1990.

Pion-Berlin, D., "The National Security Doctrine, Military Threat Perception, and the 'Dirty War' in Argentina," *Comparative Political Studies* 21, 3, 1988, pp. 382–407.

Politzer, P. (ed.), *Fear in Chile: Lives under Pinochet*, New York: Pantheon Books, 1989.

Policzer, P., *The Rise and Fall of Repression in Chile*, South Bend, IN: Notre Dame University Press, 2009.

Robin, M., *Escuadrones de la muerte: La escuela francesa*, Buenos Aires: Sudamericana, 2005.

Roniger, L. and Sznajder, M., *The Legacy of Human Rights Violations in the Southern Cone*, Oxford: Oxford University Press, 1999.

Roniger, L. and Waisman, C. H. (eds), *Globality and Multiple Modernities: Comparative North American and Latin American Perspectives*, Brighton: Sussex Academic Press, 2002.

Sanford,V., *Buried Secrets: Truth and Human Rights in Guatemala*, New York: Palgrave Macmillan, 2003.

Schabas, W., *Genocide in International Law*, Cambridge: Cambridge University Press, 2000.

Schirmer, J., *The Guatemalan Military Project: A Violence Called Democracy*, Philadelphia, PA: University of Pennsylvania Press, 1998.

Shaw, M., *What is Genocide?* Malden, MA: Polity Press, 2007.

Sheinin, D., *Argentina and the United States: An Alliance Contained*: Athens, GA: University of Georgia Press, 2006.

Simpson, J. and Bennett, S., *The Disappeared*, London: Robson Books, 1985.

Smith, P., *Talons of the Eagle*, Oxford: Oxford University Press, 2000.

Streeter, S. M., *Managing the Counterrevolution: The United States and Guatemala, 1954–1961*, Athens, OH: University Center for International Studies, 2000.

Timerman, J., *Prisoner without a Name, Cell without a Number*, Madison, WI: University of Wisconsin Press, 2002.

Traverso, E., *La violencia nazi. Una genealogía europea*, Buenos Aires: FCE, 2002.

Ungar, M., *Elusive Reform: Democracy and the Rule of Law in Latin America*, Boulder, CO: Lynne Rienner, 2002.

Valentino, B. A., *Final Solutions: Mass Killing and Genocide in the Twentieth Century*, Ithaca, NY: Cornell University Press, 2004.

Verbitsky, H., *The Flight: Confessions of an Argentine Dirty Warrior*, New York: New Press, 1996.

Verdeja, E., "Reparations in Democratic Transitions," *Res Publica* 12, 2, June 2006, pp. 115–36.

Weitz, E. D., *A Century of Genocide: Utopias of Race and Nation*, Princeton, NJ: Princeton University Press, 2003.

Wolfendale, J., *Torture and the Military Profession*, Basingstoke: Palgrave Macmillan, 2007.

Wright, T., *State Terrorism in Latin America: Chile, Argentina, and International Human Rights*, Lanham, MD: Rowman & Littlefield, 2007.

Young, G., *SIDE: La Argentina Secreta*, Buenos Aires: Planeta, 2006.

Zea, L., *Latin America and the World*. Norman, OK: University of Oklahoma Press, 1969.

Index

Abu Ghraib 125–8, 130–1
accountability: consequences of too much 170; Guatemala 176; importance of in transitional societies 170; and prosecutions 171
ACCU (United Self-defence of Cordoba and Urabá) 162
Akayesu, Jean-Paul 69, 95
Alfonsín, Raúl 172–3
Allende, Salvador 6, 29–30, 64, 68, 112, 173, 196
Alliance for Progress (1961) 26–7
Almada, Martín 116
amnesties 170–1, 173, 177–8, 199, 218
Amnesty International 117
amnesty laws: Argentina 172–3; Chile 174, 201
Anaya, Herbert 128–9
Andean Initiative 155
anti-communism: Argentina 139; Guatemala 83; as pretext for military attacks 8; SOA indoctrination 162, 190; US-led crusade against 3, 5, 107, 111
Arancibia Clavel, Enrique 115
Árbenz Guzmán, Jacobo 6, 9, 26, 121, 133, 218
Arce, Luz 198
Arellano, Sergio 71
Arevalo, President 133
Argentina: abductees 33; amnesty laws 172–3; CORREPI 182, 187–8; death squads 187; death toll 184; detention centres 46, 141, 144, 146; disappearances 142, 182, 190; and the equality principle 50; genocide in court descriptions 110; implications of defining criteria of genocide 58–60; impunity laws 145; indictments 47, 51 (*see also* Garzón indictment);

institutionalization of state terror 47; Kissinger's visit 143, 189; left-wing groups 45; Madres de Plaza de Mayo 131, 173; Malvinas/Falklands War 36, 145, 172; memorialization of the dictatorship 145–6; military coup 45–7, 137–9; national security doctrine 32–3; Office of Public Safety 190–1; Operation Condor involvement 115–16, 118, 192; Operativo Independencia 45–6; as political haven 30; prosecutions 189; repressive practices 46, 140–2; Rosario 139–41, 143–5, 187; shantytowns 187–8; society's complicity/indifference 143–5; targets of the repression 140–3; torture methods 46–7; transition 171–3; Triple A 45, 115, 139–40, 185, 190; US links and support 36, 173, 190
Argentine police: capabilities 190; exemption from civilian jurisdiction 187; *gatillo fácil* (trigger happy) 183, 187; militarization 183, 191; participation in genocide 184–6; professionalist tropes 191–2; violence 186–9, 192
Aristegui, Carlos María 186
Armenian genocide 1, 153
arms transfers: role in US Cold War policy 155; US–Colombia 155
Arruda, Marcos 131
Arslanián, León 188–9
Arzú, Álvaro 83, 220
assassinations: Chile 31, 35, 115, 200–4; Colombia 152, 154, 158–60; Guatemala 34, 217, 219, 221–2, 224; Operation Condor 31, 111, 113–15; SOA links 38; Tucapel Jimenez 200–4
AUC (United Self-defense of Colombia) 162

CPSIA information can be obtained
at www.ICGtesting.com
Printed in the USA
FFOW01n1505190115
10394FF